Potential Crop Production

A Case Study

Potential Crop Production

A Case Study

Edited by

P. F. Wareing
University College of Wales
Aberystwyth

and

J. P. Cooper
Welsh Plant Breeding Station
Aberystwyth

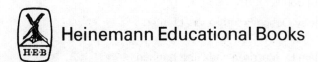 Heinemann Educational Books

Heinemann Educational Books Limited

London Edinburgh Melbourne Toronto Johannesburg Auckland
Singapore Ibadan Hong Kong Nairobi New Delhi

ISBN 0 435 62990 5

Published by Heinemann Educational Books Limited
48 Charles Street, London W1X 8AH

Designed and typeset by Design Practitioners Limited
Sevenoaks Kent

Printed in Great Britain by Morrison and Gibb Limited
London and Edinburgh

Preface

This book is based on the papers given at a symposium on 'Potential Crop Production in Britain', held in Aberystwyth in July 1969. The object of the symposium was to examine the environmental limitations to crop production in Britain and to assess the biological potential of different crops and systems of production. It was considered that the recent upsurge of interest in productivity problems had already yielded sufficient new basic information to permit a detailed study of potential production in different regions of Britain, which might well serve as a case study for a similar approach in other countries.

Crop production is basically the conversion of the environmental inputs of solar energy, carbon dioxide, water, and soil nutrients into economic end-products in the form of human or animal foodstuffs or industrial raw materials. The sequence adopted in the symposium was firstly to consider the environmental limitations to production in terms of the seasonal input of solar radiation, water, and soil nutrients, and the seasonal changes of soil and air temperature, in an attempt to decide which are the main limiting environmental factors in different regions.

The next step was to examine the response of crop plants to these environmental factors in terms of such important processes as photosynthetic activity, the structure of the crop and its use of water and nutrients, and hence to assess the potential efficiency of the plant in converting the seasonal inputs of energy, water, and soil nutrients into economic yield.

Such an assessment of the efficiency of the plant itself was then extended to consider the biological potential of particular types of crop throughout the year, when grown without limitations of water or soil nutrients, and under optimum managements. This made it possible to assess the comparative efficiency of different crops, including arable crops, grassland, horticultural crops, and forests, in converting these environmental inputs, and also to compare the efficiency of these crops with those of natural ecosystems. The comparable conversion rates of energy and protein obtained by processing through different types of farm animal were then considered and finally, the extent to which these processes could be replaced by synthetic foodstuffs.

In practice, however, the production of individual crops must be integrated into balanced farming systems, and it is important to relate the potential biological production of a particular crop to the economic yield obtained in a particular system. The most effective systems will, of course, differ with the regional environment and the symposium included examples from three contrasting environments; hill-land areas, the drier, mainly arable, lowlands of the south and east of Britain, and the wetter, predominantly grassland areas of the north and west.

Finally, the impact of recent technical developments on the realization of this potential production needs to be considered, and here techniques of harvesting and processing are becoming important. The plant breeder can modify the response of crop plants to their environment, and also to the requirements of the processor and consumer. Recent techniques for the control of pests and diseases, the use of herbicides, and of specific compounds to control plant growth have had profound effects on systems of management, as has the provision of new types of machinery for cultivation and harvesting. Further, the technical requirements of new forms of food processing pose their own requirements in terms of quality of the crop, uniformity of maturity date, and adaptation to mechanical harvesting.

This sequence of approach involved workers from many disciplines and, as will be clear from the following chapters, resulted in a wide divergence of treatments, varying from detailed mathematical models of photosynthetic processes to the practical aspects of particular farming systems, and the organization of food processing and forecasting of future consumer demands. During the course of the symposium, it was most encouraging to find how workers in very different disciplines were able to make contact and discuss the implications of their particular work in terms of potential crop production. Consequently, we felt that such an interdisciplinary approach might well merit publication as a case study of the way in which investigations on the environmental limitations to production and the biological responses of the plant to these environmental factors can provide information on the potential of the individual crop and of the farming systems to which it contributes.

Such an approach provides the necessary biological information on which economic or social decisions can be made. For instance, even in Britain, with a technically advanced agriculture, it is clear that the potential production for most crops is considerably greater than the average yield, making it technically possible either to produce much more food or, alternatively, to produce the same amount on a reduced acreage, a possibility which may be important in view of increasing demands for land use for other purposes.

We are grateful to the Royal Society for a grant for supporting the meeting so worthwhile. In particular we wish to thank Dr. Ian Rhodes for his cheerful and valuable assistance with the symposium itself and the ensuing publication.

P.F. Wareing

J.P. Cooper

Contents

Preface   v

List of contributors   xi

Introduction

Chapter 1. Future trends in British Agriculture   1
by W.E. Jones, (Chief Agricultural Adviser, Ministry of Agriculture, Fisheries, and Food)

The Crop Plant and its Environment

2. Regional and local environments   6
by W.H. Hogg (Meteorological Office, N.A.A.S., Bristol)

3. Microclimatology and crop production   23
by J.L. Monteith and J.F. Elston (University of Nottingham and University of Reading)

4. Photosynthesis and energy conversion   43
by B. Acock, J.H.M. Thornley and J. Warren Wilson (Glasshouse Crops Research Institute, Littlehampton)

5. Size, structure, and activity of the productive system of crops   76
by D.J. Watson (Botany Department, Rothamsted)

6. Water as a factor in productivity   89
by H.L. Penman (Physics Department, Rothamsted)

7. Root systems and nutrition   100
by R. Scott Russell (A.R.C. Letcombe Laboratory, Wantage)

Biological Potential of Crops

8. A dynamic model of plant and crop growth   116
by C.T. de Wit, R. Brouwer and F.W.T. Penning de Vries Agricultural University, Wageningen)

9. Physiological factors limiting the yield of arable crops   143
by Gillian N. Thorne (Botany Department, Rothamsted)

10. Potential production of grassland   159
by Th. Alberda (Institute for Biological and Chemical Research on
Field Crops and Herbage, Wageningen)

11. The potential production of forest crops   172
by E.D. Ford (Department of Forestry and Natural Resources,
University of Edinburgh)

12. Horticulture in 2000 A.D.   187
by J.P. Hudson (Long Ashton Research Station, University of
Bristol)

13. Novel sources of energy and protein   202
by Magnus Pyke (The Distillers Company Ltd., Menstrie)

14. Efficiency of food production by the animal industries   213
by W. Holmes (Wye College, University of London)

15. Comparative production of ecosystems   228
by P.J. Newbould (New University of Ulster, Coleraine)

Systems of Production in Contrasting Environments

16. Efficiency of hill sheep production systems   239
by J. Eadie and J.M.M. Cunningham (Hill Farming Research
Organization, Edinburgh)

17. Farming systems below 25 in (635 mm) rainfall   250
by E.R. Bullen (Ministry of Agriculture, Fisheries and Food,
London)

18. Farming systems with more than 30 in (760 mm) rainfall   260
by P.J. Jones (Bridget's Experimental Husbandry Farm, Winchester)

19. The determination of production systems   266
by J.D. Ivins (School of Agriculture, University of Nottingham)

Future Technical Developments

20. Plant breeding: arable crops   273
by J. Bingham (Plant Breeding Institute, Cambridge)

21. Plant breeding: forage grasses and legumes   295
by J.P. Cooper and E.L. Breese (Welsh Plant Breeding Station,
Aberystwyth)

22. Control of pests and diseases   319
by S.H. Crowdy (Department of Botany, University of Southampton)

23. Mechanisation   331
by K.E. Morgan (Department of Agriculture, University of Reading)

24. Chemical control of plant growth   343
by B.J. Heywood (May and Baker Ltd., Dagenham)

25. Environmental limitations in crop production for the quick-freezing industry   351
by J.W. Bundy (Birds Eye Foods Ltd., Walton-on-Thames)

Conclusions

26. Potential crop production in Britain — some conclusions   362
by P.F. Wareing (Department of Botany, University College of Wales, Aberystwyth)

Author Index   379

Subject Index   384

List of Contributors

Acock, Dr. B. — Glasshouse Crops Research Institute, Littlehampton, Sussex.

Alberda, Dr. Th. — Institute for Biological and Chemical Research on Field Crops and Herbage, Wageningen, Netherlands.

Bingham, J. — Plant Breeding Institute, Trumpington, Cambridge.

Breese, Dr. E.L. — Welsh Plant Breeding Station, Plas Gogerddan, Aberystwyth.

Brouwer, Dr.R. — Laboratory of Physiological Research, Agricultural University, Wageningen, Netherlands.

Bullen, E.R. — Ministry of Agriculture, Fisheries and Food, London.

Bundy, J.W. — Birds Eye Foods Ltd., Walton-on-Thames, Surrey.

Cooper, Dr. J.P. — Welsh Plant Breeding Station, Plas Gogerddan, Aberystwyth.

Crowdy, Prof. S.H. — Department of Botany, University of Southampton.

Cunningham, Dr.J.M.M. — Hill Farming Research Organization, Edinburgh.

Eadie, J. — Hill Farming Research Organization, Edinburgh.

Elston, Dr. J.F. — Department of Agricultural Botany, University of Reading.

Ford, E.D. — Department of Forestry and Natural Resources, University of Edinburgh.

Heywood, Dr. B.J. — May and Baker Ltd., Dagenham.

Hogg, W.H. — Meteorological Office (at National Agricultural Advisory Service, Westbury-on-Trym, Bristol.

Holmes, Prof. W. — Wye College, University of London, Near Ashford, Kent.

Hudson, Prof. J.P. G.M., M.B.E. — Long Ashton Research Station, University of Bristol.

Ivins, Prof. J.D. — School of Agriculture, University of Nottingham.

Jones, P.J. — Bridget's Experimental Husbandry Farm, Martyr Worthy, Winchester.

Jones, W.E. — Chief Agricultural Adviser, Ministry of Agriculture, Fisheries and Food, London.

Monteith, Prof. J.L. — School of Agriculture, University of Nottingham.

Morgan, K.E. — Department of Agriculture, University of Reading.

Newbould, Prof. P.J. — New University of Ulster, Coleraine, N. Ireland.

Penman, Dr. H.L., F.R.S. — Physics Department, Rothamsted Experimental Station, Harpenden, Herts.

Penning de Vries, F.W.T. — Laboratory for Theoretical Production Ecology, Agricultural University, Wageningen, Netherlands.

Pyke, Dr. Magnus — The Distillers Company Ltd., Glenochil Research Station Menstrie, Clackmannanshire.

Scott Russell, Prof. R. — Agricultural Research Council, Letcombe Laboratory, Wantage, Berks.

Thorne, Dr. Gillian, N. — Botany Department, Rothamsted Experimental Station, Harpenden, Herts.

Thornley, Dr. J.H.M. — Glasshouse Crops Research Institute, Littlehampton, Sussex.

Wareing, Prof. P.F., F.R.S. — Department of Botany, University College of Wales, Aberystwyth.

Warren Wilson, Dr. J. — Glasshouse Crops Research Institute, Littlehampton, Sussex.

Watson, Dr. D.J. — Botany Department, Rothampsted Experimental Station, Harpenden, Herts.

Wit, Dr. C.T. de — Laboratory for Theoretical Production Ecology, Agricultural University, Wageningen, Netherlands.

1. Future Trends in British Agriculture

W. E. Jones
Chief Agricultural Adviser, Ministry of Agriculture, Fisheries, and Food

In considering the potential crop production of Britain it is important to appreciate the changes that have occurred in British agriculture in recent times and to attempt to identify those factors which are likely to influence the pace of development in farm production processes.

Progress in the development of agriculture depends to a large extent on the output of the research services and the speed at which scientific findings can be translated into profitable farming systems. In this country it is becoming increasingly difficult, in terms of scientific manpower and finance, to supply the kind of research that meets the needs of modern farming. Governments can be expected to consider the level of investment in agricultural research from the standpoint of the aims and objectives of food production policies, and will certainly expect that research projects be directly geared to tackle the emerging problems which seem to prevent the achievement of the aims of those policies. It follows, therefore, that the selection of projects for research, particularly applied or mission-orientated research, demands the rapid identification and clear definition of the specific factors in current and future farming systems which inhibit the efficient use of farm resources, i.e. land, capital and labour. It is in this way that agriculture fulfills its role in an industrial economy such as ours.

In post-war British agriculture there has been a continuous and steady rise in agricultural output in most of the main commodities; wheat production has nearly doubled, barley production has more than trebled, home production of meat has trebled, the output of milk has increased by nearly 1000 million gallons (about 4000 million kg) and in fact the output of the farming industry has increased by one-third between 1950 and 1967.

This overall increase in physical production has been achieved without a corresponding increase in the resources used by farmers. Whilst production has been rising, the labour force has been falling; for the period under review the labour force has declined consistently by approximately 25 000 workers per annum; in fact the productivity of labour has advanced by about 5 per cent per annum, which is better than most of the major industries in the non-agricultural sector of the United Kingdom.

This increase in efficiency has, in part, been due to the assistance given by the government through price guarantees, production grants and other means of support; and in part due to the increased pressures which agriculture has been subjected to in order to remain competitive; but mainly due to advances in technology and to new scientific discoveries which have been applied to farming practices. These new techniques have resulted in the evolution of highly specialized and intensive systems of production, demanding a higher degree of expertise on the part of the producer. There has been a steady growth of very large units involving substantial capital investment and needing high standards of management both in the business and technical sense. The demands of the food industries for a steady supply of uniform products for processing and packaging for sale through supermarkets have forced producers to gear production to market requirements.

One of the most striking developments in the period has been the tremendous increase in the cereal acreage. The main reasons for this have been the higher yields resulting from the advent of improved varieties, better methods of weed and pest control, the use of new chemicals and new methods of cultivation, and improvements in machinery and equipment for harvesting and storage. Many farmers have learned that specialized systems based on cereal growing in combination with one or two other enterprises are more profitable and easier to manage than traditional mixed farming.

Simplified systems of this kind are now firmly established. They offer great advantages, but the departure from traditional fertility-building rotations obviously has its risks. In such situations, pest and disease incidence are a constant hazard, and the provision of optimum soil conditions for plant growth becomes more difficult. The problems which arise under such systems can be very complex, demanding a highly scientific approach. This pattern applies to all intensive fields of production such as poultry and egg production, intensive veal production, and continuous cereal growing. Indeed these trends are repeated in the agricultural industries of all the developed countries. Furthermore these new specialist production techniques demand a high injection of capital to allow for the scale of enterprise necessary to make them commercially profitable.

In spite of all this, British agriculture is still a very heterogeneous industry, and while its overall productivity has increased, the impact of the changes I have mentioned is by no means spread evenly throughout its individual segments and producers have not benefited equally from them. Although there has been a trend towards larger units, the agricultural industry is still essentially composed of a large number of relatively small self-contained units which manifest a wide disparity in efficiency and hence in the standards of living achieved. Farm incomes vary greatly as between the large farmer and the smaller farmer and between the farmer on better land and the farmer on poorer land. There is also a wide variation between incomes of farmers operating similar systems under comparable conditions. There are differences in income of considerable magnitude and these are due to a variety of causes, such as an inability to borrow sufficient capital to effect desirable improvements, but in the main they are due to inefficient use of available resources.

The broad aim of government agricultural policy in the United Kingdom in the post-war period has been to promote and maintain, by the provision of guaranteed prices and assured markets for the main farm commodities, 'a stable and efficient agricultural industry capable of producing such part of the nation's food and other agricultural produce as in the national interest it is desirable to produce in the United Kingdom, and of producing it at minimum prices consistent with proper remuneration and living conditions for farmers and workers in agriculture and an adequate return on capital invested in the industry'. Certain modifications have been made in the methods of supporting commodity prices, due to pressures of supplies from increases in home production and in overseas supplies. Thus the guaranteed prices for wheat, barley and milk were related to a 'standard quantity', defined as the amount of output which it was thought should be produced domestically, consistent with commitments to traditional overseas suppliers. This meant that prices to producers were likely to be reduced if the standard quantities were exceeded.

These measures, coupled with the fact that margins of profit in some of the commodities were declining, led to difficulties for the smaller family farm. So in 1958 the government introduced the Small Farmer Scheme. The basis of this Scheme was that eligible small farmers would receive grant-aid in return for operating a farm plan, approved by the advisers of the extension service.

So the growth in productivity in British agriculture has been stimulated partly by government policy and partly by natural evolution in response to outside pressures. It has been achieved through better management, better husbandry and the adoption of new technical advances. In the early 1950s the whole of the United Kingdom farming industry was geared to increasing production as an end in itself. This was a period of food scarcity, and expansion of output was the prime objective of both government and farmers. Indeed the margin between costs and income was such that the expansion of output on the individual farm automatically provided higher profits for the farmer in most farming situations.

It was during the early 1950s that the farming industry was relieved of war-time restrictions. Animal foodstuffs fertilisers and machinery became more plentiful again, and there followed an unprecedented upsurge of production, which has continued to this day. This trend, coupled with revolutionary changes beyond the farm gate, created an entirely new situation for the farmer. Influences and developments outside the farm boundary acquired a new significance, and agricultural economics and management analysis became just as important as, and certainly more urgent than, the rotation of crops and soil analysis. The steady and continuous improvement in the efficiency of farm production in the United Kingdom in the last two decades was the product of the application of the results of scientific research and technology, through increased government investment in agricultural research, strengthened Extension Services and the promotion of grant-aid schemes related to farm planning and productivity. These measures have encouraged the development of industrialized-type farming and increased the difficulties of the small family farmers. However, the special government measures now taken to encourage co-operation, rationalization of farm structure and the compensation/pension scheme for amalgamating farms will enable many of them to remain in the industry and enjoy a standard of living comparable to the rest of the community, and enable the rest of them to leave.

If the estimate that world population will have doubled by the end of this century prove to be correct then we are bound to see an unprecedented demand for food. In the United Kingdom it can safely be assumed that the loss of land to agriculture, together with a rise in population, will require a level of home food-production double what it is today. One can foresee the need to intensify the kind of research that will raise the yield per acre of crops, improve the efficiency of conversion of food stuffs by all classes of livestock, reduce waste at all stages of production, storage, processing and distribution, and, above all, increase the output per man employed.

The gaps in our knowledge of the biological processes concerned with plant and animal production are many and varied, but it is the rate of progress in filling these gaps that will determine success or failure in meeting the foreseeable rise in demand for food and, indeed, in solving the problems of world malnutrition. The yields from vast areas of cereal crops are greatly reduced because of the ravages of fungal diseases and pests. There is an urgent need for a deeper understanding of the physiology of the mechanism of resistance of plants to disease, so that new resistant varieties can be successfully bred. There is insufficient knowledge about the biochemical changes associated with tuber-formation in potatoes and the development of the sugar-beet root; in animal production, traditional extensive systems are being replaced by large intensive units, and certain diseases, formerly under control, may well assume serious economic proportions. Already, the emergence of chronic respiratory diseases have caused serious losses in the intensive production of broiler chicken, pigs and beef under intensive conditions of management. There are fundamental problems, impeding the development of more efficient food production and accounting for vast losses of food the world over; it is towards their solution that the efforts of research, extension and education must be directed.

More effective dissemination of scientific findings is also a matter which needs urgent attention. The pace of technical development in agriculture is accelerating all the time, and the problems associated with advising farmers (and governments) are likely to become more difficult and complex in the future. This is so because each new scientific or technical advance adds to the range of possible alternative situations, which in turn emphasises the need for closer collaboration between scientists, extension workers and educationists. Such collaboration could lead to the establishment of organisations or mechanisms, at both national and international levels, to determine what programmes of research and development are worth doing in terms of the resources that can be spared and the foreseeable benefits that could be expected in scientific, economic and farming terms.

2. Regional and Local Environments

W.H. Hogg
Meteorological Office, N.A.A.S., Bristol

Introduction

This account of regional and local environments in relation to potential crop production is based on the collection of standard macroclimatic data, supplemented by mesoclimatic data which have been obtained over short periods for special purposes. No attempt will be made to deal with microclimate or to define the climate experienced by the growing crop. The object is to examine the variations in the atmospheric environment in which plants may be grown and which appear to be of relevance to the question of crop production.

Probably almost every item of standard meteorological data on record has some relevance to plant production, even if only negative, but clearly these differ very much in importance. As a starting point we may regard crop production as essentially the conversion of solar energy, water and soil nutrients into economic end-products, so that solar radiation and precipitation (or other methods of expressing plant water needs) may be regarded as primary controls in potential crop production. The effects of variations in solar radiation on other elements such as air temperature and soil temperature are also relevant to plant development and growth at different times in the crop life [24] and these may also be included as primary controls. Sunshine data, which are often used as a substitute for radiation data, may also be included here.

As secondary controls we may include advected energy, which can be very important in the early areas of Britain, and topographic modifications of the environment, which may be favourable or not. Finally, as tertiary

Table 2.1
Major controls affecting regional and local environments for plant production

Primary	Solar energy, precipitation and other methods of expressing water need
	Sunshine, air temperature, soil temperature
Secondary	Advected energy
	Topographical modifications, e.g., hill climates
Tertiary	Weather favourable to plant disease
	Isolated phenomena causing damage or crop reduction

controls, we have selected climatic elements which may be particularly important in the development of plant diseases and, also, isolated phenomena such as frost which can cause severe loss of crop when they occur (Table 2.1).

Because of the distribution of weather stations and also because of the difficulties of generalization over extensive upland areas, for some of the topics discussed there is more information for England and Wales than for Scotland. Where possible this has been overcome by indicating the main trends in Scotland.

Primary Controls

Solar Radiation

In the absence of all other restrictions, crop growth would be determined by the amount of solar radiation received and Monteith [24] has estimated that in terms of total incident radiation the maximum possible efficiency of photosynthesis is about 8 per cent. In practice the efficiency is much less, and Holliday [17] gives figures for the United Kingdom showing biological yields for various crops approximating to a one per cent conversion of energy, but with economic yields at only about one-third of this for some crops.

The solar constant, i.e. the total solar radiation at normal incidence outside the atmosphere at mean solar distance, is approximately 2 cal cm^{-2}

Table 2.2
Monthly and annual mean values of total radiation on a horizontal surface in cal cm^{-2} day^{-1} and percentage ratio of direct/total radiation

	Jan	Feb	Mar	Apr	May	June	July	Aug	Sept	Oct	Nov	Dec	Year
Lerwick													
Total	24	70	140	268	347	397	351	277	184	86	32	15	183
% Direct	25	31	36	41	38	38	34	34	38	32	27	18	36
Eskdalemuir													
Total	47	94	159	266	361	384	340	277	205	116	56	34	195
% Direct	35	34	36	39	42	41	35	35	39	38	37	33	38
Cambridge													
Total	59	101	185	274	384	440	377	325	245	144	70	47	221
% Direct	35	33	40	37	42	46	38	40	44	41	36	35	41
Aberporth													
Total	63	114	227	334	453	496	429	377	272	153	73	51	253
% Direct	34	36	42	45	48	50	43	46	47	41	33	36	45
Kew													
Total	50	87	178	263	377	422	367	321	243	139	65	40	213
% Direct	29	33	42	41	46	48	40	44	46	43	36	30	43

Note: The Aberporth data are incomplete for 1957 and 1958.

min^{-1}. The radiation received on a horizontal surface on the earth is largely determined by latitude, but variations in cloudiness prevent the distribution from being purely zonal. There are few long-period routine measurements of radiation for Britain and there are many gaps in our knowledge of the detailed distribution. Day [6] has prepared monthly maps based largely on periods of three to five years and Taylor and Smith [29] have given estimates of radiation and illumination for eighty-six stations, based on sunshine and visibility. As a basis for this discussion, we shall use averages for the period 1957-66 for five stations which have been computed in the Meteorological Office (Table 2.2).

Figure 2.1 shows the annual variation for Lerwick and Aberporth, roughly representative of the extremes recorded in Britain. Two points stand out, the general tendency to a greater intensity of radiation in the south (Kew is probably somewhat affected by its proximity to London) and the consistently high values for Aberporth. The maps by Day [6] and maps of distribution of bright sunshine suggest that these high values are more the result of its coastal location than of its position in the west of the country—we have no records from the east coast. Also, the proportion of radiation which is received directly increases southwards so that there is a good deal more spatial variation in direct radiation than in diffuse, although

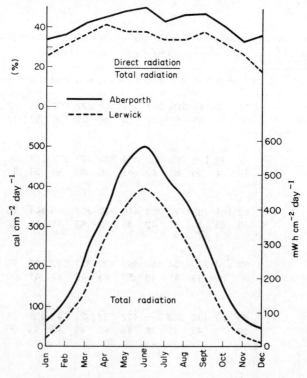

Figure 2.1   Annual variation of radiation at Lerwick and Aberporth, 1957-66.

the mean annual values of diffuse radiation exceed those for direct radiation at all stations.

The recent large-scale production of Golden Delicious apples in southern France is dependent on the use of irrigation but the high yields appear to be the result of high solar radiation. Table 2.3 gives the approximate values of total radiation in January, July and the year as read from maps published by Budyko [4].

Table 2.3
Approximate values of total radiation

	January (kcal cm^{-2} month^{-1})	July (kcal cm^{-2} month^{-1})	Year (kcal cm^{-2} year^{-1})
Southern England	2	13	90
Southern France	4	18	120

In the midsummer there is some 40% more radiation in the south of France than in the apple growing areas of England. The average yield of Cox in England is around 400 bushels acre^{-1} (18 000 kg ha^{-1}) and comparison with Dutch yields of both varieties suggests that this is equivalent to about 600 bushels acre^{-1} (27 000 kg ha^{-1}) of Golden Delicious. This compares with averages for Golden Delicious of around 900 bushels acre^{-1} (40 000 kg ha^{-1}) from the Rhône valley, an increase of some 50 per cent.

Crop Water Needs

Until some twenty years ago it was generally assumed that rainfall was sufficient for crop production in this country. While we are fortunate in that severe droughts seldom occur, the work of Penman [25] and its subsequent development in practical terms has underlined the desirability of supplementary water for a wide range of crops. The main restrictions on irrigation are now water supply and charges, so that in the end crop production may be limited by economic factors.

The average annual rainfall map shows a rise from about 500 mm (20 in.) in parts of Cambridgeshire to 5000 mm (200 in.) in the wettest parts of the Lake District, demonstrating a wide variation in regional environments in relation to crop water needs. These are values from the standard rain-gauges, which underestimate the rainfall actually reaching the ground [27].

To use these crude rainfall amounts to differentiate crop environments leads to some exaggeration because of the contrasts in rainfall regime between the wetter and drier parts of the country. Most of the rainfall in the winter half-year October to March may be considered wasted in relation to plant growth, even though a certain proportion of stored water may be used for subsequent irrigation. In the wettest parts of the country, the typical west-coast rainfall regime shows a well defined maximum in the winter half-year which has over 60% of the annual precipitation (62½% in places). In drier areas the annual distribution is more even and approximates closely to 50% in each season.

The water used by plants must be considered in relation to the rainfall in order to estimate whether there is likely to be any shortage, and M.A.F.F. Technical Bulletin 16 [22] gives a map showing the average potential transpiration for April to September at average county heights. This varies from 275-300 mm (11-12 in.) in parts of the Scottish highlands to 450-470 mm (18-18½ in.) in a number of eastern counties south of the Wash. The variation over the country is thus very much less than for rainfall, and this is true also for variation from year to year. Long-term irrigation needs computed from Penman-type water balance sheets for a period of years may be used to indicate how far natural rainfall falls short of the full plant water needs. It is, however, clearly impossible to talk of the irrigation needs of crops in general, and both the period when irrigation is likely to be of benefit and the water holding capacity of the soil must be considered. To meet these points, Hogg [14] has constructed maps giving long-term irrigation needs for England and Wales using various parameters for fifteen periods within the growing season with four possible irrigation plans to allow for differences in rooting depth and the moisture-holding capacity of the soil. Many of these could be used to pick out regional differences in the moisture environment for individual crops, and as contrasting examples we may use grass and mature fruit trees.

For grass, unless there is more than 210 mm (8 in) of readily available moisture per metre depth of soil (2½ in. per foot), it has been recommended that 25 mm (1 in.) of irrigation should be applied whenever the soil moisture deficit reaches 25 mm (1 in.) during April-September, restoring the soil to field capacity. On this basis, the climatological irrigation needs are very high, reaching an average of about 225 mm (9 in.) a year in parts of the Isle of Wight and some coastal areas of north Kent and Essex. Impossibly large quantities would thus be needed for maximum production of grass, and on purely practical grounds we may restrict the irrigation period to April-August and give somewhat less weight to the driest years. Even so, the needs are still very high and somewhat arbitrarily the 125 mm (5 in.) isopleth is selected as giving the minimum value with which we need here concern ourselves. This roughly corresponds with the 70% line given by Coppock [5] in his map showing the percentage of crops and grass, with more than 70% of the grass acreage to the north and west. Such an approach can be justified in that grass is so plentiful to the west and north of this line that we can regard potential production as reached in relation to moisture; only to the south and east is the use of irrigation likely to lead to increased production. If we call this area *dry* in relation to grass production, it is reasonable to designate the south-east corner of England as *very dry* and the line of 175 mm (7 in.) of average annual irrigation need has been used, Figure 2.2.

For mature fruit trees with a rooting depth of 60-120 cm (24-48 in.) grown in a soil with up to 210 mm of readily available moisture per metre depth of soil (2½ in. per foot), it is recommended that 50 mm (2 in.) of irrigation is applied at a soil moisture-deficit of 75 mm (3 in.) during May to August. The needs are, of course, less than for grass, but still quite high, rising to 150 mm (6 in.) a year in parts of the south and east. The isopleth for an average annual need of 75 mm (3 in.) has been selected as the basic line here as most of the country's orchards are to the south and east of this. Recent work at Luddington [9] shows that there are increases of growth and yield after irrigation, which suggests that the whole of the otherwise suitable apple and pear-growing areas of the country is short of water for full growth potential and must therefore be designated *dry*; the most extensive and most important areas lie within a *very dry* area, to the east of 113 mm (4½ in.) average annual need line.

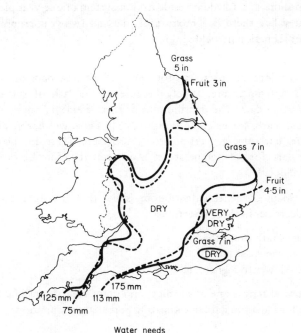

Figure 2.2 *Designation of water needs for grass and mature fruit trees, England and Wales.*

Another approach is possible in relation to grass, the estimation of grass growing days as described by Hurst and Smith [19]. A grass growing day is defined as any day from April 1 to September 30 when the soil moisture deficit does not exceed 50 mm (2 in.) and they have used county averages of rainfall and potential transpiration to provide a long-term average map. The values are expressed as average number of days lost to grass growth, April to

September, and they are less than ten west and north of a line running from the Exe estuary northwards along the Welsh border, swinging eastwards from Denbighshire, south of the Peak district and north-east to the North Riding coast. At the other extreme there are more than forty days lost along the Essex and north Kent coasts. These are clearly underestimates, as the data have been subject to smoothing in relation to both time and space, but their general validity, if not their absolute values, is supported by good correlation with regional milk-yields.

Finally, there are occasions of excess rainfall which lead to reduction in crop potential, quite apart from the damage caused by flooding. For example, apple and pear trees may suffer severe root damage, with possible death of the trees, following excessive rainfall in autumn and winter and particularly in October. This was especially noticeable in Dorset and Somerset in 1960-61. Also, strawberries in some early areas of the country must be managed in different ways according to the rainfall expected, so that the bulk of the fruit from Hampshire and Cheddar result from a system of one-year plants, but in the Tamar valley there is a mixture of one and two-year cropping, with a consequent reduction in yield.

Related Elements

Many descriptions of macro-environments in the past have been based on sunshine and temperature, largely because of the lack of sufficient long-period radiation data. The distributions of these elements can easily be seen in published maps, for example Booth [2, 3]. These will not be discussed at length here, but some general points will be made. There are, however, few published data for soil temperature, which will therefore be dealt with in rather more detail.

Sunshine. Maps of general distribution show that the duration of bright sunshine decreases in three directions:

> (a) from south to north,
> (b) from the coast inland,
> (c) from lower to higher land.

In practical terms, one of the most important uses of sunshine data is as a substitute for radiation data in estimating potential transpiration.

Air Temperatures. We have no exact knowledge of the range of temperature environments over Britain, and most published maps obscure this by the process of reducing recorded temperatures to sea-level. Estimates of this range have been made from the maps published by Booth [3], using a lapse rate of $0.6°C$ per 100 m. They are given in Table 2.4 for sea-level temperatures as read from the maps and also on the assumption that we may be interested in environments up to 1000 m.

Clearly, in the differentiation of macro-environments of temperature, altitude is of the same order of importance as all other factors together.

Temperature data have often been used to give estimates of the period when mean temperature is above a stated threshold. One of the more common thresholds is 5-6 °C (41-43 °F) and the period above this is sometimes referred to as length of growing season, though it is in no sense a biological measurement. Hogg [12] has given a map for England and Wales based on the period with mean monthly temperature above 6 °C approx. (42 °F) which shows that the duration varies from about 200 days in the highest areas to 365 days in the south-west (though the method of computation leads to overestimation at this end of the scale). An interesting feature of this distribution is the lack of variation over much of the eastern half of England. This is the result of using macroclimatic data, and undoubtedly there is a good deal of variation resulting from the mesoclimatic factors of slope and aspect.

Table 2.4
Range over Britain of mean monthly temperatures in January and July based on M.S.L. temperatures and on estimates of actual values up to 1000 m

	January	July
M.S.L.	8° to 3°C (46.5 to 37.5°F)	18° to 12.5°C (64.5 to 54.5°F)
Up to 1000 m	8° to -3°C (46.5 to 26.5°F)	18° to 7.5°C (64.5 to 45.5°F)

Further north, this period decreases to about 220 days in the Shetlands, but it is down to 180-200 days at a number of places around 300 m in the highlands, and is considerably less at greater altitudes. On the island of Tiree, it is as long as 314 days, somewhat longer than in Aberystwyth.

Soil Temperatures. During the early part of the season, particularly during germination, soil temperatures are more relevant than air temperatures. Although readings of 10 cm and 20 cm (4 and 8 in.) soil temperatures have been made at agrometeorological stations for many years there has been no comprehensive analysis of these data. The following account is based on a preliminary investigation using monthly means at 10 cm for the period 1959-67. Two points need to be emphasized, firstly, the readings are taken at 0900 G.M.T. and are not far removed from the diurnal minimum (there is some variation from month to month) and, secondly, the temperatures are influenced by the type of soil and its physical condition, particularly the proportion of air and water. No attempt is made to allow for this in the following account.

Figure 2.3 on the following page, shows the annual variation of soil temperature at eight places from which the main features of variations in environment are apparent. Near the west coast of Britain, the January and July temperatures decrease from 4.9, 16.5 °C (40.8, 61.7 °F) at Cambourne in Cornwall to 1.9, 14.7 °C (35.4, 58.4 °F) at Auchincruive in Ayrshire, the decrease being more marked in winter than in summer. In the east, the change is from 2.2, 17.8 °C (35.9, 64.1 °F) at Wye in Kent to 1.2, 13.7 °C (34.1, 56.6 °F) at Craibstone in Aberdeenshire, a greater decrease in summer than in winter. The effect of altitude is shown by the comparison between Gogerddan, 31 m, and Llety-evan-hen, 290 m, and is most marked in summer, when the July difference is 3 °C (5.4 °F) over 7 km is comparable with the difference between Wye and Craibstone, some 700 km apart. The figures below each graph show the length of the period in days when the temperature exceeds 6 °C approx. (42 °F) and 10 °C (50 °F). Mayer and Poljakoff-Mayber [23] have compiled data which indicate that seed germination after sowing is usually fastest between 15 and 25 °C (59-77 °F), depending on species, although the minimum for cereals is about 3 °C (37 °F). It is clear that in parts of Britain the chances of long periods when the soil temperature at 10 cm exceeds 15 °C are quite small. For 6 °C the range is from 309 days in Cornwall to 199 in Aberdeenshire, with corresponding values of 187 and 129 for a 10 °C threshold. However, these figures are based on 0900 G.M.T. temperatures and Gloyne [7], has pointed out that the diurnal variation of temperature at 10 cm was of the order of 8-10 °C (15-18 °F) on dry sunny days during spring and summer in south Devon. Many small seeds would not be as deep as 10 cm, and a short period survey at Luddington E.H.S. showed that in September the 5 cm soil temperatures could be 3-4 °C (5-7 °F) warmer, according to soil type, than those at 10 cm in the middle of the day.

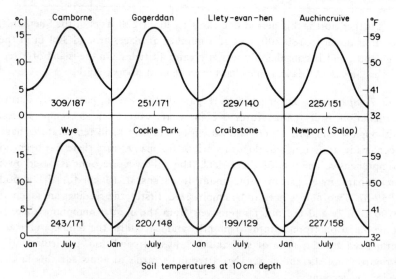

Soil temperatures at 10 cm depth

Figure 2.3   Annual variation of soil temperature at 10 cm depth for selected stations. The values beneath each curve give the period in days with mean temperature above 6 °C. approx. (42°F) and 10°C (50°F).

Secondary Controls

Advection

The movement of air over the earth is the result of temperature differences set up by spatial variation in the intensity of solar radiation, combined with the rotation of the earth. As a result of this movement there is some redistribution of energy, both as sensible heat and as latent heat which is released on condensation of water vapour, though this often occurs at considerable altitudes and does not directly affect plant life, except in relation to rainfall. The horizontal transfer of heat is known as advection, in contrast to convection, the vertical redistribution. The general planetary wind circulation and the distribution of ocean currents are such that, in our latitudes, the west coasts of continents are considerably warmer during winter than are places further east. Maps and tables given by Conrad in Köppen and Geiger [21] show that to the west of the British Isles, in longitude 10-20°W, there is a positive temperature anomaly of more than 15 °C in January.

The effects of advection are felt over the whole of the British Isles, but they are most marked in the early areas of the west which are well known for the somewhat specialized crops they produce. More important from the point of view of crop potential, the fact that winter temperatures are often above 5-6°C implies that in some years there is little, if any, cessation of growth and that more than one crop a year can be grown and harvested. For example, in the south west a typical rotation is early potatoes followed by December/January heading winter cauliflower or spring cabbage for cutting during the same period; the land is then planted again with early potatoes. Another combination is winter cauliflower followed by barley or some other farm crop.

Even in the west there are variations in earliness and Table 2.5, based on maps by Day [6], gives approximate values of solar radiation at places in the west of England and Wales which show that the effect of latitude must be combined with that of west coast location.

Table 2.5
Approximate values of mean daily total of solar radiation (diffuse plus direct) on a horizontal surface in cal cm^{-2}

	January	February	March	April
Scilly	65	140	240	410
S.W. Cornwall	60	140	220	390
Pembroke Coast	60	120	220	390
Anglesey	50	120	210	370

Further details of the effect of the environment on factors which are climatically important to early crop production in Britain are given in Hogg [15], and some of these points are discussed below.

Differences in temperature between inland areas and sites on the east or west coasts are largely due to differences in minimum temperature, but the advantages of coastal districts in the west over those in the east are due as much, if not more, to maximum rather than minimum temperature.

The graphs in Figure 2.3 suggest an advantage for the west over the east in relation to winter and spring soil temperatures. In more detail, the 10 cm soil temperatures over a period of some twenty years show that the far south-west is typically two to three weeks earlier than Long Ashton, near Bristol: in exceptional years there is no difference and occasionally it amounts to four or five weeks. The criterion used was the week in which the soil temperature at 0900 G.M.T. last fell below 6 °C approximately (42 °F).

These favourable winter and spring temperatures lead to a diminished frost risk, and over the period January 1956-65 the average frost frequency during January-March was:

Isles of Scilly	3.6	Gulval (nr. Penzance)	10.6
Dale Fort (Pembs)	13.2	Holyhead	21.8

Moving east along the south coast, the chance of frost increases fairly rapidly, for example 17.6 at Torquay and 28.4 at Southampton.

Further north, the contrast between the east and west coast in Scotland is shown by comparable values of 14.1 at Tiree and 36.6 at Leuchars, near the coast of Fifeshire.

Topographical Modifications

The major topographical modifications to the mesoclimate result from variations in altitude, slope and aspect. Considering the British Isles as a whole, the most general modification is altitude. Hill climates exist over much of Wales, northern England and Scotland, and Gloyne [8] has summarised the most important features of these in north Britain.

In the hills, significantly different mesoclimates will result from the very different intensities of radiation received on different slopes and aspects, and diagrams published by Knoch [20] show that in 50°N the maximum possible radiation on steep southerly and northerly slopes differs by a factor of about 2.

Other causes may affect radiation locally, and Rees [26] discusses this for the Glasshouse Crop Research Institution at Rustington, near the south coast. He states that more radiation is recorded there than is accounted for by the increase of sunshine along the coast. It is suggested that on sunny days convection clouds will build up a short distance inland, probably aided by the presence of the South Downs, and that additional (reflected) radiation is received along the coastal strip.

Hughes & Munro [18] have given climatic data for 1967 for four places between 4 and 40 km from the Cardigan Bay coast, and they have kindly provided radiation data on which Table 2.6 is based. The estimates given here are derived from records for 3 or 4 years, and occasionally for 2 or 5.

For places not far from the coast, the reduction of radiation with altitude is clear, but at Pant-y-dŵr many of the monthly values are close to those for Gogerddan. This is no doubt due to a reduction in cloudiness because of its distance from the coast; in spite of its altitude, the average annual rainfall at Pant-y-dŵr is only about 11 mm (46 in.) compared with 10 mm (42 in.) at Gogerddan.

Table 2.6
Monthly mean values of radiation on a horizontal surface for stations in Wales

	Alt. (m)	Distance inland (km)	Jan	Feb	Mar	Apr	May	June	July	Aug	Sept	Oct	Nov	Dec
			(cal cm^{-2})											
Gogerddan	30	4	46	95	176	284	341	379	346	308	209	123	68	39
Llety-evan-hen	290	11	36	81	145	243	311	307	317	278	168	78	54	33
Syfydrin	335	14	32	76	129	227	276	337	308	279	177	101	55	28
Pant-y-dŵr	305	40	37	86	147	241	297	359	370	284	206	114	61	39

Little need be said on the temperature and rainfall in the hills. The reduction of temperature shortens the period with mean temperature above 6 °C approximately (42 °F) and in England and Wales the start is delayed until mid-April with a duration of some 200 days [13]. As in all maritime climates, the flat form of the annual temperature curve implies that it needs only a small difference in altitude to produce a fairly marked difference in this period, and Gloyne [8] gives a rate of 4 days per 30 m (100 ft) in the north of England and south of Scotland.

The increase of rainfall in the hills is well known and, as much of the winter precipitation occurs as snow, the growth of spring pastures may be delayed. On the whole, in hill areas an excess of rainfall is more likely than a deficiency, and one of the ways in which crop potential will be lessened is by the effects of poor drainage and the formation of peat soils.

Wind is an important feature of hill climates, and Gloyne [8] gives maps which emphasize the general windiness of Britain, based largely on observation from low-level areas. The effect of wind in upland areas is certainly to limit the range of crops and to reduce the yield of those which are grown; the effect on trees is often visually obvious. There have been no experiments on the effect of shelter (or exposure) on grass, and we are forced to rely on evidence from lowland horticulture. Hogg and Carter [10] showed a significant increase of 27 per cent in the yield of lettuce over three years at Luddington, although it is one of the least windy areas of the country. This supports earlier views that maximum crop potential is likely to be reached in the less windy areas, or in those which have been sheltered. It is unlikely that this is due solely to wind — in more sheltered areas some reduction in turbulent mixing appears to modify the general mesoclimate in a way favourable to the plant. Hogg [12] has shown that the provision of shelter hedges in Cornwall may raise afternoon air temperatures at heights of 60 cm

(2 ft) around 1 °C in spring and summer and soil temperatures at depths 20 cm (8 in.) by rather less than this. On indivdual days the effect on temperature may be considerably greater, according to the general weather and particularly the wind direction.

There are few systematic observations to indicate to what extent existing land forms provide shelter for areas in their lee. This geomorphic shelter, if it can be isolated from other effects, particularly altitude and other types of shelter, may be proportional to a crop potential index. At Rosewarne in Cornwall, for example, sites not more than 30 m below the general plateau level of about 80 m (250 ft) have runs-of-wind 13-15 per cent lower than on the plateau, within a horizontal distance of 500 m (1650 ft) [11].

One other major effect of topography is to modify the distribution of frosts, and this will be discussed in relation to the physical factors which can cause damage or crop reduction.

Tertiary Factors

Diseases

The course of many crop diseases is much affected by the weather, and therefore crop potential is also affected. Potato blight is probably the most common disease for which the dependence of the epidemiology on the weather is well understood in this country [1]. The most important factors in this relationship are that the blight appears in the crop as the result of infected tubers and the pathogen is normally present, awaiting only the occurrence of favourable weather. The two most important weather parameters concerned are temperature and humidity — the rate of growth of the fungus depends on temperature, and infection requires a film of moisture on the leaf. Beaumont [1] defined a critical period as one of forty-eight hours when:

(a) Temperature does not fall below 10 °C (50 °F),
(b) Relative humidity does not fall below 75%,

after which blight is likely to develop, provided foci of the disease are present, generally within about fourteen days.

It is possible to investigate the occurrence of these Beaumont periods to give some idea of the disease risk. Table 2.7 gives values for the past ten years (June-August) for some places in south-west and south-east England.

These indicate the possibility of major variations of potential production for particular crops, both from year to year and also over fairly small distances. A word of warning is necessary here, in that the knowledge of the occurrence of a critical period also permits spraying to reduce damage and to increase potential. Also, a good 'blight year' is also a good growing year, so that loss of yield from disease may be counterbalanced by higher potential yield.

Apple scab is a similar disease in that the inoculum is widely present so that attacks occur when the leaves are wet for a period, and the severity of these attacks depends on temperature. Smith [28] has demonstrated that in place of leaf wetness we may use the concept of days with high humidity, i.e. days when the relative humidity does not fall below 90 per cent His map for June and July shows clear topographic links, especially the relative paucity of such days in the lee of the Welsh mountains and the Pennines.

Table 2.7
Hours of Beaumont periods, June-August, 1959-68

	1959	1960	1961	1962	1963	1964	1965	1966	1967	1968	Mean
St. Mawgan (Nr. Newquay)	535	1073	633	865	1212	1270	1226	576	1293	1010	969
Plymouth	575	792	450	776	1298	1215	1379	830	1207	792	931
Exeter	381	341	6	336	599	261	350	142	242	332	299
Bristol	329	388	49	53	369	204	456	228	331	307	271
Abingdon (Berks)	63	67	0	0	153	61	153	251	88	165	100

Another group of weather-dependent diseases depends on pathogens which do not complete their life cycle in Britain and which have to be imported. For example, black (stem) rust of wheat does not occur unless the uredospores are transported from other areas, from north Africa and southern Europe early in the season or from central Europe later on. Here we are concerned with a quite complex interaction between the phenology of the pathogen and of wheat crops in the source and target areas. In the end, these are linked by a meteorological accident, the occurrence of a particular wind at the right time to carry the spores to a crop capable of being infected.

Other Phenomena
In the same context, we may think of other meteorological accidents which can cause marked reductions in crop yields. Of these, the most obvious example is frost which in extreme cases can wipe out a crop over a fairly wide area in a night. This is particularly true of certain high-value crops, for example fruits and vegetables, which are being grown fairly close to their climatic limits of production. Clearly the question of topographic influences may be very important here, particularly when dealing with the radiation frosts which occur on still, clear nights in spring. The effect of land form on air flow on such nights and the collection of cold air in frost hollows needs no further elaboration here. It is logical to think of a regional frost risk for major areas of production, based on macroclimatic data, with superimposed local

frost-risks due to topography. As examples, Table 2.8 uses long period data
from Long Ashton Research Station to provide regional data for Somerset,
and a farm some 65 km (40 miles) distant for local data, based on a three
year mesoclimatic survey.

To indicate severity, different threshold temperatures have been used in
these frost definitions, and for blackcurrants it is assumed that there will be a
complete loss of crop after an air frost of $-2.2\,°C$ or worse in April and May
and a partial loss (say 50 per cent) between this and $-1.1\,°C$. Apart from
frost, one could reasonably expect a crop of 3 tons/acre in the district. Over ten
years the regional frost risk will reduce the potential from 30 tons to 18 tons,
and on the farm in question local effects will further reduce it to 12 tons.
Over a long term, we may tentatively suggest that for this crop, there is a
regional frost risk equivalent to 40 per cent of expected production which on
a given farm is increased by a further 20 per cent [16].

Table 2.8
Number of years in ten with frost after March 31

Temperature	Regional	Farm
0 (°C)	8.7	10
-1.1	5.3	6.6
-2.2	2.8	4.7

Many other examples may be given of meteorological accidents which
lead to occasional severe, if localized, loss of crop potential, including gales,
flood and hail.

ACKNOWLEDGEMENT
Acknowledgement is made to the Director-General of the Meteorological
Office for permission to publish this chapter.

REFERENCES
  1. BEAUMONT, A. 'The dependence on the weather of the dates of
     outbreak of potato blight epidemics', *Trans. Br. mycol. Soc.*, 1947, **31**,
     41-53.
  2. BOOTH, R.E. '1931-60; Average monthly, seasonal and annual maps of
     bright sunshine over the British Isles', *Clim. Mem. Met. Off.*, *1961*, **42A**,
     p.1, pls. 17.
  3. BOOTH, R.E. '1931-60; Monthly, seasonal and annual maps of mean
     daily maximum, mean daily minimum, mean temperature and mean
     temperature-range over the British Isles', *Clim. Mem. Met. Off.*, 1968,
     43A, pp.3, pls. 72.

4. BUDYKO, M.I. 'Solar radiation and the use of it by plants', in *Agroclimatological methods*, Unesco Symp. Nat. Resc. Res. 7, Reading 1968, 39-53.

5. COPPOCK, J.T. *An agricultural atlas of England and Wales*, London Faber and Faber, 1964, pp. 255.

6. DAY, G.J. 'Distribution of total solar radiation on a horizontal surface over the British Isles and adjacent areas', *Met. Mag., Lond.* 1961, **90**, 269-84.

7. GLOYNE, R.W. 'An examination of some observations of soil temperatures', *J. Br. Grassld Soc.*, 1950, **5**,157-77.

8. GLOYNE, R.W. 'Some climatic influences affecting hill-land productivity', *Proc. Symp. Eur. Grassld. Fed., Aberdeen*, 1968, 1-7.

9. GOODE, J.E. and INGRAM, J., (Personal communication), 1969.

10. HOGG, W.H. and CARTER, A.R. 'Shelter screens at Luddington 1957-59', *Expl. Hort.*, 1962, **7**, 47-51.

11. HOGG, W.H. 'Measurements of the shelter-effect of land-forms and other topographical features, and of artificial windbreaks', *Scient. Hort.*, 1964-65, **17**, 20-30.

12. HOGG, W.H. 'Climatic factors and choice of site with special reference to horticulture', *Symp. Inst. Biol.* 1965, **14**, 141-55.

13. HOGG, W.H. 'The growing season in England and Wales', *Agric. Mem. Met. Off.*, 1965, **116**, pp. 5.

14. HOGG, W.H. *Atlas of long-term irrigation needs for England and Wales*, London; M.A.A.F., N.A.A.S., 1967, vi + Pls. 300.

15. HOGG, W.H. 'Meteorological factors in early crop production', *Weather, Lond.* 1967, **22**, 84-118.

16. HOGG, W.H. 'The analysis of data with particular reference to frost surveys: suggestions on the expression of results in economic terms', *Proc. W.M.O. Region. Training Sem. Agromet.*, 1968, 343-50.

17. HOLLIDAY, R. 'Solar energy and consumption in relation to crop yield', *Agric. Prog.* 1966, **41**, 24-34.

18. HUGHES, ROY and MUNRO, J.M.M. 'Climatic and soil factors in the hills of Wales in relation to the breeding of special herbage varieties', *Proc. Symp. Eur. Grassld Fed., Aberdeen*, 1968, 109-12.

19. HURST, G.W. and SMITH, L.P. 'Grass growing days' in *Weather and Agriculture*, Pergamon Press, Oxford: 1967, 147-55.

20. KNOCH, K. 'Die Landesklimaaufnahme Wesen and Methodik', *Ber. dt. Wetterd.* 1963, **85**, 1-64.

21. KÖPPEN, W. and GEIGER, R. (editors) *Handbuch der Klimatologie*, Band I, Teil B, *Die klimatologischen Elemente und ihre Abhängigkeit von terrestrischen Einflüssen.* Berlin, 1936, pp. 556.

22. M.A.F.F. LONDON, 'Potential transpiration', *Tech. Bull. Minist. Agric. Fish. Fd.* 1967, **16**, v + 77.

23. MAYER, A.M. and POLJAKOFF-MAYBER, A. *The germination of seeds*, Oxford: Pergamon Press, 1963, pp. 236.

24. MONTEITH, J.L. 'Physical limitations to crop growth', *Agric. Prog.* 1966, **41**, 9-23.
25. PENMAN, H.L. 'Natural evaporation from open water, bare soil and grass', *Proc. R. Soc. Ser. A.* 1948, **193**, 120-45.
26. REES, A.R. 'Solar radiation on the south coast of England', *Q.Jl. R. met. Soc.*, 1968, **94**, 397-401.
27. RODDA, J.C. 'The systematic error in rainfall measurement', *J. Instn. Wat. Engrs.* 1967, **21**, 173-7.
28. SMITH, L.P. 'The duration of surface wetness', *Proc. 15 Int. hort. Congr., Nice,* 1962, **3**, 478-83.
29. TAYLOR, S.M. and SMITH, L.P. 'Estimation of averages of radiation and illumination', *Met. Mag., Lond.*, 1961, **90**, 289-94.

3. Microclimatology and Crop Production

J.L. Monteith and J.F. Elston
Universities of Nottingham and Reading

Introduction

Early publications in microclimatology emphasised the contrast between conventional climatological records at screen height and the more extreme type of climate found at the surfaces of soil and of vegetation. Formal analysis of measurements from the field was mainly concerned with the heat and water balance of natural surfaces, and later with different procedures for calculating the rate of evaporation from a crop. The subject entered a new phase when methods were developed to measure the carbon dioxide exchange of field crops, and when light gradients in plant communities were used to estimate photosynthetic rates. Eventually, it may be possible to predict dry-matter production, like evaporation, from a knowledge of the microclimatic and physiological features of a crop canopy, but development of the subject has been inhibited by a lack of measurements, in sharp contrast to the proliferation of theoretical models.

The study of evaporation and photosynthesis in relation to the physical environment of crops has opened up a new dimension in crop ecology, but it is still much easier to measure the environment to which a crop is exposed in the field than to predict how it will respond to specific features of its environment at each stage of development. One obstacle to progress is a disparity in time scales: microclimatological analyses are usually limited to periods of a few hours or days, whereas the behaviour of a crop during any stage in the growing season may reflect changes in the environment weeks or even months before. A more obvious problem is the separation of a very complex physiological and biochemical system into components which respond to discrete elements of the physical environment. The root of the problem is an obvious lack of contact between physicists and biologists, and Milthorpe [27] was critical of both: ' . . . the biologist has recoiled in horror from the very thought of attempting to understand the physics of the lower atmosphere, and the micrometeorologist has sadly neglected some of the more important principles of plant growth'. Penman [35] added this comment: 'The gap must be closed from both sides but where the biologist is eager and willing to learn, the physicist is shy, or indifferent'. Ignoring epithets, the biologist and physicist responsible for this review have tried to close a small part of the gap by exploring some less familiar aspects of microclimatology in relation to crop production.

Responses to Microclimate

Figure 3.1 is an attempt to generalize the main relations between micro-climate and the response of crops commonly grown in Britain: barley, wheat, potatoes, sugar beet and grass. Dominant features of the macroclimate have already been discussed (p. 6) but it is worth recalling that the average solar radiation during summer months is about 17 MJ m^{-2} day^{-1} *, that maximum screen temperatures seldom exceeded 25 °C at any side, and that mean winter temperatures range from about 7 °C in south-west England to 3 °C in Aberdeenshire. Figure 3.1 is divided in two parts and the strength of a response is represented by a corresponding number of circles. The upper part of the figure (full circles) show the *direct* effect of microclimatic elements on evaporation and the water balance, photosynthesis and the carbon dioxide balance, and the pattern of growth and development.

	Water balance	CO_2 balance	Growth and development
Radiation	● ● ●	● ● ● ●	● ●
Temperature	●	●	● ● ● ●
Sat. deficit	● ● ●		
Wind	●	●	●
CO_2		●	
Water balance	———	○ ○	○ ○ ○ ○
CO_2 balance		———	
Growth	○ ○	○ ○	———

Figure 3.1   (Strength of response is indicated by number of circles.)

The income of *radiation* exerts a dominant control over the rates of both photosynthesis and transpiration. For a single leaf, the relation between the rate of gross photosynthesis and the absorption of visible radiation (0.4 to 0.7μm can be well represented by a simple hyperbolic relation (p. 43). For a closed crop canopy, the response to light will be more nearly linear than the response of a single leaf because of the contribution from shaded leaves exposed to weak light. The rate of evaporation from a crop can be expressed theoretically as the sum of two terms, one proportional to the net amount of radiation absorbed by the canopy and one proportional to the saturation deficit measured above the canopy. In practice, the saturation deficit is so strongly correlated with the receipt of radiation that the rate of evaporation is closely proportional to absorbed radiation. Since the rates of photo-synthesis and transpiration are both nearly proportional to radiation over a wide range of light intensities, dry-matter production and crop water use are

* or about 400 cal cm^{-2} day^{-1}

strongly correlated and appear to be proportional when plotted cumulatively [29, 36].

The average temperature and saturation deficit of the free atmosphere change from day to day with changes of air mass, but diurnal changes significant in the microclimate of a crop are closely related to diurnal changes of radiation. *Temperature* is much less important than radiation in determining the daily pattern of photosynthesis and evaporation but rates of growth and development are closely linked to the temperature regime, and some mechanisms of control will be discussed in the next section. In ecological texts, *saturation deficit* is often regarded as a measure of the evaporating power of the air, but within the microclimate of a crop or forest, differences of saturation deficit at the same income of radiation are a measure of the availability of water for transpiration: when the transpiration rate is restricted by a shortage of water, the air tends to be dry and *vice versa*. In these circumstances, measurements with small evaporation pans and Piche evaporimeters are dangerously ambiguous.

Changes of *wind speed* from day to day or from site to site are unlikely to have much effect on the rates of transpiration or photosynthesis of field crops [28, 32] but experience from hilly and coastal regions as well as the evidence from wind-tunnel studies suggests that the mechanical action of wind may inhibit growth and development in a way that is not clearly understood. The lodging of rain-soaked crops by gusty winds frequently reduces the yield of cereals in Britain but has received little attention from microclimatologists.

The concentration of *carbon dioxide* is seldom an important discriminant of photosynthetic rates in the field because it is commonly between 280 and 300 v.p.m. within the canopy of a crop during daylight hours [45]. Lower concentrations during the day require an improbable combination of high rates of assimilation with low radiation intensities and low wind speeds [32]. Concentrations of 400 v.p.m. or more are often recorded at night when the CO_2 respired by a crop and the soil is trapped near the ground by a stable layer of air, but there is usually a rapid drop in concentration after sunrise. No figures have been published to show the seasonal or geographical variation of carbon dioxide concentration over Britain. Scandinavian measurements reported by Bischof [3] showed that mean concentrations at the surface decreased from a maximum of about 350 v.p.m. in spring to a minimum of about 300 v.p.m. in autumn, in phase with seasonal changes of photosynthesis by crops and vegetation.

The lower part of Figure 3.1, with open circles, shows the interaction of physiological processes with microclimatic factors which must be taken into account when crop production is related to microclimate over the whole growing season. For example, the water stress of plant leaves depends on the differences between the loss of water by transpiration and its uptake by roots. As water stress begins to increase during a period of dry weather, leaves expand more slowly and the rate of photosynthesis slows too as stress becomes more severe [9]. Conversely, if the growth of leaves is limited either by a shortage of water or by low temperature, the rates of transpiration and photosynthesis per unit field area will be lower during the early stages of growth, though on a leaf area basis the rates may be little changed. The effects of water stress on crop growth have been studied in great detail but most field work on the effects of temperature has been comparatively primitive, employing mean air temperatures and ignoring important differences between soil and air temperature or between plant organs and the surrounding air. But what is 'important' in this context? We shall examine this question by looking first at the behaviour of crop plants in experiments where temperature has been controlled, and then at some features of the thermal regimes they are exposed to in the field. An exhaustive review of plant growth in relation to temperature has been published by Langridge and McWilliam [23], but when microclimatologists write about temperature measurements in the field [25, 39, 52, 53] the biological implications usually get rather cursory treatment.

Responses to Temperature

It is convenient to use a standard notation for the analysis of the growth of a crop, e.g.

Standing dry weight of crop per unit ground	W	
Total leaf area index	L	
Rate of dry matter production per unit ground	C	$= dW/dt$
Net assimilation rate	E_A	$= (dW/dt)/L$
Relative leaf growth rate	R_L	$= (dL/dt)/L$
Relative growth rate	R_W	$= (dW/dt)/W$
Leaf area: plant weight ratio	L/W	

(i) Vegetative Growth

Assimilation and Respiration. The extent to which the rate of photosynthesis of a leaf changes with temperature depends partly on the nature of the environment and partly on physiological conditions. In the field, the photosynthetic rate on dull days will be proportional to light intensity because it is limited by a photochemical process, and the temperature dependence of photosynthesis will therefore be slight ($Q_{10} \simeq 1$). In bright sunshine, the photosynthetic rate of leaves at the top of a canopy will usually be proportional to the concentration of carbon dioxide in the surrounding air, and will therefore be limited by the diffusion of carbon dioxide molecules to the chloroplasts. This process also has a Q_{10} close to unity. In general, the photosynthetic rate of a healthy field crop growing in Britain will be nearly independent of foliage temperature, at least between 10 and 25 °C.

If we supply excess light and carbon dioxide in the laboratory then we limit the rate of assimilation by a biochemical process such as the activity of an enzyme, which is strongly dependent on temperature. It is possible that the effects of light and carbon dioxide saturation could be simulated by depriving a plant of water or nutrients thus rendering the biochemical steps rate-limiting. Crops growing on a poor or dry soil may have relatively small rates of photosynthesis, anomalously dependent on temperature.

The rate of aerobic dark respiration increases with temperature between 10 and 25 °C and the Q_{10} of this process is often between 2.0 and 2.5 [26]. Evidence from the temperature dependence of the carbon dioxide compensation point (Γ) suggests that the evolution of carbon dioxide in the light will also proceed faster at higher temperatures [20]. However, as respiration is only a small fraction of photosynthesis during the early phase of growth, the increase of respiration with temperature is not usually large enough to depress the *net* rate of photosynthesis until leaf temperature exceeds 25 or 30 °C.

The effect of temperature on the net photosynthetic rate over periods of days or weeks can be discussed in terms of the net assimilation rate (E_A), but the evidence is somewhat conflicting and different behaviour has been reported for a number of species. Gregory [19] found that high day temperatures and low night temperatures increased E_A of barley and noted that the negative correlation with mean night temperature was greater than would be expected from a decrease in respiration alone. Similar responses were found by Black [4] in subterranean clover and by Stoskopf, Klinck and Steppler [41] in oats. All these experiments were outside the laboratory. However, Davidson and Milthorpe [14] working with cocksfoot, and Terry [48] with sugar beet, found that E_A was relatively independent of temperature, and Warren Wilson [54] showed that between 10 and 25 °C the Q_{10} for rape and sunflower was approximately 1. Most workers agree that E_A is much more closely related to the level of illumination than to temperature, so in terms of microclimate in the field, the distribution of radiant energy within the canopy determines the rate of dry matter production *per unit leaf area* during vegetative growth. However, as the rate at which dry matter is produced *per unit field area* depends partly on the leaf area and rate of leaf expansion as well as on the net assimilation rate, it is necessary to examine the effects of temperature on relative growth rates.

Relative Growth. Gregory [19] showed that the relative leaf growth rate (R_L) of barley was positively correlated with mean day temperature and negatively correlated with night temperature, but there is considerable evidence that the elongation of plant leaves and stems increases with temperature during the night as well as in daylight [e.g. 59]. Warren Wilson [54] showed that the Q_{10} of leaf expansion for rape and sunflower decreased from a large value of 3 to 4 at 10 °C to rather more than 1 at 25 °C. These values were calculated from growth room experiments in which plants were kept at a constant temperature, but Bull [10] was able to demonstrate the strong temperature dependence of R_L on temperature in the field. During the early stages of growth, R_L of field beans (*Vicia faba*) was closely related both to mean and to maximum air temperatures and for maximum daily temperature $T\,^{\circ}C$, values of Q_{10} = 2.0 and R_L (10) = 0.055 day^{-1} were derived from the expression

$$R_L\,(T) = R_L\,(10)\,Q^{\,(T\text{-}10)/10}$$

Measurements by other workers on barley, wheat, sugar beet and potatoes fitted the same relation with rather more scatter.

The effect of temperature on leaf growth is mediated by changes in the rates of cell division and expansion [7, 14, 47] and between 10 and 25°C an increase of temperature increases the final size of leaves as well as the rates of unfolding and expansion. The similarity of the Q_{10} for leaf expansion and for respiration suggests that over a limited range of temperature, a constant fraction of respiratory energy may be employed in the production of new leaf tissue.

Provided leaf area increases linearly with plant weight, leaf area to plant weight ratio (L/W) is the time-integral of R_L (temperature dependent) divided by E_A (independent of temperature). The ratio should therefore increase with temperature during the early stage of growth. Many experiments confirm the existence of this response; Warren Wilson [54] for example, found that L/W for rape and sunflower increased from about 0.7 to 1.5 dm^2 g^{-1} between 10 and 34 °C. The ratio of leaf weight to total plant weight was more or less constant over this range, while the specific leaf area (leaf area per unit leaf weight) more than doubled.

The relative growth rate of a plant R_W is the product of E_A (more or less temperature independent) and L/W (temperature dependent) so R_W should increase with temperature in the same way as L/W and R_L. This happens; R_W doubled between 10° and 25 °C in rape and sunflower [54].

To summarise, growth room and field experiments on temperate crops show that E_A is strongly dependent on the income of radiation but is often nearly independent of temperature between 10 and 25 °C. Conversely, extension growth is strongly dependent on temperature but is not limited by levels of illumination exceeding about 5 MJ m^{-2} day^{-1} [5, 33]. The interrelation of factors in growth analysis and their dependence on temperature is illustrated diagrammatically in Figure 3.2.

Root Temperature. The dominant importance of root temperature as a determinant of crop growth was demonstrated by Brouwer [7] who grew seedlings of eight crop species at root temperatures between 5 and 40°C but with the shoots maintained at 20°C. For all the species, the dry matter production over a period of 20 days increased rapidly up to a maximum achieved between 20 and 30 °C and then decreased sharply with a further increase of temperature.

The response of plant growth to root temperature supports a general hypothesis advanced by Brouwer [8] that the shoot and root of a growing plant exist in a state of dynamic equilibrium in which the size of the shoot determines the supply of assimilates and the size of the root determines the uptake of water and minerals. Any change of the environment which has the same effect as increasing the size of the shoot will induce a compensating increase in root size to restore equilibrium, and an increase in the effective size of the root will increase shoot growth. The observation that an increase of soil temperature between 5 and 25 °C increases plant weight suggests that there is a more rapid intake of water and/or nutrients by warmer roots, though the formation and movement of growth regulators may also be involved [8, 34, 42]. Conversely, increasing the temperature of leaves from 10 to 25 °C does not increase their effective size because the assimilation rate is almost independent of temperature so that dry matter production is likely to be much less dependent on air temperature than on soil temperature. This conclusion has extremely important implications for the growth of plants in the field, where soil and air temperatures are seldom identical, and in growth rooms, where differences of several degrees centigrade may persist for several hours after changing from a 'day' to a 'night' temperature, or after switching lights on or off.

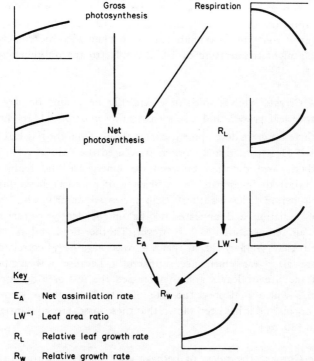

Figure 3.2 *The response to temperature of the processes governing dry-matter production. The graphs show the type of response, with temperature plotted on the x axis and the response of the process on the y axis.*

(ii) Later Growth

The first stage of growth is characterized by rapid increases both of dry matter and of leaf area. When there is not enough foliage to intercept all the incident light, E_A is relatively large and depends on isolation. The production of dry matter per unit field area is also a function of leaf area index and therefore depends on temperature as well as on radiation. There is usually a second stage in the growth of an annual crop beginning with the development of an inflorescence or a storage organ. In this phase, the leaf area is near its maximum; dry matter production depends on the assimilation rate and hence on the supply of light energy; and the partitioning of assimilates is a complex function of temperature. The behaviour of different species needs separate discussion.

Sugar Beet and Potatoes. In potatoes, the time from emergence to tuber formation is least in short days and at relatively low temperatures and high rates of isolation [6, 40]. The yield of tubers is largest when day temperatures are held about 20 to 25 °C and night temperatures about 10 to 15 °C [6, 58]. Growth of storage roots in sugar beet is most rapid in shortening days and decreasing temperatures, conditions common in autumn when the soil may be warmer than the air. Ulrich [51] found the greatest fresh weight of roots and maximum sucrose contant at a day temperature of 23 °C and a night temperature of 14 °C similar to the optimum range for potatoes.

Temperate Cereals. Flower initiation, generally depending on day length, limits further leaf growth and tillers either flower or die [11]. Thereafter, photosynthate for grain development comes mainly from the flag leaf or from the ear itself [1]. Rothamsted workers have used the ratio of grain yield to photosynthetic area duration between ear emergence and maturity (the grain/leaf ratio) to investigate the efficiency of photosynthesis during the grain-filling period. The grain/leaf ratio increased linearly with the daily income of radiation and appeared to be independently correlated with maximum air temperature [57]. However, Thorne, Ford and Watson [49, 50] found that grain yield at harvest was *negatively* correlated with temperature after ear emergence, apparently because low temperatures prolonged the life of leaves and so increased the leaf area duration. Low temperatures will also depress the rate of respiration of the stem and of senescent organs and it has been shown that these losses are substantial during maturation [30, 56].

Temperate Grasses. The tillers of herbage grass plants go through the same cycle of vegetative growth, induction and initiation as the annual cereals [13]. However, the growth of inflorescences cannot represent the same drain on carbohydrate resources in the grasses as it does in cereals. The thermal response of growth in the vegetative phase can be interpreted in terms of differences in R_L and L/W as already discussed [2, 14, 16]. There seems to be little information about the effects of temperature on the rate of accumulation of dry matter in plants that are clearly in a reproductive phase.

General Scheme. Figure 3.3 is a very simplified description of the influence that temperature is likely to exert on the growth of storage organs through a number of inter-related processes:

(i) maintenance of the photosynthetic surface favoured by low *leaf* temperatures [49] ;

(ii) conversion of starch to sucrose in sugar beet and potato cells also favoured by low *leaf* temperatures [26] ;

(iii) translocation of sugars favoured by high *stem* temperatures [43] though the process may adapt to low temperatures [44] ;

(iv) expansion of the storage organ which appears to increase with the temperature of the *organ* at least between 10 and 20°C [e.g. 12, 46, 57] ;

(v) conversion of starch to sugar in the storage organ favoured by low *root* temperature in sugar beet [47] ;

(vi) loss of carbohydrate by respiration which increases with temperature, although this may be associated with high net growth rates of storage organs.

This scheme ignores the possible effects of temperature on the synthesis and translocation of growth regulators and on circadian rhythms. However, it is consistent with the observation that sugar beet and potatoes to grow best in a fluctuating temperature which may help to satisfy the conflicting requirements for starch hydrolysis and growth, whereas cereals grow well at constant temperatures high enough to promote rapid swelling of the grain but low enough to avoid premature senescence of flag leaves and awns. Figure 3.3. emphasizes that the response of crop yield to temperature depends on the inter-relation of many processes governing dry-matter production, growth of leaf area and development at particular stages in the life of a crop. Not only are the absolute temperatures of individual organs important, but diurnal ranges of temperature and temperature difference between different plant organs must be considered too.

		Temperature		
		'source'	'pipe'	'sink'
Prolonged leaf life		low		
(starch → sucrose)		low		
Translocation			high	
Storage organ growth	(*i*) sink size			high
	(*ii*) respiration loss			low

Fig. 3.3   Simple scheme to show how temperature may affect the rate of growth of a storage organ through a number of processes.

Aspects of Microclimatology

The last section reviewed some of the evidence, both from growth rooms and from the field, that temperature is a major factor in determining plant growth. We shall now look briefly at some aspects of thermal microclimate relevant to crop production.

(i) Soil Temperature

During the growing season, the diurnal change of soil temperature lags behind the net radiation at the soil surface. At a depth of 5 to 10 cm, maximum soil temperature is often reached about two hours after maximum air temperature and throughout the late afternoon, evening and night, the soil stays warmer than the air immediately above it. After sunrise, the soil warms relatively slowly, staying cooler than the air throughout the morning and early afternoon.

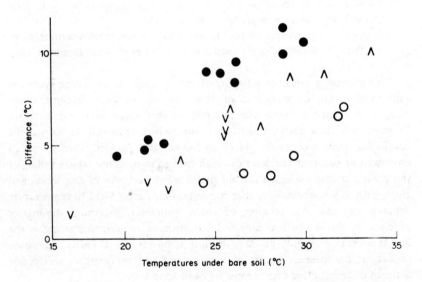

Figure 3.4 Difference between soil temperature measured two hours after noon at 10 cm under bare soil and under potatoes; after van Eimern [52].

In a spring-sown crop, the diurnal range of soil temperature is likely to reach a maximum for the season during sunny days before the canopy develops to shade the soil. Figure 3.4, taken from the work of van Eimern [52], shows the difference between soil temperatures measured two hours after noon in a potato field and under bare soil. Below plants that were 25 cm tall in late June, the soil temperature on sunny days was about 7 °C less than under the bare plot, and on cloudy days the difference was about 3 °C. When the canopy reached its maximum density in late July, the corresponding temperature differences were 11 ° and 5 °C. Figure 3.5 shows that a sward of grass was even more effective in damping the diurnal temperature wave, but the similarity in shape of the four curves shows that the fractional decrease of range for each type of cover was almost independent of depth.

As a broad generalization, the shade provided by crop foliage keeps plant roots cool during the day and warm at night. Modification of the soil temperature regime by the presence of a crop canopy introduces an important element of negative feedback into the relation between micro-climate and the growth of leaves and roots. The extent of this feedback may be one factor determining yield both in crops like potato which mature at a time when leaf area is decreasing rapidly and in sugar beet which maintains a fuller leaf cover until harvest.

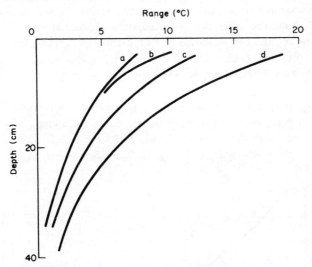

Figure 3.5 Diurnal range of soil temperature under different covers:
(a) grass; (b) wheat; (c) potatoes; (d) bare soil; after van Eimern,
[52].

(ii) Shoot Temperatures
In a crop canopy, leaves, stems and inflorescences tend towards an equilibrium temperature at which heat gains are balanced by heat losses. During the day, when stomata are open, the transpiration from leaves is often rapid enough to keep tissue temperatures with 1 or 2 °C of ambient air temperature: heat gained by the absorption of radiation is almost equal to the loss of latent heat. If stomata close because there is a shortage of water, leaves in bright sunshine may get 5 °C or more hotter than the ambient air so that the decrease in latent heat loss is made good by an increase in convective loss. Under a cloudless sky at night, leaves cool 1 or 2 °C below air temperature: heat loss by radiation is almost equal to the heat gained from warmer air

blowing over the leaf. Examples of foliage heat balance in relation to microclimate can be found in numerous papers by Gates [18].

Nearly all calculations of leaf temperature assume steady-state conditions, but leaves in the field change temperature constantly in response to changes of wind speed and of radiation income. Some of these fluctuations may be physiologically significant. Evans [17] reports a growth room experiment in which tomato plants grew faster when climatic 'noise' of about ± 2.5 °C was superimposed on a smooth temperature cycle. Considering spatial as well as secular differences of temperature, Evans urged micrometeorologists to pay more attention to recording the temperatures of plant tissue because 'Leaves petioles, stems, roots, fruits and growing points may all be at different temperatures, and the growth of plants may well be influenced by and adapted to these differences'.

As an example of a theoretical estimate rather than a measurement, Figure 3.6 shows the difference of temperature between an ear of barley and the ambient air, and between awns and air, calculated for radiative exchanges in bright sunshine (right-hand of figure) and for a clear sky at night (left-hand). Awn temperatures are overestimated because evaporative cooling is neglected and recent porometer measurements by P.V. Biscoe (unpublished) suggest that their transpiration rate may be substantial. It appears from the diagram that during the time the grains are filling, they may be several degrees warmer on average than the awns which provide a large fraction of the carbohydrate for grain formation. Here again, thermal

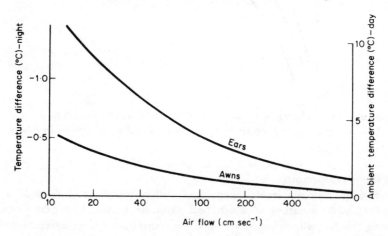

Figure 3.6 *Temperature of (a) ears and (b) awns of barley with respect to ambient air temperature. Ears and awns were assumed to be cylinders at right angles to the airflow and with diameters of 1.0 and 0.1 cm respectively. Net radiation was assumed to be + 450 Wm^{-2} during the day (right-hand axis) and − 60 Wm^{-2} at night (left-hand axis).*

microclimate may be a determinant of yield, but there is no experimental evidence to test this hypothesis.

A Model of Temperature and Growth

The rate of photosynthesis of a field crop can be expressed in terms of a 'field efficiency' defined as the ratio of energy stored in photosynthetic products to the energy of incident radiation, both referred to unit field area. The field efficiency is the product of two components:

(i) ϵ_c, the ratio of energy absorbed by the photosynthetic apparatus to the radiation incident on the canopy, per unit field area. This ratio will depend on leaf area index and on canopy architecture;

(ii) ϵ_l, the ratio of energy stored in photosynthetic products (taking account of respiration losses) to the radiation absorbed by the photosynthetic apparatus.

In models that relate photosynthetic rates to light distribution, ϵ_c and ϵ_l are usually assumed constant over the period of calculation and are therefore restricted to a static canopy with a fixed leaf area index. Dynamic models of the type described by de Wit (p. 117) take account of the way ϵ_c increases as the leaves expand to form a closed canopy, and this stage of the analysis is firmly based on experimental evidence. By contrast, very few measurements are available to show how ϵ_l changes during the season. In a crop whose leaves senesce rapidly, changes of ϵ_l may be just as important as changes of ϵ_c in determining the final yield. Until more information is available on changes of photosynthetic efficiency in the field, there is little to gain from developing elaborate new models of crop growth, and with this rationalization a very simple model will be developed here. Over a period in which ϵ_c increases as a result of leaf expansion, the accumulation of dry matter will depend on the relative leaf growth rate and hence on soil temperature. Similarly the value of ϵ_l at any stage in crop development will depend on temperature, because leaves will senesce faster and will respire faster as air temperature increases.

To explore the relation between assimilation and temperature during the early stages of crop growth only, ϵ_c will be written

$$\epsilon_c = 1 - e^{-KL} \tag{3.2}$$

where K is an absorption coefficient depending on leaf geometry and ranging from 1.0 for species with predominantly horizontal leaves to 0.3 for species with predominantly vertical leaves [31].

Measurements on the vegatative growth of maize [60], and of soybeans [38], show that the rate of dry-matter production C was proportional to ϵ_c, implying that ϵ_l was effectively constant. Making this assumption,

$$C = \epsilon_c C_m \tag{3.3}$$

where C_m is a maximum rate of dry matter production achieved with a closed canopy. Over a period of time τ, the accumulated dry weight will be

$$W = \int_0^\tau C \, dt = C_m \int_0^\tau \epsilon_c \, dt \tag{3.4}$$

If the relative leaf growth rate R_L ($= (dL/dt)/L$) is determined by temperature, the leaf area at a time t can be expressed as a multiple of the area L_0 at $t = 0$, i.e.

$$L = L_0 e^{\bar{R}_L t}$$

and if the growth rate at $10°C$ is R_L (10), then

$$R_L = R_L (10) \, Q^{(T - 10)/10} \tag{3.6}$$

Then combining equations (3.2) to (3.6) it is possible to calculate the rate of expansion of the leaf surface, the efficiency of dry-matter production ϵ_c ($= C/C_m$) and the increase in standing dry weight, all in relation to time and temperature. Figure 3.7 illustrates the performance of a crop for which the following parameters were assumed:

R_L (10)	= 0.05 day^{-1}	[10]	
Q_{10}	= 2		
K	= 0.7	(characteristic of cereals)	
L_0	= 0.1		

To reach any given value of L, the product $R_L t$ must be constant, so the leaf area after τ days at $20°C$ is equal to the area after 2τ days at $10°C$. Similarly, the value of C/C_m after τ days doubles for a $10°C$ increase of temperature. A rather different relation holds for the accumulation of dry matter: over any period of τ days at $20°C$, the standing dry weight will be *half* the weight after 2τ days at $10°C$ ($C_m \, \tau \, \bar{\epsilon}_c = 0.5 \, C_m \, 2\tau \, \bar{\epsilon}_c$). These calculations illustrate the extent to which low soil temperatures in spring are likely to restrict the growth of crops in all parts of Britain.

At a later stage, expansion of the leaf surface may slow either as a result of mutual shading or when assimilate is diverted from leaf growth to the development of a reproductive or storage system. Growth room and field experiments are needed to establish the range of leaf area indices over which the model is valid for different species growing in different environments.

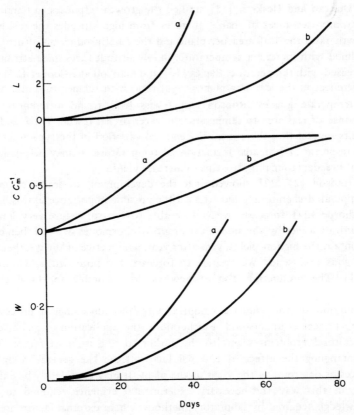

*Fig. 3.7   Estimated growth of a crop at mean soil temperatures of (a) 20°
and (b) 10°C. L is leaf area index; C/C_m relative crop growth
rate; W standing dry matter in kg m^{-2}. For assumed parameters
see text.*

Conclusions

A final limit on the productivity of a crop grown in Britain must be set by the
total amount of photosynthetically-active radiation received in a year.
However, as Watson [55] emphasized, the efficiency with which that energy
can be used depends upon the size, structure and duration of the crop
canopy. The rate at which leaves expand, especially during the early stages of
growth when the leaf area index is low, is therefore an important determinant
of crop production over the whole year (as distinct from the potential rate of
production during the main period of growth). As leaf expansion is very
sensitive to temperature, within the range of the British climate, it is worth
considering whether crop production could be increased by changing the
response of crop plants to their thermal environment. Such changes might be
achieved either genetically or chemically.

Duncan and Hesketh [15] studied the growth responses to temperature of twenty-two races of maize. In races from high altitudes the relative leaf growth rate, the leaf area per plant and the total production of dry matter declined with increasing temperature. In low altitude races these attributes all increased with temperature. Eagles [16] and MacColl and Cooper [24] found differences in the leaf area/plant weight ratio with temperature in a number of temperate grasses. Robson and Jewiss [37] found differences in the response of leaf area to temperature in races of tall fescue. These and other results suggest that there is much genetical variation in the type and scale of the response of leaf area formation to temperature. It may be possible for plant breeders to manipulate this to increase yield.

Hudson [21, 22] showed that the development of leaf area may be manipulated chemically, and stressed the possible importance of this. Earlier, Milthorpe [27] forecast; 'we will be able to control before very long, the growth of leaves by the simple use of growth hormones. We will then be able to obtain the highest yields, year after year, irrespective of the weather which the gods may send.' We hesitate to forecast, but note, with F.G. Gregory [19]: 'The production also of new varieties suitable for local climatic conditions must always remain a matter of pure empiricism, unless the interaction of the climatic complex with the physiological processes of distinct races is understood. Furthermore, the application of physiology to agricultural problems seems to the author to find its most fertile field in disentangling the effect of external factors from the general interplay of processes determining the yield of the plant. It may confidently be expected that in this way the necessary experimental evidence required to check knowledge acquired by laboratory methods, where external factors are as far as possible varied one at a time, will be obtained.

Investigations of this kind are singularly lacking . . . . '

REFERENCES

1. ARCHBOLD, H.K. 'Physiological studies in plant nutrition. XIII Experiments with barley on defoliation and shading of the ear in relation to sugar metabolism', *Ann. Bot. NS* 1942, 6, 487-531.
2. BEEVERS, L and COOPER J.P. 'Influence of temperature on growth and metabolism of rye grass seedlings. I. Seedling growth and yield components', *Crop Sci.*, 1964, 4, 139-143.
3. BISCHOF, W. 'Periodical variation of the atmospheric CO_2 content in Scandinavia', *Tellus,* 1960, 12, 216-226.
4. BLACK, J.N. 'The interaction of light and temperature in determining the growth rate of subterranean clover *(Trifolium subterranean* L.)', *Aust. J. Biol. Sci.*, 1955, 8, 330-343.
5. BLACKMAN, G.E. 'Influence of light and temperature on leaf growth', in Milthorpe, F.L. *The Growth of Leaves.* London: Butterworths, 1957, 151-167.

6. BORAH, M.N. and MILTHORPE, F.L. 'Growth of the potato as influenced by temperature. *Indian J. Pl. Physiol.* 1962, **5**, 53-72.

7. BROUWER, R. 'Influence of temperature of the root medium on the growth of seedlings of various crop plants', *Inst. Biol. Sch. Ond. van Lanbouw. Wag. Med.*, 1962, 175.

8. BROUWER, R. 'Distribution of dry matter in the plant', *Inst. Biol. Sch. Ond. van Landbouw. Wag. Med.*, 1962, 203.

9. BROUWER, R. 'Some physiological aspects of the influence of growth factors in the root medium on growth and dry matter production', *Inst. Biol. Sch. Ond. Landbouw. Wag. Med.*, 1963, 212.

10. BULL, T.A. 'Expansion of leaf area per plant in field bean (*Vicia faba* L.) as related to daily maximum temperature', *J. appl. Ecol.*, 1968, **5**, 61-68.

11. BUNTING, A.H. and DRENNAN, D.S.H. 'Some aspects of the morphology and physiology of cereals in the vegetative phase', in Milthorpe, F.L. and Ivins J.D., *The Growth of Cereals and Grasses* London: Butterworths, 1966, 20-38.

12. BURT, R.L. 'Some effects of temperature on carbohydrate utilization and plant growth', *Aust. J. Biol. Sci.* 1966, **19**, 711-714.

13. CALDER, D.M. 1966 'Inflorescence induction and initiation in the Gramineae', in Milthorpe, F.L. and J.D. Ivins *The Growth of Cereals and Grasses'*, London: Butterworths, 196, 59-73.

14. DAVIDSON, J.L. and MILTHORPE, F.L., 1965 'The effect of temperature on the growth of Cocksfoot (*Dactylis glomerata* L.)', *Ann. Bot. NS*, 1965, **29**, 407-417.

15. DUNCAN, W.G. and HESKETH, J.D., 'Net photosynthetic rates, relative leaf growth rates and leaf numbers of 22 races of maize grown at eight temperatures', *Crop Sci.*, 1968, **8**, 670-674.

16. EAGLES, C.F. 'The effect of temperature on vegetative growth in climatic races of *Dactylis glomerata* in controlled environments', *Ann. Bot. NS*, 1967, **31**, 31-39.

17. EVANS, L.T. 'Extrapolation from controlled environments to the field', in Evans, L.T. *Environmental Control of Plant Growth*, London: Academic Press, 1963, 421-435.

18. GATES, D.M. 'Transpiration and leaf temperature', *A. Rev. Pl. Physiol.*, 1968, **19**, 211-238.

19. GREGORY, F.G. 'The effect of climatic conditions on the growth of barley', *Ann. Bot.*, 1926, **40**, 1-26.

20. HEATH, O.V.S. and MEIDNER, H. 'Compensation points and carbon dioxide enrichment for lettuce grown under glass in winter', *J. exp. Bot.*, 1967, **18**, 746-751.

21. HUDSON, J.P. 'Effects of weather on plant behaviour', *Nature, Lond.*, 1958, **182**, 1337-1340.

22. HUDSON, J.P. 'Weather, crops and man', Inaugural Lecture, Univ. of Nottingham, 1959.

23. LANGRIDGE, J. and McWILLIAM, J.R. 'Heat response of higher plants',

in Rose, A.H. *Thermobiology*, London and New York: Academic Press, 1967.

24. MacCOLL, D. and COOPER, J.P. Climatic variation in forage grasses. III. Seasonal changes in growth and assimilation in climatic races of *Lolium, Dactylis* and *Festuca', J. appl. Ecol.,* 1967, **4**, 113-127.

25. MATTSSON, J.O. 'Microclimatic observations in and above cultivated crops', *Lund studies in Geography*, 196, Ser. A No. 16.

26. MAYER, B.S., ANDERSON, D.B. and BOHNING, R.H., *Introduction to plant physiology*, Princeton: van Nostrand, 1960, 541.

27. MILTHORPE, F.L. 'Plant growth and the weather', Inaugural lecture, Univ. of Nottingham, 1955.

28. MONTEITH, J.L. 'Evaporation and environment', *Symp. Soc. exp. Biol,* 1965, No. 19, 205-234.

29. MONTEITH, J.L. 'The photosynthesis and transpiration of crops', *Expl. Agric.,* 196, **2**, 1-14.

30. MONTEITH, J.L. 'Analysis of the photosynthesis and respiration of field crops from vertical fluxes of carbon dioxide', in Proc. of the Copenhagen Symp. *Functioning of terrestrial ecosystems at the primary production level*, 1968, 349-358.

31. MONTEITH, J.L. 'Light interception and radiative exchange in crop stands', in *Physiological aspects of crop yield* ,Madison: American Society of Agronomy, 1969.

32. MONTEITH, J.L., SZEICZ, G. and YABUKI, K. 'Crop photosynthesis and the flux of carbon dioxide below the canopy', *J. appl. Ecol.,* 1964, **1**, 321-337.

33. NEWTON, P. 'Studies on the expansion of the leaf surface. II. The influence of light intensity and daylength', *J. exp. Bot.,* 1963, **14**, 458-482.

34. NIELSON, K.F. and HUMPHRIES, E.C., 1966 'Effects of root temperature on plant growth', *Soils and Fert.,* 196, **29**, 1-7.

35. PENMAN, H.L. 1962 'Weather and Crops', *Qt. J. R. met. Soc.,* 1962, **88**, 209-219.

36. PENMAN, H.L. 'Water as a factor of productivity', in *Potential Crop Production* (Ed. J.P. Cooper & P.F. Wareing), Heineman, London: 1970.

37. ROBSON, M.J. and JEWISS, O.R. 'A comparison of British and North African varieties of tall fescue *(Festuca arundinacea)*. III. Effects of light, temperature and daylength on relative growth rate and its components', *J. appl. Ecol.,* 1968, 191-204.

38. SHIBLES, R.M. and WEBER, C.R. 'Interception of solar radiation and dry matter production by various soybean planting patterns', *Crop Sci.,* 1966, 6, 55-59.

39. SHUL'GIN, A.M. 'The temperature regime of soils', *Israel Program for Scientific Translations, Jerusalem*, 1965, 218.

40. SLATER, J.W. 1963 'Mechanisms of tuber initiation', in Ivins, J.D. and Milthorpe, F.L. *The Growth of the Potato*, London: Butterworths, 1963,

114-120.

41. STOSKOPF, N.C., KLINCK, H.R., and STEPPLER, H.A. 'Temperature in relation to growth and net assimilation rate of oats', *Can. J. Pl. Sci.* 1966, **46**, 397-404.

42. SUTTON, C.D. 'Effect of low soil temperature on phosphate nutrition of plants – a review', *J. Sci. Fd. Agric.*, 1969, **20**, 1-3.

43. SWANSON, C.A. 1959 'Translocation of organic solutes', in Steward, F.C. Plant Physiology, A Treatise, vol. 2 pp. 481-551, 1959, New York.

44. SWANSON, C.A. and GEIGER, D.R., 'Time course of low temperature inhibition of sucrose translocation in sugar beets', *Pl. Physiol., Lancaster*, 1967, **42**, 751-756.

45. TAMM, E. and KRZYSCH, G., 'Zum Verlant des CO_2-Gehaltes des Luft', *Z. Acker – u. PflBau.*, 1961, **112**, 253-278.

46. TERRY, N. 'The effect of light and temperature on the growth of sugar beet', M.Sc. Thesis, Univ. of Nottingham, 1963.

47. TERRY, N. 'Physiology of sugar beet in relation to temperature', Ph.D. Thesis, Univ. of Nottingham, 1966.

48. TERRY, N. 1968 'Developmental physiology of sugar beet. I. The influence of light and temperature on growth', *J. exp. Bot.*, 1968, **19**, 795-811.

49. THORNE, G.N. FORD, M.A. and WATSON, D.J. 'Effects of temperature variation at different times on growth and yield of sugar beet and barley', *Ann. Bot. NS*, 1967, **31**, 72-101.

50. THORNE, G.N. FORD, M.A. and WATSON, D.J. 'Growth development and yield of spring wheat in artificial climates', *Ann. Bot. NS*, 1968, **32**, 425-446.

51. ULRICH, A. 'The influence of temperature and light factors on the growth and development of sugar beets in controlled climatic environments', *Agron. J.*, 1952, **44**, 66-73.

52. VAN EIMERN, J. 'Untersuchungen uber das Klima in Pflanzengestan den', *Ber. dt. Wetterd, Offenbach*, 1964, No. 96.

53. VAN WIJK, W.R. *Physics of plant environment*, Amsterdam: North-Holland Publishing Co., 1963, 382.

54. WARREN WILSON, J. 'Effect of temperature on net assimilation rate', *Ann. Bot. NS*, 1966, **30**, 753-761.

55. WATSON, D.J. 'Factors limiting production', in Yapp, W.B. and Watson, D.J. *The Biological Productivity of Britain*, London: Institute of Biology, 1958, 25-32.

56. WATSON, D.J., THORNE, G.N. and FRENCH, S.A.W., 'Analysis of growth and yield of winter and spring wheats', *Ann. Bot. NS.*, 1963, **27**, 1-22.

57. WELBANK, P.J., WITTS, K.J. and THORNE, G.N., 'Effect of radiation and temperature on efficiency of cereal leaves during grain growth', *Ann. Bot. NS*, 1968, **32**, 79-95.

58. WENT, F.W. *The experimental control of plant growth*, Waltham, Mass:

Chronica Botanica, 1957, 343.

59. WILLIAMS, C.N. and BIDDISCOMBE, E.F. 'Extension growth of grass tillers in the field', *Aust. J. agric. Res.*, 1965, **16**, 14-22.

60. WILLIAMS, W.A., LOOMIS, R.S., DUNCAN, W.G., DOVRAT, A., and NUNEZ, A.F. 'Canopy architecture and the growth and grain yield of corn', *Crop Sci.*, 1968, **8**, 303-308.

4. Photosynthesis and Energy Conversion

B. Acock, J.H.M. Thornley, and J. Warren Wilson
Glasshouse Crops Research Institute, Littlehampton, Sussex

Introduction

The efficiency of photosynthesis in converting light energy into chemical energy varies from about 20 per cent to less than 1 per cent, depending on the type of crop and the environment. Maximum potential crop production will be achieved only if the efficiency of photosynthetic conversion of daylight is as high as possible, since photosynthesis is the ultimate physiological limitation to crop production and since it is not economically feasible to supplement daylight artificially.

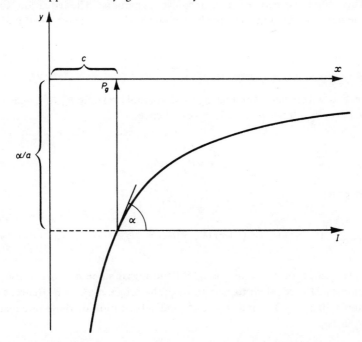

Fig. 4.1. Dependence of gross photosynthetic rate (P_g) of a leaf on light flux density (I), as described by a rectangular hyperbola (equations 4.1 and 4.2).

In symbols, the ratio P/I should be maximized, where P is the rate of CO_2 uptake by the photosynthesising system and I is the incident light flux density ('light' is used in this chapter to mean total radiation in the 400-700 nm waveband, often called photosynthetically active radiation). To express this energy conversion non-dimensionally, as an efficiency, P/I is multiplied by the heat of combustion of the photosynthetic products formed from unit CO_2 uptake. To understand how type of crop and environment affect photosynthetic efficiency or P/I, it is necessary to know how they affect the functional relation of P to I.

For single leaves, the equation

$$P_g = \frac{\alpha I}{1 + aI} \tag{4.1}$$

relating gross photosynthetic rate P_g to light flux density incident on the leaf I, where α and a are constants, has been used by several authors to describe the light response curve for leaf photosynthesis [3, 17] and has been adopted in most models of crop photosynthesis [7, 10, 11, 12, 25, 30, 32, 42, 43, 48]. α is the initial slope of the curve at low I, and α/a is the asymptotic value of P_g at saturating light (Figure 4.1).

This curve is part of a rectangular hyperbola. The equation for a rectangular hyperbola in the fourth quadrant with coordinates x and y which are also the asymptotes (Figure 4.1) is

$$xy = -q$$

where q is a constant. The rectangular hyperbola relating P_g to I meets the origin $I = 0$, $P_g = 0$ where $x = c$, $y = -\alpha/a$; hence

$$x = I + c$$
$$y = P_g - \alpha/a$$

Substituting,

$$(I + c)(P_g - \alpha/a) = -q \tag{4.2}$$

Since the slope of the curve is q/x^2, the initial slope $\alpha = q/c^2$; also, as equation (4.2) is required to pass through the origin, $c(\alpha/a) = q$. Hence it can be shown that $c = 1/a$ and $q = \alpha/a^2$, and substitution of these in equation (4.2) yields

$$(I + 1/a)(P_g - \alpha/a) = -\alpha/a^2$$

which, on simplification, is equation (4.1).

Equation (4.1) has been widely used because it is simple, it fits many data quite well, and the parameters α and α/a are biologically meaningful.

However, it has limitations:

(i) It is generally used as an empirical relationship without theoretical justification.
(ii) The constant a includes effects of both environment and leaf characteristics.
(iii) The equation ignores respiration and its interaction with photosynthesis.
(iv) Effects of CO_2 concentration are not included explicitly. Although variation in CO_2 concentration is small for field crops, it is important for experimental studies of photosynthesis as well as for crops grown in glasshouses in which CO_2 enrichment is practised commercially.

This chapter presents a model of photosynthesis and respiration which is intended to avoid these limitations; it summarizes treatments by other authors; it shows how equations derived for the proposed model can, by introduction of successive assumptions, be related to treatments by other authors and eventually to equation (4.1); it extends these equations for single leaves to the more complex situation of the crop canopy; and it presents computations of the photosynthetic efficiency of leaves and canopies as determined by characteristics of the leaf, canopy and environment.

Photosynthesis of Single Leaves

A Model of Net Photosynthesis with Coupled Photosynthesis and Respiration

In this section, a simple model of leaf photosynthesis is described, and equations based on this model are developed. A qualitative discussion is given of how this model simulates some of the transient effects observed in photosynthesis.

The Leaf. There are two main types of process occurring in photosynthesis:

(i) the physical process of diffusion of CO_2 from the outside air into the leaf cytoplasm;
(ii) the chemical reactions taking place in the leaf cytoplasm.

In the model, it is assumed that all diffusive resistance is located in one surface of the leaf (if desired, this diffusive resistance can be resolved into component resistances in parallel and series). It is further assumed that there is a uniform internal environment, so that, for example, light flux density and CO_2 concentration are uniform throughout the leaf cytoplasm. This last assumption ignores any compartmentation that might exist; for instance, photosynthesis and respiration might occur at physically distinct sites separated by an appreciable diffusive resistance.

The thickness of the leaf (d) enters into the model because the rate of diffusion depends on surface area, whereas the rate of chemical processes depends on cytoplasmic volume. Previous authors have not written leaf thickness explicitly into their equations. This procedure might lead one to ascribe differences in photosynthetic efficiency to differences in leaf biochemistry, whereas in fact they might merely reflect a difference in leaf thickness.

Diffusion. If C and C_i are the concentrations of CO_2 in the air and the leaf cytoplasm respectively, then the net photosynthetic rate (P_n) per unit area (counting one surface only) of leaf is

$$P_n = \frac{C - C_i}{r_d} \qquad (4.3)$$

where r_d is the total diffusive resistance.

It is to be noted that C of equation (4.3) should be corrected for the solubility of CO_2 in the leaf cytoplasm at the appropriate temperature. For example, at $20°$ C and standard atmospheric pressure, 90.1 m^3 of CO_2 will dissolve in 100 m^3 of water, so that the atmospheric concentration of CO_2 should be multiplied by $90.1/100$. This correction will be neglected in the theoretical development, although it should not be forgotten as gas solubilities in water are strongly temperature dependent. (*Note added in proof*: Professor O.V.S. Heath has kindly drawn our attention to a discussion of gas solubilities by E.R. Leonard [27].)

Photosynthesis. The scheme described below is an extension of the model of Rabinowitch [37].

In the present model the first reaction that a CO_2 molecule can undergo after diffusing into the leaf cytoplasm is an irreversible combination with an acceptor molecule A:

$$CO_2 + A \xrightarrow{\;k_1\;} A\ CO_2 \qquad (4.4)$$

k_1 and the parameters k_i to be introduced below are rate constants, some of which are probably temperature dependent. The bound CO_2 may then be fixed by reaction with X^*, a product of some photochemical or biochemical reactions:

$$A\ CO_2 + X^* \xrightarrow{\;k_2\;} A + G + X \qquad (4.5)$$

where G indicates a carbon product, and X is the alternative form of X^*. It seems preferable not to try and identify X or X^* with a particular biochemical substance (such as chlorophyll, pyridine nucleotide or ATP); for the present purpose it is only necessary that X represent the controlling element or bottleneck in what is undoubtedly a very complicated sequence of linked reactions. The intermediate carbon product G may then be utilized or stored, so that

$$G \xrightarrow{\quad k_3 \quad} \text{utilization and store} \qquad (4.6)$$

Light of flux density I is involved (although not necessarily directly as indicated here) in the production of X^* from X:

$$X + I \xrightarrow{\quad k_4 \quad} X^* \qquad (4.7)$$

$$X^* \xrightarrow{\quad k_5 \quad} X \qquad (4.8)$$

The pathway in (4.8) allows X^* to return by decay or degradation to the state X. This process might be chemical, or due to fluorescent or non-radiative decay.

Respiration. The respiratory process will be summarized in two reactions. The first of these produces the carbon intermediate G from a large store S:

$$S \xrightarrow{\quad k_6 \quad} G \qquad (4.9)$$

and in the second reaction the carbon intermediate G is converted to CO_2:

$$G + X \xrightarrow{\quad k_7 \quad} CO_2 + X^* \qquad (4.10)$$

Photosynthesis and respiration have the species X, X^*, CO_2 and G in common; they will therefore interact, the strength and consequences of this interaction depending upon the rate constants and other parameters.

Oxygen does not appear explicitly in this scheme, so the present model cannot account directly for a reduction in respiration at low oxygen tension. This effect might be mimicked by assuming that one or more of the rate constants depends upon oxygen tension, but extension of the model to include oxygen is straightforward.

Qualitative Behaviour and Possible Modifications. Next, the interactions and type of behaviour that might result from equations (4.4) − (4.10) as a result of changes in light flux density will be discussed. In the dark, X^* is produced by respiration (4.10); it can revert to X either by decay (4.8) or by fixing CO_2 (4.5). Although the model thus predicts some residual CO_2 fixation in the dark, there will be a net flow of CO_2 out of the leaf. If light is now applied at low flux density, a suitable choice of k_4, k_5 and k_7 will result in a large increase in X^*, and hence the production of carbon intermediate G (4.5). The level of G will build up until the outflow of G by (4.6) and (4.10) is equal to the inflow of G by (4.5) and (4.9). This increased respiration (4.10) will have a different dependence upon the rate constants in the light from that in the dark, and the observation of a different temperature dependence would not be surprising [13, 23]. If the light is switched off, X^* will decrease sharply, with perhaps only a small relative increase in X, and as G is well above its steady state dark level a burst in CO_2 emission will result.

Earlier in the chapter, mention was made of possible compartmentation of the processes of photosynthesis and respiration. Various levels of compartmentation are possible. Compartmentation of CO_2 might be achieved by superscripting the CO_2 used in photosynthesis CO_2^P in (4.4), and that produced by respiration CO_2^R in (4.10). It would then be necessary to replace (4.3) by two equations, the first dealing with gross photosynthetic rate $P_g = (C - C_i^P)/r_d$ and the second with respiration $R = (C_i^R - C)/r_{d'}$, where $r_{d'}$ is the diffusion resistance from the site of respiration to the leaf exterior. A further separation of photosynthesis and respiration could be achieved by supposing that the intermediate carbon products of photosynthesis (G of (4.5) and (4.6)) are quite different or separate from the carbon intermediates involved in respiration (G of (4.9) and (4.10)). Compounds superscripted G^P and G^R could be used to describe this more complicated situation. Finally, photosynthesis and respiration might be separated completely if, in addition, X and X^* of (4.5), (4.7) and (4.8) are assumed to be different or separate from X and X^* of (4.10). There would then be no interaction between the processes of photosynthesis and respiration.

Since photosynthesis occurs in the chloroplasts and much respiration takes place in the mitochondria which are physically separate organelles, a more realistic form of compartmentation might completely separate X, X^*, G and C_i for photosynthesis and respiration but allow them to interact by diffusing across some inter-organelle pathway. Various schemes showing the diffusion pathways that might be involved in the movement of CO_2 to and from the sites of photosynthesis and respiration have been proposed [e.g. 26, 33]. However these deal only with the movement of CO_2 which is a small molecule and probably diffuses much more rapidly than the larger molecules represented by X, X^* and G. Also, any gaseous phase in the inter-organelle pathway will absolutely block the movement of X, X^* and G but not of CO_2.

It will be clear that by suitable choice of rate constants, and by assuming the absence or presence of compartmentation in different parts of the system, the nature and degree of the interactions between respiration and photosynthesis can be varied. It is hoped that this scheme, with appropriate variations, will permit the simulation of photosynthesis and respiration in both the C-3 photosynthetic pathway typical of temperate species and the C-4 pathway typical of tropical grasses.

Equations of Motion. First, we define

$$A_0 = A + A\,CO_2 \tag{4.11}$$

and

$$X_0 = X + X^* \tag{4.12}$$

By inspection of (4.3) — (4.10), the first-order differential equations describing the system are:

$$\frac{dC_i}{dt} = \frac{C - C_i}{dr_d} - k_1 A C_i + k_7 G X \tag{4.13}$$

$$\frac{dA}{dt} = - k_1 A C_i + k_2 (A_0 - A)(X_0 - X) \tag{4.14}$$

$$\frac{dG}{dt} = k_2 (A_0 - A)(X_0 - X) - k_3 G + k_6 S - k_7 G X \tag{4.15}$$

$$\frac{dX}{dt} = k_2 (A_0 - A)(X_0 - X) - k_4 I X + k_5 (X_0 - X) - k_7 G X \tag{4.16}$$

These four equations completely determine the behaviour of the four variables C_i, A, G and X, given a set of initial conditions. Net photosynthesis is then computed using (4.3).

The Steady State. In the steady state, all time derivatives are equal to zero, so that equations (4.13)— (4.16) become

$$0 = \frac{C - C_i}{dr_d} - k_1 A C_i + k_7 G X \tag{4.17}$$

$$0 = - k_1 A C_i + k_2 (A_0 - A)(X_0 - X) \tag{4.18}$$

$$0 = k_2 (A_0 - A)(X_0 - X) - k_3 G + k_6 S - k_7 G X \tag{4.19}$$

$$0 = k_2 (A_0 - A)(X_0 - X) - k_4 I X + k_5 (X_0 - X) - k_7 G X \tag{4.20}$$

The straightforward approach is to assume that C and I are given, and to solve these four equations for C_i, A, G and X and then use (4.3) to give P_n. However, when doing this, clumsy polynomials are obtained, and unwanted solutions (for example with negative concentrations) are generated along with the physically acceptable ones. An easier computational method is to assume that A and X are given, assigning them values between 0 and A_0, and 0 and X_0 respectively, and then calculate G, I, C_i, C and finally P_n. From (4.19),

$$G = \frac{k_2 (A_0 - A)(X_0 - X) + k_6 S}{k_3 + k_7 X} \tag{4.21}$$

giving G in terms of A and X, all other quantities in (4.21) being given. Using this value of G, the light flux density is then derived from (4.20)

$$I = \frac{k_2 (A_0 - A)(X_0 - X) + k_5 (X_0 - X) - k_7 G X}{k_4 X} \tag{4.22}$$

The CO_2 concentration in the leaf cytoplasm (C_i) is given by (4.18):

$$C_i = \frac{k_2(A_0 - A)(X_0 - X)}{k_1 A}$$

and the external CO_2 concentration (C) is obtained from (4.17):

$$C = C_i + dr_d(k_1 A C_i - k_7 G X) \qquad (4.23)$$

This expression can also be used even if it is assumed that the stomatal resistance (which is one component of r_d) is a function of internal CO_2 concentration (C_i) or of some other variable.

Finally, net photosynthetic rate is given by equation (4.3).

Asymptotic Behaviour. With saturating light ($I = \infty$) and saturating CO_2 ($C = \infty$), $X = 0$ and $A = 0$, and the net photosynthetic rate is given by

$$P_n (I = \infty, C = \infty) = dA_0 k_2 X_0$$

giving the maximum possible value of P_n.

At a given CO_2 concentration P_n can be saturated with respect to light, and the behaviour of $P_n(I = \infty, C)$ which is a function of C can be examined. This relation is described by a hyperbola which, if no compartmentation is introduced, passes through the origin.

Similarly, the curve of $P_n(I, C = \infty)$ versus I is a hyperbola which does not pass through the origin.

Estimation of the Parameters. The model described above contains eleven adjustable constants. These are k_1, k_2, k_3, k_4, k_5, $k_6 S$, k_7, A_0, X_0, r_d and d. The values of some of these, such as r_d and d, are moderately well-known. Later on in this paper, the present model is reduced to Rabinowitch's scheme for photosynthesis, and in this scheme two parameters appear whose magnitudes are fairly well-known. These are

$$\text{photochemical efficiency, } \alpha = \frac{dk_2 k_4 A_0 X_0}{k_5}$$

and $\text{carboxylation resistance, } r_x = \dfrac{1}{dk_1 A_0}$

The rate constant k_1 might be considered to be an association constant for an enzyme-substrate reaction, and where such rate constants have been measured, they typically lie in the range $10^6 - 10^9 M^{-1} s^{-1}$ [28, p.275]. The product $k_2 X^*$ might be expected to have the magnitude of a typical enzyme-substrate complex dissociation constant, that is $10 - 10^4 s^{-1}$. If A_0 is an enzyme of molecular weight 10^5 then a cytoplasmic concentration of 0.1 g 1^{-1} corresponds to $A_0 = 10^{-6}$ M.

Simple considerations of this sort greatly restrict the permissible range of the many parameters of the model. In some preliminary simulation studies, the following values have been somewhat arbitrarily taken as a starting point*:

$$k_1 = 10^7 \text{ M}^{-1} \text{ s}^{-1}, \qquad k_5 = 10 \text{ s}^{-1}, \qquad X_0 = 10^{-5} \text{ M},$$
$$k_2 = 10^8 \text{ M}^{-1} \text{ s}^{-1}, \qquad k_6 S = 10^{-6} \text{ M s}^{-1}, \qquad r_d = 10^3 \text{ s m}^{-1},$$
$$k_3 = 10^{-2} \text{ s}^{-1}, \qquad k_7 = 10^2 \text{ M}^{-1} \text{ s}^{-1}, \qquad d = 0.5 \times 10^{-3} \text{m},$$
$$k_4 = = 2 \times 10^{-3} \text{ m}^2 \text{ J}^{-1}, \qquad A_0 = 10^{-6} \text{ M},$$

With these values, one can evaluate (transforming to more familiar units): photochemical efficiency = 4.4×10^{-6} gCO_2 J^{-1}, carboxylation resistance = 200 s m^{-1}, and the maximum rate of photosynthesis in saturating light and CO_2 = 22×10^{-3} gCO_2 m^{-2} s^{-1}. Simulation of transients in photosynthesis and respiration should be a stringent test of the model.

Some Published Models of Photosynthesis and Respiration
Many of the discussions of photosynthesis found in the literature (apart from work using models based on electrical circuit analogues which does not attempt to simulate the biochemical processes) have their origin either in the formalism put forward by Maskell [29], or that suggested by Rabinowitch [37], the latter approach being probably that most used. However, various simplifications are possible from these basic models, and one frequently encounters expressions of which the origin and theoretical basis are not entirely clear. In this section the equations used by several authors are discussed, it is shown how these can be reduced to simpler forms, the different treatments are compared, and finally it is shown how the model of coupled photosynthesis and respiration presented in the previous section can be reduced to Rabinowitch's scheme.

General Comments Concerning Respiration. Net photosynthetic rate P_n is the difference between gross photosynthetic rate P_g and the respiration rate R, so that

$$P_n = P_g - R \qquad (4.24)$$

---

*CO_2 concentrations (C and C_i), which are here expressed in units of molarity to conform with the biochemical treatment, are later expressed as volume ratios.

Also, diffusion and carboxylation resistances are later described by a conductance τ (equation 4.51), expressed in units of gCO_2 m^{-2} s^{-1}. To obtain τ from a resistance r, at a temperature of TK and a pressure of p N m^{-2}, one may use the relation

$$\tau = \frac{19.77}{r} \times \frac{273}{T} \times \frac{p \times 10^{-5}}{1.013}$$

These terms have not been precisely defined, and the quantities they represent differ between experiments according to the measuring methods used. For instance, when (4.24) is applied to the results of an experiment in which CO_2 exchange is measured, P_g comprises all the CO_2-consuming reactions of the leaf (not all of them necessarily photosynthetic) and R comprises all the CO_2-producing reactions. P_n is the net rate at which CO_2 diffuses into the leaf, and using the previous notation,

$$P_n = \frac{C - C_i}{r_d} \qquad (4.25)$$

Two ways of dealing with respiration are commonly encountered. In the first of these, the products of respiration are assumed to be kept apart from the substrates for photosynthesis, and there is a separate diffusion path for escape of respiratory CO_2 from the leaf. In this case the use of (4.25) is not valid (see the comments earlier on compartmentation), P_g can be calculated by neglecting R entirely, and then P_n is obtained by simply subtracting R from P_g (4.24). Equation (4.25) is only applicable if C_i is uniform throughout the leaf.

In the second way of dealing with respiration, the respiratory CO_2 is not separated from the CO_2 for photosynthesis. It is now not valid to calculate P_g neglecting R, and then simply subtract R to give P_n, for a result of respiration is to increase C_i, which generally has the effect of increasing P_g. It is necessary to solve equations (4.24) and (4.25) simultaneously. This can be achieved by assuming that P_g is a particular function of I and C_i, and using (4.25) to eliminate C_i from (4.24), giving a relation connecting P_n, I and C. It is to be noted that the inclusion of a constant respiration affects photosynthesis, without producing a back reaction of photosynthesis upon respiration.

Summary of the Models. In this section we shall follow other authors in omitting the explicit effects of leaf thickness, although the role played by leaf thickness will become clear when a discussion is given of how the model described in the previous section reduces to Rabinowitch's scheme.

Expressions have been rewritten so that they deal with net photosynthetic rate where applicable, and appropriate changes in notation have been made to give consistency.

(i) Maskell [29] adopts what he describes as Warburg's [45] picture of the photochemical phase in which the net photosynthetic rate P_n is given by

$$P_n = \frac{\alpha I C_i}{C_i + K_c} - R = \frac{C - C_i}{r_d} \qquad (4.26)$$

where K_c and α are constants. It will be noticed that the gross photosynthetic rate has a Michaelis-Menten type of dependence on C_i. Eliminating C_i one can derive from (4.26)

$$0 = P_n^{\,2} r_d - P_n \,(\alpha I r_d + K_c + C - R r_d) + \alpha I C - R(K_c + C) \qquad (4.27)$$

This is the equation of a non-rectangular hyperbola for the $P_n : I$ and $P_n : C$ curves (Figure 4.2).

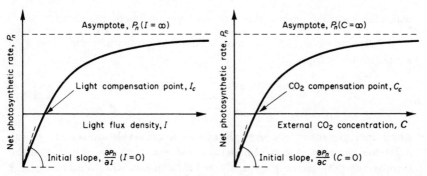

Fig. 4.2   *Dependence of net photosynthetic rate on light flux density and CO_2 concentration. (Key, Table 4.1).*

Table 4.1
Key to Figure 2, showing the characteristics of the hyperbolae obtained using three different models (equations 4.27, 4.31 and 4.35). Rabinowitch's model (third row) takes no account of respiration so that $R = 0$ and $P_g = P_n$ in equation (4.31).

	$P_n(I = \infty)$	$P_n(C = \infty)$	$\frac{\partial P_n}{\partial I}(I = 0)$	$\frac{\partial P_n}{\partial C}(C = 0)$	I_c	C_c
Maskell model	$\dfrac{C}{r_d}$	$\alpha I - R$	$\dfrac{\alpha}{1 + \dfrac{K}{C + R r_d}}$	complicated expression	$\dfrac{R(K + C)}{\alpha C}$	$\dfrac{RK}{\alpha I - R}$
Rabinowitch model $R = 0$	$\dfrac{C}{r_d + r_x}$	αI	α	$\dfrac{1}{r_d + r_x}$	0	0
Rabinowitch model with respiration $R \neq 0$	$\dfrac{C - R r_x}{r_d + r_x}$	$\alpha I - R$	α	complicated expression	$\dfrac{RC}{\alpha(C - R r_x)}$	$\dfrac{\alpha I R r_x}{\alpha I - R}$

The Maskell model can be reduced in two ways. The first of these is to put $r_d = 0$ (this is equivalent to putting $C_i = C$) giving the equation

$$P_n = \frac{\alpha I C}{C + K_c} - R \qquad (4.28)$$

P_n is then linearly dependent upon the flux density I at constant C, and the $P_n : C$ curve is a rectangular hyperbola which saturates at $P_n = \alpha I$ and whose initial slope is $\alpha I/K_c$. The second way of reducing (4.27) is to put $K_c = 0$. Equation (4.27) then factorizes to give two straight lines

$$\left.\begin{array}{l} P_n = C/r_d \\[2mm] P_n = \alpha I - R \end{array}\right\} \qquad (4.29)$$

which represent the limiting factor response postulated by Blackman.

(ii) Rabinowitch [37] takes no account of respiration. The expression equivalent to (4.26) is

$$P_g = \frac{\alpha I C_i/r_x}{\alpha I + C_i/r_x} = \frac{C - C_i}{r_d} \qquad (4.30)$$

where the constant r_x is commonly called the carboxylation resistance. The difference between Maskell's model and Rabinowitch's model is that, if the cytoplasmic CO_2 concentration (C_i) is held constant, then Maskell assumes that gross photosynthetic rate is linearly proportional to I, whereas Rabinowitch's model gives a hyperbolic dependence on I. Eliminating C_i one obtains

$$0 = P_g^{\ 2} r_d - P_g\,(\alpha I(r_d + r_x) + C) + \alpha I C \qquad (4.31)$$

It will be seen that (4.31) is obtained from (4.27) by putting $R = 0$, and by replacing K_c by $\alpha I r_x$. Once again, (4.31) defines a family of non-rectangular hyperbolae (Figure 4.2).

This model may again be reduced in two ways: firstly by putting $r_d = 0$, giving

$$P_g = \frac{\alpha I C/r_x}{\alpha I + C/r_x} \qquad (4.32)$$

so that both the $P_g : I$ and the $P_g : C$ curves are rectangular hyperbolae. Secondly, two limiting straight lines are obtained by putting $r_x = 0$:

$$\left.\begin{array}{l} P_g = C/r_d \\[2mm] P_g = \alpha I \end{array}\right\} \qquad (4.33)$$

(iii) It is straightforward to include a constant respiration (R) in the Rabinowitch model. Equation (4.30) becomes

$$P_n = \frac{\alpha I C_i/r_x}{\alpha I + C_i/r_x} - R = \frac{C - C_i}{r_d} \qquad (4.34)$$

With this modification, equation (4.31) is replaced by

$$0 = P_n{}^2 r_d - P_n \, (\alpha I(r_d + r_x) + C - R r_d) + \alpha I C - R(\alpha I r_x + C) \quad (4.35)$$

which again defines a family of non-rectangular hyperbolae (Figure 4.2).

This equation can be reduced in the usual way. Putting $r_d = 0$, the rectangular hyperbolae

$$P_n = \frac{\alpha I C / r_x}{\alpha I + C / r_x} - R \qquad (4.36)$$

are obtained. Putting $r_x = 0$ gives two limiting straight lines

$$\left.\begin{array}{l} P_n = C / r_d \\[2mm] P_n = \alpha I - R \end{array}\right\} \qquad (4.37)$$

(iv) Hill & Whittingham [21] apparently follow the approach of Maskell closely, although without considering explicitly the role of light. For example, the first equation on p.47 of their book

$$P_n = P_g{}^{C = \infty} \, \frac{C_i}{C_i + K_c} - R = \frac{C - C_i}{r_d} \qquad (4.38)$$

is identical with equation (4.26) of this discussion if αI is replaced by $P_g{}^{C = \infty}$, the maximum rate of gross photosynthesis obtained with saturating CO_2.

(v) Equation (11) of Monteith [31, p. 106]

$$P_g = \frac{C}{r_d \, (1 - P_g / \alpha I) + r_x + C / \alpha I} \qquad (4.39)$$

is identical with (4.31) of this discussion which is derived from the model of Rabinowitch. However, Monteith does not apply this equation to his data; he simplifies the equation to that of a rectangular hyperbola, stating that at both high and low light flux densities it is valid to neglect the term containing the diffusive resistance.

(vi) Chartier [9] uses the model of Rabinowitch (neglecting respiration) to derive the usual non-rectangular hyperbola relating P_g, C and I. For example, equations (8) and (3) of Chartier are identical with (4.30) of the present discussion, and equation (11) of Chartier is identical with our equation (4.31).

Chartier [10] goes on to discuss photosynthesis in a canopy. He uses a rectangular hyperbola to describe the dependence of P_g on I, and he obtains this from (4.31) of the present discussion by assuming the first term on the right-hand side, $P_g^2 r_d$, can be dropped to give (cf. Chartier [10] equation 3);

$$P_g = \frac{\alpha I C/(r_d + r_x)}{\alpha I + C/(r_d + r_x)} \qquad (4.40)$$

However, it is not clear that this approximation is valid, for as $\alpha I \gg P_g$ (see Figure 4.2), the second term on the right-hand side of equation (4.31) $(P_g \alpha I r_d)$ will always be at least as large as the first term on the right-hand side; one should therefore either drop the first two terms $(P_g^2 r_d$ and $P_g \alpha I r_d)$ by putting $r_d \approx 0$, or retain them both.

Chartier deals with respiration by simply subtracting a constant respiration term from the gross photosynthesis. As discussed earlier, this procedure implies that respiration and photosynthesis occur in separate compartments.

(vii) In his recent book Heath [15, pp.124-6] discusses Maskell's treatment of photosynthesis and respiration, and in his equation (4.5) he uses a relation put forward by Maskell. In our symbols

$$P_n = \frac{C}{r_d + \text{photochemical resistance}} \qquad (4.41)$$

An expression of this type is given on p.519 of Maskell [29]. In order to look at the shape of some curves, Heath makes the assumption that

$$\text{Photochemical resistance} = l/I$$

where l is a constant, so that the above relation becomes

$$P_n = \frac{C}{r_d + l/I} = \frac{CI}{l + r_d I} \qquad (4.42)$$

This expression predicts that P_n is directly proportional to C at all light intensities. Also, Heath's model differs from others in predicting

$$\frac{\partial P_n}{\partial C}(C = 0) = \frac{1}{r_d + l/I} = \text{a function of } I$$

whereas Rabinowitch's model without respiration gives

$$\frac{\partial P_g}{\partial C}(C = 0) = \frac{1}{r_d + r_x} = \text{a constant}$$

for example see Figure 4.2.

(viii) Brown [5] uses

$$P_g = K_b I C_i \qquad (4.43)$$

where K_b is a constant. This is a simpler form than has been used in any of the models described above, and it is likely to give a reasonable description of the system only over restricted ranges of I and C_i. From this expression, an equation is derived in which net photosynthetic rate is linearly proportional to C, but has a hyperbolic dependence upon I [5, equation 5], as in Heath's treatment (4.42).

Discussion of the Various Models. A comparison of equation (4.26) (Maskell) and equation (4.30) (Rabinowitch) shows that in Maskell's expression, if C_i is held constant, P_g can increase without limit as I increases, whereas with (4.30) (Rabinowitch) P_g will saturate at constant C_i as I increases. The latter behaviour would seem to be more reasonable, although (4.26) might give a fair description over the range of light flux densities commonly encountered. A similar criticism can be levelled at Rabinowitch's model which predicts that P_g can increase without limit as both I and C_i are increased. Once again, one must remember that although the lack of a limitation to P_g would seem to be a theoretical deficiency, it might not be important to the experimentalist.

A more serious drawback to the foregoing models is the assumption that respiration is constant and is unaffected by light flux density or internal CO_2 concentration. At the time when these earlier models were developed, this was generally thought to be the case, although now there seems little doubt that respiration is not the same in the light and in the dark. A model that allows the two processes of photosynthesis and respiration to interact seems to be preferable.

Reduction of the Present Model to the Rabinowitch Model. In order to obtain Rabinowitch's result from the model presented at the beginning of this chapter, it is necessary to assume that the reducing power produced by light is linearly proportional to the light flux density (e.g. [9], equation 7). In the present scheme, X^* plays the equivalent role of reducing agent, and using (4.20) with $X_0 = X + X^*$,

$$X^* = \frac{(k_4 I + k_7 G)X_0}{k_2 (A_0 - A) + k_5 + k_4 I + k_7 G} \qquad (4.44)$$

In order to obtain a simple proportionality between X^* and I, we must take

$$\left. \begin{array}{l} k_4 I \gg k_7 G \\ k_5 \gg k_4 I \\ k_5 \gg k_2 (A_0 - A) \end{array} \right\} \qquad (4.45)$$

giving
$$X^* = k_4 X_0 I / k_5 \qquad (4.46)$$

These approximations are equivalent to neglecting respiration and to giving X^* a fast decay process.

Putting (4.46) into (4.18) and solving for A,

$$A = \frac{k_2 A_0 k_4 X_0 I / k_5}{k_1 C_i + k_2 k_4 X_0 I / k_5} \tag{4.47}$$

and putting this into (4.17) with $k_7 \approx 0$,

$$\frac{C - C_i}{dr_d} = \frac{k_1 k_2 A_0 k_4 X_0 C_i I / k_5}{k_1 C_i + k_2 k_4 X_0 I / k_5} \tag{4.48}$$

If we write photochemical efficiency

$$\alpha = d k_2 k_4 A_0 X_0 / k_5 \tag{4.49}$$

and carboxylation resistance

$$r_x = 1 / d k_1 A_0$$

then we obtain equation (4.30), namely

$$P_g = \frac{\alpha I C_i / r_x}{\alpha I + C_i / r_x} = \frac{C - C_i}{r_d}$$

It will be noticed that photochemical efficiency and carboxylation resistance depend upon leaf thickness, and it might be more appropriate to describe the biochemistry by the parameters α/d and $r_x d$ which are independent of leaf thickness.

Summary of Simpler Equations for Gross Photosynthesis, and Modifications for Net Photosynthesis

Simplifying assumptions applied to the model proposed above can give equations for gross photosynthetic rate at three progressively simpler levels:

(i) Assuming fast decay of X^* and neglecting respiration yields the non-rectangular hyperbola which is also given by Rabinowitch's treatment (equations 4.31, 4.39):

$$P_g = \frac{\alpha I C / r_x}{\alpha I + C / r_x + (\alpha I - P_g) r_d / r_x} \tag{4.50}$$

This equation has been used by Chartier [9] to fit data for turnip leaves.

(ii) Assuming in addition either that r_d is negligible (Monteith [31]) or that the term $P_g^2 r_d$ is negligible (Chartier [10]) yields a rectangular hyperbola:

$$P_g = \frac{\alpha I C / r}{\alpha I + C / r}$$

where r is r_x for Monteith and is $(r_d + r_x)$ for Chartier. This equation is used by Monteith [32] and Chartier [10]; and Budyko [8] uses an equivalent expression:

$$P_g = \frac{\alpha I \tau C}{\alpha I + \tau C} \qquad (4.51)$$

where τ (= $1/r$) is the conductance for CO_2 transfer in photosynthesis.
(iii) Equation (4.51) simplifies to equation (4.1)

$$P_g = \frac{\alpha I}{1 + aI}$$

if τ and C are constant, and to

$$P_g = \frac{\tau C}{1 + kC} \qquad (4.52)$$

if α and I are constant. Equation (4.52) has been used by Hesketh [17], Hesketh & Moss [19] and Chartier [9].

A non-rectangular hyperbola (level i above) differs from a rectangular hyperbola (levels ii and iii) in having the asymptotes at other than a right angle; its equation takes the form

$$(x - py)y = -q$$

instead of

$$xy = -q$$

The non-rectangular hyperbola of equation (4.50) allows for variation in the curvature of a photosynthetic response curve having a fixed initial slope and asymptote: the greater is the ratio of r_d/r_x the sharper is the curve and the more it departs from a rectangular hyperbola (equation 4.51).

These equations at three levels refer to P_g; however, P_n is the quantity normally measured, and it is more relevant to crop production. As a result, many authors concerned with fitting equations to measured photosynthetic rates have modified the equations for P_g to refer to P_n. Two alternative methods have been used.

The first and more common method assumes that

$$P_n = P_g - R_d$$

where R_d is the measured dark respiration rate. This gives, for equation (4.51),

$$P_n = \frac{\alpha I \tau C}{\alpha I + \tau C} - R_d \qquad (4.53)$$

This treatment amounts to raising the horizontal axis of the response curves of photosynthesis to light and CO_2.

The second method [3, 19, 20, 46] introduces the light compensation point (I_c) and, by extension, the CO_2 compensation point (C_c):

$$P_n = \frac{\alpha(I - I_c)\,\tau(C - C_c)}{\alpha(I - I_c) + \tau(C - C_c)} \qquad (4.54)$$

This treatment amounts to displacing the vertical axes of the light and CO_2 response curves.

These two methods can be applied to other equations for P_g, from the non-rectangular hyperbola (equation 4.50) to the simplest forms (equations 4.1, 4.52). Both are arbitrary procedures which allow curves to be fitted to Pn data but do not represent realistically the interaction of photosynthesis and respiration; this requires a more complex model such as that presented earlier.

In what follows, the second method of treating P_n (through I_c and C_c) is adopted in preference to the first (through R_d). It has the advantage of permitting the light respiration rate in CO_2-free air to differ from the dark respiration rate, but at the expense of adding two parameters instead of one. Equation (4.54) has infinite discontinuities at combinations of I and C falling on the straight line

$$0 = \alpha(I - I_c) + \tau(C - C_c)$$

This fault is not serious, since such low values of C rarely occur in nature, but it underlines the arbitrary character of this type of treatment for P_n.

Computations and Data

Equations Fitted to Amaranthus edulis Data. To examine the adequacy with which some of the treatments described above relate P_n to I and C, equations were fitted to the extensive measurements on *Amaranthus edulis* published by El-Sharkawy, Loomis & Williams [14]. All data have been converted to SI units, and light flux density has been calculated on the assumption that 1 ft-c is equivalent to 0.045 J m^{-2} s^{-1} (400-700 nm). The common units for C (ppm, vpm and μl l^{-1}) are not part of the SI. An appropriate SI unit is m^3 CO_2 m^{-3} air, but as this expression is cumbersome C has been expressed below as a dimensionless volume ratio, so that 5 x 10^{-6} is equivalent to 5 vpm.

The continuous curves in Figure 4.3 are for the non-rectangular hyperbola (equation 4.50) for P_g, modified to apply to P_n:

$$P_n = \frac{\alpha(I - I_c)\,(C - C_c)/r_x}{\alpha(I - I_c) + (C - C_c)/r_x + (\alpha(I - I_c) - P_g)\,r_d/r_x} \qquad (4.55)$$

The fitting procedure, which assumed that the leaf characteristics α, r_d, r_x, I_c and C_c did not vary with I and C, was as follows:

(i) Mean values of I_c and C_c were estimated from intercepts of P_n plotted against I and C respectively.

(ii) P_n was plotted against $P_n/(I - I_c)$, and straight lines fitted visually indicated a mean value of the initial slope α from their intercepts with the $P_n/(I - I_c)$ axis. Similarly, plots of P_n against $P_n/(C - C_c)$ were used to estimate a mean value of the initial slope $1/(r_d + r_x)$, i.e. τ. Extrapolation of the same fitted straight lines to intercepts on the P_n axis yielded estimates of the asymptotes $(C - C_c)/(r_d + r_x)$, i.e. $\tau(C - C_c)$, and $\alpha(I - I_c)$; estimates of τ and α obtained from these asymptotes tended to be higher than those from the initial slope intercepts, except at low values of I and C, indicating that a hyperbolic relation did not fit perfectly. The 'initial slope' estimates of α and τ were used in preference to the 'asymptote' estimates, because a good fit at low and moderate values of I and C was thought desirable.

(iii) The method proposed by Chartier [9] was then used to estimate r_x and, by difference, r_d.

The curves fit the data satisfactorily except at the three highest values of P_n, for intense light and above-ambient CO_2 concentration.

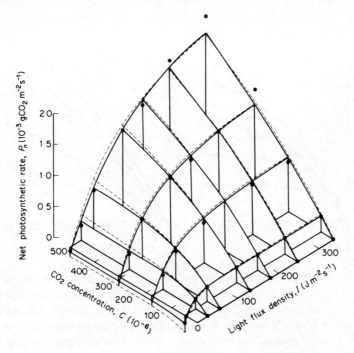

Figure 4.3 Dependence of net photosynthetic rate of Amaranthus edulis leaves on light flux density and CO_2 concentration; from data of El-Sharkawy, Loomis, and Williams [14]. Original data indicated by dots; fitted non-rectangular hyperbolae (equation 4.55) shown by continuous curves, and fitted rectangular hyperbolae (equation 4.54) by broken curves.

For these data r_x was estimated as about one-fifth of the total resistance $(r_d + r_x)$. Estimates of $r_x/(r_d + r_x)$ which were calculated from other A. edulis data tended to be higher; however, the estimation involves various errors and assumptions which do not encourage confidence in it.

Broken curves in Figure 4.3 are for the rectangular hyperbola (equation 4.54). If 'initial slope' estimates of α and τ had been adopted in this case the curves would have been substantially below the actual data except at low I and C; accordingly the values of α and τ were estimated by an iterative procedure, yielding a compromise between the 'initial slope' and 'asymptote' estimates. The curves fit the data fairly well, but the curvature is too great at high C, and the initial slope of the light response curves is about 50 per cent too great, resulting in excessive values for dark respiration.

Variation in Leaf Characteristics. These equations assume that the photosynthetic characteristics of a leaf do not vary with I and C. In fact r_d rises because of stomatal closure at low I [6] and high C [34] ; and I_c increases at low C, and C_c at low I [16] . Hence because the equations are based on average values of leaf characteristics, fitted curves may deviate from measured values of P_n at extremes of I and C.

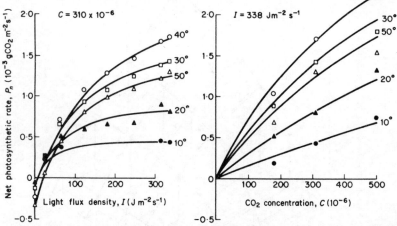

Figure 4.4   Effect of temperature on the dependence of net photosynthetic rate of Amaranthus edulis leaves on light flux density and CO_2 concentration; from data of El-Sharkawy, Loomis, and Williams [14]. Curves have been fitted using equation (4.54) with a CO_2 compensation point of zero; other photosynthetic characteristics as follows:

Temperature ($^\circ$C)	Photochemical efficiency, α (10^{-6} gCO$_2$ J^{-1})	Conductance τ (gCO$_2$ m^{-2} s^{-1})	Light compensation point, I_c (J m^{-2} s^{-1})
10	15	1.6	4
20	15	3.2	6
30	15	6.5	8
40	15	8.4	9
50	15	5.5	22

Average values are nevertheless useful, and α and τ are valuable indicators of photosynthetic capacity. Three types of variation in these photosynthetic characteristics can be distinguished:

(i) Short-term changes occur within minutes as a response to leaf water status or temperature. Effects of temperature on *A. edulis* are shown in Figures 2 and 3 of El-Sharkawy *et al.* [14]; their results are consistent with temperature influencing τ (and I_c) but not α. Expressed graphically (Figure 4.4), temperature affects the asymptote of the light response curve but not the initial slope, whereas it affects the initial slope of the CO_2 response curve but not the asymptote.

(ii) Over longer periods of days or weeks, ageing and growing conditions affect leaf characteristics. Data in Figure 4 of El-Sharkawy *et al.* [14] show that α and τ for old leaves and for shade leaves were roughly half of the values for recently expanded sun leaves. Potassium deficiency and water stress also reduce τ [36, 38].

(iii) Genetic differences in photosynthetic characteristics are illustrated in Table 4.2 for six species selected to represent a range of types. These values are for leaves grown in high light, and of an age expected to give high photosynthetic rates; α and τ were estimated from initial slopes of light and CO_2 response curves. It seems that α varies less than τ; the range for α in Table 4.2 is under three-fold, agreeing with the range $7.4 - 20.3 \times 10^{-6}$ gCO_2 J^{-1} listed for sixteen crop species by Hesketh [17] and Monteith [32]; while the over five-fold range for τ roughly agrees with the range $2.0 - 10.6$ gCO_2 m^{-2} s^{-1} quoted for thirteen species by Monteith. Somewhat lower values of α and τ occur in certain native species, especially woody ones [5, 24]. Varietal differences in α and τ have been found by Bjorkman and Holmgren [4] and Brun and Cooper [6]. The association between high τ and low C_c, in species with the C-4 photosynthetic pathway (the first two listed in Table 4.2) is probably not fortuitous.

Table 4.2
Photosynthetic characteristics of leaves of various species

Species	Photochemical efficiency, α $(10^{-6}$ gCO_2 $J^{-1})$	Conductance, τ $(gCO_2\,m^{-2}\,s^{-1})$	Light compensation point, I_c $(J\,m^{-2}\,s^{-1})$	CO_2 compensation point, C_c (10^{-6})
Zea mays	9.7	6.1	10.7	2
Amaranthus edulis	14.1	5.2	7.6	3
Helianthus annuus	10.0	3.7	12.6	37
Trifolium pratense	10.2	3.5	5.6	39
Stylosanthes humilis	7.7	3.3	6.0	48
Acer saccharum	20.3	1.1	4.1	50

Data from: [3, 14, 17]

Effects of Light, CO_2 and Leaf Characteristics on Computed Photosynthesis and Energy Conversion. In order to display the interacting effects of α, τ, I,

and C on P_n, equation (4.54) was used to compute P_n for several values of
the leaf characteristics and for values of I up to 500 J m^{-2} s^{-1} (bright
sunlight) and C up to 1000 x 10^{-6} (1000 vpm or about three times ambient
concentration). Figure 4.5 plots the response surface of P_n to I and C for
leaves of four types; all have $I_c = 6$ J m^{-2} s^{-1} and $C_c = 5$ x 10^{-6}, but two levels
of α and τ are compared. The difference in τ has a greater effect on P_n than
the difference in α, merely because a five-fold difference in value was taken
instead of two-fold. Increase in α tends to steepen the surface perpendicular
to the C axis more than that perpendicular to the I axis, and increase in τ has
the opposite effect, but both raise the response surface generally.

Figure 4.5 is of interest in relation to CO$_2$ enrichment for glasshouse
crops. Firstly, it indicates that the increase in P_n obtained by CO$_2$

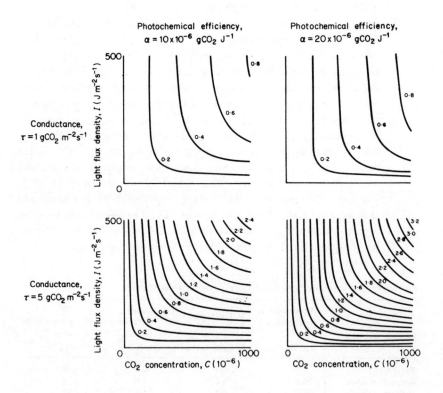

Figure 4.5 *Dependence of net photosynthetic rate on light flux density and
CO$_2$ concentration, computed from equation (4.54) for leaves
having two values of photochemical efficiency and two values of
conductance. Net photosynthetic rate (10^{-3} gCO$_2$ m^{-2} s^{-1}) is
expressed as response surface contours.*

enrichment can equally be obtained by increase in τ which, if it can be achieved by breeding, is simpler than CO_2 enrichment. Secondly, it shows that the absolute increase in P_n resulting from a given increase in C rises with increasing I and falls with increasing C; and is greater for higher values of α and (except at low I coupled with high C) for higher values of τ.

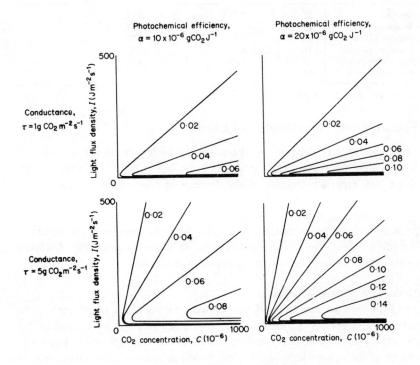

Figure 4.6 *Response surface contours showing the dependence of the efficiency of light energy conversion on light flux density and CO_2 concentration for leaves of the four types represented in Figure 4.5.*

Higher light results in greater P_n, but the light is not used as efficiently as at lower flux densities. Figure 4.6 shows the efficiency of energy conversion, calculated on the basis that 1 g of CO_2 yields 0.682 g of photosynthate and that the heat of combustion of the latter is 15 700 J g^{-1}. For leaves with the same photosynthetic characteristics as those in Figure 4.5, the greatest efficiency is at a light flux density that increases with increase in C and τ and with decrease in α, but is of the order of 20 J m^{-2} s^{-1}. The maximum efficiency at normal C is about $0.05 - 0.10$, but CO_2 enrichment to 1000 x 10^{-6} doubles this. These computed values agree in order of magnitude with experimental data (Table 4.3).

Table 4.3

Maximum efficiencies of light energy conversion for leaves of various species at normal CO_2 concentration

Species	Light flux density, I ($J m^{-2} s^{-1}$)	Net photosynthetic rate, P_n ($10^{-3} gCO_2 m^{-2} s^{-1}$)	Efficiency of light energy conversion
Zea mays	22	0.25	0.12
Amaranthus edulis	48	0.50	0.11
Helianthus annuus	19	0.17	0.10
Trifolium pratense	31	0.39	0.13
Stylosanthes humilis	17	0.09	0.06
Acer saccharum	13	0.03	0.03

Data from: [3, 14, 17, 19, 44]

Photosynthesis of a Canopy of Leaves

Crop productivity depends on the photosynthetic rate of the canopy as a whole. This photosynthetic system is far more complex than that of the single leaf, especially because of the decrease in I with depth in the canopy. There is also a gradient in C with depth, but this is relatively small and is ignored below, as are other components such as leaf age and posture and the presence of organs other than leaves. In principle there is no difficulty in including such effects, but limitations of space require the following treatment of canopy photosynthesis to be kept simple.

Model of Net Photosynthesis

The light flux density averaged over a horizontal plane at a given depth in the canopy (I') depends on the leaf area index (L) above this level and on the extinction coefficient (K) which is a measure of the light-intercepting efficiency of the canopy leaf area. K tends to fall as leaves become more erect, or grouped in clumps, or as their scattering coefficient increases; all these features reduce efficiency of light interception.

Monsi & Saeki [30] have shown that for many canopies the decrease in I' with depth in the canopy follows approximately the Beer-Lambert law

$$I' = I_0 \exp(-KL) \tag{4.56}$$

where I_0 is the light flux density on a horizontal plane above the canopy. The light flux density I incident on an inclined leaf is on average less than that on a horizontal surface I' at the same level, and Saeki [39] proposed that

$$I = KI_0 \exp(-KL)/(1-m) \tag{4.57}$$

where m is the transmission coefficient of the leaf. This expression makes various approximations [see 1, 2, 40] but has been widely adopted [e.g. 22, 35, 43] and has the advantage of simplicity.

By substituting equation (4.57) into equation (4.54) and integrating with respect to L equation (4.58) is obtained (the assistance of Mr. R.C. Hoare in deriving this equation is acknowledged) relating the net photosynthetic rate of the canopy per unit area of ground ($P_{n,c}$) to parameters of

(i) climate (terms I_0, C);
(ii) canopy structure and optical properties (terms L, K, m);
(iii) leaf photosynthetic characteristics (terms α, τ, I_c, C_c):

$$P_{n,c} = \alpha \bigg/ \left[\left\{ \frac{K\alpha}{\tau(C - C_c)} \right\} \left\{ 1 - \frac{\alpha I_c}{\tau(C - C_c)} \right\} \right]$$

$$\times \ln \left[\left[\left\{ 1 - m \right\} \left\{ 1 - \frac{\alpha I_c}{\tau(C - C_c)} \right\} + \left\{ \frac{\alpha I_0 K}{\tau(C - C_c)} \right\} \right] \right.$$

$$\div \left. \left[\left\{ 1 - m \right\} \left\{ 1 - \frac{\alpha I_c}{\tau(C - C_c)} \right\} + \left\{ \frac{\alpha I_0 K \exp(-KL)}{\tau(C - C_c)} \right\} \right] \right]$$

$$- \alpha I_c L \bigg/ \left\{ 1 - \frac{\alpha I_c}{\tau(C - C_c)} \right\} \tag{4.58}$$

Computations and Data on Photosynthesis and Energy Conversion. It is not possible to discuss here the interactions of all nine parameters in equation (4.58), but Figure 4.7 displays some effects of climate (I_0 and C) and canopy characteristics (K and L) for leaves of one type only ($\alpha = 10 \times 10^{-6}$ gCO$_2$ J^{-1}; $\tau = 1$ gCO$_2$ m^{-2} s^{-1}; $I_c = 6$ J m^{-2} s^{-1}; $C_c = 5 \times 10^{-6}$; $m = 0.1$).

The response surfaces for $K = 0.4$, a value indicating relatively inefficient interception of light, show that increase in L results in greater $P_{n,c}$ at high I_0, because of increased light interception, but results in smaller $P_{n,c}$ at low I_0, because the lower leaves are below their compensation point. The response surfaces for $K = 1.2$, a value corresponding to efficient light interception by a mosaic of planophile leaves, indicate by contrast a higher $P_{n,c}$ at low L for all levels of I_0, while at higher values of L the $P_{n,c}$ is lower than for $K = 0.4$, because there is more shading of lower leaves. Thus the optimal L is high (above 8) when K is low and I_0 is high, but falls as K increases and I_0 decreases.

The increase in $P_{n,c}$ resulting from a given increase in C rises with increasing I_0 and falls with increasing C, as for single leaves. It also rises with increase in L to an extent depending on I_0, C and K; and it rises with increase in K at low L and I_0 but falls with increase in K at high L and I_0.

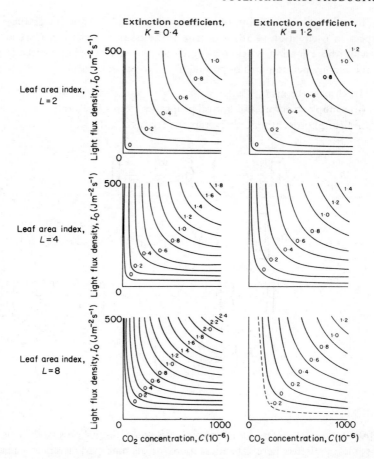

Figure 4.7 Dependence of net photosynthetic rate of a canopy per unit ground area $(10^{-3}\ gCO_2\ m^{-2}\ s^{-1})$ on light flux density and CO_2 concentration, computed from equation (4.58) and expressed as response surface contours, for canopies having three values of leaf area index and two values of extinction coefficient.

The values of α and τ on which these response surfaces are based are not high, and Table 4.4 shows the effect of increased α and τ on $P_{n,c}$ in fairly strong light ($I_0 = 300\ J\ m^{-2}\ s^{-1}$) and normal CO_2 concentration ($C = 300 \times 10^{-6}$).

Figure 4.8 shows that computed efficiencies of energy conversion for the canopy of leaves ($\alpha = 10 \times 10^{-6}\ gCO_2\ J^{-1}$; $\tau = 1\ gCO_2\ m^{-2}\ s^{-1}$) are smaller than for comparable single leaves (Figure 4.6) at low I_0, especially when high L is associated with high K, owing to the respiratory losses by lower leaves; however, the energy conversion at high I_0 is greater than for single leaves (except when high L is associated with high K), presumably because a greater area of leaf is illuminated than for a single leaf layer though at a lower average I. In the range $L = 2$ to 8, the maximum efficiency at normal C is about 0.01

— 0.05. The optimum I_0 for efficiency of energy conversion is roughly 100 J m^{-2} s^{-1}, considerably higher than the optimum I for single leaves; it increases with C and especially with L.

Table 4.4
Net photosynthetic rate of the canopy (10^{-3} gCO_2 m^{-2} s^{-1}) under high light (300 J m^{-2} s^{-1}) and normal CO_2 concentration (300×10^{-6}), as affected by photochemical efficiency α, conductance τ, leaf area index L, and extinction coefficient K, for leaves with a transmission coefficient of 0.1 and compensation points of I_c = 6 J m^{-2} s^{-1} and C_c = 5 x 10^{-6}; computed from equation (4.58).

τ(gCO$_2$ m^{-2} s^{-1})		1		5	
α (10^{-6} gCO$_2$ J^{-1})		10	20	10	20
K	L				
	2	0.43	0.50	1.07	1.56
0.4	4	0.75	0.91	1.63	2.50
	8	0.96	1.25	1.91	3.01
	2	0.45	0.51	1.30	1.75
1.2	4	0.55	0.65	1.44	2.00
	8	0.29	−0.03	1.22	1.54

Observed efficiencies of energy conversion for canopies at normal C (Table 4.5) are somewhat higher than those in Figure 4.8, probably because of more favourable τ.

In conclusion, it is clear that crop photosynthesis depends on so many aspects of microclimate, canopy structure and leaf characteristics (all oversimplified in the present treatment) that their interactions cannot be foreseen intuitively and can be predicted only by detailed quantitative analysis. Existing models of crop photosynthesis assume a relation between leaf photosynthetic rate and light (equation 4.1) which is too empirical to provide insight into the characteristics of leaf microstructure and bio-chemistry that determine photosynthetic potential. The model of leaf photosynthesis proposed tentatively in this paper seeks to provide a more realistic treatment. Much further work will be needed to provide a satisfactory model of respiration in leaves and other organs.

Few quantitative data are available on variation of leaf photosynthetic characteristics with cultivar, leaf age, and conditions during growth. However, it has been shown that selection can increase the photosynthetic potential of leaves. Increased photosynthesis can also be achieved by modifying the environment: in glasshouses, supplementary heat and CO_2 have potent effects, and for field as well as glasshouse crops, improved soil nutrient and water status enhance photosynthesis. Finally, appropriate choice of sowing dates, spacings and other management practices can help to maximise photosynthesis. Only when breeding, environmental modification and management practices are correctly integrated to give optimal leaf characteristics, microclimate and canopy structure will maximum efficiency of energy conversion be achieved.

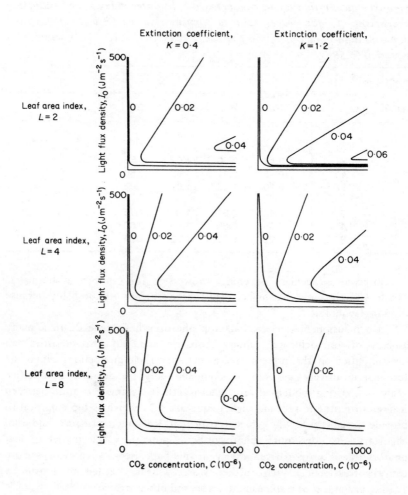

Figure 4.8 Response surface contours showing the dependence of the efficiency of light energy conversion on light flux density and CO_2 concentration for canopies having three values of leaf area index and two values of extinction coefficient; leaf photosynthetic characteristics as for Figure 4.7

Table 4.5

Efficiencies of light energy conversion of various canopies under high light and normal CO_2 concentration

Species	Light flux density, I_0 ($J\ m^{-2}\ s^{-1}$)	Net photosynthetic rate, $P_{n,c}$ ($10^{-3}\ gCO_2\ m^{-2}\ s^{-1}$)	Efficiency of light energy conversion
Glycine max	314	2.60	0.088
Zea mays	440	2.78	0.068
Medicago sativa	450	1.86	0.044
Trifolium repens	405	0.83	0.022

Data from: [18, 41, 47]

Summary

The efficiency of photosynthetic conversion of light energy into chemical energy is determined by the relation between incident light and leaf photosynthetic rate. The simple relation (equation 4.1) commonly used in computing crop photosynthesis has certain limitations.

A more realistic model of the physical and chemical processes of photosynthesis and respiration and their interaction is developed (equations 4.3-4.10): it describes steady-state and transient behaviour given a knowledge of light flux density, CO_2 concentration, leaf thickness, and other parameters. Successive approximations can reduce this model to that of Rabinowitch and, eventually, to the common, simple relation.

Other published models of photosynthesis are summarised and discussed. A non-rectangular hyperbolic response curve of photosynthesis to light has sometimes been derived, but has usually been simplified to a rectangular hyperbola for fitting to data; these two forms have been fitted to published data for *Amaranthus edulis* leaves. Also, the variations in fitted parameters with temperature and between species are discussed.

The interactions of light, CO_2 concentration, leaf characteristics and canopy structure on photosynthesis are too complex to visualize intuitively. However, computations based on a model are presented to show the effects of these factors on net photosynthetic rates and photosynthetic efficiencies of leaves and entire canopies. Such computations suggest how crop productivity may be increased by breeding for appropriate plant characteristics, by modifying the environment (especially in glasshouses), and through spacing and other management practices.

DEFINITIONS OF SYMBOLS

C	CO_2 concentration in the air	
C_c	CO_2 concentration at the compensation point	see page 60
C_i	CO_2 concentration in the leaf	
d	leaf thickness	m
I	light flux density incident on the leaf	$J\ m^{-2}\ s^{-1}$
I_c	light flux density at the compensation point	$J\ m^{-2}\ s^{-1}$
I_0	light flux density in horizontal plane above canopy	$J\ m^{-2}\ s^{-1}$
I'	light flux density in horizontal plane beneath leaf area index L	$J\ m^{-2}\ s^{-1}$
K	extinction coefficient of canopy	
L	leaf area index of canopy	
m	transmission coefficient of leaf	
P_g	gross photosynthetic rate per unit leaf area	$gCO_2\ m^{-2}\ s^{-1}$
P_n	net photosynthetic rate per unit leaf area	$gCO_2\ m^{-2}\ s^{-1}$
$P_{n,c}$	net photosynthetic rate of canopy per unit ground area	$gCO_2\ m^{-2}\ s^{-1}$
R	respiration rate per unit leaf area	$gCO_2\ m^{-2}\ s^{-1}$
R_d	dark respiration rate per unit leaf area	$gCO_2\ m^{-2}\ s^{-1}$
r_d	diffusive resistance to CO_2 transfer in photosynthesis	$s\ m^{-1}$ or
r_x	carboxylation resistance to CO_2 transfer in photosynthesis	$m^2\ s\ gCO_2^{\ -1}$
α	photochemical efficiency	$gCO_2\ J^{-1}$
τ	conductance to CO_2 transfer	$m\ s^{-1}$ or $gCO_2\ m^{-2}\ s^{-1}$

REFERENCES

1. ACOCK, B.A., THORNLEY, J.H.M. and WARREN WILSON, J. 'Spatial variation of light in the canopy', in *Prediction and Measurement of Photosynthetic Productivity*, (Proc. IBP/PP Tech. Meeting, Trebon), Wageningen, 1970.

2. ANDERSON, M.C. 'Stand structure and light penetration. II. A theoretical analysis', *J. appl. Ecol.*, 1966, 3, 41-54.

3. BEGG, J.E. and JARVIS, P.G. 'Photosynthesis in Townsville lucerne (*Stylosanthes humilis* H.B.K.)', *Agr. Meteorol.*, 1968, 5, 91-109.

4. BJORKMAN, O. and HOLMGREN, P. 'Adaptability of the photosynthetic apparatus to light intensity in ecotypes from exposed and shaded habitats', *Physiol. Plant.*, 1963, 16, 889-914.

5. BROWN, K.W. 'A model of the photosynthesizing leaf', *Physiol. Plant.*, 1969, 22, 620-37.

6. BRUN, W.A. and COOPER, R.L. 'Effects of light intensity and carbon dioxide concentration on photosynthetic rate of soybean', *Crop Sci.*, 1967, **7**, 451-7.

7. BUDAGOVSKII, A.I. and ROSS, Y.K. 'Principles of the quantitative theory of photosynthesis by crop stands', in *Photosynthesis of Productive Systems*, (transl. N. Kaner, ed. J.L. Monteith), Jerusalem: Israel Program for Scientific Translations, 1967, 37-43.

8. BUDYKO, M.I. 'Solar radiation and the use of it by plants', in *Agroclimatological Methods* (Proc. 7th Symp. nat. Resources Res., Reading), Paris: UNESCO, 1968, 39-53.

9. CHARTIER, P. 'Etude theorique de l'assimilation brute de la feuille', *Ann. Physiol. veg.*, 1966, **8**, 167-95.

10. CHARTIER, P. 'Lumiere, eau et production de matiere seche du couvert vegetal', *Ann. agron.*, 1967, **18**, 301-31.

11. DAVIDSON, J.L. and PHILIP, J.R. 'Light and pasture growth', in *Climatology and Microclimatology* (Proc. 11th Symp. Arid Zone Res., Canberra), Paris: UNESCO, 1958, 181-7.

12. DUNCAN, W.G., LOOMIS, R.S., WILLIAMS, W.A. and HANAU, R. 'A model for simulating photosynthesis in plant communities', *Hilgardia*, 1967, **38**, 181-205.

13. EL-SHARKAWY, M. and HESKETH, J. 'Photosynthesis among species in relation to characteristics of leaf anatomy and CO_2 diffusion resistances', *Crop Sci.*, 1965, **5**, 517-21.

14. EL-SHARKAWY, M.A., LOOMIS, R.S. and WILLIAMS, W.A. 'Photosynthetic and respiratory exchanges of carbon dioxide by leaves of the grain amaranth', *J. appl. Ecol.*, 1968, **5**, 243-51.

15. HEATH, O.V.S. *The Physiological Aspects of Photosynthesis*, London: Heinemann, 1969, 310.

16. HEATH, O.V.S. and MEIDNER, H. 'Compensation points and carbon dioxide enrichment for lettuce grown under glass in winter', *J. exp. Bot.* 1967, **18**, 746-51.

17. HESKETH, J.D. 'Limitations to photosynthesis responsible for differences among species', *Crop Sci.*, 1963, **3**, 493-6.

18. HESKETH, J. and BAKER, D. 'Light and carbon assimilation by plant communities', *Crop Sci.*, 1967, **7**, 285-93.

19. HESKETH, J.D. and MOSS, D.N. 'Variation in the response of photosynthesis to light', *Crop Sci.*, 1963, **3**, 107-10.

20. HESKETH, J.D. and MUSGRAVE, R.B. 'Photosynthesis under field conditions. IV. Light studies with individual corn leaves', *Crop Sci.*, 1962, **2**, 311-5.

21. HILL, R. and WHITTINGHAM, C.P. *Photosynthesis*, London: Methuen, 1957, 175.

22. HIROI, T. and MONSI, M. 'Dry-matter economy of *Helianthus annuus* communities grown at varying densities and light intensities', *J. Fac. Sci. Tokyo Univ.* III, 1966, **9**, 241-85.

23. HOLMGREN, P. and JARVIS, P.G. 'Carbon dioxide efflux from leaves in light and darkness', *Physiol. Plant.*, 1967, **20**, 1045-51.

24. HOLMGREN, P., JARVIS, P.G. and JARVIS, M.S. 'Resistance to carbon dioxide and water vapour transfer in leaves of different plant species', *Physiol. Plant.*, 1965, **18**, 557-73.

25. KUROIWA, S. 'Theoretical evaluation of dry-matter production of a crop canopy under insolation- and temperature-climate: a summary', in *Agroclimatological Methods* (Proc. 7th Symp. nat. Resources Res., Reading), Paris: UNESCO, 1968, 331-2.

26. LAKE, J.V. 'Respiration of leaves during photosynthesis. I. Estimates from an electrical analogue', *Aust. J. biol. Sci.*, 1967, **20**, 487-93.

27. LEONARD, E.R. 'Studies in tropical fruit. VI. A preliminary consideration of the solubility of gases in relation to respiration', *Ann. Bot.*, 1939, **3**, 825-43.

28. MAHLER, H.R. and CORDES, E.H. *Biological Chemistry*, London: Harper & Row, 1966, 872.

29. MASKELL, E.J. 'Experimental researches on vegetable assimilation and respiration. XVIII. The relation between stomatal opening and assimilation – a critical study of assimilation rates and porometer rates in leaves of cherry laurel', *Proc. R. Soc.* B, 1928, **102**, 488-533.

30. MONSI, M. and SAEKI, T. 'Uber den Lichtfaktor in den Pflanzengesellschaften und seine Bedeutung fur die Stoffproduktion', *Jap. J. Bot.*, 1953, **14**, 22-52.

31. MONTEITH, J.L. 'Gas exchange in plant communities', in *Environmental Control of Plant Growth* (ed. L.T. Evans), New York: Academic Press, 1963, 95-111.

32. MONTEITH, J.L. 'Light and crop production', *Fld Crop Abstr.* 1965, **18**, 213-9.

33. MOSS, D.N. 'Respiration of leaves in light and darkness', *Crop Sci.*, 1966, **6**, 351-4.

34. PALLAS, J.E. 'Transpiration and stomatal opening with changes in carbon dioxide content of the air', *Science*, 1965, **147**, 171-3.

35. PEARCE, R.B., BROWN, R.H. and BLASER, R.E. 'Photosynthesis in plant communities as influenced by leaf angle', *Crop Sci.*, 1967, **7**, 321-4.

36. PEASLEE, D.E. and MOSS, D.N. 'Stomatal conductivities in K-deficient leaves of maize (*Zea mays.*, L.)', *Crop Sci.*, 1968, **8**, 427-30.

37. RABINOWITCH, E.I. *Photosynthesis and Related Processes*, 2, (1), New York: Interscience, 1951, 603-1208.

38. RACKHAM, O. 'Radiation, transpiration and growth in a woodland annual', in *Light as an Ecological Factor* (6th Symp. Brit. Ecol. Soc., ed R. Bainbridge, G.C. Evans and O. Rackham), Oxford: Blackwell, 1966, 167-85.

39. SAEKI, T. 'Interrelationships between leaf amount, light distribution and total photosynthesis in a plant community', *Bot. Mag., Tokyo*, 1960, **73**, 55-63.

40. SAEKI, T. 'Light relations in plant communities', in *Environmental Control of Plant Growth* (ed. L.T. Evans), New York: Academic Press, 1963, 79-92.
41. SAKAMOTO, C.M. and SHAW, R.H. 'Apparent photosynthesis in field soybean communities', *Agron. J.*, 1967, **59**, 73-5.
42. TOOMING, H. 'Mathematical model of plant photosynthesis considering adaptation', *Photosynthetica*, 1967, **1**, 233-40.
43. VERHAGEN, A.M.W., WILSON, J.H. and BRITTEN, E.J. 'Plant production in relation to foliage illumination', *Ann. Bot.*, 1963, **27**, 627-40.
44. WAGGONER, P.E., MOSS, D.N. and HESKETH, J.D. 'Radiation in the plant environment and photosynthesis', *Agron. J.* 1963, **55**, 36-9.
45. WARBURG, O. 'Uber die Geschwindigkeit der photochemischen Kohlensaurezersetzung in lebenden Zellen. I.', *Biochem. Z.*, 1919, **100**, 230-70.
46. WARREN WILSON, J. 'Maximum yield potential', in *Transition from Extensive to Intensive Agriculture with Fertilizers* (Proc. 7th Colloquium Int. Potash Inst., Israel) Berne: IPI, 1971 (in press).
47. WILFONG, R.T., BROWN, R.H. and BLASER, R.E. 'Relationships between leaf area index and apparent photosynthesis in alfalfa (*Medicago sativa* L.) and ladino clover (*Trifolium repens* L.)', *Crop Sci.*, 1967, **7**, 27-30.
48. de WIT, C.T. 'Photosynthesis of leaf canopies', *Versl. Landbouwk. Onderz.*, No. 663, 1965, 57.

5. Size, Structure, and Activity of the Productive System of Crops

D.J. Watson
Rothamsted Experimental Station, Harpenden, Herts.

The yield of a field crop depends on all that happens to it during its previous growth, so if our aim is to understand how, and by how much, yield can be increased, we need information on the changes that occur throughout the growth period, on how they depend on properties of the plant and are affected by environmental factors, and to what extent the state of the crop at any stage influences the final yield. From such information, rational judgements should become possible on how to alter the form or development of the plant by breeding, or how to change the environment by husbandry procedures or adjust the relation of plant development to seasonal climatic change, to increase yield.

Apart from water, the economic yield of a crop consists mainly of carbon compounds, formed by photosynthesis in leaves, and used in the growth of the plant organs that have economic value. So to understand how economic yield is determined, we need to know how the crop performs as a photosynthetic system, i.e. how the size and structure of the system, and its efficiency, change with time during the growth period. The size and efficiency of the system can be measured by leaf area index and net assimilation rate, respectively, but its structure is more difficult to define; it depends on the number, size and shape of leaves, their distribution throughout the crop profile and on their posture.

Although economic yield is correlated with total dry-matter yield, it does not necessarily continue to increase proportionally with increase in total dry weight; it may depend not only on how much photosynthate can be supplied to the economically useful parts of the plant, but also on how much photosynthate these parts are able to accept. The system that determines economic yield, therefore, consists of sources and sinks of photosynthate, that is, the leaves and the parts that have economic value. There is now much evidence that in some conditions the leaves can produce more photosynthate than the sinks can receive, so that economic yield depends partly on the capacity of the sinks, and not wholly on the output of the photosynthetic system. Excess photosynthate may accumulate elsewhere in the plant, or its movement out of the leaves may be restricted, and in some species this slows photosynthesis. Thus, the sinks may sometimes regulate the rate of photosynthesis.

All the growing parts of the plant in stems, roots and leaves are sinks for photosynthate, except that young leaves become self-supporting before they are fully expanded. Many plants produce bulky tissues in roots or stems that accumulate sugars or polysaccharides and act as perennating organs; fruits and seeds also act as important sinks for photosynthate. In agricultural plants other than grasses or forage crops, these organs are the economically useful parts. They have been greatly increased in size or number by selection, and their composition has been changed to increase the concentration of constituents that are suitable for food. Consequently these useful parts, such as potato tubers, sugar-beet roots and cereal grains, have become the dominant sinks during the period when they are growing.

It seems obvious that such a productive system will operate most efficiently when the size and structure of the crop canopy (the amount and arrangement of leaf surface) is such that light interception and CO_2 assimilation are maximal while the sinks are active, when the capacity of these sinks in storage organs or seeds is adequate to accept the photosynthate provided by the leaves, and when expenditure of dry matter on the rest of the plant (stems, petioles and roots) is no more than is necessary to support the leaves in an efficient arrangement and supply sufficient mineral nutrients and water.

To determine whether the growth of the useful plant parts at any time is controlled by the supply of photosynthate or by the sinks, it would be necessary to change one or other of them, and measure how the growth of the useful parts is affected. In a field crop, production of photosynthate cannot suddenly be increased, but it can be decreased by shading or partial defoliation. Similarly, the demand for photosynthate by the sinks cannot suddenly be increased, but it can be decreased by removing part of them. This would be easy, though laborious, with above-ground parts such as cereal spikelets, but more difficult or impossible with underground sinks such as tubers or roots. Nor would such a decrease in the sinks be a valid test of whether they were controlling growth unless the whole supply of photosynthate continued to be available to the remaining sinks. The results of such tests might often be difficult to interpret because the supply of photosynthate and the demand by the sinks may sometimes, perhaps often, be in balance or nearly so, and then change in either would affect the growth rate of the useful parts. Also, the efficiency of the conducting tissues between sources and sinks may affect the rate at which photosynthate moves and so affect the apparent strength of the sinks.

It is difficult to discuss the source/sink relationship because an adequate terminology is lacking, and because methods have not been devised for measuring the attributes of sinks that determine their activity. If the activities of sources and sinks could be manipulated independently in the ways suggested, the *sink strength* of a crop might be measured as the rate of growth in dry weight of the useful plant parts per unit area of land when the supply of photosynthate is in excess, i.e. when increase or small decrease in the supply does not affect the rate of growth. *Sink capacity* might then be defined as the integral of sink strength over the period of intake of photosynthate, when this is stopped by internal factors of the sinks, i.e. by failure of supply. This is equivalent to the potential yield of the useful plant parts. Measurements of sink strength or sink capacity so defined might help to distinguish the causes of varietal differences in economic yield, or effects of climate or different husbandry methods.

Some attempts have been made to study how economic yield depends on the activity of sinks, by partial defoliation or removing sinks [2], but not enough has been done to establish how sink strength changes during growth. In what follows, therefore, the rate of change in dry weight of the economically useful parts is taken as a measure of sink performance, and whether or not it is determined by sink strength or supply of photosynthate or both is a matter for conjecture.

The object of the rest of this chapter is to describe the changes with time in the productive systems of five crops of different species grown at Rothamsted, as indicated by the changes in leaf area index, net assimilation rate, total dry weight, and the dry weight of the useful parts, and to discuss how they influence economic yield and how they depend on environmental factors.

Table 5 1
Details of the experiments

Crop	Variety	Date of sowing or planting	Date of harvest	Yield	
				Grain	
				(cwt acre^{-1})	(t ha^{-1})
Winter wheat [1]	Cappelle-Desprez	20 October	8 August	45.0	5.65
Spring wheat [1]	Jufy I	8 March	15 August	38.1	4.78
Barley [2]	Proctor	22 March	17 August	52.7	6.61
				Roots	
				(tons acre^{-1})	(t ha^{-1})
Sugar beet [3]	Sharpe's Klein E	31 March	3 November	18.8	47.2
				Tubers	
				(tons acre^{-1})	(t ha^{-1})
Potato [4]	King Edward	2 May	13 October	17.8	44.7

[1] Watson, Thorne and French, 1963; [2] Watson, Thorne and French, 1958; [3] Goodman, 1968; [4] Dyson, 1965.

The crops selected from the few on which appropriate measurements were made (Table 5.1) are from experiments, and treatments within experiments, that gave the heaviest yields for each species; they are from plots with most fertilizer. The varieties grown in these experiments are still in common use, and are included in the N.I.A.B. lists of recommended varieties, except for Jufy I spring wheat; Proctor barley is much less widely grown than formerly. The yields were good for the time when the crops were grown, but more than 60 cwt acre^{-1} (7.5 tonne ha^{-1}) of wheat and 20 tons acre^{-1} (50 tonne ha^{-1}) of potatoes have since been obtained at Rothamsted and heavier yields of potatoes and sugar beet can be produced on lighter soils than the clay loam of Rothamsted farm.

The Photosynthetic System

Size : Leaf Area Index

The leaf area index L (Figure 5.1), of the cereal crops include the areas of exposed leaf sheaths in addition to the leaf laminae. Throughout the autumn and winter L of winter wheat remained very small and did not attain a value of I until the end of March, twenty-three weeks after sowing. The early growth of spring wheat and barley was much faster; they had leaf area indices of 1 in May, about eight weeks after sowing. Subsequently, L of all three cereals increased faster to maxima of nearly 9 for winter wheat at the end of May, 7 for spring wheat in mid-June and 11 for barley in early July. The interval between the time when $L = 1$ and maximum L was 10 weeks for winter wheat, 6 weeks for spring wheat and 8 weeks for barley. The maxima occurred about a week before the date of 50 per cent ear emergence of winter wheat, coincident with it in spring wheat, and a few days after it in barley. From the maxima, L decreased very rapidly to zero in August. Leaf area of wheat was lost more slowly during June and July than later, but with barley the loss was more uniform and much faster than in wheat; in two weeks at the end of July L of barley decreased from more than 8 to 1.5. The intervals between maximum L and harvest were 10 weeks for winter wheat, 9 weeks for spring wheat and 6 weeks for barley.

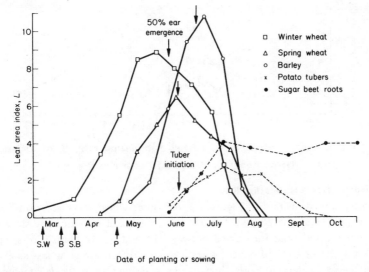

Figure 5.1 Changes with time in the leaf area index, L, of different crops.

Sugar beet and potato did not have leaf area indices of 1 until mid-June, 11 weeks after sugar beet was sown but only 6 weeks after the potatoes were planted. The wide spacing of the sugar-beet seedlings accounts for their slower initial growth in L than of the spring cereals. The potato tubers were chitted before planting; this and the much larger size of potato tubers than of sugar-beet seeds explain the much shorter time they took to establish L of 1. Subsequently, L of sugar beet increased faster than L of potatoes. It reached 4 in mid-July and continued close to this value until harvest in November. L of potatoes also reached its maximum of nearly 3 in mid-July, but then decreased steadily throughout the next two months, until by the end of September all leaves were dead.

Thus, the cereal crops produced much more leaf surface than sugar beet or potatoes, most of it during the period from May to July, whereas sugar beet and potatoes had most from July onwards. The differences in leafiness are shown by the following values of leaf area duration (L integrated over the growth period, in weeks) : winter wheat 106, spring wheat 61, barley 78, sugar beet 68, potatoes 26. Another important difference was that sugar beet maintained near maximal values of L over a long period, whereas maximal L of the cereals and potatoes were peak values between periods of rapid increase and decrease.

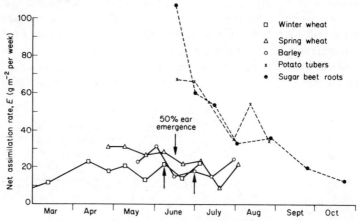

Figure 5.2 Changes with time in the net assimilation rate, E, of different crops. Arrows show the dates of 50% ear emergence.

Efficiency : Net Assimilation Rate

The net assimilation rate E, Figure 5.2, of winter wheat increased from very small winter values of 20 g m^{-1} week^{-1} in April, and subsequently showed no obvious time trend but varied between 12 and 22. In May, E of spring wheat was larger than of winter wheat, but the difference grew less as E of spring wheat decreased, with fluctuations matching those in E of winter wheat grown in the same experiment. The larger E of spring wheat than of winter wheat in May-June was probably the result of less mutual shading of leaves than was associated with the larger L of winter wheat [16]. E of barley in May was similar to that of spring wheat, but in June it decreased to values close to those of winter wheat, possibly also through differences in L. E before and after ear emergence did not differ consistently, but the last values of all three crops were larger than the previous ones.

E of sugar beet in June was more than 100 g m^{-2} week^{-1} and of potatoes nearly 70 g m^{-2} week,$^{-1}$ but both decreased to 35 g m^{-2} week^{-1} at the end of August, and sugar beet to 12 g m^{-2} week^{-1} in October.

Structure : Profile of Leaf Area Index

The distribution of leaf area down the crop profile was not measured in these experiments, but the results of stratified samplings of the foliage of similar crops [11] show that the species differ greatly in the structure of their leaf canopies. Cereals had little leaf area in the bottom 20 cm of the profile; most of it was nearly uniformly distributed in the upper part of the crop above 20 cm from the ground in May, above 40 cm in June and above 60 cm in July. Most leaf area of sugar beet was in the layer between 20 and 40 cm from the ground; the amount per unit height decreased rapidly towards the top of the crop, and was also small in the botom 20 cm layer. The leaf area of potato was nearly uniformly distributed throughout the profile in July, but later it increased steadily from top to bottom of the crop. No doubt there are also differences in leaf angle associated with these differences in distribution of leaf area.

Sink Performance : Growth of the Useful Parts.

The growth of cereal grains begins at fertilization, a few days after the ears emerge, Figure 5.3. Potato tubers are initiated as swellings at the tips of stolons. These events occurred within a period of three weeks in June. The growth of sugar-beet storage roots has no well defined beginning, as the root initial is already present in the seed, but the peripheral meristems responsible for lateral expansion of the storage roots begin to appear about six weeks after germination [4]. The dry weight of sugar-beet roots was very small at the beginning of June, and began to increase faster in the middle of the month. Thus, the sinks for photosynthate in the useful parts of all the crops began to be active at nearly the same time, in spite of the wide differences between crops in sowing or planting date, in growth pattern and habit and in morphology of the useful parts.

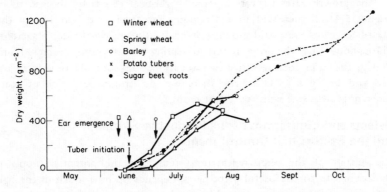

Figure 5.3 Changes with time in the dry weight of the useful plant parts.

The dry weight of cereal grains at any time was estimated as the difference between the dry weight of ears and the final dry weight of chaff (parts of the ear other than grain) which changes only slightly during the growth of the grain. Unfortunately, the dry weights of barley ears were not determined in the early stages of their growth. Initially wheat grains grew very slowly, presumably because the physical size of the sinks, and their strength, was small, but after two weeks growth rapidly increased to a maximum and then decreased. Winter wheat grains ceased to grow at the end of July, and spring wheat grains in early August; subsequently, both lost weight before harvest, presumably by respiration. Throughout June and and July the dry weight of sugar-beet roots and potato tubers were comparable to those of the cereal grains, but they continued to increase much longer; they were apparently still increasing in weight at the final harvest.

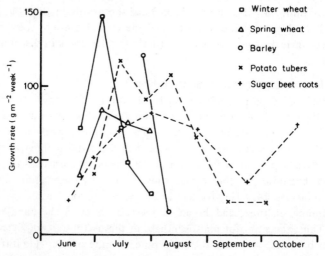

Figure 5.4   Changes with time in the growth rates of the useful plant parts.

The growth rates of cereal grains, sugar-beet roots, and potato tubers (Figure 5.4) all increased to a maximum and then decreased, except that sugar-beet roots were still growing at nearly the maximal rate in October. Throughout July the growth rate of spring wheat grains decreased only slowly; the rates for successive two-weekly periods after 27 June were 166, 148 and 137 g m^{-2}. Otherwise there was no prolonged period of nearly constant growth rate with any of the crops.

Defects and Limitations of the Productive System, and the Factors that Control them

The output of the photosynthetic system, and the potential supply of photosynthate to the useful plant parts, depends on how much of the light falling on the crop is intercepted by the leaves. When the leaf area index is large enough to intercept all of it, or so much of it that the illumination of the lowest leaves is sufficient only to offset their respiratory loss, the crop growth rate (C) is greatest, and further increase in L may cause little change, or more rarely, a decrease in C. Optimal L, the value at which C reaches a peak or a ceiling value, depends on the daily radiation; it also depends on the structure of the leaf canopy. For the crop to produce most dry matter, L should be as close as possible to the optimum throughout the growth period. Although, unfortunately, there is little precise information on the values of optimal L for different crops, or how they change with seasonal change in radiation it is clear that none of the crops achieved this desirable condition. All started with periods of very small L, and all but sugar beet reached a similar state at the end of their growth periods. There is some inconclusive evidence that optimal L for wheat or barley may be about 9 in mid-summer. The winter wheat and barley crops reached values close to this for a short time, but during most of their growth, including nearly all the period after ear emergence, and during the whole growth of the spring wheat crop, L was sub-optimal. The same is true for the potato crop, for which optimal L may be about 3 [6] or 4 [5]. Optimal L of sugar beet is probably between 3.5 and 4 [8] and L of the sugar-beet crop was close to this from mid-July to October. Larger values of L than these optima have been recorded for potato and sugar-beet crops, but not for cereals, so it seems that most good crops by current standards have enough, or more than enough, leaf area to intercept nearly all the incident light at some time during their growth. For maximum dry-matter production, it is especially important that this should occur in May, June and July when there is most radiation per day; this happened with the cereals, but sugar beet had sub-optimal L until nearly the end of July, and the largest L of potato, probably still sub-optimal, also occured in late July.

The differences in optimal L between the cereals and the root crops presumably reflect differences in the structure of their leaf canopies. A large part of the leaf lamina area and the whole of the leaf sheath area of cereals is held vertically, and in the period after ear emergence the sheaths form an increasing part of the green leaf area and eventually the greater part, whereas fully expanded leaves of potato and sugar beet have a nearly horizontal posture. So unit leaf area index of cereals intercepts less light, and the incident light is spread over more leaf area, of cereals than of sugar beet and potato.

The changes with time in net assimilation rate (E, Figure 5.2) reflect both the seasonal change in daily radiation and the changes in mutual shading of leaves associated with change in L. Thus, E of winter wheat increased from January to early April but not later, whereas E of spring wheat and barley decreased from May to July, presumably because the rapid increase in L decreased the illumination of much of the leaf surface. Similarly, E of sugar beet and potato decreased rapidly from large values in June, because daily radiation became less and leaf shading more, through increase in L.

That the sinks in the useful parts of all the different crops began to be active at nearly the same time may be somewhat fortuitous, and does not imply a common relation to seasonal climatic factors. Ear emergence of cereals and tuber initiation of potato depend on the date of sowing or planting and on environmental factors. Thus, delaying the sowing of spring wheat by three weeks, from 11 April to 2 May, delayed ear emergence by one week, from 21 to 27 June (unpublished data of P.J. Wellbank) and nitrogen fertilisation delays tuber initiation and early growth [7, 10].

The similarity in the starting time of the sinks is also a consequence of differences in their botanical nature; cereal grains are reproductive structures that do not start to grow until flowers are produced and fertilized, whereas tubers and storage roots are vegetative structures that appear early in the growth of the crop much sooner after sowing than cereal grains. The same differences determine that the photosynthetic system of cereal crops contribute to filling the grain during less than half of its existance, and only about half the total leaf area duration (39 per cent for the winter wheat, 54 per cent for the spring wheat and 45 per cent for barley) supports grain growth, whereas potato tubers and sugar-beet storage roots are present during more than three-quarters of the growth period, which includes an even larger fraction of the total leaf area duration.

Immediately after fertilization, cereal grains are very small and L is near maximal, so the movement of photosynthate into the grains is probably limited by their sink strength; the leaves produce far more than the grains can accept, and the dry weight of shoots continues to increase for about four weeks [16] but some of the dry matter accumulated in the shoots may later pass to the grains [3]. During this time the growth rate of the grains increases (Figure 5.4) as their size and, presumably, their sink strength increases. Afterwards, the increase in sink strength apparently overtakes the supply of photosynthate which is decreasing because L is rapidly becoming smaller. The fact that the slower decrease in L of spring wheat than of winter wheat is accompanied by slower decrease in grain growth rate supports this interpretation.

The similar changes with time in tuber growth rate (Figure 5.4) probably have a more complex explanation. After tubers are initiated, all parts of the plant continue to increase in size and weight, so the tubers compete for photosynthate with sinks in the stems and roots. This implies that growth of the tubers at this time must depend both on the strength of their sinks in relation to others elsewhere in the plant, and on the supply of photosynthate. It may explain how increased nitrogen supply delays tuber growth soon after their initiation, but later increases it; increased nitrogen may increase the sink strength of other parts of the plant more than of the tubers, but later the greater leaf area supplies more photosynthate to the tubers as well as to stems and roots [7]. Presumably tuber growth rate at first increased with time (Figure 5.4) because both sink strength and supply of photosynthate increased, and which of these was dominant is not obvious. The slowing of tuber growth after mid-August (Figure 5.4) presumably reflects the decrease in L by senescence and death of leaves, but the death of the haulms may itself be a consequence of the demand by the tubers.

Radley [12] found that the tuber bulking rate (rate of increase in tuber fresh weight per unit land area) was remarkably constant over a range of L from 1 to 4, and apparently independent of weather, suggesting that for most of the growth period the sink strength of tubers determined their growth rate; if so, their sink strength was constant in spite of their increase in size. However, Bremner and Radley [6] found tuber yield to be closely correlated with leaf area duration calculated within an upper limit of 3, which suggests that the supply of photosynthate, not the strength of the sinks, controls tuber growth when L is less than 3. There is no evidence in Figure 5.4 of a constant tuber growth rate. Although it seems clear that many potato crops have an excess of leaf surface in July or August, in the sense that change in leaf area index does not affect tuber growth rate, it is uncertain whether this is because L is greater than that necessary for complete light interception, or because dry matter production and movement into the tubers is limited by their sink strength.

The relation between sources and sinks of photosynthate in the sugar-beet crop, also, is still obscure. Cross-grafts between tops and roots of sugar beet and spinach beet showed that with both varieties, grafts of tops on spinach-beet roots had smaller E than grafts on the larger sugar-beet roots [13]. It now seems possible that even the large roots of sugar beet impose a restriction on photosynthesis by its leaves. Humphries and Watson [9] found that when sugar-beet seedlings were raised in a growth room at $20\,^{\circ}C$ with continuous light or 16 h photoperiod, and transplanted to the field at the end of April, the transplants had a larger dry-weight ratio of roots: tops than plants grown from seed sown in the field, and eventually gave a larger yield of roots. As they had similar maximum L and leaf area duration, the larger yield of the transplants was caused mainly by increased E which persisted throughout the growth period.

However, the sink strength of the root does not wholly control the amount of photosynthesis by the leaves; E continues to decrease with decrease in daily radiation throughout the growth period. Also, the root yield of different crops is closely correlated with leaf area duration, presumably because invironmental factors affect both L and the size of the roots similarly. For example, nitrogen fertilizer increases both, but L more than root weight [8], so it is possible that the decrease in E by nitrogen may partly be an effect of the sinks, and not wholly of greater mutual shading of leaves.

This discussion shows that there are several sources of inefficiency in the productive systems of these crops. Only light received from June onwards contributed to growth of the useful parts. The cereals did more photo-synthesis in the earlier part of the year than potatoes or sugar beet, but dry matter produced at this time remained in the shoots and did not enter the grain. Consequently, the dry-weight yield of the useful parts per cent of total dry weight was much less for cereals than potatoes or sugar beet: winter wheat (grain) 34 per cent, spring wheat 36 per cent, barley 51 per cent, potato (tubers) 84 per cent, sugar beet (roots) 63 per cent. During much of the short period when the useful parts were growing, leaf area was too small to intercept all the incident light, and only sugar beet had a prolonged period when L was near optimal. Leaf area of potato and sugar beet was most deficient when there was most daily radiation. In cereals, the activities of sources and sinks of photosynthate during grain filling were badly adjusted; the photosynthetic system was larger at first and rapidly decreased in size, whereas the sink strength was initially small but increasing. Heavy potato crops apparently have an excess of leaf area during much of the tuber growth period, and the sinks in sugar-beet roots have some control over the entry of photosynthate that may restrict the output of the leaves. The leaves of cereals and potato are senescent and leaf area index rapidly decreases during the later stages of growth of grain or tubers; the yield of tubers, but perhaps not of grain, might be increased if the leaves survived longer.

The changes with time in the productive system of the cereal crops, and in the relation between sources and sinks for photosynthate, are consequences of the determinate growth of the shoots; after the terminal bud initiates the inflorescence, no more leaves can be produced. All leaves are expanded by the time of fertilization, and some have already died, so that leaf area index is nearly maximal at this time but later decreases as the remaining leaves die. Thus, the supply of photosynthate to the developing grains of wheat and barley comes from a rapidly deteriorating photosynthetic system. The inefficiency of this arrangement is shown by contrast with maize [1]. Maize ears are produced from lateral buds, and though leaf production is subsequently stopped by the development of the male inflorescence, the leaves produced above the ear continue to supply the grains with photosynthate much longer than in wheat or barley. The practical significance of the final decay of the photosynthetic systems of cereals and potato is presumably that the grains and tubers pass into a dormant state appropriate for prolonged storage. The timing of the changes has presumably been adjusted by selection to fit the seasonal climatic cycle and permit harvesting at a convenient time. Sugar-beet roots go to the factories for processing as soon as possible after harvest, so there is no need for them to be stored with minimal change for long periods, and the productive system can with advantage remain active until the end of the growth period.

Finally, this account of the changes with time in the size and performance of the productive systems of different crops should include some discussion of how they depend on the environment. That they do so is implied by the wide variation in crop yield from year to year and from place to place. Some effects of environment are obvious; thus, the supplies of nutrients and water from the soil affect the size of the whole plant including both sources and sinks of photosynthate, but not necessarily in the same proportion. For example, nitrogen fertilizer applied to a cereal crop increases both leaf area index after anthesis, and the number of ears or grains per ear, to an extent depending on when it is applied. The effect of physical factors of the environment, particularly radiation and temperature, on the productive system are less clear. Much is known of how they affect photosynthesis, something of how they affect leaf production, expansion and survival, but much less of their influence on sink strength. They may control flowering and so determine the existence of the important sinks when economic yield consists of fruit or seeds. Temperature and daily radiation in the period before initiation of spikelets by apical meristems of wheat, and radiation between initiation and anthesis, affect the number of grains per ear [14]. Welbank, Witts and Thorne [17] showed that the grain:leaf ratio of cereal crops is affected almost equally by mean daily radiation and mean temperature in the period after anthesis, and concluded that the temperature effect is on the sink strength of the grains, not on photosynthesis. If the activity of sinks depends on cell division or expansion, or on metabolic processes, temperature may be the external factor that most affects it. More work in controlled environments on these and other aspects of the relation between sources and sinks and their dependence on environmental factors is urgently needed.

REFERENCES

1. ALLISON, J.C.S. 'A comparison between maize and wheat in respect of leaf area after flowering and grain growth', *J. agric. Sci.*, 1964, **63**, 1-4.

2. ALLISON, J.C.S. and WATSON, D.J. 'The production and distribution of dry matter in maize after flowering', *Ann. Bot.* 1966, **30**, 365-81.

3. BIRECKA, H. and DAKIC-WLODKOWSKA, L. 'Photosynthetic activity and productivity before and after emergence in spring wheat', *Acta. Soc. Bot. Pol.*, 1966, **35**, 637-62.

4. BOUILLENE, R., KRONACKER, P. and ROUBAIX, J. de, 'Etapes morphologiques et chimiques dans le cycle vegetatif de la betterave sucriere', *Inst. Belge Am. Bett.* 1940, **8**, 87-162.

5. BREMNER, P.M., EL SAEED, E.A.K. and SCOTT, R.K. 'Some aspects of competition for light in potatoes and sugar beet', *J. agric. Sci.*, 1967, **69**, 283-90.

6. BREMNER, P.M. and RADLEY, R.W. 'Studies in Potato Agronomy. II. The effects of variety and time of planting on growth, development and yield', *J. agric. Sci.*, 1966, **66**, 253-62.

7. DYSON, P.W. 'Analysis of growth and yield of the potato crop with particular reference to nutrient supply', Ph. D. Thesis, University of London, 1965.

8. GOODMAN, P.J. 'Physiological analysis of the effects of different soils on sugar beet crops in different years', *J. appl. Ecol.*, 1968, **5**, 339-57.

9. HUMPHRIES, E.C. and WATSON, D.J. 'Effect of seedling treatment on growth and yield of sugar-beet in the field', *Ann. appl. Biol.*, 1969, **64**, 385-93.

10. IVINS, J.D. 'Agronomic management of the potato', in *The Growth of the Potato*, eds. J.D. Ivins and F.L. Milthorpe, London: Butterworth, 1963.

11. LEACH, G.J. and WATSON, D.J. 'Photosynthesis in crop profiles measured by phytometers', *J. appl. Ecol.* 1968, **5**, 381-408.

12. RADLEY, R.W. 'The effect of season on growth and development of the potato', in *The Growth of the Potato*, eds. J.D. Ivins and F.L. Milthorpe, London: Butterworth, 1963.

13. THORNE, G.N. and EVANS, A.F. 'Influence of tops and roots on net assimilation rate of sugar beet and spinach beet and grafts between them', *Ann. Bot.*, 1964, **28**, 499-508.

14. THORNE, G.N., FORD, M.A. and WATSON, D.J. 'Growth, development, and yield of spring wheat in artificial climates', *Ann. Bot.*, 1968, **32**, 425-45.

15. WATSON, D.J., THORNE, G.N. and FRENCH, S.A.W. 'Physiological causes of differences in grain yield between varieties of barley', *Ann. Bot.*, 1958, **22**, 321-52.

16. WATSON, D.J., THORNE, G.N. and FRENCH, S.A.W. 'Analysis of growth and yield of winter and spring wheat', *Ann. Bot.*, 1963, **27**, 1-22.

17. WELBANK, P.J., WITTS, K.J. and THORNE, G.N. 'Effect of radiation and temperature on efficiency of cereal leaves during grain growth', *Ann. Bot.*, 1968, **32**, 79-95.

6. Water as a Factor in Productivity

H.L. Penman
Rothamsted Experimental Station, Harpenden, Hertfordshire

Introduction

There are several ways of measuring crop production but in an assessment of potential it is probably best to start with the botanist's concept of yield as meaning the growth of the whole plant, and to regard the separation into wanted and unwanted parts as a separate problem that deserves its own special research activity. Any such measure of total botanical yield can be converted into an energy equivalent, using 4000 cal g^{-1} as an acceptable general average for all kinds of plant material. From this an important geographical variable can be eliminated by expressing the growth (as energy) as a fraction of the total income of solar radiation during the life of the crop. To give scale, for this chapter and others, Table 6.1 shows the great range in efficiency (ϵ) of fixing solar radiation for cereals, between a very large

Table 6.1
Range of achievement and possibilities

System or source		Efficiency x 10^{-4}	
Subsistence farming	Average	4—10	Most of the hungry nations
	Probable best	8—20	
Ranch farming	Average	10—20	Satisfied: adequate output
	Probable best	20—40	with minimum effort
Intensive farming	Average	25—35	Industrialized: seeking maximum
	Probable best	60—100+	return for large capital investment
Experiments (season)		80—150	
Experiments (few weeks within season)		150	
Experiments (few days within season)		200—400	
Experiments (in very feeble light)		400—700	
Theoretical upper limit		800—1000	

From Penman [7].

theoretical upper limit, and a very small value in subsistence farming. British achievement is in the third line, at about $\epsilon = 35 \times 10^{-4}$ as an average, but most good farmers can get twice as much, and some, like experimenters at research stations, can get three times this average efficiency. As a first objective in improving crop production the exercise of skill and good management in exploiting what is already known should be able to raise the average to the 'good' level: for research, the desired standard should be $\epsilon \cong 100 \times 10^{-4}$. In ordinary farming units this represents about 5 tons per acre (12.5 t ha^{-1}) of dry matter annually (grass, grain plus straw) or about 20 tons per acre (about 50 t ha^{-1}) of economic yield for root crops.

Water Use and Efficiency

In metric units, the formal equation for efficiency is

$$QY = \epsilon R_I \qquad (6.1)$$

where Q is the heat of formation of plant material (4000 cal g^{-1}),
   Y is the yield (g cm^{-2}),
   R_I is radiation income (cal cm^{-2}).

Equation (6.1) is a definition. Equation (6.2) is a summary of experience, limited both in crops studied and in range of climate, that over the main growing season, and *while water supply is not limiting plant growth,*

$$QY = \alpha E_T \lambda \qquad (6.2)$$

where E_T is the accumulated potential transpiration for the period (cm),
   λ is the latent heat of vaporization of water (590 cal g^{-1}),
   α is a constant, dependent on management variables other than water supply.

Equations (6.1) and (6.2) are not independent: there is a very direct relationship between E_T and R_I, easily summarized for south-east England as: when water supply is not limiting, of the summer radiation from the sun, one-quarter is reflected by a green crop, and one-half of the remainder is used in evaporating water. From measurements, the ratio is 0.38 and hence

$$\alpha = \epsilon/0.38$$

Substituting in either of the yield equations, and expressing Y in tonnes ha^{-1}, and E_T in centimetres of water, then the yield/transpiration equation, in field units, is

$$Y/E_T = 39\epsilon \text{ tonnes ha}^{-1} \text{ cm}^{-1} \qquad (6.3)$$

To about one per cent, 1 tonne ha^{-1} cm^{-1} = 1 ton $acre^{-1}$ in^{-1}, so that in English units an adequate approximation is

$$Y/E_T = 800\epsilon \text{ cwt acre}^{-1} \text{ inch}^{-1} \qquad (6.3a)$$

Table 6.2
Expected growth and response to irrigation in Britain farming

Efficiency Description	ϵ x10^4	Dry matter for E_T = 15 in (380 mm) cwt acre^{-1} (t ha^{-1})	Maximum response to irrigation, cwt acre^{-1} in^{-1} (t ha^{-1} cm^{-1})
Average	33	40 (5.0)	2.7 (0.13)
Good	67	80 (10.0)	5.4 (0.26)
Very good	100	120 (15.0)	8.0 (0.40)

This gives a measure of the rate of loss of yield incurred by lack of water when water is needed, and for a given summer total of E_T it gives a measure of maximum yield to be expected for any value of ϵ. The first inference is to be tested in the course of the paper: the second is demonstrated in Tables 6.2 and 6.3 for an assumed value of E_T = 15 inches. Table 6.2 gives three special cases of equation (6.3a): Table 6.3 is from Agricultural Statistics, 1966/67 [1], giving average yields of some crops for England and Wales for the ten years 1956 to 1966. It must be noted that the agreement between the averages of Table 6.3, and 'average' in Table 6.2 is *not* a discovery; the average values of Table 6.2 are in fact derived from Table 6.1 — at *c.* 35 x 10^{-4} — for cereals in Britain, with barley dominant. What is important, to be carried forward, is that potatoes, wheat and lucerne provide similar values (and probably temporary grass, too, after allowing for a shorter growing season), but sugar beet does not. Of the common British farm crops sugar beet is by far the most efficient in fixing solar radiation (in terms of *total* growth), and it may well be the best in the world.

Table 6.3
Some average yields: England and Wales, 1956 to 1966

Crop	From Table No.*	Yield (Y), cwt acre^{-1} (t ha^{-1})	
Potatoes (Tubers: assume 0.25 DM)	54	46	(5.75)
Sugar Beet (Washed roots: assume 0.25 DM)	57	62 + tops	(7.75 + tops)
Barley (Grain and estimated straw)	52 and 56	39	(4.87)
Wheat (Grain and estimated straw)	52 and 56	45	(5.62)
Lucerne	57	41	(5.12)
Temporary grass	55	31	(3.87)

*refers to table no. in *Agricultural Statistics, 1966/67* [1].

When is Water Needed?

Water supply affects productivity in many ways, of which five are important for the healthy plant.

(a) When all the soil profile is too dry there may be loss of turgor in the leaves, stomatal closure, and a decrease in both assimilation and transpiration.

(b) At an intermediate stage there may be enough water, deeper in the profile, to maintain transpiration, but not enough in the cultivated layer to permit nutrient uptake and maintain growth.

(c) During an extended period of drought the feeding roots in the cultivated layer may die, or the top may wither, or both. The first rain (or irrigation) may not produce any major growth response until the plant has acquired new working parts.

(d) Occasionally — it has been detected in sugar beet and kale — almost the opposite can happen: there may be a flush of growth after a period of drought dormancy.

(e) Excess water, among other possible harmful effects, may cause leaching of nutrients and decrease yield thereby.

Of these, (d) can be left aside as a worthwhile subject for research, and examples of (c) and (e) will be given later. Combination of (a) and (b) is possible through a simple hypothesis [2, 3, 4, 5] to specify when water is needed. Starting from field capacity, the later imbalance of evaporation and rainfall produces a soil moisture deficit, D, given by

$$D = E - R$$

It is assumed that up to a limiting value, D_l say, the availability and accessibility of water and nutrients are adequate for full growth; beyond D_l it is assumed that growth (but not transpiration) stops completely. This drastic over-simplification has two commendable aspects. First, it leads directly to sound bases for irrigation recommendations in terms farmers can understand and exploit; second, it matches the present crudeness of field records of growth, which are not good enough to test any more elaborate hypothesis.

During the summer, the deficit changes irregularly because of irregular rain (or irrigation), and at some time it will reach a (potential) maximum — D_m, say. After this the general trend will be a decrease in deficit, i.e. the soil profile gets wetter, and in this period there will be no restriction on plant growth, whatever the absolute value of the deficit. It is easy to show that the effective part of the total potential evaporation (E_A as part of E_T) is given by

$$E_A = E_T - (D_m - D_l) \text{ for } D_m > D_l \qquad (6.4)$$

Note that up to the time at which D_m is reached this equation is simply

$$E_A = E_T + D_l - D_m$$
$$= (E_T + D_l) - (E_T - R_m)$$

where R_m is the rainfall up to the time at which D_m is reached, i.e.

$$E_A = D_l + R_m \qquad (6.5)$$

In words, until this time the crop can use only what falls as rain (and any irrigation) plus what is usefully stored in the soil at the outset. After D_m is passed the amount of rain is not a factor; there is more than enough to meet the later transpiration demand. For full-season studies, it is preferable to use equation (6.4), when $D_m > D_l$. For $D_m < D_l$, then

$$E_A \cong E_T$$

In field units, the form of equation (6.2) now becomes

$$Y = kE_A$$
or
$$= k(E_T + D_l - D_m) \qquad (6.6)$$
$$Y/E_T = k(1 + D_l/E_T - D_m/E_T) \qquad (6.6a)$$

offering several ways of extracting information from field results. The yield is known, and E_T and D_m are calculated from the weather records. When zero time is known with some certainty (not possible for annual crops) a plot of Y against $E_T - D_m$ should give a straight line of slope k with an intercept at $Y = 0$ that gives a value of D_l. This is very rarely possible, and in general a guide to the value of D_l is more easily obtained in other ways — by inspection and trial. Where an approximate estimate of a 'zero' time can be made (near emergence when known) equation (6.6a) is helpful, plotting Y/E_T against D_m/E_T, in which an error in E_T is not very important. Such a plot should show a horizontal line over the range $D_m < D_l$ (where $E_A \cong E_T$) and then a line of constant negative slope equal to k, the value of the ordinate for the horizontal section. The correctness of the line-fitting is demonstrated by the equality of the two values of k, and then the change from horizontal to sloping gives the value of D_l. This is a rather severe test to impose on field measurements, and this sort of diagram is more useful for teaching than for analysis.

Experiments

Nearly all of the remainder of this chapter is based on eighteen years' results from an irrigation experiment at Woburn, mainly from the first nine years [3, 4, 5]. A survey of the second nine years is now in preparation [8, 9, 10], and some results will be quoted though they are provisional. Records for two crops will be used for grass, where the dry matter yield is an acceptable estimate of total botanical yield; and for potatoes, where one quarter of the tuber yield is probably an adequate estimate for testing the predictions of Table 6.2.

(a) Grass

(i) *Woburn and Hurley — up to 1959.* Two contemporary experiments on irrigation of grass lasted for several years on the same swards. At Woburn, Bedfordshire, Cocksfoot (S 37) was sown in April 1954 and cuts were made at about three-week intervals during the six following summers. At Hurley, Berkshire, Rye-grass (S 23) and White Clover (S 100), established in 1951, came under experiment at the end of 1955, and cuts were made each summer at about four-week intervals up to November 1959 [11]. At both places one irrigation treatment kept the soil near field capacity throughout; at both there were three intensities of nitrogen fertilizer, coincident in amount and form, with a zero treatment at Hurley but not at Woburn.

Table 6.4

Mean growth rate per unit increment in potential transpiration
($100 \, kg \, ha^{-1}$ per 1 cm transpiration)

Site	Sward	N_0	N_1	N_2	N_3
Woburn	Cocksfoot	—	1.9	2.4	2.8
Hurley	Rye-grass/Clover	1.8	2.0	2.4	3.0

(N_1 19; N_2 38; N_3 76 kg ha^{-1} N per cut)

Over the six summers and five winters of the Woburn experiment the accumulated dry matter increased very nearly linearly with accumulated potential transpiration [4, Figure 2], the slope of the line depending on nitrogen dressing (Table 6.4). At Hurley, there were not complete weather records, and my calculations of transpiration were based on Kew values — 40 km to the east. The corresponding plot is on the left of Figure 6.1, for two of the treatments, and the slopes are in Table 6.4. Within the known uncertainties, these two experiments have given the same result. The efficiency for N_3 was near 85×10^{-4} at both places (the Hurley values are on the right of Figure 6.1), and from equation (6.3) the expected maximum possible response to irrigation is 0.33 t ha^{-1} cm^{-1}: the tabled value is near 0.30 t ha^{-1} cm^{-1}. The agreement of the two estimates is acceptably good. The measured responses were generally smaller, but differences were removed after making allowance for the limiting deficit. At Woburn, for this treatment, the value needed was $D_l = 5$ cm, as the size of the soil moisture deficit that can be tolerated without any check to growth. For the other nitrogen treatments (N_1 and N_2) somewhat smaller values of D_l were needed and when applied to the whole range of watering treatments all the information available became coherent [4, Figure 3]. In detail, thses plots of yield against E_A revealed that there was still a small winter gap in which some other parameter is needed to supplement potential evaporation as a growth index.

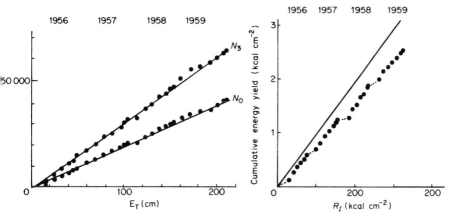

Fig. 6.1   *Total growth of ryegrass/white clover at Hurley on irrigated plots.*
            Left: yield as dry matter.   (N$_0$ = no applied nitrogen
                          N$_3$ = 76 kg ha^{-1} nitrogen per cut)
            Right: yield as energy equivalent. (The diagonal line indicates a
            conversion rate of 1%.)
            (Yields from Stiles and Williams, [11]
              E$_T$ = potential evaporation
              R$_I$ = radiation income
            (From Penman [6].)

(ii) *Woburn — after 1959.* During the second nine years at Woburn there was a two-year crop of Italian Ryegrass (S 22) cut fourteen times between October 1959 and October 1961. In the summer of 1960 everything followed the previous pattern, but 1961 was anomalous. There was considerable need for irrigation in a season when weed invasion decreased yields, so that the best efficiency was only 70×10^{-4}, i.e. the expected maximum possible response to irrigation was near 0.27 t ha^{-1} cm^{-1}. The observed value was at least 50 per cent more, and this is regarded as a demonstration of point (c) listed earlier, that in a period of drought unirrigated plants may reach a state of senescence in which they cannot exploit rain when it does fall. Applied to one set of treatments, this idea leads to the conclusion that the wasted rainfall on the unirrigated plots was 8.5 cm (in a period where the total rain was 14 cm), i.e. the measured farming benefit came from 15.2 cm of irrigation (paid for) plus this 8.5 cm (free) made effective only because the supplementary irrigation was applied.

For three years, 1962-64, there was an experiment on lucerne. Except in the spring of establishment it did not respond to irrigation, but another result is of great interest. Plotting accumulated yield against potential evaporation (as for the left of Figure 6.1) gave three straight lines of about equal slope ($0.26 \text{ t ha}^{-1} \text{ cm}^{-1}$) but clearly not one straight line. The winter gaps were very obvious (as on the right of Figure 6.1). Guessing that soil temperature might be a limiting factor in winter, it was found that the gaps could be bridged if the growth rate was zero below $4.5°C$ (at 30 cm depth); in time, this was from the end of November to late March in 1963, and to early March in 1964.

(b) Potatoes: Woburn

Early potatoes (Ulster Chieftain, 1951-53) and main crop potatoes (Majestic 1954-56) were grown at two intensities of nitrogen fertilizer. The responses to irrigation were made coherent by assuming a limiting deficit of 2.5 cm and, fortuitously, both sets of results could be represented on the same diagram of yield against adjusted potential transpiration, E_A, [5, Figure 1], the slopes being; N_1, $1.75 \text{ t ha}^{-1} \text{ cm}^{-1}$; N_2, $2.02 \text{ t ha}^{-1} \text{ cm}^{-1}$. Without any forcing, the intercepts on the axis at zero yield were the same, at about 9.5 cm.

A similar experiment on early potatoes (Arran Pilot, 1960-62) had management variables included, thereby eliminating some watering treatments, and as the seed tubers were severely damaged by frost before planting in 1962, only two years' results are worth consideration. The intensities of nitrogen fertilizer were 20 per cent greater than in 1951-53 (N_1, $0.5 \rightarrow 0.6$; N_2, $1.0 \rightarrow 1.2 \text{ cwt acre}^{-1}$ N), and, probably because of this, absolute yields were a little greater, but the slopes of the lines — with some uncertainty — are effectively the same as before (N_1, 1.8; N_2, $2.1 \text{ t ha}^{-1} \text{ cm}^{-1}$). Again, they coincide on the E_A axis, and the increased yield is represented by a displacement of this point of intersection to $E_A \cong 7$ cm, as though the Arran Pilot got an earlier start to growth than either the Ulster Chieftain or the Majestic (by the equivalent of about ten days summer growth). The best measured responses to irrigation (in 1961) were 1.8 and 2.0 t ha^{-1}, for N_1 and N_2, indicating that the limiting deficit for potatoes is indeed small, and that keeping the soil close to field capacity is a sound guide to irrigation practice in most English summers.

There can be exceptions. In wet summers irrigation will not be needed, but occasionally the early summer may be dry enough to justify irrigation, and late summer may be wet enough to obviate any further need. It has happened once in eighteen years that in another main-crop potato experiment, in 1966, early watering and subsequent rain were in amounts that produced drainage (estimated at 6.3 cm in total) from the irrigated plots and none from the control plots, with 2.5 cm drainage before the end of June. For the only time in the whole experiment there was a significant decrease in yield reasonably attributable to irrigation, in amount about equal to the effect of halving the nitrogen content of the basal fertiliser (i.e. in a ratio near 1.8/2.1 — see above). Hence 'keeping the soil close to field capacity' needs the qualifying remark that some buffering deficit should be retained to guard against the possibility of heavy rain within a few days of an irrigation operation.

Assuming the dry matter content was one quarter of the tuber yield, the whole crop efficiencies were 115 and 145 x 10^{-4} for N_1 and N_2 treatments respectively, greater than for grass, and better than the 'very good' of Table 6.2. The measured responses of 1.8 and 2.0 t ha^{-1} cm^{-1} correspond to 9 and 10 cwt $acre^{-1}$ $inch^{-1}$ (cf. 8 in Table 6.2) as dry matter.

Discussion

Water is not a nutrient, and though it is usually convenient to talk about 'responses' to irrigation, it is sometimes helpful to think in terms of what is lost by not having water there when it is needed. The role of water is to provide a desired environment for the roots that will ensure maximum efficiency of photosynthesis in the leaves. In a well-drained soil this desired environment exists over a range of water content, expressed either as a quantity (as throughout this chapter) or as a potential (scientifically, better; operationally, very difficult to use). This range is quantified by the 'limiting deficit' used in formal analysis and in interpretation of field results, and is the basis of advice on when to irrigate and how much to apply. Broadly, the values are known for the important farm, vegetable and fruit crops. When the soil water-content is maintained within this range, then crop yields are limited by other factors, and there are hints that skill and experience applied uniformly to a range of crops will produce about the same *botanical* yield for most of them. So — as a point for discussion — what started as a simple energy ratio to give a figure to 'efficiency' has some sort of constancy within a given farming system, and the ϵ of equation (6.3) might be thought of as an index of the system (as in Table 6.1). Then the 'factor' of the title takes on its algebraic meaning, and equation (6.3) can be written as

$$Y = (39\epsilon)E_T$$

where the quantity in brackets is a synthesis of all factors other than water, and the equation will apply within the optimum range of soil water content. Outside this range, transformed to

$$\Delta Y/I = 39\epsilon$$

the equation gives a measure of response to irrigation. For the present this can be regarded as a hypothesis — standing up fairly well to the tests that are being imposed from the Woburn results — with an important implication. The yield (or the response) is a product, not a sum, i.e. water cannot be used to make good some defect elsewhere in management, and the better this other management is, the better will be the return from judicious irrigation.

Summary

Production is defined as total botanical yield, and efficiency, ϵ, as the ratio of the yield, as energy equivalent, to the solar radiation income. For average British farming $\epsilon \simeq 35 \times 10^{-4}$. For some crops it is known that when water is not limiting, the yield, Y is proportional to the potential transpiration, E_T, which is closely related to the solar radiation. With assumptions, a growth equation is derived (water not limiting) as

$$Y/E_T = 39\epsilon \text{ t ha}^{-1} \text{ cm}^{-1}$$

and, (water limiting) a response equation,

$$\Delta Y/I = 39\epsilon \text{ t ha}^{-1} \text{ cm}^{-1}$$

where I is necessary irrigation. Irrigation is defined as necessary only after the soil moisture deficit has passed a limiting value D_l, and only until it reaches a potential maximum value for the season, D_m. Then the growth equation becomes

$$Y = k(E_T + D_l - D_m)$$

with $k = \Delta Y/I$

Experimental results are given for two well-fertilized crops (grass and potatoes) to justify the assumptions and test the inferences. For grass $\epsilon \simeq 90 \times 10^{-4}$, and irrigation responses are as predicted for $D_l \simeq 5$ cm. For early potatoes, $\epsilon \simeq 140 \times 10^{-4}$ and irrigation responses correspond to $D_l \simeq 2.5$ cm. Judicious irrigation will give most help to the best management.

REFERENCES
1. MINISTRY OF AGRICULTURE, FISHERIES AND FOOD, *Agricultural Statistics, 1966/67*, London: H.M.S.O.
2. PENMAN, H.L. 'Weather and water in the growth of grass', in *The Growth of Leaves*, Ed. F.L. Milthorpe, London: Butterworth, 1956.
3. PENMAN, H.L. 'Woburn irrigation, 1951-59. I. Purpose, design and weather', *J. agric. Sci. Camb.*, 1962, **58**, 343-348.
4. PENMAN, H.L. 'Woburn irrigation, 1951-59. II. Results for grass', *J. agric. Sci. Camb.*, 1962, **58**, 349-364.
5. PENMAN, H.L. 'Woburn irrigation, 1951-59. III. Results for rotation crops', *J. agric. Sci. Camb.*, 1962, **58**, 365-379.
6. PENMAN, H.L. 'Climate and crops', *Mem. Proc. Manchr. lit. phil. Soc.*, (1967-8) **110**, 1-13.
7. PENMAN, H.L. 'The earth's potential', *Sci. J.*, 1968, **4** (no. 5), 42-7.

8. PENMAN, H.L., 'Woburn irrigation, 1960-68. IV. Design and interpretation', *J. agric. Sci. Camb.*, 1970, **75**, 69-73.
9. PENMAN, H.L., 'Woburn irrigation, 1960-68. V. Results for leys', *J. agric. Sci. Camb.*, 1970, **75**, 75-88.
10. PENMAN, H.L., 'Woburn irrigation, 1960-68. VI. Results for rotation crops', *J. agric. Sci. Camb.*, 1970, **75**, 89-102.
11. STILES, W. and WILLIAMS, T.E. 'The response of a rye-grass/white clover sward to various irrigation regimes', *J. agric. Sci. Camb.*, 1965, **65**, 351-364.

7. Root Systems and Nutrition

R. Scott Russell
Agricultural Research Council, Letcombe Laboratory, Wantage, Berkshire

Introduction

If plants are provided with a uniformly favourable rooting medium throughout their lives, the quantities of water or nutrients which reach shoots are often little affected by quite severe pruning of roots, as those which remain absorb more rapidly; this has been well illustrated in water culture by Brouwer and Kleinendorst [7]. In these circumstances root development appears to be a rather squandrous procedure which dissipates metabolites which could more usefully increase the photosynthetic area or those organs which are of immediate economic interest. It might therefore be thought that studies of root form and function are likely to make at best a minor contribution to increasing the productivity of crops. Other evidence gives superficial support for this view. Recent spectacular achievements in plant breeding have depended little, if at all, on the selection of rooting characteristics and the nutrient requirements of plants can be satisfied at an economic cost by the use of fertilizers. Although many important questions about the behaviour of nutrients in soil remain unanswered, there can be no disagreement with a statement in a recent review by Cooke [11] that 'fertilizers free us completely from one natural limitation to crop production — the supply of plant nutrients from soil'. Moreover information which already exists on the response of crops, and especially grassland, to fertilizers hold promise of further considerable increases in productivity; this question has been so comprehensively discussed by Cooke (*loc. cit.*) that further comment is unnecessary.

None the less there is another side to the story — crop yields are often limited by water supply even in this country; root penetration is restricted by unfavourable soil conditions, soil-borne pests and diseases reduce yield; waterlogging for even quite limited periods sometimes has serious effects. To what extent can these limitations be mitigated by a fuller understanding of the performance of plant roots and their reaction to the soil? Will it become possible in breeding programmes to take account of rooting characteristics which enable fertilizers and water to be utilized more efficiently? It seems timely to consider such questions even though we may not yet be able to provide definite answers. Lately some of the obstacles to the detailed study of performance of root systems have been at least partially circumvented and the inadequacy of some of our former views has been demonstrated by practical experience. For example, weed control has made it possible to grow some crops successfully without the laborious tillage which was formerly regarded as essential for adequate plant growth.

Morphology of Root Systems and the Efficiency of Absorption

One of the main difficulties in defining the characteristics of root systems which make them efficient absorbing organs has been the paucity of data on the extent to which nutrients can be absorbed and translocated by different parts of them. Recently this subject has received more attention. Bowen and Rovira [6] immersed root systems in nutrient solutions labelled with radioactive tracers, and by electronic scanning detected uptake by different tissues. In our laboratory we have preferred a method developed from that first described by Kramer [28] ; short lengths of intact roots are sealed across the diameter of suitably incised plastic tubing (usually 3.5 mm diameter) through which labelled nutrients are circulated, while the remainder of the root system is provided with a nutrient solution of similar concentration but unlabelled [42]. Thus it is possible to observe not only retention of the labelled nutrient in the treated zones but also translocation to other parts of the plant; conclusions on the former question reached by this method are in reasonable agreement with those of Bowen and Rovira. In three-week old barley plants the uptake of both phospate and calcium* is approximately constant per unit volume of root tissue in the unbranched apical parts of seminal and nodal axes and in primary laterals, so that uptake per unit surface area is considerably higher in the thicker root members. The ratio in which the two ions are absorbed and translocated is not constant throughout the root system; in this respect the basal parts of axes contrast particularly with the younger tissues [9]. Provided that the cortex has remained intact, phosphate enters the basal zone approximately as readily as near the apex and an appreciably higher fraction is translocated, but little calcium is translocated from the older tissues (Table 7.1). It appears that the small transfer of calcium is due to its inability to penetrate the cortex [10] ; contrary to earlier suggestions, the thickening of the endodermis does not create a barrier to ion transfer.

The results of numerous experiments, in which uptake and translocation have been measured in nine types of segment from widely different parts of barley root systems, makes it possible to revise earlier estimates [42] of the contribution of different types of root member to the nutrition of the entire plant (Table 7.2). Although the limitations of the data must be emphasised, it is encouraging that direct measurements of uptake by the entire root system

---

* Both in these experiments and in the soil studies which are described later in this chapter, the uptake of calcium was inferred from measurements of isotopes of strontium (either ^{85}Sr or ^{89}Sr). The reasons for so doing, and the justification for inferring the behaviour of calcium from that of strontium in the two types of study, have been discussed elsewhere [44].

Table 7.1

Uptake and translocation of phosphate and calcium[1] from 3.5 mm segments of seminal roots of barley plants in 24 hours in solution culture.

Concentrations of Solution:	H_2PO_4 3 x 10^{-6} M Ca++ 1.25 x 10^{-6} M	
	Position of Segment (cm from apex)	
	1 cm	44 cm
Uptake (pico moles/segment)		
Phosphate: treated segment	395	335
translocated	53	241
Calcium: treated segment	89	58
translocated	51	2.0
Translocation (% of uptake)		
Phosphate	12	42
Calcium	36	3
Ratio: Phosphate/Calcium	1	120

From Clarkson et al [10].

(1) based on tracer experiments with strontium, see footnote, p. 101.

are in reasonable agreement with those which would be calculated from Table 7.2. Less detailed experiments with rubidium and potassium suggest that the pattern of uptake of these ions resembles that for phosphate [12]. However, it must be emphasised that these conclusions refer only to situations when ample and uniform nutrient supply is provided to the entire root system.

The form and rate of extension of cereal root systems grown with an adequate nutrient supply in water culture [23] appears to be comparable to that observed in Weaver's [51] classic studies on plants grown in deep and friable soils. Thus the foregoing results may be applicable to cereals growing in such conditions in soil, provided that other factors of the environment do not modify root form and ions can move freely through the soil, so that all root members are exposed to the same external concentration. This later condition may be satisfied for calcium because the soil solution is often adequate to supply the requirements of plants, but this is not so with phosphate as its rate of diffusion through soil to the root surface is likely to limit uptake [3]. The greatest diffusion 'drag' would be experienced by the root members of largest diameter; if ions moved freely to the root surface, their uptake per unit surface area would be greatest. Present information on the rate of diffusion relates mainly to the bulk soil [35], and considerable error might be introduced if rhizosphere organisms and root exudates cause an appreciable modification in the rate of diffusion close to the root surface. It is to be hoped that a procedure recently described by Nye and his colleagues [17] will provide direct evidence on this question. An indirect basis for suggesting the possible mangitude of the effect of diffusion on roots of different size is, however, possible from diffusion theory [14]; this suggests that if (a) absorption varies with the concentration at the root surface and, (b) the rate of diffusion in soil were so slow that, near the root surface, the concentration of phosphate in the solution phase is reduced almost to zero, uptake by seminal and nodal axes might be reduced by factors of perhaps 3 and 6 respectively relative to that of the laterals, shown in Table 7.2. Modifying the estimates for phosphate in the table on this basis, it appears that laterals could be responsible for about two-thirds of the total quantity which reaches shoots. The same would be true of other ions which diffuse slowly.

Table 7.2
Contribution of different types of root member to the uptake of phosphate and calcium by barley plants (var. Maris Badger) 2-3 week old

	Seminal axes	Nodel axes	Laterals
Dimensions of root systems			
Length cm	420	380	4910
Mean diameter mm	0.40	0.62	0.18[1]
Volume cm^3	0.53	1.15	1.75
Percentage contribution to total uptake			
Phosphate	15	34	51
Calcium[2]	10	31	59
Percentage contribution to shoot content in 24 h.			
Phosphate	27	40	33
Calcium[2]	5	35	60

(1) Mean diameter of primary and secondary laterals is approximately 0.2 mm and 0.1 mm respectively. Primary laterals account for over 90% of total lateral length.
(2) See footnote p. 101.
Based on Russell and Sanderson [42] Clarkson, *et al* [9] and Clarkson and Sanderson [10].

The importance of root hairs under such conditions deserves consideration. In solution culture their contribution is clearly small — not only are they poorly developed but uptake occurs freely in parts of the root system from which they are absent. However, it can be readily calculated that the development of root hairs would considerably enhance the absorption of phosphate from soil when diffusion is rate-limiting [34], provided that the root hairs make intimate contact with the soil and the rate of diffusion in the soil they penetrate is similar to that some distance from the root. Some observations in soil are suggestive that root hairs contribute to nutrient uptake [29] but they would be compatible also with diffusion through soil to the root cylinder being accelerated in the zone in which the root hairs develop. There is at present no direct evidence on this question and, especially because of the large effects which microorganisms can exert on the form of root hairs [6], it seems prudent to regard their contribution to nutrient uptake as an open question.

Irrespective, however, of the significance of root hairs, it is evident that if the diffusion of an ion in soil is so slow that it causes the concentration close to absorbing surfaces to fall considerably below that in the bulk soil, the efficiency of the finer root members will be enhanced relative to the thicker axes. Thus ions which contrast in their mobility in the soil may be absorbed in differing ratios by roots of contrasting thickness. Significant differences in the ratio to which phosphate and calcium are absorbed from different depths in uniform soil have been demonstrated for a number of crops [33]. The extent to which this is accountable to physiological processes in the plant as opposed to diffusion in the soil is at present uncertain, but it is evident that uptake of a single ion species cannot be regarded as a reliable index of root activity.

The Significance of Root Depth

If the supply of nutrients and water were uniform and abundant throughout the soil, the desirable form of the root system can be readily defined — it should be finely divided and of just sufficient size to satisfy the requirements of the shoot, its depth of penetration being unimportant provided that it gives adequate anchorage. Under the normal conditions of agriculture, however, the situation is very different. The advantage of deep root systems in dry conditions has been long recognized; in even quite short periods of drought the surface soil can become so depleted of water that the development of roots, or the absorption of nutrients by those which are already present, can be greatly restricted, if indeed they survive. But until

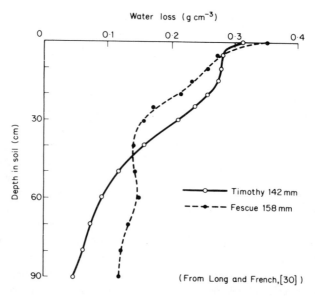

Fig. 7.1   Uptake of water by Timothy and Meadow Fescue from different depths in the soil under dry summer conditions.

recently the quantitative study of such questions has been both difficult and laborious. Fortunately, new methods now make it possible to study more directly and reliably relationships between the growth and performance of roots, and the profiles of water and nutrients in the soil. The neutron moderation procedure [30] can eliminate much uncertainty in the measurement of soil moisture, though the relatively long range of neutrons is a disadvantage when it is desired to follow steep gradients of water over small distances closer to the soil surface, but other methods are then applicable. Figure 7.1 from Long and French [30] shows the contrasting patterns of loss of water from soil, measured by the neutron method, under Meadow Fescue and Timothy during dry summer conditions. The deeper rooted Fescue drew considerably more water from the lower zones which contained more water.

By injecting radioactive tracers to different depths in soil, Newbould [33] demonstrated the extent to which the absorption of phosphate can vary with soil water. The uptake of both phosphate and calcium from 5 cm below the ground surface was closely correlated with the water content of that zone; when water was ample, it contributed nearly as much phosphate and calcium as the total drawn from 10, 20 and 40 cm but, in dry periods the proportionate contribution of the surface zone was approximately halved.

Because variations in the supply of water and nutrients in the soil not only influence absorption but also can profoundly affect the form of the root system, information on the distribution of living roots is essential for the detailed interpretation of measurements of the uptake of water and nutrients from different depths. The limitation of methods which depend on washing root systems free from soil is evident despite the elegant and laborious work of many investigators, from Weaver [51] to de Roo [13]. Often the most obvious difficulties are to distinguish living roots from those which are dead, and to recover all the fine roots which are particularly important in absorption; sometimes also the roots of the crop may be confused with those of botanically similar weeds. An alternative procedure which involves injecting rubidium-86 into shoots and subsequently measuring its activity in soil cores has therefore been investigated [43]. Rubidium is highly mobile in plants and, although its concentration in expanding apical tissues is greater than elsewhere, it has been shown that for annual plants the quantity of roots in an appreciable volume of soil, e.g. a 5 cm cube, can be inferred from the quantity of rubidium-86 it contains. The energetic gamma radiation of this nuclide permits direct measurement of soil samples a few kg in weight without chemical preparation. For this reason the procedure has advantage over the use of phosphorus-32 as described by Racz et al [39]. In Figure 7.2, the distribution of barley roots measured in this way is compared with their uptake of phosphate and calcium from different depths in a uniform soil.

It may be expected that in the future the refinement and combination of these techniques will provide much fuller information on the relationship between the depth of root systems and their efficiency as absorbing organs under different circumstances. The results of this work may well be of

considerably greater importance in relation to the utilization of water than
nutrients; whereas fertilizers are increasingly freeing us from dependence of
soil nutrients, water is likely to become an increasingly scarce commodity. It
has been estimated, for example, that irrigation could be beneficial
throughout those parts of Britain where the average rainfall is below about 35
inches (89 cm) [31]. Moreover, the more extensive use of fertilizers may
increase the requirement for water. Thus, Penman [38] showed, that on the
light soil of Woburn, additional water was necessary for spring wheat to
respond to extra nitrogen. The possibility that important relationships remain
to be discovered between the depth of root systems and their efficiency for
utilising fertilizers should not, however, be discounted. For example, the
extent and depth to which roots penetrate and ramify may influence their
ability to intercept fertilizers.

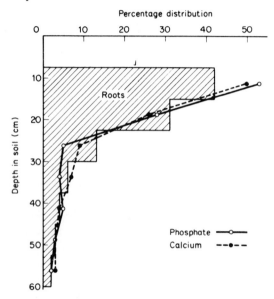

Fig. 7.2   Distribution of barley roots in the soil measured by the
            rubidium-86 method, compared with their uptake of phosphate
            and calcium from different depths.

'Critical Periods' of Root Growth

The total depth which a root system eventually attains may be less important
than the rapidity at which it becomes established at the minimum depth
where the supply of moisture and nutrients will not be interrupted. The need
to give particular attention to root performance at certain stages of growth is
also indicated by the fact that nutrient uptake per unit volume of root may
vary considerably with time, depending primarily on the demands of the
shoot; different nutrients contrast in this respect. Thus when barley is grown
with an ample nutrient supply in solution culture, the uptake of potassium

per unit volume of root can show a three-fold decrease between the second and fourth week of growth though the rate for phosphate is approximately constant [23]. As yet there is little quantitative basis for defining these 'critical periods', though they may often occur early in the life of the plant, especially when the surface soil dries out rapidly or, with direct drilled crops, when the establishment of roots in the soil beneath the planting slit can be of particular importance. A marked contrast between the approaches which are appropriate for the analysis of the growth of shoots and roots is thus evident; because shoot growth is often approximately exponential throughout the vegetative period, the mean growth rate is often of major interest. A further contrast may also be noted; whereas the increase in mass of shoots is often of primary concern during the vegetative phase, with roots interest centres mainly on their performance as absorbing organs.

Variability in Root Form

The considerable variability in root form which arises from genetic and environmental causes directs attention to the possibility that the efficiency of root systems may be enhanced by selection or by the control of environmental factors. The difficulties of exploiting these opportunities should, however, not be underestimated. The practical problems which could be created for the plant breeder by considering an additional set of charactistics is obvious, and beyond this the considerable interactions which occur between different factors which affect root growth — environmental and genetic — can cause difficulties in interpretation. The problem is made more difficult by our meagre knowledge of the complex control mechanisms which determine the growth of roots and their relationships to shoots [27, 50]. It is possible here only to note some of the major causes of variability and their more conspicuous effects.

Much information on intervarietal differences in the characteristics of root systems was recently reviewed by Troughton and Whittington [48]; significant interactions between nutrient and variety have been demonstrated in cereals both with respect to the size and the form of root systems [22]; intervarietal differences in disease resistance also occur, for example between varieties of flax with respect to *Fusarium oxysporum* [52]. Recently in solution culture, considerable differences in the length of root axes have been demonstrated between cereal varieties. A comparison of Proctor barley with two short-strawed varieties and one South African variety with a contrasting photoperiodic requirement is illustrated in Table 7.3; there is evidence of considerable differences, especially in the length of root axes, and these bear no simple relationship to differences in the size of shoots. The long and short-rooted varieties differ less in the development of laterals on the basal parts of the axes than in the length of the relatively unbranched apical sections (Figure 7.3). Since uptake occurs largely through laterals, the practical significance in these differences seems likely to depend on whether the development of laterals on the basal parts of the longer axes will be

stimulated if conditions near the soil surface limit the activity of laterals
which have developed in that zone.

Table 7.3

*Comparison of root structure of barley varieties after 2—3 weeks in solution
culture with ample nutrient supply*

	Weeks after germination	Proctor	Algerie 48[1]	Seto Hadaka[2]	Swanneck[3]
Dry weight (mg)					
Shoots	2	27	46	23	40
	3	91	136	60	117
Roots	2	7	8	4	8
	3	40	53	19	51
Ratio: Root/Shoot	2	0.26	0.17	0.17	0.20
	3	0.43	0.33	0.30	0.36
Seminal Roots[4]					
Total root system	3	0.97	0.85	0.95	0.82
Mean length of root axes(cm)	2	12	11	10	14
Seminal	3	25	39	17	40
Nodal[4]	3	5	11	2	9

— based on Hackett and Stewart [25].

(1) Short strawed — from North Africa
(2) Short strawed — from Japan
(3) Similar height to Proctor — from South Africa
(4) At week 2 seminal roots accounted for entire root system

The supply of carbohydrates and other metabolites from shoots and the
uptake of water and nutrients are some of the most obvious physiological
factors which influence the development of root systems. It is, for example,
familiar that the ratio of roots to shoot can be depressed when the quantity
of carbohydrate available for downward translocation is low. Not only the
size but also the form of roots may be affected by metabolic conditions; thus
potassium deficiency can particularly restrict the development of laterals in
cereals [22]. When the supply of water and nutrients varies within the
rooting zone, as occurs frequently in the field, further complications can
occur. Whereas in some soils the addition of nutrients to the upper soil layers
enhances uptake in that region only, in other soils the performance of the
entire root system may be changed [33]. Moreover, high local concentrations
of nutrients can cause the proliferation of roots so that uptake occurs largely
from that zone [36].

Other factors in the soil exert an equally profound effect. The importance
and complexity of mechanical impedance is now well established [4, 20].
Arrays of glass beads (ballotini) of varying size through which aerated culture
solution is circulated provide a convenient way for exposing roots to

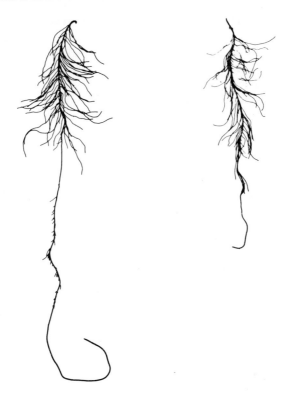

Fig. 7.3   *Seminal root axes of* **left** *Barley var. Swanneck and* **right** *var.*
Proctor after three weeks growth in solution culture.

definable mechanical stress, other factors of their environment being
unaffected. When the development of barley roots is restricted in this way,
root hairs are found to within 1 mm of the apex. The shape of the apices is
frequently much distorted, and the root axes assume a 'zig-zag' form as a
result of their passage between the beads. The development of root hairs
occurs predominantly on the inner or concave surfaces at the points of
curvature, while laterals are by contrast initiated on the outer or convex side
within a millimetre or two of the apex [18]. How typical these effects are of
other species is unknown, but it is of interest that they are broadly
comparable with those described over sixty years ago by Snow [47]. Since
the root hairs anchor the root within a very short distance of the apex, it is
difficult to accept the view that the axial force exerted by a root as it
penetrates the soil can be inferred from that required to hold the basal part of
the root in a fixed position when the apex elongates [16]. Moreover, a
consideration of the form of root apices subject to mechanical impedance
makes it seem improbable that any mechanical probe could measure reliably
the radial and axial forces to which the apical root cells are subjected; the
effect of the root cap is an aspect on which information is particularly

meagre. None the less, useful empirical relationships between the resistance of the soil and the ability of roots to penetrate it can be established with penetrometers [16] ; and measurements of the bulk density of soil can also provide a useful guide [49] , unless other factors, such as soil water, exert a dominant influence.

The most characteristic effects of uniform mechanical impedance to the entire root system appears to be the development of short, relatively thick root axes with a proliferation of laterals [8] . Frequently under field conditions, impedance may not be uniform — cracks, worm holes or the pathways of dead roots can provide opportunities for ready penetration through otherwise unfavourable soil. The extent to which the growth of those root axes which reach such channels compensates for the restricted development of the remainder of the root system is not known. Little information is available about the effects of the morphological changes caused by impedance on the efficiency of nutrient uptake, but preliminary results obtained in artificial systems suggest that uptake per unit weight or volume of root is little affected, even when the mean length of root axes has been drastically reduced [19] . It seems, therefore, that the main effect of impedance may be to limit the zone of soil which roots explore, and that there will be little effect on the plant if the supply of water and nutrients is adequate in this restricted range. This may explain in part why cereal crops can be grown successfully without cultivation of the soil when weeds are controlled with paraquat, even though root penetration is reduced. Although, until recently, a well-prepared seed bed was usually regarded as imperative for successful agriculture, there has long been evidence that heavily compacted soil is not necessarily deleterious and sometimes is even beneficial; over thirty years ago Heath [26] reported the latter situation with cotton. His paper concluded with the admission that the result could not be satisfactorily accounted for and that a more rigorous physiological analysis was necessary. This remains true, and it seems likely that no single explanation is applicable under all conditions; Passioura and Leeper [37] have suggested that, when manganese is deficient in neutral soils, close contact between roots and soil due to compaction may facilitate the solubilisation of MnO_2 by reducing substances on the root surface.

Another aspect of the root environment on which it has become necessary to revise some earlier views is soil aeration. The irrepairable damage which root systems can suffer through even short periods of anaerobiosis, caused by waterlogging, cannot be attributed solely to the direct effects of the shortage of oxygen or the increased concentration of carbon dioxide; the explanation appears to lie mainly in the production of numerous toxic substances [21] . Recently it has been shown that the evolution of ethylene may be of much significance; waterlogged soils both in the laboratory and the field can generate concentrations of this gas which can inhibit root elongation under laboratory conditions [46] ; information on the susceptibility of different species would be of considerable interest. Evidence that toxic gases arise in the soil is not as novel as was believed when this finding was published recently. In 1935 Nielson-Jones [32] published a brief statement, only lately located, that gas generated in soil could cause epinastic curvature in tomato perioles; ethylene was mentioned as a possible agent, but its presence was not demonstrated — this would have been a formidable task in the absence of modern analytical methods.

Time permits only passing reference to some of the multifarious activities of soil microorganisms. Those which do not become intimately associated with plant roots will not be considered, despite their considerable effect on the availability of nutrients and on soil structure. In solution culture competition for nutrients, especially phosphate, can occur between roots and microorganisms which are present on their surfaces or in their outer cortical layers [1, 41]; except when plants are grown under rigidly sterile conditions, relationships between external concentration, pH and absorption may be so profoundly modified by microorganisms that it is necessary to review the validity of theoretical interpretations which were based on observations in non-sterile conditions. The significance of such effects when plants are grown in soil is at present uncertain, but other important effects of rhizosphere organisms are evident — some stimulate root extension, others retard it; both lateral branching and the development of root hairs can be affected [6]. The mechanisms responsible are largely unknown, but it has been shown that these organisms can release a wide range of biologically active substances including auxins, vitamins, and gibberellins, while some rhizosphere organisms are capable of suppressing pathogenic microorganisms [15]. The nature of the rhizosphere flora differs widely between species [5], reflecting presumably the contrasting composition of root exudates [40]. The variation in the activity of the microflora which can be induced by changes in the metabolic status of plants possibly arises from the same cause [2]. Information on the total extent and significance of organic substances released by roots is, however, regrettably meagre. It has been suggested that the weight of exudates may exceed that of the roots which release them and that some 1000 m^3 of gel-like substances may be produced from root caps per hectare of a crop each year [45], but considerable uncertainty besets these estimates. Nonetheless it is evident that, until root exudates have been studied much more fully, it will be impossible to interpret many questions concerning not only the rhizosphere, but also the diffusion of ions near roots and effects on soil structure.

Finally the effects of mechanical injury deserve comment. Under laboratory conditions, the removal of the apical meristems on cereal root axes causes a considerable increase in both the length and diameter of laterals which develop close to the point of decapitation [23]. This response (Figure 7.4) is reminiscent of the release of apical dominance in shoots and suggests the importance of the root apex in hormonal control. It is thus to be expected that when root apices are injured — and they are particularly susceptible to attack by some pathogens [14] — the ability of the root system to exploit the soil may be much modified. It seems probable that this type of effect may contribute to the proliferation of roots near fertilizer granules, to which reference has already been made – root injury could then facilitate nutrient uptake, but usually the restriction of the rooting range is likely to reduce its capacity to absorb water and nutrients. Thus the fact that, under favourable circumstances, roots systems are frequently larger than is necessary to support shoots may have the important practical consequence that their size remains adequate when subjected to a degree of injury.

Fig. 7.4   Modification in development of laterals on Barley root axes caused by removal of apical 1 cm of axis 12 days previously.

Conclusions

Our knowledge of the performance of root systems has recently increased in a number of directions. However, the paucity of information on many important aspects is evident – for example on mechanism of hormonal control, the significance of root exudates and microorganisms at the root/soil interface. It is at present premature to predict the extent of the contribution which research on root systems may eventually make to increasing the productivity of crops, but the desirability of attempting to do so is evident since the supply of water and nutrients from the soil is not infrequently a major factor limiting the capacity of shoots to convert solar energy into organic forms. Two broad approaches deserve consideration – the selection of genetically desirable root types and the identification of soil conditions in which root development is most conducive to efficient and economic crop production. The practicability of avoiding laborious tillage operations particularly deserves consideration.

Some requirements for the profitable investigation of these matters can be identified. A dual approach linking research under controlled conditions in the laboratory with field experiments is perhaps even more necessary than in the study of plant shoots. The environment in which roots grow is from some points of view more variable and complex, and artificial laboratory model systems often provide the only feasible way of studying the effects of individual factors and elucidating the underlying mechanisms. However, because the environment affects the form and function of roots so profoundly the significance of conclusions reached in the laboratory must remain in doubt until they have been tested under a representative range of conditions in soil. A further requirement is also obvious, namely that full account should be taken of relationships between roots and shoots; without this no adequate analyses of the growth and performance of root systems — or for that matter shoots — is possible.

Acknowledgements
During the preparation of this review I have been much indebted to a number of my colleagues in the Letcombe Laboratory, especially Dr. D.A. Barber and Dr. D.T. Clarkson. I am also most grateful to Dr. G.W. Cooke, Rothamsted Experimental Station, and Mr. P.H. Nye, University of Oxford, who provided copies of papers which were not yet published.

REFERENCES
1. BARBER, D.A. 'Micro-organisms and the inorganic nutrition of higher plants', *A. Rev. Pl. Physiol.*, 1968, **19**, 71-88.
2. BARBER, D.A. and FRANKENBURG, U.C. 'The influence of carbohydrate status on the absorption of phosphate by barley plants under sterile and non-sterile conditions', *Agricultural Research Council Letcombe Laboratory, Report ARCRL 18.* 1968, 39-40.
3. BARBER, S.A. 'A diffusion and mass-flow concept of soil nutrient availability', *Soil Sci.*, 1962, **93**, 39-49.
4. BARLEY, K.P. and GREACEN, E.L. 'Mechanical resistance as a soil factor influencing the growth of roots and underground shoots', *Adv. Agron.*, 1967, **19**, 1-43.
5. BEREZOVA, E.F. 'Significance of root system micro-organisms in plant life', *in Plant Microbe Relationships*, Prague: Czechoslovakia Academy of Sciences, 1965.
6. BOWEN, G.D. and ROVIRA, A.D. 'The influence of micro-organisms on growth and metabolism of plant roots', *in Root Growth*, London: Butterworths, 1969.

7. BROUWER, R. and KLEINENDORST, A. 'Effect of root excision on growth phenomena in perennial ryegrass', Jaarb, Inst. biol. scheik. Onderz. LandbGewass., 1965, 11-20.

8. CANNON, W.A. *Physiological features of roots, with especial reference to the relation of roots to aeration of the soil.* Carnegie Institution of Washington Publ. 368, 1925.

9. CLARKSON, D.T., SANDERSON, J. and RUSSELL, R.S. 'Ion uptake and root age', *Nature,* 1968, **220**, 805-806.

10. CLARKSON, D.T. and SANDERSON, J. In prep., 1970.

11. COOKE, G.W. 'Using chemicals to increase soil productivity', in *Society of Chemical Industry Symposiom,* Lancaster, 1969

12. CRANK, J. *Mathematics of Diffusion.* Oxford: Oxford University Press, 1956.

13. DE ROO, H.C. 'Tillage and root growth', in *Root Growth,* London: Butterworths, 1969.

14. DILLON WESTON, W.A. and GARRETT, S.D. *'Rhizoctonia solani* associated with a root rot of cereals in Norfolk', *Ann. appl. Biol.,* 1943, **30**, 79-82.

15. DOMSCH, K.H. 'Microbial stimulation and inhibition of plant growth', *Trans. 9th Internation Congr. Soil Sci.,* 1968, **3**, 455-463.

16. EAVIS, B.W. and PAYNE, D. 'Soil physical conditions and root growth', in *Root Growth,* London: Butterworths, 1969.

17. FARR, E., VAIDYANATHAN, L.V. and NYE, P.H. 'Measurement of ionic concentration gradients in soil near roots', *Soil Sci.,* 1969, **107**, 385-391.

18. GOSS, M. In prep., 1970.

19. GOSS, M. and WALTER, C. 'The effect of mechanical reistance on the growth of plant roots', *Agricultural Research Council Letcombe Laboratory, Report ARCRL 19,* 1969, 27-28.

20. GREACEN, E.L., BARLEY, K.P. and FARRELL, D.A. 'The mechanics of root growth in soils with particular reference to the implications for root distribution', in *Root Growth,* London: Butterworths, 1969.

21. GREENWOOD, D.J. 'Effect of oxygen distribution in the soil on plant growth', in *Root Growth,* London: Butterworths, 1969.

22. HACKETT, C. 'A study of the root system of barley. I Effects of nutrition on two varieties', *New Phytol.,* 1968, **67**, 287-300.

23. HACKETT, C. and HOLLOWAY, A.M. 'Rates of growth and nutrient uptake of the barley root system', *Agricultural Research Council Letcombe Laboratory Report ARCRL 17,* 1967, 11-13.

24. HACKETT, C. 'Quantitative aspects of the growth of cereal root systems', in *Root Growth,* London: Butterworths, 1969.

25. HACKETT, C. and STEWART, H.E. 'A comparison of the root systems of these exotic varieties of barley with the root system of the barley variety Proctor', in *Agricultural Research Council Letcome Laboratory Report, ARCRL 18,* 1968, 20-22.

26. HEATH, O.V.S. 'A study in soil cultivation. The effects of varying soil

consolidation on growth and development of rain-grown cotton', *J. agric. Sci.*, 1937, **27**, 511-554.

27. HESS, C.E. 'Internal and external factors regulating root initiation', in *Root Growth*, London: Butterworths, 1969.

28. KRAMER, P.J. 'Relative amounts of mineral absorption through various regions of roots', in *A Conference on Radioactive Isotopes in Agriculture*, Michigan State Univ., East Lansing, 1956, 287-295, (TID-7512), USAEC.

29. LEWIS, D.G. and QUIRK, J.P. 'Phosphate diffusion in soil and uptake by plants. III P31-movement and uptake by plants as indicated by P32-autoradigraphy', *Plant & Soil*, 1967, **26**, 445-453.

30. LONG, I.F. and FRENCH, B.K. 'Measurement of soil moisture in the field by neutron moderation', *J. Soil Sci.*, 1967, **18**, 149-166.

31. NATIONAL RESOURCES (TECHNICAL) COMMITTEE *Irrigation in Great Britain*. London: H.M.S.O., 1962.

32. NEILSON-JONES, W. 'Organic soils and epinastic response', *Nature*, 1935, **136**, 554.

33. NEWBOULD, P. 'The absorption of nutrients by plants from different zones in the soil', in *Ecological Aspects of the Mineral Nutrition of Plants*, No. 9, Blackwell: Oxford, 1969.

34. NYE, P.H. 'The measurement and mechanism of ion diffusion in soil. I The relation between self-diffusion and bulk-diffusion', *J. Soil Sci.*, 1966, **17**, 16-23.

35. NYE, P.H. 'The use of exchange isotherms to determine diffusion coefficient in soil', *Trans. 9th Int. Congr. Soil Sci.*, 1968, **1**, 117-126. *Soil* 1968, **1**, 117-126.

36. OHLORGGE, A.J. 'Some soil-root-plant relationships', *Soil Sci.*, 1962, **93**, 30-38.

37. PASSIOURA, J.B. and LEEPER, G.W. 'Soil compaction and manganese deficiency', *Nature*, 1963, **200**, 29-30.

38. PENMAN, H.L. 'Woburn irrigation, 1951-59', *J. agric. Sci.*, 1962, **58**, 343-379.

39. RACZ, G.J., RENNIE, D.A. and HUTCHEON, W.L. 'The P32 injection method for studying the root system of wheat', *Canad. J. Soil Sci.*, 1964, **44**, 100-108.

40. ROVIRA, A.D. 'Plant root exudates and their influence upon soil micro-organisms', in *Ecology of Soil-borne Plant Pathogens*, International Symposium, University of California, Berkeley, 1963, 170-186.

41. ROVIRA, A.D. and BOWEN, G.D. 'Phosphate incorporation by sterile and non-sterile plant roots', *Aust. J. biol. Sci.*, 1966, **19**, 1167-1169.

42 RUSSELL, R.S. and SANDERSON, J. 'Nutrient uptake by different parts of the intact roots of plants', *J. exp. Bot.*, 1967, **18**, 491-508.

43 RUSSELL, R.S. and ELLIS, F.B. 'Estimation of the distribution of plant roots in soil', *Nature*, 1968, **217**, 582-583.

44. RUSSELL, R.S. and NEWBOULD, P. 'The pattern of nutrient uptake in root systems', in *Root Growth*, London: Butterworths, 1969.

45. SAMTSEVICH, S.A. 'Active secretions of plant roots and their importance', *Fiziol. Rast.*, 1965, **12**, 837-846.
46. SMITH, K.A. and RUSSELL, R.S. 'Occurrence of ethylene, and its significance, in anaerobic soil', *Nature*, 1969, **222**, 769-771.
47. SNOW, L.M. 'The development of root hairs', *Bot. Gaz.*, 1905, **40**, 12-48.
48. TROUGHTON, A. and WHITTINGTON, W.J. 'The significance of genetic variation in root systems', in *Root Growth*, London: Butterworths, 1969.
49. TROUSE, A.C. Jr. and HUMBERT, R.P. 'Some effects of soil compaction on the development of sugar cane roots', *Soil Sci.*, 1961, **91**, 208-217.
50. VAADIA, Y. and ITAI, C. 'Interrelationships of growth with reference to the distribution of growth substances', in *Root Growth*, London: Butterworths, 1969.
51. WEAVER, J.E. *Root development of field crops*, New York: McGraw-Hill, 1926.
52. WOOD, R.K.S. *Physiological plant pathology*, Oxford: Oxford University Press, 1966.

8. A Dynamic Model of Plant and Crop Growth

C.T. de Wit
Laboratory for Theoretical Production Ecology, Agricultural University
Institute for Biological and Chemical Research on Field Crops and Herbage
(I.B.S.), Wageningen, The Netherlands.

R. Brouwer
Laboratory of Physiological Research, Agricultural University, Wageningen,
The Netherlands.

F.W.T. Penning de Vries
Laboratory for Theoretical Production Ecology, Agricultural University,
Wageningen, The Netherlands.

Introduction

The development of an elementary crop growth simulator (ELCROS), designed according to the general principles of biological model-building [24] has been discussed earlier [4, 25], with special attention to the functional balance between the growth of the shoot and the root.

It is assumed that the individual plant or the whole crop contains a pool of reserves (RES), largely in the form of carbohydrates. Photosynthesis (PHR) is the only source of these reserves which are then used for respiration (RSP), increase in structural root weight (GRW), in structural leaf weight (GLW) and in structural stem weight (GST). The rates of these changes are represented by valve symbols in the relational diagram of Figure 8.1. Photosynthesis and respiration transfer material from and to the environment, but the growth rates transfer carbohydrates from the reserve pool to the structural weight of the roots (WRT), leaves (WLV) and stem (WST), i.e. into organic material that cannot be used as reserves. The levels or contents of these integrals are represented within rectangles in Figure 8.1, which also indicates the way in which root growth may depend on environmental conditions. Soil temperature is determined by direct observation or from the meteorological part of the programme and the relative growth rate of the roots (RGRR) is calculated for the particular species concerned. This is not a growth rate which can be used directly to compute the increase in root weight, but an auxiliary value necessary for further computations, and as such is presented in a circle in Figure 8.1. The possible rate of increase in root weight (PGRW) is now calculated by multiplying the relative growth rate

* based on a paper given to the Conference on the Productivity of Photosynthetic Systems. Part I: Models and Methods. Trebon, Czechoslovakia, September, 14-21, 1969.

(RGGR) by the weight of those roots (WRT) which are still young enough to be capable of growth (C). This possible growth rate, again an auxiliary value, is only realized as an actual rate of increase in root weight (GRW) when there are sufficient reserves. In this method of presentation (Figure 8.1), the flow of organic material (kg CH_2O ha^{-1} day^{-1}) is presented by full lines and the flow of information by dotted lines. In view of the daily cycle of environmental conditions, it is assumed that the rates calculated for a particular moment do not change appreciably over a period of about an hour, so that hourly time steps can validly be used in this simulation model.

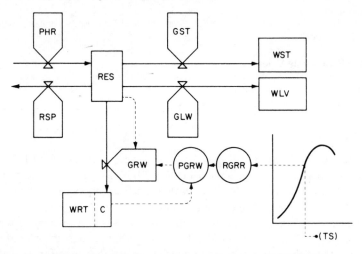

Fig 8.1   The relational diagram of the central part of ELCROS.

Operating versions of this simulation programme (ELCROS) are available in the languages DYNAMO and CSMP/360 [9]. The latter will be used in the present chapter. At the present time a simulation programme of this type must be regarded more as a guide to research than as a final solution, since many *ad hoc* assumptions regarding the physiological mechanisms underlying plant and crop growth still have to be made. The present chapter will discuss some of the more important of these mechanisms, paying special attention to the rates of photosynthesis, of leaf growth and of respiration. The interrelations between shoot and root growth have been treated elsewhere [4].

Photosynthetic Rate

(i) Physiological Aspects
The photosynthetic rate of a crop depends on the amount of incoming light energy, the area and distribution of leaves in the canopy and the photosynthetic properties of the individual leaves.

The calculation of the photosynthetic rate of the crop at a particular instant is carried out in two stages. Firstly, the light distribution over the individual leaves of a crop has to be calculated, and secondly, the photosynthetic rate of the crop has to be obtained by integration of the photosynthetic rate of each leaf calculated from its photosynthesis function.

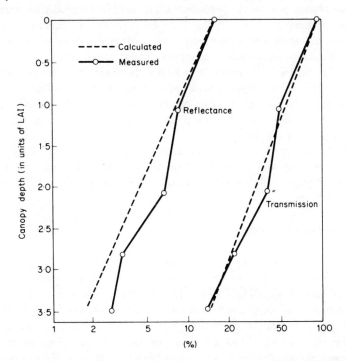

Fig. 8.2   Calculated and measured transmission and reflection in a maize crop with a leaf area index of 3.5; from Idso and de Wit [8].

The evaluation of the light distribution is a purely geometrical problem, which by now has been largely solved. Figure 8.2, for instance, shows the measured and calculated transmission and reflection rates inside a maize crop, the calculated values being based on measurement of the reflection and transmission coefficients of individual leaves and on the leaf distribution function. Although the architecture of the canopy may vary during the growth of a crop, the influence of variation in leaf arrangement should not be over-emphasized. For instance, the leaf distribution function of a grass canopy varies from very erectophile in short swards in spring to very planophile in long swards in autumn. However, assuming that the photosynthesis function remains the same, this large difference in leaf distribution would lead, under Dutch conditions, to a difference in gross photosynthesis of only $25 - 50$ kg CH_2O ha^{-1} day^{-1}, out of a total of about 375 kg ha^{-1} day^{-1} [23].

The influence of the photosynthesis function of the individual leaves is more important, because of its greater variability. If the maximum photosynthetic rate of the individual leaves increases by 100%, but the photo-synthetic rate at low intensities remains the same, then the photosynthesis of the crop may increase by about 50 per cent [23].

The photosynthetic rate of a leaf will depend to a considerable extent on its age or position along the stem, but such effects cannot as yet be incorporated in the simulation programme, since the distribution of leaves of different ages through the crop canopy is usually not known.

In the present programme (ELCROS), therefore, these effects of ageing are neglected and the instantaneous photosynthesis rate is calculated by the numerical method described by de Wit [23], which assumes that each leaf has a definite life-span, but that the photosynthesis function does not change during the life of the leaf.

In this programme the instantaneous effect of temperature on photo-synthesis is taken into account, but no account is taken of any effect of the temperature regime during the formation of leaves on their subsequent rate of photosynthesis.

(ii) Programming Aspects

The numerical calculation of crop photosynthesis from the basic data for each hour of simulation is expensive with regard to computer time. Consequently, calculations are done once and for all and summarized in a two-way table in which leaf area (ALV) and the sine of the angle of the sun are the two variables. Separate tables are used for clear and for overcast skies. The height of the sun at the hourly intervals is calculated from the latitude, the day of the year and the hour of the day according to standard astronomical formulae [23]. The condition of the sky (i.e. clear or overcast) is obtained from the meteorological section of the simulation programme, and the leaf area from the leaf growth section of the programme. The estimates of crop photosynthesis for maize given in Table 8.1 are based on the assumptions that leaf distribution is slightly plagiophile [23], that the scattering coefficient is 0.2, and that the leaf photosynthesis rate is given by

$$(LI/(.365 + LI)) \times 84.5 \text{ kg } CH_2O \text{ ha}^{-1} \text{ h}^{-1}$$

in which LI is the light intensity absorbed in cal cm^{-2} min^{-1}. This function has been calculated for 23°C, but similar calculations can be made for other temperatures, and in fact the instantaneous effect of temperature for maize may be accounted for quite accurately by the following multiplication factors:

Temp. °C	0	5	10	15	20	25	30	35	40	45
Factor	0	0	0.28	0.54	0.79	1.03	1.08	1.08	0.99	0.45

It is at present assumed in ELCROS that leaf temperature equals air temperature at a standard height i.e. at 10 cm above a soil surface covered with turfgrass, and that root temperature has an amplitude of 0.45 times that of air temperature and lags two hours behind it. The temperature of the growing point is assumed to be intermediate between soil and air temperature, depending on its position with respect to the soil surface. These assumptions seem reasonable, and can only be improved upon by simulating simultaneously the growth of the crop and the micro-climate.

Table 8.1
Crop photosynthesis rates of maize as dependent on leaf area index (ALV) and the sine of the angle of the sun for clear (C) and overcast (O) skies.

ALV	0	0.1	0.2	0.3	0.4	SINE 0.5	0.6	0.7	0.8	0.9	1.0	SKY
0	0	0	0	0	0	0	0	0	0	0	0	C
	0	0	0	0	0	0	0	0	0	0	0	O
1	0	7.0	15.5	21.0	25.0	28.2	31.2	34.0	36.0	38.3	40.0	C
	0	1.7	3.2	5.5	7.2	8.5	10.7	12.5	14.0	15.6	16.8	O
2	0	9.0	20.0	28.2	35.0	41.5	47.2	52.1	56.2	60.4	63.7	C
	0	2.0	4.5	7.2	10.0	12.7	15.2	17.9	20.2	22.7	24.5	O
3	0	10.2	21.3	31.0	39.5	47.0	54.5	61.4	66.7	72.6	77.1	C
	0	2.4	5.2	8.5	11.5	14.5	17.5	20.5	23.0	26.1	28.2	O
4	0	10.5	22.0	32.0	42.0	50.0	58.5	65.9	72.5	79.1	84.4	C
	0	2.5	5.7	9.0	12.2	15.5	18.5	21.8	24.7	27.7	29.9	O
5	0	10.8	22.5	32.4	42.2	50.5	59.0	68.2	74.0	82.5	88.3	C
	0	2.5	5.8	9.2	12.4	15.8	18.8	22.3	25.4	28.5	30.7	O
6	0	11.1	22.9	32.7	42.3	51.0	59.5	69.3	75.5	84.3	90.4	C
	0	2.6	5.9	9.4	12.6	16.0	19.2	22.6	25.6	28.8	31.1	O
7	0	11.4	23.3	33.1	42.4	51.5	60.0	69.8	76.5	85.2	91.5	C
	0	2.6	6.0	9.5	12.7	16.1	19.3	22.7	25.7	29.0	31.3	O
8	0	11.5	23.5	33.3	42.5	51.9	60.4	70.1	77.0	85.7	92.0	C
	0	2.6	6.1	9.6	12.8	16.2	19.4	22.8	25.8	29.1	31.4	O
9	0	11.6	23.8	33.4	42.6	52.2	60.8	70.2	77.5	85.9	92.3	C
	0	2.7	6.1	9.6	12.9	16.2	19.5	22.9	25.9	29.1	31.5	O
10	0	11.7	24.0	33.5	42.7	52.5	61.2	70.3	78.0	86.0	92.5	C
	0	2.7	6.2	9.7	13.0	16.3	19.5	22.9	26.0	29.2	31.5	O

Leaf Growth

(i) Physiological Aspects
The rate of growth of the plant or crop has usually been measured in terms of increase in weight, in length and thickness or in area, depending on the aim of the particular experiment.

The present programme (ELCROS) must take several aspects of growth into account. In the first place, it must describe the accumulation of dry matter into the structural tissues, i.e. the dry matter accumulated minus the directly available reserves, which are kept in a separate pool for distribution to the growing organs. In the second place, the rate of expansion of the leaf surface has to be known to obtain a measure of the size of the photosynthetic system. The primary determinant of growth is therefore the flow of reserves into the structure of the growing plant-parts. The rate of this flow depends on the amount of tissue capable of growth, the relative growth rate of the tissues, and the availability of essential materials for growth.

In the young seedling, all the tissue takes part in growth and, provided that all essential materials are available, growth occurs at the maximum rate for the particular temperature. This maximal rate can be conveniently expressed as the relative growth rate on the basis of total weight (RGR = $(dW/dt)/W$). In older plants, however, part of the tissue is mature and incapable of growth. In spite of this, single plants will grow exponentially when the supply of essential materials for growth increases linearly with the size of the plant.

In this case, the mature material is always a constant (and small) fraction of the total. When, however, deviations from exponential growth occur, as with mutual shading or limiting water supply, the fraction of mature material will vary and may comprise a large part of the total weight. In this case, the relative growth rate, expressed on the basis of total weight, will show variable values, although the relative growth rate of the tissues capable of growth is likely to remain constant, so long as all essential materials are present.

The amount of tissue capable of growth can be estimated from the pattern of leaf growth of the plant or crop. At constant temperature, the consecutive leaves of a maize plant, like most other species [21], appear at a constant rate, and at any one time only the last three visible leaves are increasing in size (Figure 8.3) [6]. From experiments with bean plants, it appears that the leaves next in age, which do not grow in the intact plant, can resume growth when the youngest leaves are removed. This generally-accepted consequence of the removal of sinks [7] probably occurs also in maize, although in this species the complete youngest leaves cannot be removed without damaging the whole plant. The removal of only the visible leaves does not affect the meristem nor the growth of the youngest leaves, since both cell division and cell extension take place within the sheaths of the older leaves [16].

This pattern of leaf growth can be illustrated by considering a maize plant with ten visible leaves, numbered from 1 (the oldest) to 10 (the youngest). Leaves 10, 9 and 8 are growing at about the same rate [6] and are assumed to be fully capable of growth. Leaves 1 to 5 will not grow any more even if the shoot apex is completely destroyed, although their axillary buds can develop into new tillers. The intermediate leaves, 7 and 6, can resume growth to a certain extent only. The fraction of tissue fully capable of growth thus decreases with the age of the plant, and this effect has to be introduced into the simulation programme.

A maize plant growing at a temperature of 20°C may take 2.3 days

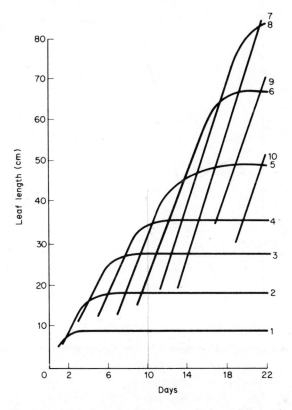

Fig. 8.3   *The increase in length of successive leaves of the maize plant with time; only three leaves are growing at the same time. From Grobbelaar [6].*

between the initiation of two successive leaves, so that, following the above assumptions, it is only the tissue which has been produced in the last 4 x 2.3 i.e. 9.2 days which is still fully capable of growth. Within this period the plant weight increases at least ten-fold, which means that only 10 per cent of the total weight consists of mature tissue. Hence no large errors are introduced into the first estimate of the relative growth rate by using total plant weight as a basis for calculation, provided that the plants have been growing exponentially with a constant supply of such essential materials for growth as carbohydrates, water and minerals. In the present version of the simulation programme (ELCROS) the mineral supply is assumed to be optimal throughout for all plant parts. However, although water is assumed to be optimally available to the roots, local water stress may occur in the transpiring parts, due to resistance in the plant. The extent of this water stress can be estimated by comparing the amount and activity of the roots which are present with the amount and activity of those required to maintain full turgidity of the leaves, taking into account the transpiration rate [4].

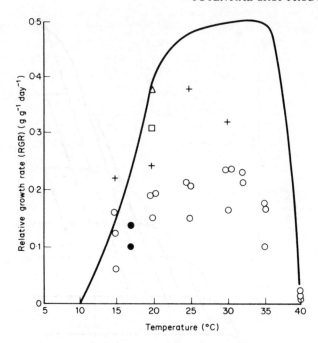

Fig. 8.4   *Relative growth rates of maize tops and roots under various*
conditions (see text), and the estimated relation between temp-
erature and the relative growth rate of young tissue, when well
supplied with carbohydrates and at full turgidity.

The effect of temperature on relative growth rates, derived from various
experiments, is given in Figure 8.4, and it can be seen that there is
considerable variation in relative growth rate over the range 15 to 30 °C. This
variation is due to various other limitations to growth. The open circles (o)
indicate the relative growth of the roots of plants which were kept with their
shoots at a temperature of 20 °C. As Figure 8.5 shows, between 20° and
30 °C, the carbohydrate content of these plants was low, and growth was
therefore limited by lack of reserves. The relative growth rate of whole plants,
growing at various temperatures under comparable conditions is probably also
subject to this limitation, although water stress in the above ground parts of
the plants may also be operating.

To overcome these limitations, plants were transferred from a nutrient
solution with nitrogen to one without nitrogen. Shoot growth was now
inhibited by shortage of nitrogen, resulting in an increased carbohydrate
content and an enhanced growth rate of the roots [3]. The relative growth
rate of the roots calculated for a five-day period after transfer is shown as an
open square (□) in Figure 8.4. Prolonged growth without N gives plants with a
relatively well-developed root system and a high carbohydrate content, the
growth of the leaves being limited only by the N supply. Supplying N

removes this limitation almost immediately, so that for a time leaf growth proceeds uninhibited by the lack of carbohydrates, or minerals, or even by water stress, since the large water-absorbing area of the roots compared with the smaller transpiring surface of the shoots, decreases the resistance to transfer of water. The relative growth rate of the shoots under such conditions is plotted as a triangle (△) in Figure 8.4 [3]. Even this high value may not, however, represent the maximum possible, since as a result of the previous check in shoot growth, the plant contains a relatively high percentage of older tissue.

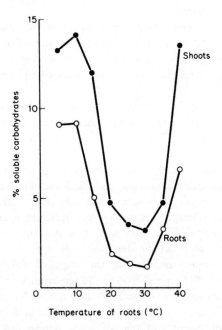

Fig. 8.5   *The influence of root temperature on the carbohydrate content of maize, at a shoot temperature of 20°C; from Grobbelaar [6].*

An indication of the maximum growth rates possible may be obtained from the values for young seedlings, still dependent on the materials in the seeds, which are shown as crosses (+) in Figure 8.4. Even in this case, however, there is still some doubt whether all essential materials for growth were optimally available, since Kny [12] showed that removing either the roots or the shoots from seedlings resulted in a faster growth of the remaining part, and Brown and Rickless [5] observed relative growth rates of 2.4 day^{-1} for the root tips of cucumber grown *in vitro*. Hence, even the highest values found in the present experiments may not indicate the maximum possible relative growth rates of young tissue grown without any limitations due to lack of reserves, water stress or shortage of minerals. Bearing in mind that maize cannot grow at temperatures below 11 °C, that under favourable conditions the optimum temperature for growth appears to be at least 35 °C, and that the maximum possible growth rates were probably rarely achieved, the response of relative growth rate to temperature used in the present simulation programme (ELCROS) is given by the curve drawn in Figure 8.4. The use of this curve provides satisfactory comparisons of simulated and actual growth rates, but may need modification when more information is available on the maximum growth rates possible under non-limiting conditions.

(ii) Programming aspects

Even using the above physiological information in the simulation programme, it is still necessary to make *ad hoc* assumptions regarding some details of the operations, and one great advantage of attempting to construct such a programme is that it reveals quite clearly many of the important gaps in our knowledge.

Since the capacity of leaves for growth depends on their age, it is necessary to keep track of the age distribution of the leaf material in terms of its stage of development. This stage of development can be quantitatively characterized as follows.

Silking of maize in the field occurs at practically the same date, irrespective of the density of planting, which indicates that the rate of leaf initiation is independent of the size of the individual plant. Since, at constant temperature and daylength, the rate of leaf initiation is also independent of the number of leaves already formed, it is possible to specify a rate of development of maize which depends only on the external variables, daylength and temperature. Taking the stage of development (DVS) at seedling emergence as zero and that at the appearance of the male flower as one, the rate of development (DVR) may be expressed in units of day^{-1}.

The relation between this rate of development and temperature for one Dutch variety of maize and one of oats, determined under controlled conditions at fourteen hours daylength, is shown in Figure 8.6(a). The temperature of the growing point (TG) can be computed from data in the meteorological section of the programme, and using the language CSMP as mentioned earlier, the rate of development for each moment may be calculated from:

$$DVR = AFGEN (DVRTB,TG)$$

FUNCTION DVRTB = (-5.,0.), (10.,0.), (15.,0.011), (20.,0.025), . . .
(30.,0.04), (35.,0.04), (40.,0.004), (60.,0.004)

The curve of Figure 8.6(a) for maize is here characterized by the pair of values of the function DVRTB, the first number of each pair being the value of the independent variable TG and the second number being the rate of development (DVR). The AFGEN function states that the value of the rate of development is obtained by interpolation in DVRTB with TG as the independent variable. The stage of development (DVS) is now obtained by

$$DVS = INTGRL (0, DVR)$$

a CSMP function that indicates that the initial value of DVS at seedling emergence is zero, the rate of change is DVR and that DVS is obtained by integration.

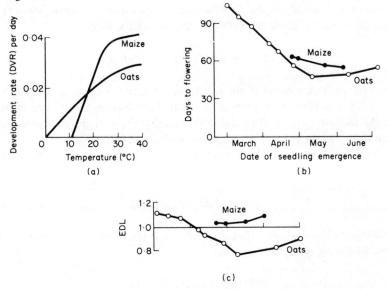

Fig. 8.6   (a) *The relation between temperature and development rate*
                (DVR) of a maize and oat variety at a daylength of 14 hours.
           (b) *The relation between date of seedling emergence and time*
                from emergence to flowering in the field in the Netherlands.
           (b) *The classical concepts of optimum and ceiling leaf area index*
                on the assumption that respiration is proportional to total
                dry matter.

The actual number of days from seedling emergence to flowering of maize and oats sown at successive intervals in the field is shown in Figure 8.6(b), while Figure 8.6(c) gives the ratio of the actual and the computed vegetative period. For maize, this ratio is very close to one, indicating that under Dutch field conditions maize behaves as a day-neutral plant. However, in oats the ratio is larger than one before the half of April and smaller then one thereafter, indicating that the oat plant is sensitive to daylength under Dutch conditions. A simulation of the influence of daylength will, however, have to be based on a thorough study of the relevant literature.

To determine the age distribution of the leaf material in terms of the stage of development at its time of formation, a function which may be called a 'box-car train' is introduced into the programme, as shown in Figure 8.7. The rate of growth is integrated in the first box-car of the train, and each time the stage of development is increased by a factor 0.04, the content of the last box-car is discarded and that of the others is transferred to the car with the next highest number. Hence, just before a transfer, the 1st, 2nd and 3rd and 31st box-cars contain the leaf material that is $0 - 0.04$, $0.04 - 0.08$, $0.08 - 0.12$, ... $1.2 - 1.24$ units old in terms of stage of development. When the plant has reached the stage of 0.4, only the first ten box-cars of the train contain leaf material. In the CSMP version of ELCROS this operation which gives the weight of the leaves (WLVB) may be referred to as

$$WLVB = TRAIN\ (31,GLW,DVS,0.04)$$

The symbol WLVB refers to the weight of the leaves in the box-car-train, 31 denotes the number of box-cars in the train, GLW denotes the increase in leaf weight and the symbols DVS and 0.04 state that the contents are transferred each time that the stage of development is advanced by 0.04 unit.

The total weight of the leaves (WLV) may now be obtained from the expression

$$WLV = SUM1\ (31,WLVB)$$

a function which indicates that the contents of the thirty-one box-cars in the train WLVB are summed.

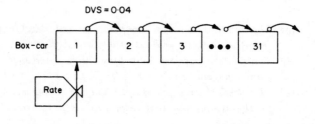

Fig. 8.7   *Diagram of a 'box-car-train' to determine the age distribution of growing material.*

On the basis of the number of leaves that are capable of growth at a particular time, it may be assumed that the capacity for growth of the contents of the thirty-one box-cars of the train WLVB may be expressed as follows, showing the effect of maturity (EMA).

$$EMA\ (1-31) = 5 \times 1.,0.88,0.67,0.43,23 \times 0.02$$

This means that the contents of the first five box-cars are fully capable of growth, that the contents of the last twenty-three box-cars have retained only a rudimentary capacity for growth (by means of dormant axillary buds), and that the ability to grow decreases linearly from the fifth to the ninth box-car. Hence, the weight of the leaves that are capable of growth (WLVC) may be obtained from

$$WLVC = SUM2\ (31,WLVB,EMA)$$

a function which means that WLVC is the sum of the thirty-one products of the content of each box-car of the train WLVB and its EMA-value.

To calculate the amount of growth of the leaves, the relative growth rate of the leaves (RGRL) must first be calculated from the air temperature (TA) around the plants as

$$RGRL = AFGEN(RGRTB,TA)$$

$$FUNCTION\ RGRTB = (-5.,0.),\ (10.,0.),\ (15.,0.17),\ (20.,0.25),\ \ldots$$
$$(25.,0.56),\ (40.,0.22),\ (45.,0.08)$$

in which the RGRTB function is similar to the curve in Figure 8.4.

The maximum possible growth of the leaves (PGLV) i.e. when there are no limitations of water stress or carbohydrate shortage, is now given by

$$PGLV = WLVC\ x\ RGRL$$

In considering the influence of the reserve percentage (RPR), it is assumed that at a reserve percentage of 0, growth is zero, and at a value of 4 per cent, growth is at its maximum rate; in other words, the growth constraint of the leaves due to lack of reserves (GCLR) is

$$GCLR = LIMIT\ (0.,1.,RPR/4.)$$

This function makes GCLR equal to 0 or 1, when RPR is smaller than 0 or larger than 4 respectively, and otherwise takes the value of RPR/4.

It follows from Figure 8.1 that the total reserves in the plant are given by the integral

$$RES = INTGRL\ (0.,PHS - RSP - GLW - GRW - GST).$$

and that the reserve percentage equals RPR = RES/TWT, in which TWT is the total weight of the plant or crop.

A similar growth constraint due to lack of turgidity can be calculated from the relative amount of roots. If it is now assumed that growth is limited by the smallest of these constraints, then the actual growth rate in terms of leaf weight (GLW) is

$$GLW = PGLW\ x\ AMIN1\ (GCLR,GCLT)$$

Finally, it is important to consider the rate of increase of leaf area. A simple assumption is that the increase in leaf area is proportional to the increase in leaf weight, so that leaf area may be found from leaf weight, using a factor of about 750 kg ha^{-1} (7.5 mg cm^{-2}).

However, the specific leaf area (i.e. the amount of leaf surface per unit leaf weight) is greatly influenced by environment conditions. The influence of water and soil nutrients can be neglected in the present treatment, since the main purpose of the ELCROS programme is to stimulate the growth of the crop under optimal conditions of water and nutrient supply. The supply of carbohydrates to the growing leaves, however, has a large influence on their morphology. For instance, if it takes thirty days for seedling emergence to flowering and fifteen leaves are formed within this period, there is only a two days supply of carbohydrates available for each leaf. At a plant density of 100,000 plants ha^{-1} and a carbohydrate production of 200 kg ha^{-1} day^{-1}, this amounts to an average 4 g of carbohydrates per leaf. If, however, the plant density is doubled the carbohydrate supply per leaf is reduced to 2 g, and if the plant density is halved the supply is increased to 8 g. A leaf of 8 g is not only longer and wider, but also thicker than a leaf of 2 g, an effect which is catered for in the ELCROS programme by including the specific leaf weight (WARL) which varies from 500 kg ha^{-1} (5 mg cm^{-2}) for an average growth rate of 1 g per leaf per day or lower, to 1000 kg ha^{-1} (10 mg cm^{-2}) for an average growth rate of 4 g per leaf per day or higher. Maize plants, for instance, usually possess comparatively thin leaves when they are young or densely planted, or grown at low light intensities in growth rooms, and comparatively thick leaves when widely spaced in the field.

At any particular moment, therefore, the growth of the leaf area (GLA) may be calculated as

$$GLA = WARL \times GLW$$

which in turn is integrated in a 'box-car-train' to give the area of the leaves (ALVB),

$$ALVB = TRAIN (31, GLA, DVS, 0.04)$$

Although the main factors which influence specific leaf weight can be qualitatively introduced in this way, the whole question of leaf morphology provides a good example of an area where the critical physiological basis for the simulation programme is still lacking.

Respiration

(i) Physiological Aspects
It is often assumed that the respiration rate of a crop at any particular temperature is proportional to the amount of leaf tissue. This assumption leads to the well-known graph (Figure 8.8(a)) which indicates the optimum area of the leaves (ALV) at which net photosynthesis is at its maximum, and the ceiling leaf area, at which photosynthesis is fully counterbalanced by respiration. The use of this assumption in the simulation programme leads to inconsistent results. If respiration per unit plant material is assumed to be

low, then the programme predicts yield levels similar to those observed in the field, but also predicts respiration rates under controlled conditions which are far smaller than those obtained by experiment. If it is assumed that respiration per unit plant material is higher, the predicted respiration rates under controlled conditions agree with the observed values, but the predicted ceiling yields in the field are far too small.

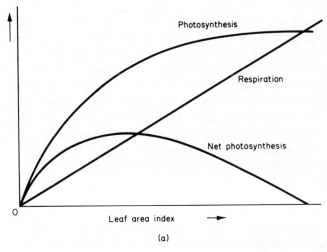

(a)

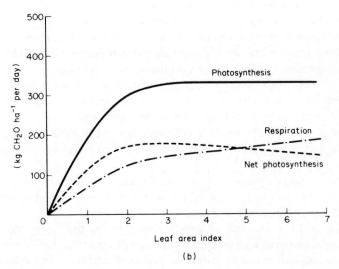

(b)

Fig. 8.8   (a) The classical concepts of optimum and ceiling leaf area index on the assumption that respiration is proportional to total dry matter.

(b) Photosynthesis, respiration, and net photosynthesis in relation to leaf area index, as measured in Trifolium repens at 20°C; from McCree and Troughton [15].

Recently, McCree and Troughton [15] have shown conclusively that respiration rates of crops are not proportional to the weight of the vegetative material (or to the area of the leaves), but are in fact related to the photosynthesis rate of the crop surface (Figure 8.8(b)). The incorporation of this information into explanatory models of crop growth requires more detailed physiological and biochemical knowledge of the relevant growth processes.

There is abundant evidence that in plants respiration is regulated to meet changing metabolic demands through an intimate coupling of respiration to phosporylation [1]. Many processes in the cell, like synthesis, growth and solute transfer, need energy which is obtained from the conversion of adenosine triphosphate (ATP) to adenosine diphosphate (ADP) and inorganic phosphate (IP). The APD and IP are required for glycolysis, and this process would be brought to a standstill if all available ADP were converted into ATP, as indicated by experiments with uncoupling agents such as dinitrophenol. These substances destroy the coupling between oxidation and phosphorylation of ADP, but ATP breakdown is unaffected and the result is an increased supply of ADP.

In actively growing tissue, the drain of respiratory intermediates and the consumption of ATP is high, so that the respiration rate in these tissues is likely to be greater than in older tissue in which ATP turnover is lower, whereas the stimulation by DNP is likely to be smaller in the younger tissues. In fact, in carrot slices the actual respiration decreased from 100 per cent of the uncoupled rate in young material to about 30 per cent in older, whereas the rate of respiration in the uncoupled state (+ DNP) remained the same [1]. This suggests that the amount of enzymatic material did not change with age, and that respiration was in fact geared to the needs of the plant.

In a recent paper Beevers [2] has distinguished between (i) growth respiration, associated with synthetic events, (ii) maintenance respiration, associated with protein turn-over in older cells and with repair and maintenance of inherently unstable cell-structures and (iii) idling respiration, concerned with hydrolyses of ATP in which there is no useful outcome to the plant.

In the ELCROS programme, the coefficient of growth respiration is expressed as the weight lost during the synthesis of one unit of weight of structural material, and may be estimated in various ways.

Firstly, at $25\,^{\circ}C$ the relative growth rate of young tissue, well supplied with essential materials for growth, may account to about $0.5\ \text{day}^{-1}$, whereas the relative respiration rate of such tissue is about $0.25\ \text{day}^{-1}$. In the absence of maintenance and idling respiration this would indicate a growth respiration coefficient of about 0.5, a value within the range reported for animal growth [11, 17].

Alternatively, the efficiency of synthesis of structural materials, on a weight basis can be calculated from the biochemical pathways of synthesis. Assuming that all the products of photosynthesis are channelled through glucose and that N is supplied as NO_3, it can be calculated that the formation of 1 g each of proteins, fats, polymers of sugars and the uptake of 1 g of minerals requires about 2.35, 2.94, 1.15 and 0.1 g of glucose, respectively. Hence, for the formation of 1 g of tissue, consisting of 25 per cent protein, 6 per cent fat, 59 per cent polymers of sugars and 10 per cent of minerals, about 1.45 g of glucose is necessary. From these calculations, it follows that the weight of the CO_2 produced is about 0.5 times the weight of plant tissue formed, which agrees with the value of 0.33 reported by McCree [14], for the ratio between respiration and net photosynthesis. Since there is no indication that biochemical pathways depend on temperature, it is assumed that the growth respiration coefficient is independent of temperature, an assumption which seems to be confirmed in recent experiments with maize seedlings.

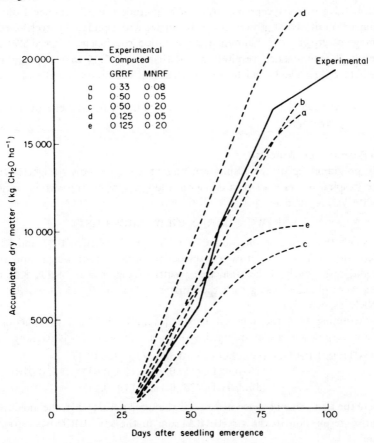

Fig. 8.9   Actual and simulated growth of maize in Ames (Iowa) in 1963; experimental data from Shibles [20]; respiration factors from McCree [14].

At present, it is difficuly to separate maintenance and idling respiration, but it can be tentatively assumed that both are proportional to the amount of enzymatic material. According to Price [18], this uncoupled respiration rate, in the presence of optimal substrate, oxygen and uncouplers, amounts to 200-300 μlO$_2$ h^{-1} mg^{-1} protein-N at 25 $^\circ$C. The value corresponds to a relative uncoupled respiration rate of 0.28 kg CH$_2$O (kg dry matter)$^{-1}$ day^{-1} for tissue with 4 per cent protein-N. From the values given by Price [18] a Q_{10} of 2.2 can be assumed for the uncoupled respiration rate over a wide temperature range.

Earlier observations [10, 13, 19] have suggested that the respiration rate of mature leaves, expressed as a fraction of the uncoupled respiration rate, is about 0.25, but the data of McCree [14] suggest a value of about 0.08.

Clearly the maintenance respiration coefficient is still not well defined, but an idea of its acceptable order of magnitude can be obtained from the comparison of actual growth curves for maize with simulated curves based on a range of growth and maintenance respiration coefficients (Figure 8.9). The use of a maintenance respiration coefficient of 0.25 in the programme predicts ceiling yields which are less than half the values actually observed, but the lower coefficients for the growth and maintenance respiration (GRRF and MNRF) calculated by McCree [14] result in predicted yields of the right order of magnitude.

(ii) Programming Aspects

The programming of the respiration rate of a crop is now straightforward. The respiration rate associated with the growth of the various organs (RSPAWG) is taken as:

$$\text{RSPAWG} = \text{GRRF} \times (\text{GLW} + \text{GRW} + \text{GST})$$

in which the growth respiration factor (GRRF) is taken as 0.33 and GLW, GRW and GST are the growth rates of leaf weight, root weight and stem weight, respectively. (The simulated results of Figure 8.10, 8.11, 8.12 and 8.13 were obtained using earlier estimates of 0.2 and 0.125 for GRRF and MNRF respectively).

Assuming that the relation between temperature and the uncoupled relative respiration rate of an organ with 1 per cent organic N is given by

FUNCTION URRTB = (-50.,0.0061), (0.,0.0093), (5.,0.014), . . .
                 (10.,0.021), (15.,0.031), (20.,0.047), (25.,0.070), . . .
                 (30.,0.104), (35.,0.15.,), (50.,0.14)

where the first value between brackets is the temperature, then the uncoupled relative respiration in the air (URRA) and in the soil (URRS) is obtained from

$$\text{URRA} = \text{AFGEN (URRTB, TA)}$$

$$\text{URRS} = \text{ARGEN (URRTA, TS)}$$

where TA and TS are the air and soil temperature respectively.

From observation it is assumed that in a well-fertilized maize plant, the nitrogen content of the leaves (NLV), of the roots (NRT) and of the stem (NST) decrease for successive 'box-cars' of their train according to

NLV (1-31) = 10 x 4 . . . , 5 x 3.9, 3 x 3.8, 2 x 3.7, 3.6, . . .
         3.5, 3.4, 3.3, 3.2, 3.1, 2.9, 2.8, 2.7, 2.6

NST (1-31) = as for leaves
NRT (1-31) = 1% lower than for leaves.

Thus, the uncoupled respiration rate of the whole crop is

URRC = URRA(SUM2(31,WLVB,NLV) + SUM2(31,WSTB,NST)) . . .
      + URRS (SUM2(31,WRTB,NRT))

The respiration associated with maintenance is then

RSPAWM = MNRF x URRC

in which the maintenance respiration factor (MNRF) is taken as 0.08.

Comparison of Simulated and Observed Results

An example of the operation of the present simulator programme (ELCROS) some simulated results will be discussed and compared with actual experiment observations.

As mentioned earlier, ELCROS operates using a time step of one hour, i.e. every hour all rates of changes are re-calculated and integrated. Hence in the course of one day, all calculations are performed twenty-four times.

The simulated results for the growth of maize for a period of twenty-four hours, during its nineteenth day after emergence are presented in Figure 8.10. At midnight, the reserve percentage is decreasing, accompanied by decreased growth rates. At the onset of light, the reserve percentage increases again, followed by increased growth rates first of the leaves, then of the roots. At the beginning of the dark period, there is a rather sudden increase in the growth of the leaves; this is a result of the decrease in transpiration, accompanied by an increase of turgidity. The growth rate soon drops again due to the decrease of the reserve level.

The respiration is coupled to the growth rate and therefore lags behind the photosynthesis rate. The small increase in photosynthesis and transpiration during the day reflects the increase in leaf surface, the leaf area index being slightly greater than 1. The relative growth rates of the shoot and root during the day are 0.16 and 0.10 g g^{-1} day^{-1} respectively. The shoot-root ratio is also increasing somewhat because of increased mutual shading. These relative growth rates are comparable with the actual values observed in maize under the same conditions (Figure 8.4), indicating that net photosynthesis, rather than the capacity to grow, governs the rate of growth. Figure 8.11, which compares actual and simulated data for the growth of maize, shows that the present programme simulates the influence of temperature on the rate of growth and development resonably well, although the rate of development of the plants used in this particular experiment deviated from that introduced into the programme earlier.

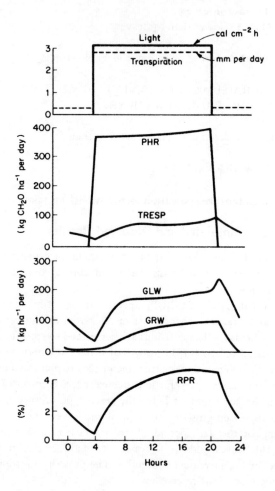

*Fig. 8.10   The simulated photosynthesis (PHR), respiration (TRESP), trans-
piration (TRANSP), growth of leaves (GLW) and of roots (GRW),
and reserve percentage (RPR) of maize under controlled conditions during a 24 hour period. (29 January, 1969; air temperature
20 °C, soil temperature 20 °C, relative humidity 65%, daily
photosynthesis 272 kg ha^{-1}, daily respiration 55 kg ha^{-1}, total
weight 1146 kg ha^{-1}, leaf area 1.3 ha ha^{-1}.)*

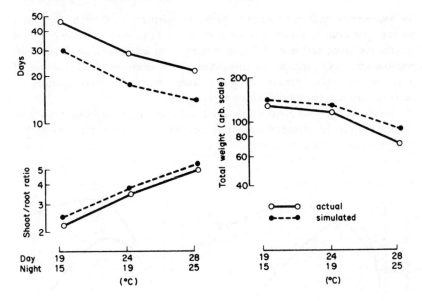

Fig. 8.11   Simulated and actual growth of maize up to the 11th leaf stage
(DVS = 0.6).

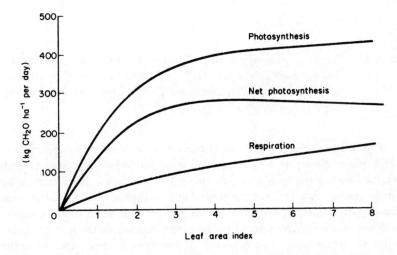

Fig. 8.12   Simulated photosynthesis, respiration, and net photosynthesis in
maize in relation to leaf area index, at a temperature of 20 °C.

The simulated relation between the leaf area index and the daily
photosynthesis, respiration, and net photosynthesis under controlled conditions is presented in Figure 8.12. These results are very similar to those
obtained from actual experiments (Figure 8.8). This similarity is a result of

the assumption that respiration is partly coupled to the growth rate, but a similar agreement is obtained when it is assumed that respiration depends on the reserve level, rather than being directly coupled to growth. These two possibilities may, perhaps, be distinguished by studying the behaviour of plants during short periods of water stress, which are accompanied by decreased growth rates and increased reserve levels.

Such a similarity between simulated and observed values could never be obtained from the assumption that respiration is mainly controlled by the amount of plant material present.

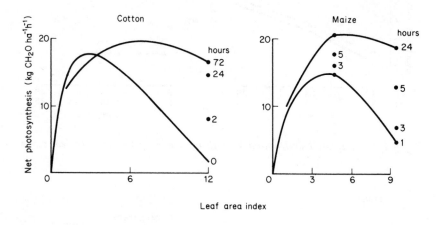

Fig. 8.13   The net photosynthesis of cotton (actual experiment) from Ludwig, Saeki, and Evans [13] , and maize (simulated experiment) at various times after increasing the leaf area index by placing single grown plants close together.

Figure 8.13 compares the results of an actual and simulated experiment in which plants grown at a wide spacing were suddenly transferred to high densities with a leaf area index of about 10. The actual experiment using cotton revelas that the net photosynthesis at high densities falls to zero directly after transfer, but that within twenty-four hours the situation is modified, so that net photosynthesis no longer depends on the leaf area index within the dense range. This is because of a decrease in respiration during the twenty-four hour period. The simulated experiment using maize reveals the same behaviour. Further analyses of the simulated data showed that mutual shading due to crowding reduced the photosynthesis per unit leaf area, resulting in a decreased reserve percentage, which was in its turn accompanied by a decreasing growth rate and a decreasing respiration rate. Because the speed of adjustment in the actual and simulated experiment is about the same, it seems likely that a similar mechanism is operating in the actual and in the simulated plants.

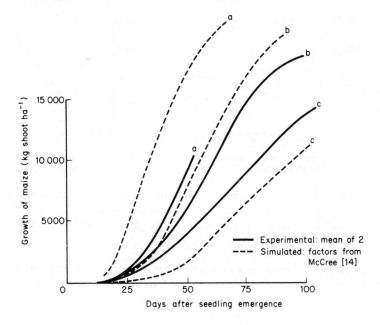

Fig. 8.14   Actual and simulated growth of maize under field conditions, (a) in California, (b) in Iowa, and (c) in the Netherlands; from Williams, Loomis, and Lepley [22], Shibles [20] and unpublished.

The actual and simulated growth rates of maize in California, Iowa and the Netherlands are presented in Figure 8.14 The simulated curves were obtained by using the latitude, seedling emergence data and weather data for the locations and years concerned. None of the other parameters were adjusted to obtain better agreement. Closed crop surfaces are reached at yields of 1500 kg ha^{-1} and the slope of the curves thereafter is termed the crop growth rate. At each of the three locations, the actual and simulated crop growth rate is roughly the same, although the differences between locations are considerable. This shows that the present version of ELCROS gives reasonable predictions for this particular characteristic.

The simulated crop in California is much earlier in reaching its grand period of growth than the actual crop, whereas the reverse is the case in the Netherlands. However, the average temperature in California during the early stages of growth was around 25 °C and in the Netherlands about 10° lower. The effect of these large temperature differences on the relative growth rate and the photosynthesis rate may well account for the differences between simulated and actual performance in California and the Netherlands. It is not clear, however, why, in the actual experiments, the periods from seedling emergence until the closed canopy of 1500 kg ha^{-1} was reached are so similar in both locations.

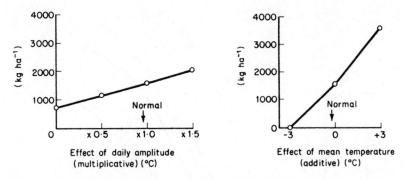

Fig. 8.15   Simulated influence of the daily amplitude and the mean of air and soil temperature on the total weight of maize in 1938 in the Netherlands (at the date when a weight of 1500 kg ha^{-1} is reached under normal conditions).

Since relatively small temperature changes within the range of 15° to 25 °C can have large effects on the growth of maize, it may well be that the large discrepancy in early growth between actual and simulated experiments are due to systematic differences between the actual micro-climate and the simulated micro-climate. The influence of changes in the daily amplitude and in the average daily temperature on the early growth of maize was therefore simulated for Dutch conditions (Figure 8.15). It appears that a difference in average temperature of only 1 °C could account for the difference obtained between the actual and simulated growth curves. Relatively large errors in temperature amplitude, on the other hand, do not appear to have much effect. Apart from this influence of temperature, it may be questioned whether, under dry conditions, as in California, the water supply during the early stages of growth has always been sufficient.

Hence, the accurate simulation of the early growth of maize depends to a large extent on the accurate prediction of the average temperature and moisture status at the surface of the soil.

REFERENCES

1. BEEVERS, H. *Respiratory metabolism in plants,* New York: Row, Peterson and Company, 1961.

2. BEEVERS, H. 'Respiration in plants and its regulation', Proc. Int. Biol. Prog. Tech. Meeting, *Productivity of Photosynthetic Systems: Models and Methods* (in press), 1970.

3. BROUWER, R., JENNESKENS, P.J. and BORGGREVE, G.J. 'Growth responses of shoots and roots to interruptions of the nitrogen supply', *Jaarb. Inst. biol. scheik. Onderz. Landb. Gewass,* 1961, 29-36.

4. BROUWER, R. and WIT, C.T. de 'A simulation model of plant growth with special attention to root growth and its consequences', in *Root Growth,* W.J. Whittington (ed.), London: Butterworth, 1969, 224-44.

5. BROWN, R. and RICKLESS, P. 'A new method for the study of cell division and cell extension, with some preliminary observations on the effect of temperature and of nutrients', *Proc. R. Soc.*, 1949, **B.136**, 110-125.

6. GROBBELAAR, W.P. 'The growth of maize pretreated at various soil temperatures', *Jaarb. Inst. biol. scheik. Onderz. Landb. Gewass.*, 1962, 33-38.

7. HUMPHRIES, E.C. 'Effect of removal of a part of the root system on the subsequent growth of the root and shoot', *Ann. Bot.*, 1958, **22**, 251-257.

8. IDSO, S.B. and WIT, C.T. de 'Light relations in plant canopies', *Appl. Optics*, 1970, **9**, 177-184.

9. I.B.M. *System/360, Continuous system modelling program* H20-0367-2. Techn. Publ. Dept., White Plains, U.S.A.

10. JAMES, W.O. *Plant Respiration*, London: Oxford Univ. Press, 1953, 282.

11. KLEIBER, M. *The Fire of Life*, New York: John Wiley and Sons, 1961.

12. KNY, L. 'On correlation in the growth of roots and shoots', *Ann. Bot.* 1894, **8**, 265-280.

13. LUDWIG, L.J., SAEKI, T. and EVANS, L.T. 'Photosynthesis in artificial communities of cotton-plants in relation to leaf area. 1. Experiments with progressive defoliation of mature plants', *Aust. J. biol. Sci.*, 1965, **18**, 1103-1118.

14. McCREE, K.J. 'An equation for the rate of respiration of white clover plants grown under controlled conditions', Proc. Int. Biol. Prog. Tech. Meeting. *Productivity of Photosynthetic Systems: Models and Methods* (in press), 1970.

15. McCREE, K.J. and TROUGHTON, J.H. 'Non-existence of an optimum leaf area index for the production rate of white clover grown under constant conditions', *Pl. Physiol. Lancaster*, 1966, **41**, 1615-1622.

16. MILTHORPE, F.L. and DAVIDSON, J.L. 'Physiological aspects of regorwth following defoliation', in *The growth of cereals and grasses*, Milthorpe, F.L. and J.D. Ivins (ed.): London: Butterworth, 241-53.

17. NEEDHAM, A.E. *The growth processes of animals* London: Pitman, 1964.

18. PRICE, C.A. 'Respiration and development of vegetative plant organs and tissues', in *Encyclopedia of Plant Physiology*, XII/2, W. Ruhland (ed.), Berlin: Springer, 1960, 491-520.

19. PRINZ ZUR LIPPE, A 'Uber den Einfluss des vorangegangen Licht-Dunkelwechsel auf die CO_2-Auscheidung der Primarblätter von Phaseolen-Multifloren in anschliessender Dunkelheit', *Z. Bot.*, 1956, **44**, 297-318.

20. SHIBLES, R.M. (Personal communication).

21. WENT, F.W. *The experimental control of plant growth*, Waltham, Mass., U.S.A.: Chronica Botanica Co., 1957.

22. WILLIAMS, W.A., LOOMIS, R.S. and LEPLEY, C.R. 'Vegetative growth of corn as affected by population density I', *Crop Sci.*, 1965, **5**, 211-215.

23. WIT, C.T. de 'Photosynthesis of leaf canopies', *Agric. Res. Rep.*, 1965, 663, 57 pp.

24. WIT, C.T. de 'Dynamic concepts in biology', Proc. Int. Biol. Prog. Tech. Meeting. *Productivity of Photosynthetic Systems: Models and Methods* (in press), 1970.

25. WIT, C.T. de and BROUWER, R. 'Über ein dynamisches Modell des vegetativen Wachstum von Pflanzenbestanden', *Angew. Bot.*, 1968, 42, 1-12.

9. Physiological Factors Limiting the Yield of Arable Crops

Gillian N. Thorne
Rothamsted Experimental Station, Harpenden, Herts.

Introduction

Many people have discussed the efficiency with which crops use CO_2 and light to produce carbohydrate. The physiological factors limiting both the rate at which dry matter is produced and the total annual production have been studied experimentally and theoretically, using mathematical models, but biologists have neglected the physiological factors limiting the yield of the useful parts of crops — the portion that interests the farmer and consumer. The general relationships of physiological factors with total or biological yield and economic yield are usually similar, but the quantitative relationships often differ. The quantitative relationships will be discussed in this paper.

The useful parts of the major British arable crops — cereals, potatoes and sugar beet — are composed almost entirely of carbohydrate and water. Also, most of the other dry matter in these and other arable produce is formed from carbon, hydrogen and oxygen, so we can regard arable crops as machines for converting CO_2 and water into carbohydrate, using the sun's energy. Mineral nutrients are needed for this process, but they can be supplied adequately from fertilizers or the soil. There is plenty of water as a raw material for synthesis of carbohydrate, and crops suffering from drought can be irrigated. But CO_2 and light are often limiting, and it is not practicable to increase them artificially in the field. So the physiological factors limiting yield are those that determine how efficiently crops convert the limited resources of CO_2 and light into carbohydrate, and how much of this carbohydrate moves into the storage organs that form the useful and economically valuable parts of the crop. These factors can be divided into

(a) the size of the leaf surface available for absorbing CO_2 and light,

(b) the rate of uptake of CO_2 per unit leaf area,

(c) the distribution of dry matter between useful and other parts of the plant.

Leaf Area

Leaf area is frequently correlated with growth and yield, and this is undoubtedly often a causal relationship. The relevant measure of leaf area to consider in relation to the final yield of total dry matter, or the useful part of most crops, is the integral of leaf area index (*L*) over the whole growth period, leaf area duration (*D*). *D* will increase if leaf area increases faster at the beginning of the growth period, if maximum *L* is increased, if *L* declines more slowly at the end of the growth period, or if the growth period is extended. Increasing *D* in one or more of these ways may increase yield.

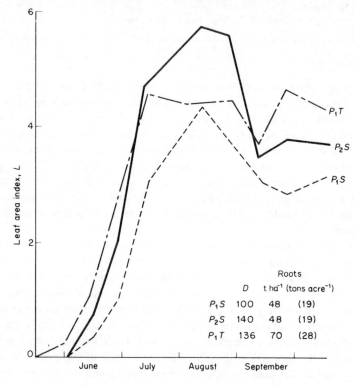

Fig. 9.1   *Change with time in leaf area index (L) of sugar beet.*
P₁ = 15 000 plants per acre (c. 37 000 plants per hectare)
P₂ = 30 000 plants per acre (c. 75 000 plants per hectare)
S = sown in the field on 23 April, T = transplanted to the field on
18 April. D = leaf area duration in arbitrary units; from Scott and
Bremner, [47].

Crop growth early in the season is often restricted because leaf area is too small to intercept all the incident radiation, and this limits final yield. In 1938, Watson and Baptiste [71] showed that sowing sugar beet earlier than was usual in agricultural practice increased yield, partly by increasing leaf area at the beginning of the growth period. Such early sowing is now normal. Scott and Bremner [47] increased early leaf growth still further by transplanting seedlings grown for five weeks in a greenhouse. With 15 000 plants per acre (37 000 ha^{-1}), the transplanted crop yielded 28 tons of roots (11 t ha^{-1} of sugar), 9 tons more than a crop sown in the open five days after transplanting. Transplanting increased D by 36 per cent. Doubling the plant population increased D by 40 per cent but did not increase the yield, probably because most of the increase in D resulted from larger L when the latter was already adequate, Figure 9.1. (see opposite). Increasing populations of sugar beet above the standard 30 000 per acre had only small effects on D and none on yield [22]. Yield of kale was also greatly increased when L early in the season was increased by sowing at the end of the previous summer [66]. Crops sown in August or September had a mean L of 2.0 at the end of May and yielded almost nine tons per acre of dry matter (22 t ha^{-1}) in the following October, whereas a commercial crop sown at the usual time in April had L of 0.06 at the end of May and yielded only 3.3 tons acre^{-1} (8.3 t ha^{-1}). The maximum leaf areas that are attained by many crops of sugar beet and potatoes seem to be adequate and it is unlikely that yields would increase if maximum L (L_{max}) were larger. Yields of sugar increased with increase in L_{max} up to 2.8 in one series of experiments [22] and up to 4.3 in another [23].

These values of optimum L_{max} were not determined precisely; yield decreased negligibly with larger values. The optimum may have been smaller in the 1966 experiments than in the 1968 ones because most of the values above 3 came from crops with more than 30 000 plants per acre. (c.f. Scott and Bremner, [47]).

An L_{max} of about 3 seems to be optimal for yield of potatoes also. When variety, seed size and spacing were varied, 57 per cent of the variation in tuber yield was accounted for by variation in D, but this increased to 80 per cent when D was calculated assuming that all values of L exceeding 3 equalled 3 [5]. As with sugar beet, closer spacing increased yield much less than it increased D: halving the spacing between plants within the rows increased D of King Edward by 20 per cent but increased yield by only 10 per cent. However, increasing the seed size increased yield similarly (by 9 per cent) although it increased D by only 4 per cent. This difference in response probably resulted from the timing of effects on L: larger seed increased L mainly in June, before it reached 3, whereas closer spacing had much of its effect in July when L was between 3 and 5 (Figure 9.2).

Presumably yield of sugar beet and potatoes fails to increase when L exceeds 3-4 because this is close to optimum L for crop growth rate, C (L at which C is maximal). Optimal L was not determined for the potato crops mentioned above; for the sugar-beet crops Scott and Bremner [47] quote 4-5 and Goodman [23] 3.5. The larger value of between 6 and 9 obtained by Watson [69], when L was varied by thinning, seems not to apply when different values of L are obtained by treatments applied continuously. Goodman found that final total dry-weight increased with increase in L_{max} beyond the optimum for C, presumably because, under these conditions, L approached the optimal value over a longer proportion of the growing period and so mean C was greater. However, the optimum value of L_{max} for yield of sugar was less than for total dry weight, and so was similar to the optimum value with respect to C.

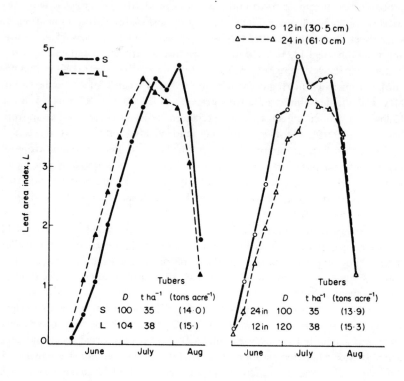

Fig. 9.2   Change with time in leaf area index (L) of King Edward potato
crops. Seed was small (S) or large (L) planted 12 in. (30.5 cm) or
24 in. (61.0 cm) apart in the rows.
D = leaf area duration in arbitrary units; from Bremner and Taha,
[5].

Increasing D by delaying senescence of the leaves is difficult to do
experimentally and hence has rarely been shown to increase yield. Applying
nitrogen fertilizer late or decreasing the temperature did delay death of wheat
leaves and increase grain yield [57, 58]. If wheat and barley leaves could be
made to stay green during more of the grain-filling period, as those of rice and
maize do, [1, 28], yields should increase considerably. There is little scope
for increasing yield and D by lengthening the growth period: for most of our
crops this already occupies all of the year when environmental conditions are
favourable for growth and photosynthesis [68].

Leaf area will not contribute equally to yield during all parts of the growth period because of environmental effects on the production and use of photosynthates. Also, the ontogenetic development of the plant may cause carbohydrate supply to be especially critical for the growth of the storage organs at certain times. Sugar-beet roots and potato tubers accumulate carbohydrate throughout most of the growth period, and the stage during which the basic annular structure of the sugar-beet tap-root is formed, or before tubers are initiated, occurs when L is only small and so contributes little to D [70]. Cereal grains, on the other hand, start accumulating carbohydrate only at anthesis, when L has reached its maximum. Leaf area before anthesis does not contribute directly to yield, and after anthesis leaves below the flag-leaf node contribute little even when well exposed to light. The evidence that L above the flag-leaf node (L_f) and the duration of this between anthesis and maturity (D_f) are the parts of total L and D relevant to grain yield has been summarised elsewhere [54]. L_f has been measured in only a few experiments [48, 59, 80] and so our knowledge of the effects of leaf area on grain yield are largely based on total L. This may not matter as L and L_f are usually fairly closely correlated.

D_f and yield would increase if the leaves survived longer (see above) and might also if L_{max} were increased, e.g. by more shoots or larger flag leaves. Optimum L_{max} for grain yield seems to be at least 10, which is greater than most of the values recorded. This is probably more than the optimal value of L_{max} for C before anthesis, which may be about 9 [72, 77], as photosynthesis of all the leaves contributes to C but of only some of them to grain yield, and the upper leaves probably shade each other less than the lower ones. The experimental evidence is largely circumstantial. For example, the decrease in grain:leaf ratio, G, (grain yield divided by post-anthesis D) with increase in L_{max} was much less than the analagous decrease in net assimilation rate with increase in L before flowering, generally considered to be caused by self-shading [73, 78]. Also, variation in grain:leaf ratio between years could be accounted for satisfactorily by environmental factors with no suggestion of a depression in G when L was large, such as would indicate that optimum L had been exceeded [81]. However, L_{max} in all these experiments never exceeded 9 and was usually less than 7. Increasing L_{max} above 10 by sowing more densely than normal did not increase grain yield of barley, although it did increase total dry weight ([31] and Kirby, personal communication). However, this may indicate that severe competition before anthesis, and not extreme self-shading after anthesis, decreased the potential ear size or sink (see below).

The evidence given above suggests that, at certain times of the year, leaf area limits the yield of arable crops and that there is scope for improvement. Increasing L early in growth would be best, except that cereals with longer survival of leaves should be valuable. Yield is unlikely to increase with maximum leaf area indexes above 3-5 for sugar beet and potato crops or above 10 for cereals, but neither is it likely to be depressed. Increasing plant density is not a profitable way of increasing leaf area.

Photosynthesis

Apart from the effects of radiation on photosynthesis, growth and yield, evidence of causal relations between yield and net uptake of CO_2 is much scarcer than of those between yield and leaf area, but small differences in CO_2 uptake may be important in determining differences in yield between crops if they persist and affect leaf area. The net CO_2 uptake by the whole plant per unit leaf area, usually estimated as net assimilation rate E, includes apparent photosynthesis (the net uptake of CO_2 by leaves in the light), respiration by the leaves in the dark, and respiration by the non-photosynthetic tissues during the whole twenty-four hours. Respiratory loss of CO_2 by crops may be a sizeable proportion of the photosynthetic gain [21]. but insufficient is known about respiration to permit discussing its role as a factor limiting yield. Moreover, many of the differences found in E are caused by differences in photosynthesis, not respiration [74, 79].

Differences in the rates of photosynthesis of crops may arise from differences in arrangement of the leaves which affect mutual shading, or from inherent differences in rates of photosynthesis due to biochemical or other 'internal' factors. Theoretically, when L is large, crops with upright leaves should photosynthesise faster per unit of leaf area than crops with horizontally disposed leaves [15, 37]. This effect has been obtained experimentally. Yield of maize was increased when the upper leaves were held erect by tying them to the stem [46]. Conversely, weighting the tips of normally erect rice leaves so that they were positioned more horizontally decreased photosynthesis in dense stands, but not when plants were widely spaced [35]. Pearce, Brown and Blaser [44, 45] obtained artificial communities with different values of L and different leaf dispositions by growing barley seedlings at different densities in boxes tilted at various angles and then placing all the boxes horizontally. The boxes of erect plants absorbed more CO_2 than boxes of inclined ones only when L exceeded 3, and especially in bright light, as predicted by Monsi and Saeki's model [37].

Differences in leaf angle between varieties of some of our arable crops may account for differences in net assimilation rate (E), as they seem to do in some grasses [9]. The greater E and yield of cultivated than of wild sugar-beet when L exceeds 1 was explained by differences in leaf arrangement [75]. Japanese varieties of rice adapted to high levels of fertilizer, presumably those that yield well when L is large, have small upright leaves [62], and such varieties grow faster at a given L than ones with more horizontally disposed leaves, because light penetrates further into the crop [24]. Small upright leaves may be equally advantageous for temperate cereals; almost all the largest-yielding varieties of wheat, barley and oats in a collection of 300 at the University of Guelph had narrow, upright leaves, whereas the smaller-yielding varieties had long, floppy leaves [51]. Detailed growth analysis of these different types has not been published.

In dense crops, even with erect leaves, E may be inversely correlated with

L because mutual shading with increase in L decreases the average intensity of light reaching the leaves and hence slows photosynthesis; e.g. the greater E of spring than of winter wheat was entirely a consequence of its smaller L [77]. A similar explanation probably accounts for the greater E of potato varieties that had smaller values of L [69]. Of course, large values of E caused in this way cannot be selected in breeding for increased yield.

The search for variations in photosynthesis within species that are not the consequence of differences in leaf arrangement, but are caused by inherent differences in the photosynthetic mechanism, has revealed many examples of plants differing in growth rate and yield but with similar rates of photosynthesis, some where rates of photosynthesis varied without affecting yield, and a few where faster photosynthesis seemed to increase growth and yield. For example, potato varieties differing greatly in plant form, date of maturity and yield had similar rates of photosynthesis [8]; photosynthetic rates of modern varieties of cultivated wheat were no greater than those of some wild ancestors [19]; higher rates of photosynthesis did account for the greater yield of one of two varieties of soybean [6] and one of two varieties of *Phaseolus vulgaris* [29, 64]. Varietal differences in photosynthesis appear more often between varieties originating from widely different climatic regions than between those adapted to similar environments. This has been observed with wheat [50], barley [43] and maize [14]. The expression of such genotypic differences may depend on the environment in which the plant was grown and photosynthesis measured; e.g. photosynthetic rates of races of maize from high altitudes were higher than of races from lower altitudes when the temperature at which the plants were grown, and photosynthesis was measured, was $15°C$, but the rates were lower at temperatures warmer than $27°C$ [14]. Similar phenomena are well documented for grasses [16, 17]. In many of these recent studies of variation in photosynthetic rates within and between species, large differences in leaf area occurred which were not correlated with rates of photosynthesis. This led Duncan and Hesketh [14] to conclude, as Watson [67] did more than twenty years earlier, that dry weight usually depends more on leaf expansion than on photosynthesis. Until recently, no differences in rate of photosynthesis had been detected between varieties of cereals grown in this country that differed in yield [33, 52, 53]. However, differences in photosynthesis which may explain differences in yield have now been found between Professor Marchal and Cappelle Desprez winter wheat, and between dwarf and tall selections of winter wheat [3, 34]. A similar difference was found by Natr [39] between some Czech varieties of winter wheat.

An exciting recent discovery that affects any consideration of photosynthesis as a factor limiting yield is that there are two groups of plants with different photosynthetic mechanisms: one with and one without photorespiration. Species without photorespiration grow and photosynthesise faster at high temperatures and light intensities than those with photorespiration. The groups differ in other respects such as leaf anatomy, the biochemical pathway of CO_2 fixation, and the response of photosynthesis to environmental factors [11, 18, 25]. Species without photorespiration are mostly tropical grasses of the chloridoid-eragrostoid and panicoid lines, such as maize, sorghum and sugar cane, whereas festucoid grasses and most dicotyledons have photorespiration [13]. If more crop species can be found which lack photorespiration, it may be possible to use them in breeding for reduced photorespiration and hence higher rates of photosynthesis and growth. When French beans were made to behave like tropical grasses by decreasing the oxygen concentration of the air from 21 per cent to 2.5 or 5 per cent, dry weight at the end of experiments lasting six or seventeen days was doubled [4].

Exceptions to the systemic division between the two types are being found. Photorespiration is absent in some, but not all, genera within the Amaranthaceae; both types also occur within the Chenopodiaceae and even within one genus, *Atriplex* [27, 60]. The two types have also been found within the genus *Panicum* [12]. Tobacco normally shows photorespiration, as do other dicotyledons, but Zelitch and Day [82] found a variety with an unusually low rate of photorespiration and also a high rate of net photosynthesis. They conclude that 'genetic manipulation of photorespiration is now feasible'.

Many other properties of plants, apart from photorespiration, have been suggested as the main one limiting the rate of photosynthesis: e.g. diffusion resistance [21] or enzyme activity [61, 65]. But Meidner [36] has suggested that unjustifiable conclusions may have been reached from some of the evidence. Doubtless more variability in photosynthetic rates will be found and used in breeding as more material is examined and the causes of the variability elucidated.

Distribution of Dry Matter

However large the total dry weight of a crop, agricultural yield will depend on the distribution of dry matter, i.e. on the proportion of the total dry weight that is found in the economically useful part — the harvest index [10]. This proportion obviously increased during domestication of cultivated species from their wild ancestors, and appears to be still doing so. It is larger in modern than in old varieties of spring barley, spring and winter wheat [76, 77] and larger still in short varieties of spring wheat derived from Norin 10 [59]. Present maximum values of harvest index may be increased still further by breeding, although there must be an upper limit. Yield of the useful parts will increase with increase in total dry weight as long as harvest index remains constant, but will not do so if the capacity of the storage organs for carbohydrate, the sink capacity, is limited. Such a limitation may restrict economic yield though not total dry-matter production, or it may slow photosynthesis and restrict total dry-matter production also. There is plenty of evidence that decreasing sink capacity decreases yield; it is more difficult to prove that yields would be increased above their present maximum values if sink capacities were increased.

Decreasing the sink capacity of potato plants by removing some of the developing tubers decreased yield, because carbohydrate that would otherwise have moved to the tubers accumulated in the tops, and because a slower net assimilation rate decreased total dry matter production [7, 41]. Similarly, E of sugar-beet 'plants', composed of sugar-beet tops grafted onto sugar-beet roots, decreased when the sink was decreased by replacing the sugar-beet root by the smaller root of spinach-beet, and also E of spinach-beet leaves was increased when the spinach-beet root was replaced by the larger sugar-beet root [56]. Analogous effects of root size have been observed in the field: sugar-beet plants transplanted from growth cabinets had greater E throughout the season than ones sown directly in the field or raised in an unheated glasshouse, apparently because the plants from the growth cabinets had a greater root:top ratio [20]. These increases in E with increase in sink capacity must be caused by higher photosynthetic rate, not lower respiration rate, because the larger proportion of the total dry weight accounted for by tubers or roots would increase respiration per unit leaf area. Decreasing sink capacity of barley by removing some developing grains caused carbohydrate that would otherwise have moved to the ears to accumulate in the stems and roots [42], but neither this treatment, nor removal of complete ears of wheat, reduced the photosynthetic rate of the flag leaf appreciably [33, 55]. However, in certain conditions, photosynthesis of wheat flag leaves can be greatly decreased by removing the ears [30].

One expression of sink capacity that has been measured in cereals is the efficiency of translocation, i.e. the proportion of the ^{14}C in a plant found in the grains following treatment of a leaf with $^{14}CO_2$. More efficient translocation has rarely been shown to increase yield directly: there was no difference between three Swedish varieties that differed in yield [49]; some varietal differences were found by Lupton [32]. but could not be associated with yield.

Yield may be limited by the sink capacity of the useful parts of crops and simultaneously by the supply of carbohydrate. E of potato plants was less in 40 per cent daylight than in full daylight, and was also decreased by removing tubers in both light intensities [41]. Grain yield of wheat was correlated with the number of grains per ear with fourteen or eighteen hours of light per day, although grain yield was less with the shorter day [57]. With four different numbers of grains on ears of wheat the remaining grains grew larger with each decrease in number because the supply of carbohydrate per grain increased, but the larger size never compensated for the smaller number, indicating that sink capacity of the individual grains, as well as the supply of carbohydrate, was limiting growth [3].

Sink capacity is an ill-defined term that describes behaviour rather than indicating the cause of that behaviour. Its physiological determinants are still unknown, though both growth substances and enzymes have been suggested. The control of the movement of assimilates by sink capacity mentioned above may be mediated by growth substances produced in the sinks e.g. auxin and gibberellins [26]. Decreases in sink capacity may slow photosynthesis because carbohydrates accumulate in the leaves; possible mechanisms are discussed by Neales and Incoll [40]. However, the soluble carbohydrate content of flag leaves of wheat changed little when their photosynthesis was altered by manipulating the sink [30]. Sinks may also control photosynthesis by producing growth substances which affect either the photosynthetic process directly [2, 63] or the concentration of relevant enzymes. For example, when source:sink relationships were changed by removing some of the leaves from young plants of dwarf beans, maize and willow, the remaining leaves photosynthesised faster and carboxylating enzymes were more active [65]. Larger quantities of enzymes may have been synthesised because more cytokinins from the roots reached the fewer leaves.

Conclusions

The yields of cereal grain, sugar, or dry matter in potato tubers obtainable at the present time from good crops represent less than 3 per cent conversion of the available visible radiation (Table 9.1), whereas the theoretical maximum is 18 per cent [38]. So theoretically there is plenty of potential for improving yield; the experimental evidence indicates that some of this potential can be realised.

Increased leaf area could increase yield, particularly if leaf growth were faster in the cool conditions of early May; greater maximum leaf area indices are unlikely to increase yield much, unless the arrangement of sugar-beet and potato leaves can be changed so that light penetrates deeper into the canopy;

Table 9.1
Percentage conversion of visible radiation into arable produce
Calculated using visible radiation = 45% total solar radiation at Rothamsted and assuming that all dry matter = glucose having heat of combustion of 3.73 kcal g^{-1}

Product	Agricultural yield (t ha^{-1})	Dry matter (ha^{-1})	Useful radiation	Energy conversion
Cereal grain	7	6	mid June-mid August	2.0%
Beet sugar	50 (roots)	8 (sugar)	June-October	1.5%
Potato tubers	50	12	June-September	2.4%

slower death of leaves of cereals and perhaps also of potato might be beneficial. However, there is little historical evidence that yields have increased through more leaf growth except indirectly: use of bolting-resistant sugar-beet gains the advantage of early sowing (see p. 144), and stiff-strawed cereals have large leaf area because they can be given much nitrogen fertilizer without lodging. Higher photosynthetic rates resulting from inherent differences in the photosynthetic mechanism, or possibly also from better-arranged leaves, could increase yield. This has rarely occurred in the past, but the variability in photosynthesis now being discovered suggests that yields will be increased this way in the future. Past experience indicates that the most likely way yields will increase is by improvement in sink capacity that will result in better dry-matter distribution, rather than greater total dry-matter production. Experimental evidence, and the recent production of new varieties with greatly increased harvest indices, such as the dwarf wheats and IR8 rice, suggest that increased sink capacity will continue to be a profitable source of improved yields. So it seems to be physiologically feasible for our arable crops to yield considerably more than they do at present; it remains for the plant breeders to realise this potential.

REFERENCES

1. ALLISON, J.C.S. 'A comparison between maize and wheat in respect of leaf area after flowering and grain growth', *J. agric. Sci. Camb.*, 1964, 63, 1-4.
2. BIDWELL, R.G.S. and TURNER, W.B. 'Effect of growth regulators on CO_2 assimilation in leaves, and its correlation with bud break response in photosynthesis', *Pl. Physiol., Lancaster*, 1966, 41, 267-70.
3. BINGHAM, J. 'Investigations on the physiology of yield in winter wheat, by comparison of varieties and by artificial variation in grain number per ear', *J. agric. Sci. Camb.*, 1967, 68, 411-22.
4. BJORKMAN, O. 'Effect of oxygen concentration on dry matter production in higher plants', *Yb. Carnegie Instn. Washington*, 1967, 66, 228-32.
5. BREMNER, P.M. and TAHA, M.A. 'Studies in potato agronomy. I. The effect of variety, seed size and spacing on growth, development and yield', *J. agric. Sci. Camb.*, 1966, 66, 241-52.
6. BRUN, W.A. and COOPER, R.L. 'Effects of light intensity and carbon dioxide concentration on photosynthetic rate of soybean', *Crop Sci.*, 1967, 7, 451-4.
7. BURT, R.L. 'Carbohydrate utilization as a factor in plant growth', *Aust. J. biol. Sci.*, 1964, 17, 867-77.
8. CHAPMAN, H.W. and LOOMIS, W.E. 'Photosynthesis in the potato under field conditions', *Pl. Physiol. Lancaster*, 1953, 28, 703-16.
9. COOPER, J.P. 'The significance of genetic variation in light interception and conversion for forage-plant breeding', *Proc. 10th int. Grassld. Congr.*, 1967, 715-20.
10. DONALD, C.M. 'In search of yield', *J. Aust. Inst. agric. Sci.*, 1962, 28, 171-8.
11. DOWNES, R.W. and HESKETH, J.D. 'Enhanced photosynthesis at low oxygen concentrations: differential response of temperate and tropical grasses', *Planta*, 1968, 78, 79-84.

12. DOWNTON, W.J.S., BERRY, J. and TREGUNNA, E.B. 'Photosynthesis: temperate and tropical characteristics within a single grass genus', *Science, N.Y.*, 1969, **163**, 78-9.

13. DOWNTON, W.J.S. and TREGUNNA, E.B. 'Carbon dioxide compensation — its relation to photosynthetic carboxylation reactions, systematics of the Gramineae, and leaf anatomy', *Can. J. Bot.*, 1968, **46**, 207-15.

14. DUNCAN, W.G. and HESKETH, J.D. 'Net photosynthetic rates, relative leaf growth rates, and leaf numbers of 22 races of maize grown at eight temperatures', *Crop Sci.*, 1968, **8**, 670-4.

15. DUNCAN, W.G., LOOMIS, R.S., WILLIAMS, W.A. and HANAU, R. 'A model for simulating photosynthesis in plant communities', *Hilgardia*, 1967, **38**, 181-205.

16. EAGLES, C.F. 'Apparent photosynthesis and respiration in populations of *Lolium perenne* from contrasting climatic regions', *Nature, Lond.*, 1967, **215**, 100-101.

17. EAGLES, C.F. and TREHARNE, K.J. 'Photosynthetic activity of *Dactylis glomerata* L. in different light regimes', *Photosynthetica*, 1969, **3**, 29-38.

18. EL-SHARKAWY, M.A. and HESKETH, J.D. 'Photosynthesis among species in relation to characteristics of leaf anatomy and CO_2 diffusion resistances', *Crop Sci.*, 1965, **5**, 517-21.

19. EVANS, L.T., HESKETH, J.D., PATON, D. and WARDLAW, I.F. 'Yield determination', *Rep. Div. Pl. Industry, C.S.I.R.O.*, 1966, 70-1.

20. FRENCH, S.A.W. and HUMPHRIES, E.C. 'Effect of seedling treatment on growth of sugar beet', *Rep. Rothamsted exp. Stn. for 1968*, 1969, 99-100.

21. GAASTRA, P. 'Climatic control of photosynthesis and respiration', in *Environmental Control of Plant Growth*, Ed. L.T. Evans, New York: Academic Press, 1963.

22. GOODMAN, P.J. 'Effect of varying plant populations on growth and yield of sugar beet', *Agric. Prog.*, 1966, **41**, 82-100.

23. GOODMAN, P.J. 'Physiological analysis of the effects of different soils on sugar-beet crops in different years', *J. appl. Ecol.*, 1968, **5**, 339-57.

24. HAYASHI, K. and ITO, H. 'Studies on the form of plant in rice varieties with particular reference to the efficiency in utilising sunlight. I. The significance of extinction coefficient in rice plant communities', *Proc. Crop Sci. Soc. Japan.*, 1962, **30**, 329-33.

25. HESKETH, J.D. 'Enhancement of photosynthetic CO_2 assimilation in the absence of oxygen, as dependent upon species and temperature', *Planta*, 1967, **76**, 371-4.

26. HEW, C.S., NELSON, C.D. and KROTKOV, G. 'Hormonal control of translocation of photosynthetically assimilated ^{14}C in young soybean plants', *Am. J. Bot.*, 1967, **54**, 252-6.

27. HOFSTRA, G. and HESKETH, J.D. 'Effects of temperature on the gas exchange of leaves in the light and dark', *Planta*, 1969, **85**, 228-37.

28. I.R.R.I. 'Plant Physiology', *Rep. Int. Rice Res. Inst. for 1966*, 1967, 18.
29. IZHAR, S. and WALLACE, D.H. 'Studies of the physiological basis for yield differences. III. Genetic variation in photosynthetic efficiency of *Phaseolus vulgaris* L', *Crop Sci.*, 1967, **7**, 457-60.
30. KING, R.W., WARDLAW, I.F. and EVANS, L.T. 'Effect of assimilate utilisation on photosynthetic rate in wheat', *Planta*, 1967, **77**, 261-76.
31. KIRBY, E.J.M. 'The effect of plant density upon the growth and yield of barley', *J. agric. Sci. Camb.*, 1967, **68**, 317-24.
32. LUPTON, F.G.H. 'Translocation of photosynthetic assimilates in wheat', *Ann. appl. Biol.*, 1966, **57**, 355-64.
33. LUPTON, F.G.H. 'The analysis of grain yield of wheat in terms of photosynthetic ability and efficiency of translocation', *Ann. appl. Biol.*, 1968, **61**, 109-19.
34. LUPTON, F.G.H. and BINGHAM, J. 'Winter wheat: Physiology of yield', *Breed, Inst. 1968*, 1969, 53-5.
35. MATSUSHIMA, S., TANAKA, T. and HOSHINO, T. 'Analysis of yield-determining process and its application to yield-prediction and culture improvement of lowland rice. LXVIII. On the relation between morphological characteristics and photosynthetic efficiency (1)', *Proc. Crop Sci. Soc. Japan*, 1964, **33**, 44-48.
36. MEIDNER, H. "Rate limiting' resistances to photosynthesis', *Nature*, 1969, **222**, 876-7.
37. MONSI, M. and SAEKI, T. 'Über den Lichtfaktor in den Pflanzengesellschaften und Seine Bedeutung für die Stoffproduktion', *Jap. J. Bot.*, 1953, **14**, 22-52.
38. MONTEITH, J.L. 'The photosynthesis and transpiration of crops', *Expl. Agric.*, 1966, **2**, 1-14.
39. NATR, L. 'The varietal differences in the intensity of photosynthesis', *Sb. Csl. Akad. Zemed. Ved. Rada C.*, 1966, **12**, 163-78.
40. NEALES, T.F. and INCOLL, L.D. 'The control of leaf photosynthesis rate by the level of assimilate concentration in the leaf: A review of the hypothesis', *Bot. Rev.*, 1968, **34**, 107-25.
41. NÖSBERGER, J. and HUMPHRIES, E.C. 'The influence of removing tubers on dry matter production and net assimilation rate of potato plant', *Ann. Bot. N.S.*, 1965, **29**, 579-88.
42. NÖSBERGER, J. and THORNE, G.N. 'The effect of removing florets or shading the ear of barley on production and distribution of dry matter', *Ann. Bot. N.S.*, 1965, **29**, 635-44.
43. ORMROD, D.P., HUBBARD, W.F. and FARIS, D.G. 'Effect of temperature on net carbon dioxide exchange rates of twelve barley varieties', *Can. J. Pl. Sci.*, 1968, **48**, 363-8.
44. PEARCE, R.B., BROWN, R.H. and BLASER, R.E. 'Photosynthesis in plant communities as influenced by leaf angle', *Crop Sci.*, 1967, **7**, 321-4.
45. ————— 'Net photosynthesis of barley seedlings as influenced by leaf area index', *Crop Sci.*, 1967, **7**, 545-6.

46. PENDLETON, J.W., SMITH, G.E., WINTER, S.R. and JOHNSTON, T.J. 'Field investigations of the relationship of leaf angle in corn (*Zea mays* L.) to grain yield and apparent photosynthesis', *Agron. J.* 1968, **60**, 422-4.

47. SCOTT, R.K. and BREMNER, P.M. 'The effects on growth, development and yield of sugar beet of extension of the growth period by transplantation', *J. agric. Sci. Camb.*, 1966, **66**, 379-88.

48. SIMPSON, G.M. 'Association between grain yield per plant and photosynthetic area above the flag-leaf node in wheat', *Can. J. Pl. Sci.*, 1968, **48**, 253-60.

49. STOY, V. 'The translocation of the C^{14}-labelled photosynthetic products from the leaf to the ear in wheat', *Physiologia Pl.*, 1963, **16**, 851-66.

50. STOY, V. 'Photosynthesis, respiration, and carbohydrate accumulation in spring wheat in relation to yield', *Physiologia Pl. Suppl. IV.*, 1965, 1-125.

51. TANNER, J.W., GARDENER, C.J., STOSKOPF, N.C. and REINBERGS, E. 'Some observations on upright-leaf-type small grains', *Can. J. Pl. Sci.*, 1966, **46**, 690.

52. THORNE, G.N. 'Varietal differences in photosynthesis of ears and leaves of barley', *Ann. Bot. N.S.*, 1963, **27**, 155-74.

53. THORNE, G.N., 'Photosynthesis of ears and flag leaves of wheat and barley', *Ann. Bot. N.S.*, 1965, **29**, 317-29.

54. THORNE, G.N., 'Physiological aspects of grain yield in cereals', in *The Growth of Cereals and Grasses*, eds. F.L. Milthorpe and J.D. Ivins, London: Butterworth, 88-105.

55. THORNE, G.N., 'Photosynthesis of flag-leaf laminae of cereals', *Rep. Rothamsted exp. Stn. for 1965*, 1966, 100-1.

56. THORNE, G.N. and EVANS, A.F. 'Influence of tops and roots on net assimilation rate of sugar beet and spinach beet and grafts between them', *Ann. Bot. N.S.*, 1964, **28**, 499-508.

57. THORNE, G.N., FORD, M.A., and WATSON, D.J. 'Growth, development and yield of spring wheat in artificial climates', *Ann. Bot.*, 1968, **32**, 425-45.

58. THORNE, G.N. and WATSON, D.J. 'The effect on yield and leaf area of wheat of applying nitrogen as a top-dressing in April or in sprays at ear emergence', *J. agric. Sci. Camb.*, 1955, **46**, 449-56.

59. THORNE, G.N., WELBANK, P.J. and BLACKWOOD, G.C. 'Growth and yield of six short varieties of spring wheat derived from Norin 10 and of two European varieties', *Ann. appl. Biol.*, 1969, **63**, 241-51.

60. TREGUNNA, E.B. and DOWNTON, W.J.S. 'Carbon dioxide compensation in members of the *Amaranthaceae* and related families', *Can. J. Bot.*, 1967, **45**, 2385-7.

61. TREHARNE, K.J. and COOPER, J.P. 'Effect of temperature on the activity of carboxylases in tropical and temperate *Gramineae*', *J. exp. Bot.*, 1969, **20**, 170-5.

62. TSUNODA, S. 'Leaf characters and nitrogen response', in *The Mineral Nutrition of the Rice Plant*, Baltimore, U.S.A.: John Hopkins Press,

401-18.

63. TURNER, W.B. and BIDWELL, R.G.S. 'Rates of photosynthesis in attached and detached bean leaves, and the effect of spraying with indoleacetic acid solution', *Pl. Physiol. Lancaster*, 1965, **40**, 446-51.

64. WALLACE, D.H. and MUNGER, H.M. 'Studies of the physiological basis for yield differences. II. Variation in dry matter distribution among aerial organs for several dry bean varieties', *Crop Sci.*, 1966, **6**, 503-7.

65. WAREING, P.F., KHALIFA, M.M. and TREHARNE, K.J. 'Rate-limiting processes in photosynthesis at saturating light intensities', *Nature*, 1968, **220**, 453-7.

66. WARNE, L.G.G. 'Potential productivity of marrow stem and thousand-headed kale', *Nature, Lond.*, 1961, **192**, 579.

67. WATSON, D.J. 'Comparative physiological studies on the growth of field crops. I. Variation in net assimilation rate and leaf area between species and varieties, and within and between years', *Ann. Bot. N.S.*, 1947, **11**, 41-76.

68. WATSON, D.J., 'Leaf growth in relation to crop yield', in *The growth of leaves*, ed. F.L. Milthorpe, London: Butterworth, 178-91.

69. WATSON, D.J., 'The dependence of net assimilation rate on leaf-area index', *Ann. Bot. N.S.*, 1958, **22**, 37-54.

70. WATSON, D.J., 'Size, structure and activity of the productive systems of crops', in *Potential Crop Production*, eds. J.P. Cooper and P.F. Wareing, London: Heinemann.

71. WATSON, D.J. and BAPTISTE, E.C.D. 'A comparative physiological study of sugar beet and mangold with respect to growth and sugar accumulation. I. Growth analysis of the crop in the field', *Ann. Bot. N.S.*, 1938, **2**, 437-80.

72. WATSON, D.J. and FRENCH, S.A.W. 'Dependence of net assimilation rate of barley on leaf-area index', *Rep. Rothamsted exp. Stn. for 1957*, 1958, 90-1.

73. WATSON, D.J. and FRENCH, S.A.W. 'Competition within a wheat crop', *Rep. Rothamsted exp. Stn. for 1960*, 1961, 94.

74. WATSON, D.J. and HAYASHI, K. 'Photosynthetic and respiratory components of the net assimilation rates of sugar beet and barley', *New Phytol.*, 1965, **64**, 38-57.

75. WATSON, D.J. and WITTS, K.J. 'The net assimilation rates of wild and cultivated beets', *Ann. Bot. N.S.*, 1959, **23**, 431-9.

76. WATSON, D.J., THORNE, G.N. and FRENCH, S.A.W. 'Physiological causes of differences in grain yield between varieties of barley', *Ann. Bot. N.S.*, 1958, **22**, 321-52.

77. WATSON, D.J., THORNE, G.N. and FRENCH, S.A.W. 'Analysis of growth and yield of winter and spring wheats', *Ann. Bot. N.S.*, 1963, **27**, 1-22.

78. WATSON, D.J. 'Competition between rows of a wheat crop', *Rep. Rothamsted exp. Stn. for 1962*, 1963, 85-6.

79. WATSON, D.J., WILSON, J.H., FORD, M.A. and FRENCH, S.A.W. 'Changes with age in the photosynthetic and respiratory components of the net assimilation rates of sugar beet and wheat', New Phytol., 1966, 65, 500-8.

80. WELBANK, P.J., FRENCH, S.A.W. and WITTS, K.J. 'Dependence of yields of wheat varieties on their leaf area durations', Ann. Bot. N.S., 1966, 30, 291-9.

81. WELBANK, P.J., WITTS, K.J. and THORNE, G.N. 'Effect of radiation and temperature on efficiency of cereal leaves during grain growth', Ann. Bot. N.S., 1968, 32, 79-95.

82. ZELITCH, I. and DAY, P.R. 'Variation in photorespiration. The effect of genetic differences in photorespiration on net photosynthesis in tobacco', Pl. Physiol. Lancaster, 1968, 43, 1838-44.

10. Potential Production of Grassland

Th. Alberda
Institute for Biological and Chemical Research on Field Crops and Herbage,
Wageningen, Netherlands.

The potential production of vegetation or of a crop can be defined as the production of dry matter over a period of time during which the roots are under optimal growing conditions as regards the supply of water, minerals and oxygen, so that the growth rate is determined by the incoming light energy. In agriculture, it is important to know the potential production of a crop, as either the total biomass produced or the agriculturally important part of it. It must be pointed out, however, that in the latter case the highest possible economic yield is often not obtained under the optimal conditions for total biomass production (e.g. grain yield). But in the grass crop, the *total* above-ground production is important, and we can attempt to provide optimal soil conditions for maximum production.

The aim of increasing production is obviously as old as agriculture itself. It is only during the second half of the last century and the beginning of this century that plant physiology and agricultural chemistry had developed far enough for the fundamental facts of crop production to be understood. This subject was treated in a very clear and elegant way by Boysen Jensen in 1932, but it was only after 1950 that a large number of papers appeared which attempted to calculate the potential production of a closed crop from the available physical and physiological data [9, 14, 16, 19]. Following these papers, attempts were made to compare such calculations with actual production values [1, 5, 13, 18]. With the development of computer techniques, an important advance has been possible in recent years [12, 20] in that all the available information from plant physiology and meteorology can be used in a programme to calculate the potential rate of dry-matter production of crops which possess certain well-defined characteristics.

It is not, however, necessary to calculate this potential production in order to obtain the highest possible production from the grass crop, as demonstrated by a letter written by W. Dickinson to Lord Portman [10] in 1847. The following statements are taken almost literally from this letter:

'I had a new method of cultivating a peculiar plant — Italian rye-grass — the result of which was as startling as it was new, whereby nine or ten crops of excellent green food had been obtained between March and December; being cut in the former month and watered with liquid manure, consisting of one-third of pure horse urine and two-thirds of water, distributed from a London street water-cart passing once over the plant immediately after the grass was cut, one watering being sufficient for one crop.

'The method I recommended was to prepare the land by ploughing, cleaning, and reducing it to a fine surface in the month of August or September, to sow by a broadcast machine two bushels of seed per acre, to harrow lightly in, handweed the first growth, and, as soon as there was about 18 inches of grass, to cut it for green food.

'I have never failed to produce every year from seven to ten crops. I have been convinced it luxuriates in a dry subsoil rather than not retentive, that it will grow rapidly in the strongest clays if not poisoned with stagnant water, that it grows fast in any light soil well irrigated with liquid manure. I have grown it in sand from the sea-shore, moistened with liquid manure. I have a full conviction that with abundance of manure, and especially liquid manure, it is possible to grow 40 or even 50 tons of rye-grass per acre in a single season.

'Knowing something of the value of urine, and the profit to be derived from it, I undertook as a preliminary step the construction of tanks. I think no man has, in the first instance, made tanks enough to contain the urine made on his farm during the winter months to be applied during the summer.

'One of these tanks, containing 1000 gallons, costs £2. 17. 6. If all the water is caught from farm horses, cows, pigs, farm servants, household servants, the tanks would be filled very quickly; and whenever the tank containing 1000 gallons of urine is properly applied to Italian rye-grass, the result will show it is not too high an estimate to calculate the tank and drains paid for.

'The first application will convince the grower of 10 acres of this grass that his present stock is insufficient to eat it. He must add to it, and thereby increase the quantity of urine considerably, and so go on to keep a much larger farming stock altogether. The often-asked question "How shall I obtain urine enough?", will cease to be asked, and the amount of solid faeces so much increased as to obviate the necessity for a constant outlay of capital to procure it.'

These statements of Dickinson can now be compared with our present knowledge of the potential of the grass crop.

Let us first consider the production of the crop. Dickinson mentions a yearly production up to 50 tons of grass per acre. Since his 'long ton' will be equivalent to 1016 kg, this yearly production amounts to 125.5 metric tons ha^{-1}, or, assuming a dry matter percentage of 15 per cent, 18.8 t dry herbage ha^{-1}. In 1967 Cooper [8] obtained a dry herbage production of 29 t ha^{-1}, while Alberda [2] obtained 22 t ha^{-1} in the Netherlands. In the following year in the Netherlands, the maximum yield was only 18 t ha^{-1}. The difference between the Welsh and the Dutch yield in 1967 was almost entirely due to some growth during the winter months in the milder climate of Wales. Assuming that the winter climate in the London area is similar to that in the Netherlands, the conclusion can be drawn that no substantial increase in dry herbage production has been achieved during more than one hundred years since Dickinson's results. This is not surprising, since calculations with de Wit's [20] computer programme showed that these levels of production are close to what can be expected on the basis of incoming light energy, with some variation due to the relative dry-matter production above and below the cutting level and to the rate of respiration. During these past 120 years our insight into the factors determining herbage production has increased, but not the maximum production itself.

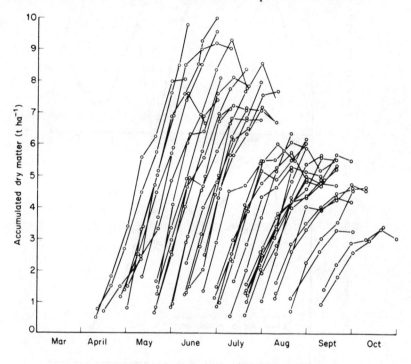

Fig. 10.1   Herbage dry-matter production of closed swards on different soils and during different years; from Alberda and Sibma [4].

The second important point in Dickinson's letter is his statement about the effect of soil conditions. If we are to obtain maximum total dry-matter production, the soil conditions must be optimal as regards the supply of water, minerals and oxygen. Dickinson supplied the necessary water and minerals in the form of diluted horse urine and observed that the type of soil was not of much importance as long as it was not 'poisoned with stagnant water'. Apparently he was guided by experience as to the amount of urine necessary for maximum production; we now know rather more about the minimum levels of the most important minerals in the plant [21], and in our fertilizer applications we were guided by this knowledge. But the result is the same; the type of soil becomes less important the closer we get to the optimal supply of water and minerals. As Figure 10.1 indicates, growth rate determinations, carried out in different years and on different soils, show only minor differences.

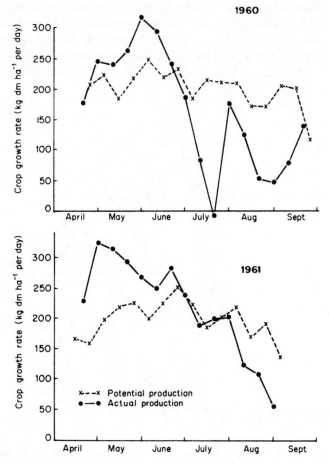

Fig. 10.2   Actual and potential growth rates during 1960 and 1961; in calculating the potential growth rate a dissimilation rate of 20% has been used; from Alberda [1].

We are also better informed about the seasonal course of dry-matter production and its relation to the incoming light energy, although there are still aspects which are far from clear. Let us first consider the rate of dry-matter production of a closed sward in relation to the incoming light energy. If the mean herbage growth rate for each ten-day period and the rate of potential production based on the incoming radiation, are plotted through the growing season (Figure 10.2), there is a distinct similarity in the shape of both curves. However, for some yet unknown reason there is a decline in the effectiveness of the light energy as the season advances. Similarly, the yield differences from year to year can often be related to differences in the amount of light energy. In the grass crop, the number of experiments on maximum production is as yet too small to state the extent of this relationship, but in several other crops, grown with high fertilizer levels, Sibma [17] found a good correlation between yield and light energy. Figure 10.3 shows the result for potatoes. The multiple correlation coefficient between annual yield and both the length of the growing period and the mean light energy is 0.96, while the partial correlation between annual yield and mean light energy is 0.76.

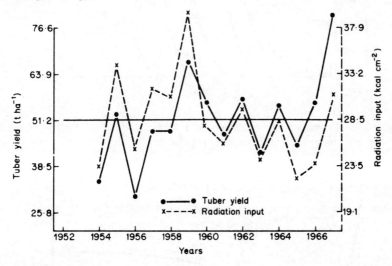

Fig. 10.3   Relation between radiation and yield of potatoes over a number of years; from Sibma [17].

The rate of dry-matter production of a closed sward has been the subject of much discussion during the last ten years. In 1961 Donald [11] condensed the available data to provide a theoretical model of the course of dry-matter production of such a sward. According to this model there is a well-defined optimum growth rate which occurs at the optimal leaf area index, i.e. the stage of development of the canopy in which nearly all the incident light is intercepted by the leaves. With a further increase in dry matter of the crop, the rate of photosynthesis of the canopy remains constant, whereas the rate of respiration increases with the amount of tissue present, until both rates eventually become equal, i.e. the growth rate becomes zero, and a ceiling yield is reached. Donald stated that experimental findings did not always agree with this model, and indeed a constant crop growth rate over prolonged periods is often found, followed by a rather sudden change to zero values [4, 7] (Figure 10.1 and Figure 10.4).

It is now clear that Donald's model is rather too simple. In the first place, there is usually no sharp optimum leaf area index. From de Wit's computer programme [20], it appears that under conditions of bright sunshine a grass

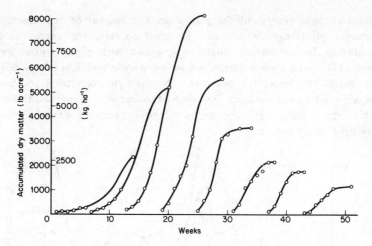

Fig. 10.4   Course of herbage production of successive cuts during the year;
drawn after data from Brougham [7].

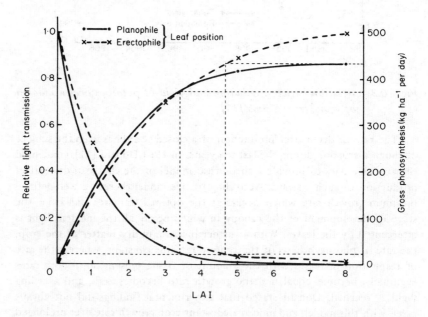

Fig. 10.5   Relative transmission (clear sky, sun at 45°) and gross photosynthesis (clear sky, end of May) of a grass crop with two extreme
leaf positions, calculated with de Wit's [20] computer programme for increasing LAI. For other characteristics of the grass
sward, see Alberda and Sibma [4].

sward intercepts more than 95 per cent of the incoming radiation at a leaf area index between 3.5 and 4.5, depending on leaf arrangement. This is the stage at which the canopy is usually considered to be closed. With a further increase in leaf area index, the rate of gross photosynthesis increases by about 15 per cent before the maximum value is obtained (Figure 10.5). In the second place, Donald assumed the rate of respiration to be linearly related to the amount of dry matter produced, and this may not always be the case [3]. McCree and Troughton [15] showed that in white clover the rate of respiration was proportional to the rate of gross photosynthesis, and not to the amount of dry matter present (Figure 10.6). This may in part be due to the dying-off of the older leaves and in part to the formation of more structural material, with less specific respiration.

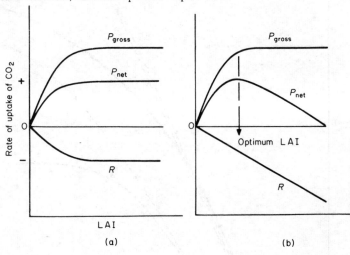

Fig. 10.6   *Theoretical CO_2 exchange rates of a plant community at various leaf area indices, if respiration rate is proportional to (a) gross photosynthesis rate, and (b) leaf area index; from McCree and Troughton [15].*

Besides these internal factors, such external factors as daylength, altitude of the sun, and mean temperature, will also have a modulating influence on photosynthesis and respiration.

When this information is introduced into the computer programme as accurately as possible, the predicted crop growth rates follow the same kind of linear relationships as actually found by experiments, (Figure 10.7). Furthermore, ceiling values of dry-matter production which decrease with the season are also predicted, again corresponding to those found in practice. However, the sudden transition from a fairly high growth rate to zero production is not predicted by the computer programme, and is still far from being explained. In practice, the ceiling yield is rarely reached, because the grass is usually cut well before this stage for reasons of chemical composition and the condition of the sward. The close agreement between the slope of the growth curves for each month (Figure 10.1) enable us to calculate mean growth rates for a closed crop canopy over the whole growing season (Table 10.1).

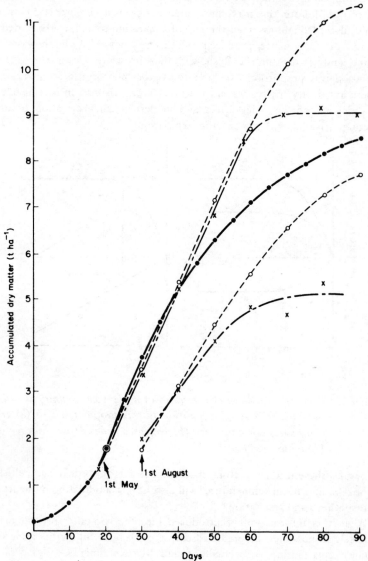

Fig. 10.7   Actual growth curves for growth periods starting 1 May and 1 August (x———x———x) together with calculated curves from de Wit's [20] computer program (o———o———o) for the same periods and a calculated curve for constant internal and external conditions (●———●———●); from Alberda and Sibma [4].

Table 10.1
Potential production for an erectophile canopy of LAI = 5, (calculated from the mean radiation input at Wageningen between 1960 and 1965) and actual production data for a grass sward over the same period

Month	April			May			June			July			August			September			October		
10-day period	10	11	12	13	14	15	16	17	18	19	20	21	22	23	24	25	26	27	28	29	30
Potential Crop photosynthesis (kg ha^{-1} day^{-1})	214	242	258	274	295	307	334	316	330	301	295	301	284	264	247	227	218	185	167	136	118
Potential herbage production (60% of above)	128	145	155	164	177	184	200	190	198	180	177	180	170	158	148	136	131	111	100	82	71
Actual herbage production	105	133	152	170	183	192	200	195	185	175	160	147	133	116	100	85	66	50	33	10	
Recovery time (days)		25			20			22			25			27			31			—	

As regards harvesting techniques, Dickinson mentions seven or ten crops in one season, ranging from March till December, and cut at a height of ± 18 inches (45 cm). In Wageningen, we have tried to cut the grass crop at a dry herbage weight of about 4 t ha^{-1}, a technique which usually involves five cuts, with the first in the beginning of May and the last in the beginning of October [2, 4]. In Cooper's experiments [8], the grass was cut seven times during the growing season, beginning in early March and ending in late October. Since, in the present experiments, the height of the grass was not measured, and since Dickinson does not mention the weight of his separate cuts, a direct comparison of seasonal production is not possible. If the grass is cut at the usual level of ± 5 cm, the greater part of the photosynthesising leaf is taken away, and there is probably a negative dry-matter balance in the remaining plant parts during the first few days after cutting. Brougham [6] has studied the regrowth of a sward after cutting at different heights to obtain differences in leaf area index directly after defoliation. His results, together with theoretical considerations, led him to conclude that the best way of managing a sward was to maintain a closed canopy either by a high cutting level with frequent cutting, or by lenient grazing. In practice, however, this method proved to be not very successful. By mowing at a high level, the sward deteriorates gradually as a result of an increasing amount of dead and decaying leaves, and with lenient grazing, dung and uring patches are left untouched, so that parts of the sward are grazed intensively and other parts not at all. We therefore arrive at the conclusion that for maximum production, the crop has to be defoliated from time to time at such a level as to remove the greater part of the lower leaf material, even though this gives a temporary reduction in growth rate.

By cutting at a level of about 2.5 cm, Brougham found that in a rye grass/clover pasture a closed canopy was restored after about three weeks. His pasture then contained more than 30 per cent clover. With a pure stand of perennial rye-grass, cut at 5 cm, we in Wageningen found a light interception of more than 95 per cent after three weeks, as shown by our light interception curves for the successive cuts, Figure 10.8. There is little difference between the various cuts, except for the last cut in September. It must be pointed out that under the present conditions, which are aimed at providing maximum production, there is no midsummer depression in yield, either in the growth rates of the closed sward or in the regrowth curves. From the growth data available, the mean recovery time to form a closed sward again can be given for different periods of the growing season (Table 10.1). From this table, it is possible to calculate the potential herbage production for any system of cutting, provided that the ceiling value is never reached.

Although the potential herbage production did not increase between the time of Dickinson's letter and our recent experiments, the actual herbage production has advanced markedly, especially after the last world-war, largely through a steadily increasing use of fertilizers. The mean grassland output in Britain and the Netherlands is at present about half the potential value, and

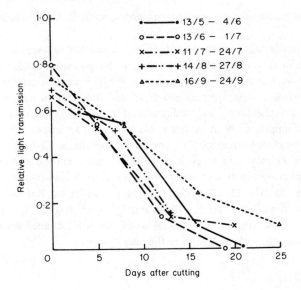

Fig. 10.8   Relative light transmission during successive regrowth periods.

we may expect that it will continue to increase. This brings us to the last aspect of William Dickinson's letter: the use of fertilizers. It is the major difference between his experiments and our own, and a very important one. Dickinson used horse urine, we have used artificial fertilizers. In Dickinson's time the question 'How shall I obtain enough urine?' was very important, whereas today the problem is rather 'How do I get rid of dung and urine?'. The labour costs of transport and use of dung and urine are so high, and artificial fertilizers relatively so cheap, that methods have been developed to get rid of the excreta of man and his domesticated animals in the cheapest possible way, first in the cities, but nowadays also in the villages and even on the farms. However, although it may be possible to get rid of the organic matter in this human and animal waste, it is much more difficult to get rid of the minerals it contains, unless we are able to precipitate them, or to transport them into the ocean. At the present time, it is probably not an overstatement to say that the major part of our vastly increasing use of artificial fertilizer flows from the land into our open inland waters, where it will have the same effect as on the land, i.e. to enhance the production rate of organic matter. In former days, ditches and streams were cleared mechanically and so a part of the mineral residues were again returned to the land. But now we clear them by chemical means, leaving the minerals *in situ*. Unless we are prepared to kill all the plant life in and along our inland waters, we may therefore expect a rapid increase of primary production, with all its consequences of oxygen depletion and destruction of animal life. Furthermore, this problem is arising at the same time as a rapidly increasing demand for inland waters for recreational purposes, such as fishing, swimming, and boating.

In considering potential production, in Britain or elsewhere, we have therefore to face the problem of locating this potential production exactly where we want it and not somewhere else. We have to consider the disposal of our agricultural waste just as much as our industrial waste. However, in dealing with the potential production of grassland, the problems are still relatively simple, since it is fairly easy to keep an important part of the minerals in closed circulation on the farm. This means that after more than 100 years we may have to go back to Dickinson's method and to construct large tanks to retain at least most of the minerals. Such tanks will, of course, cost more than the £2. 17. 6. that Dickinson paid for his. But such costs have to be met, not by the farmers alone, but by all of us, for if we neglect these problems of the disposal of mineral waste, we will be faced with far bigger and much more costly problems in the near future.

REFERENCES

1. ALBERDA, Th. 'Actual and potential production of agricultural crops', Neth. J. agric. Sci., 1962, 10, 325-333.
2. ALBERDA, Th. 'Dry matter production and light interception of crop surfaces: IV. Maximum herbage production as compared with predicted values', Neth. J. agric. Sci., 1968, 16, 142-153.
3. ALBERDA, Th. 'The influence of carbohydrate reserves on respiration, photosynthesis and dry matter production of intact plants', Proc. XI Int. Grassl. Congr., 1970, 517-522.
4. ALBERDA, Th. and SIBMA, L. 'Dry matter production and light interception of crop surfaces. III. Actual herbage production in different years as compared with potential values', J. Br. Grassl. Soc., 1968, 23, 206-215.
5. BLACK, J.N. 'An analysis of the potential production of swards of subterranean clover (Trifolium subterraneum L.) at Adelaide, South Australia', J. appl. Ecol., 1964, 1, 3-18.
6. BROUGHAM, R.W. 'Effect of intensity of defoliation on regrowth of pasture', Aust. J. agric. Res., 1956, 7, 377-387.
7. BROUGHAM, R.W. 'The effects of season and weather on the growth of a rye-grass and white clover pasture', N.Z. Jl. agric. Res., 1959, 2, 283-296.
8. COOPER, J.P. 'Energy and nutrient conversion in a simulated sward', Rep. Welsh Pl. Breed. Stn. 1967, 1968, 10-11.
9. DAVIDSON, J.L. and PHILIP, J.R. 'Light and pasture growth', in Climatology and microclimatology, Proc. Canberra Symp. 1956, 1958, 181-187.
10. DICKINSON, W. 'On a variety of Italian rye-grass', Jl. R. agric. Soc., 1847, 8, 572-582.

11. DONALD, C.M. 'Competition for light in crop and pastures', *Symp. Soc. exp. Biol.*, 1961, **15**, 282-313.

12. DUNCAN, W.G. 'A model for simulating photosynthesis and other radiation phenomena in plant communities', *Proc. X Int. Grassld Congr.*, 1967, 120-125.

13. GAASTRA, P. 'Photosynthesis of leaves and field crops', *Neth. J. agric. Sci.*, 1962, **10**, 311-324.

14. KASANAGA, H. and MONSI, M. 'On the light transmission of leaves and its meaning for the production of matter in plant communities', *Jap. J. Bot.*, 1954, **14**, 304-324.

15. McCREE, K.J. and TROUGHTON, J.H. 'Non-existence of an optimum leaf area index for the production rate of white clover grown under constant conditions', *Pl. Physiol. Lancaster*, 1966, **41**, 1615-1622.

16. MONTEITH, J.L. 'Light distribution and photosynthesis in field crops', *Ann. Bot.*, 1965, **29**, 17-37.

17. SIBMA, L. 'Relation between radiation and yield of a number of agricultural crops in the Netherlands', *Neth. J. agric. Sci.*, 1970, **18**, 125-131.

18. STANHILL, G. 'The effect of environmental factors on the growth of alfalfa in the field', *Neth. J. agric. Sci.*, 1962, **10**, 247-253.

19. WIT, C.T. DE 'Potential photosynthesis of crop surfaces', *Neth. J. agric. Sci.*, 1959, **7**, 141-149.

20. WIT, C.T. DE 'Photosynthesis of leaf canopies', *Agric. Res. Rep.*, 1965, **663**, 57 pp.

21. WIT, C.T. DE, DIJKSHOORN, W. and NOGGLE, J.C. 'Ionic balance and growth of plants', *Versl. landbouwk Onderz.*, 1963, **69**, 15, 68 pp.

11. The Potential Production of Forest Crops

E.D. Ford
Department of Forestry and Natural Resources, University of Edinburgh

Introduction

Unlike the other crops discussed in this book, forests do not contribute to man's food chain (see Pirie [21], however), and it is of little value to draw forest crops into a general comparison of crop efficiencies on the basis of the weight dry matter produced. Forestry is a major land user [16] and its efficiency as a crop system is of importance, but if comparisons are to be made between forests and other biological systems *as crops*, this can only be achieved realistically through economic analysis.

The major reason why a consideration of the potential production of forests is of importance is that it is central to the argument for intensive forestry. The proponents of intensive forestry argue that limited capital can be more efficiently deployed through such treatments as drainage and fertilization on a limited number of forests rather than through a continuous expansion of forest holdings which entails high costs of establishment [9]. This argument for intensive forestry is likely to increase if more efficient methods of applying growth improvement treatments continue to become available, particularly if they become available at a lower relative cost. Central to the argument is the assertion that yields can be increased by such treatments, but if the case for intensive forestry is to be seriously considered, it is essential that those yields which can be obtainable from applying various treatments can be predicted. We must have an understanding of the relationship between input, in terms of management effort which can be expressed as cost, and output gained in terms of timber which can be expressed in terms of price. However, before we can arrive at such an understanding, we need a quantitative appreciation of the limits set to production by factors which are outside the control of management, and a quantitative knowledge of just how management can influence growth. The particular characteristics of perennial growth and the long-term nature of forest operations mean that empirical techniques which have proved successful in establishing quantitative relationships in field crops and pasture may not be so successful for forest crops.

The Measurement of Forest Crop Growth

In Britain our crops are almost entirely of the plantation type, that is they are established as even-age crops of trees. As such a crop grows, individuals are removed at regular intervals, a technique known as thinning, and this process complicates any attempt to obtain a measure of forest production. Thinning reduces biomass and alters the amount of growth made in subsequent seasons. Normal forestry practice is not to measure production but rather to use the height of the crop as an index of its productivity, and a particular example of this approach is the calculation of *yield class*, which has been produced by the Forestry Commission for use in British forests [6].

In this particular case the height of the crop is calculated as the mean height of the forty trees of largest girth per acre, and is called the top height. A relationship has been established, from a range of sample plots, between this parameter and the volume of timber which would be produced by the stand under a specific rate of stocking and thinning. Thus height is used as an indication of productivity of the crop, yet productivity is presented as a yield class figure in volume units, (Figure 11.1).

The technique is dependent upon the use of low thinning regimes, that is the removal of trees in the lower part of the forest canopy, as opposed to crown thinning, which is the removal of tall trees. Variation does occur in the shape of stems between stands of trees of the same age and height, and the timber volume of such stands would be different. However, such form differences can be observed in the trees used to calculate top height and allowance made for its effect.

The Current Approach to Forest Crop Production

The general approach adopted in this country to forest productivity has been to consider what a particular site will produce if planted with trees. Ameliorative treatments beyond those needed to establish the crop are rarely contemplated. The attitude is 'What will this site produce?' as opposed to 'How much can we grow here?' and this has led to investigations to find the features of a site which are most important in determining the actual production which is obtained. The technique used is to measure a large number of features of the physical environment for a range of sites, and then to use multiple regression and correlation analysis to explore the relationship between these features and the productivity of the forest crop. Provided that relationships are found, this type of study can then aid forest management, facilitating the prediction of the productivity on any site from measurements of certain of its environmental characteristics.

A number of such site classification studies, as they are called, are in progress in Britain, e.g. for Sitka spruce, *Picea sitchensis* Carr. in Scotland [17], Sitka spruce, Douglas fir (*Pseudotsuga taxifolia* Britt.) and Japanese larch (*Larix leptolepis* Murr.) in north Wales [14], and Corsican pine (*Pinus nigra var calabrica Schneid.*) in southern England and Wales [7]. A number of studies have been completed in America and Europe, and it is of interest to briefly examine the type of results which have been obtained [22] .

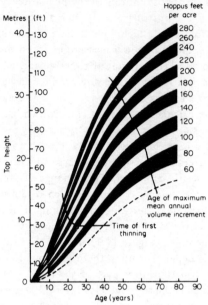

Fig. 11.1   *General Yield Class curves for Sitka spruce. The Yield Class figures refer to the maximum mean annual timber volume increments (in hoppus feet acre^{-1}, where 100 hoppus feet per acre = 8.9 m^3 ha^{-1}) which will accrue to those stands defined by the corresponding top height-age curves. Other tables have been constructed, (Forestry Commission [7]), to predict the thinning yields and final timber volume which will be obtained from a stand of known Yield Class, managed in a specified way.*

studies have been completed in American and Europe, and it is of interest to briefly examine the type of results which have been obtained [22] .

The environmental features which have been measured in site classification studies can be divided into three groups: meteorological, topographic and edaphic. In the first group are such parameters as annual or spring rainfall and the number of frost-free days per annum, in the second group slope and aspect, and in the last group a multiplicity of factors including depth of soil, measures of the physical structure of soil, such as percentage clay content, and frequently measures of the soil nutrient status.

As might be expected from the large number of factors which influence plant growth, those people involved in site classification work have had little success in determining quantitative relationships when gross climatic variation has been examined at the same time as detailed differences in soil or topography, and generally the approach has been to seek an initial stratification of sites into climatic types before attempting to find quantitative relationships between environment and productivity.

Within climatic types, by far the greatest effort has gone into attempts to find variations in productivity as a function of soil characteristics, but a striking feature of the results is that, in general, soil nutrient status has been found of less value than other soil features as an indicator of productivity. The edaphic parameters which have been found of most value are those which indicate the general condition of the rooting medium, such as depth of soil or percent clay content, rather than the soil nutrients themselves. To some extent this may be an artifact of the techniques used, either specifically of measurement, where predominantly agricultural techniques of soil nutrient analysis have been used, or more generally of the approach employed by site classification studies. Thus depth of soil is some indication of the total nutrients of a site, and because it is also an indication of other important features of the environment, e.g. water status, then it appears of greater significance in any correlation analysis than these individual factors. However, the value of soil physical characteristics in site classification studies underlines the point that the general condition of the rooting medium is of great importance in determining productivity in the forests which have been examined.

There are two contributing reasons for this. Firstly, forests are generally restricted to marginal lands. This is true throughout the world, with some notable exceptions in southern Africa [15], and it is particularly true of Britain. This restriction to marginal means that, by definition, such hazards as drought or flood are likely to be encountered, so that the general characteristics of the rooting medium are important. In these situations one is investigating limiting factors to growth rather than subtle combinations of factors which lead to maximum growth. The second reason why soil physical conditions are of such importance is that forestry in general is a low input system in economic terms. Fertilization is not widely practised and this, combined with the long duration of forest crops, means that growth becomes dependent upon the rate of nutrient release in the soil. This is a biological process which is also dependent upon what can be termed the general condition of the rooting medium.

Although site classification studies have focussed attention on the particular problems of the nutrition of the perennial crop, they are of very limited use in suggesting how the production of any site may be increased. An analysis is produced in such terms as percentage clay in the sub-soil, depth of the B horizon and percentage slope (e.g. [30]), rather than in direct measures of the factors which control plant growth, and so such studies cannot indicate in a quantitative way how growth might be improved. Site classification studies are of very limited use to anyone who wishes to consider his forest in terms of input of management commitment, e.g. fertilizer and drainage, related to outputs of timber yield. It does not begin to define what are the optimum conditions for growth. It is site-oriented rather than plant-oriented, and is geared to an analysis of factors which limit production on poor sites.

The Potential Production of Forest Crops

What is needed by foresters is an appreciation of how a forest crop grows, which would provide the basis for decisions on the economics of intensifying forest management. In considering the strategy which should be adopted to achieve such knowledge, there are a number of features peculiar to forest crops which must be borne in mind.

(a) Forest crops can be managed for a range of different production objectives, e.g. pulp or saw logs. Whilst total production in all cases might be measured as timber volume, how this timber is distributed between different sizes of tree is of vital importance, i.e. does the crop consist of a large number of small trees or a small number of large ones?

(b) There is a long duration between the establishment of the crop and its final harvesting and, as far as the biology of the crop is concerned, there are two major consequences of this.

   (i) In order to achieve a closed leaf canopy early in the life of the crop, individual trees are planted at closer spacings than it is envisaged will prevail at the final harvest. Throughout the life of the crop, the 'surplus' number of trees are gradually removed and may in fact form the major part of the yield. This removal of the trees means that the structure of the crop, and therefore of the leaf canopy, is altered at regular intervals.

   (ii) As soil cultivation is not practised during the life of the crop, there is an accumulation of leaf material on the forest floor which plays a major part in the nutrition of the crop.

(c) There are added complications to empirical experimentation with forests over and above those experienced with other crops. The size of trees means that larger uniform areas are required where treatments have to be applied. The perennial nature of the crop makes it impossible to repeat experiments with identical biological material because each crop goes through a unique sequence of climate before experimentation might start. Consequently empirical experiments can only be of limited value.

If we are to obtain an overall picture of the options open to management and the inputs required to achieve these, then we require a system for representing a complex series of interactions and which can answer a series of questions. A way in which this can be done is through the construction of a mathematical model for forest growth. De Wit [29] has described the construction of models for the growth of annual plants and crops, but because of the nature of forest operations and the particular biology of forests this approach is likely to be of value to forestry even more than to agricultural production.

The basis of a complete model would be the description of the response of plants to factors such as temperature and daylength. The different meristems of trees, leaf, cambial, apical and root, tend to show different, sometimes very distinct, phases of growth during the growth season which may be controlled by different environmental factors. This part of the model would partially define potential production in that it deals with the control mechanisms of development (for a more detailed discussion of the factors involved, see Ford and Fraser [9]. It is easily said that such knowledge should form the basis of any model, though in fact our knowledge of the basis physiology, particularly in a quantitative form, is greatly lacking. However, something of these relationships for plants in general have been dealt with by earlier contributers so that this physiological 'core' to the model will not be considered, but rather those features of forests which are determinants of forest production and which can be controlled by management during the life of the crop.

Crop Structure

Within the limits to production set by meristem control systems, solar radiation determines potential production. However, the structure and physiology of the leaf canopy are features which influence the realisation of any potential which may be defined in terms of the efficiency of the incoming radiation. In forestry, management may manipulate the leaf canopy through the process of thinning in order to achieve specific production objectives. This requirement for a particular crop structure and its likely effect on the structure of the leaf canopy could influence the realisation of any biologically determined potential. We need to know what are the important features of biology, environment and of management which determine the distribution of tree size in a forest crop, and how this distribution is related to total production.

Seen in a general context, this is a problem of variation between individuals and how it develops. The first element which needs to be considered is the distribution of sizes in the transplant stock which is used to establish the forest crop. To what extent do transplants all grow with the same relative growth rate, so that the final distribution of tree sizes merely reflects that of the transplant stock or perhaps some random alteration of it; and to what extent does true dominance develop? By true dominance is meant the process whereby one individual modifies the environment to such an extent that the relative growth rate of surrounding trees is altered, and a spacial pattern of dominance develops.

Figure 11.2 is a diagramatic representation of the development of a well-stocked, unmanaged even-aged tree population, based on work with a sweet chestnut coppice by Ford and Newbould [10]. As the woodland grows, large trees continuously expand their crowns in three dimensions. As this process takes place, some trees become overtopped; they come to hold leaves only in the lower part of the leaf canopy, their relative growth rate declines and ultimately they die. At any stage in the development of the coppice woodland, the largest number of individuals are in the small-size classes. This is partly a reflection of the initial uneven distribution of shoot sizes caused by continuous shoot formation from May to July in the first year of growth. However, in all unmanaged even-aged woodlands in light-limiting situations, one can expect that there will be a preponderance of small individuals.

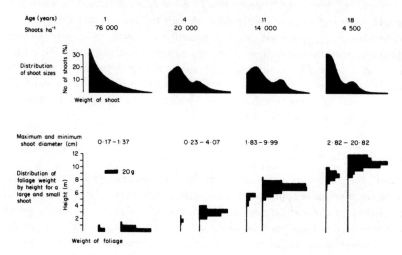

Fig. 11.2   The development of an even-aged tree population based on work with sweet chestnut coppice. The coppice grows quickly, closes canopy at about 8 years, and is normally clear-felled after 15-18 years. As the woodland grows, a distinct class of dominant shoots develops which is illustrated by the secondary maxima in the distribution of shoot sizes [10].

When a stand closes canopy, the larger the individual tree, the larger the absolute production it makes. However, where one is concerned with the total production of a stand, one needs to be concerned with the efficiency with which individual trees utilize their share of the leaf canopy. A way in which this has been investigated has been to examine the relationship between growth increment per unit of crown size and size of tree. A number of investigations into this relationship have been conducted where tree size and increment have been measured as timber volume and crown size as crown volume, surface area or projection, Figure 11.3, [1, 2]. For a review see Hamilton [12].

As would be expected, there is a general trend that the larger the crown of the individual tree, then the greater is the absolute production which it makes. However, some investigations have suggested that beyond a certain size of crown there is a loss in the efficiency of production. Thus as crown projection increases, a point is reached where increment per unit of crown projection starts to decrease. We have no generalized knowledge of at what stand or canopy size this curvilinear relationship develops, or how the situation varies between species. An explanation which has been put forward for the loss in efficiency of production by large trees is that above a certain size of crown, the ratio between the outer photosynthesizing sheath of a crown and its inner respiring section becomes important. However, regardless of the validity of this explanation, it seems that for trees above a certain size, the crown surface area/crown volume ratio is an important determinant of the efficiency of utilization of space in the stand. Consequently, to realise full potential of forests composed of this larger size of tree, manipulation of the structure of the canopy through thinning might be necessary to achieve a high crown surface area/crown volume ratio.

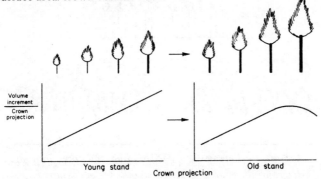

Fig. 11.3   *A postulated change in efficiency of the largest individual tree crowns as the forest grows. In stands where the largest trees exceed a certain size, they become less efficient than smaller trees in producing timber volume per unit of ground area that is covered by their crowns.*

As an unmanaged stand grows, there is a constant loss of trees through death, and it is effectively this loss which is anticipated by the process of thinning. When contemplating a thinning two questions arise.

(a) To what extent should the loss through death be anticipated, i.e. at what intensity should the stand be thinned? Within the wide limits of heavy thinning and no thinning, the volume of growing stock is not altered sufficiently to drastically affect yield.

(b) From which part of the crop should individual trees be removed? What is removed in a thinning is important because it can be sold immediately, but what is left is also important because growth in the future will be laid down on the trees which remain. The options available can be illustrated by contrasting two of the major types of thinning, low and crown, Figure 11.4. In low thinning, the natural disappearance of the small trees comprising the lower part of the leaf canopy is anticipated, whilst in crown thinning, trees are removed from the middle and larger-sized classes. Most evidence indicates that the total yield in terms of volume per acre is no greater from a series of crown thinnings than from a comparable series of low thinnings. With crown thinning, however, the volume is harvested in fewer trees of greater average diameter.

The additional increment which accrues to those trees which remain after a thinning tends to occur in the lower, and economically most valuable parts of the stem. When thinning, one of the major questions which must be decided is on which trees you wish this to happen. This aspect of thinning — the effect it has on timber quality — is extremely important.

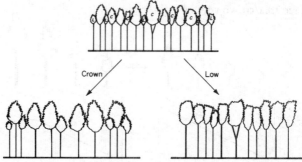

Fig. 11.4   A contrast between crown thinning and low thinning. The top diagram illustrates a stand about to be thinned. Trees which would be removed by a crown thinning are indicated by C, by a low thinning, L. The lower diagrams show the structure of the stand after a certain amount of growth has been made, after Smith [24].

Experimentation in the field of thinning has not only been confounded by the normal difficulties experienced with empirical work in forestry but also by the almost universal measurement of thinning intensity as a ratio of the timber volume removed to that remaining, with the only structural designation being low or high. Functional measures of crop or canopy structure have not been used to establish any generalized conclusions. (For a detailed consideration of thinning practice in silviculture, see Smith [24].

Crop Nutrition

The second feature which can be manipulated by management to affect the realisation of potential is nutrition. As discussed above, it appears from the work of site classification that the factors which control nutrient availability are of more importance in determining forest producitivity than the total amount of nutrients in the soil. Before considering how the nutrient levels of even-aged conifer stands have been manipulated, one should look at the basic nutrient cycle.

Millar [19] has documented the distribution and movement of nitrogen in a thirty-six year Corsican pine stand (Table 11.1). The trees were planted on bare sand at Culbin Forest, Morrayshire, and at the time of the investigation were yield class 85. The important feature to note is that the trees contain less nitrogen than the organic horizons of the soil. Average annual incorporation of nitrogen by the trees was estimated by adding to the nitrogen content of the standing trees an estimated value for the nitrogen content of the thinnings which has been removed, then dividing the total by the age of the crop. The value obtained, 6.4 lb acre^{-1} year^{-1} (7.2 kg ha^{-1} yr^{-1}) is less than 0.4 per cent of the total quantity of nitrogen within the system. The salient feature of nutrition in this type of crop is the rate at which nutrients cycle through needles, litter, then back to the needles.

Table 11.1
The distribution of organic matter and nitrogen in a 35-year plantation of Corsican Pine [18].

	Organic matter		Nitrogen content	
	lb acre^{-1}	kg ha^{-1}	lb acre^{-1}	kg ha^{-1}
Trees — Crowns	17.400	19.500	74	83
Boles	69.200	77.500	54	60
Stumps and roots	47.200	52.900	101	113
Total trees	113.800	149.900	229	257
Ground vegetation	900	1000	7	8
Forest floor (L+F+H)	43.700	49.000	287	322
Total organic matter	178.400	199.800	523	586
Sand to 3 ft. 6 in. (107 cm)			1228	1365
Total	178.400	199.800	1751	1962

The overall effect of conifer litter on soil properties leading to a general tendency to podsolization is well known [13]. However, during the course of one rotation of an even-aged conifer plantation, soil properties tend to show distinct changes. These changes have been studied by Page [20] for crops of Sitka Spruce on podsolic soils in north Wales.

From Figure 11.5 it can be seen that the young crop has little influence on soil conditions until canopy closure at a top height of about 20 (6.1 m). After this time there is a marked reduction in radiation reaching the forest floor, and consequently temperatures decrease and humidity increases. Radiation levels continue to decrease up to the time of first thinning, which is normally practised at a top height of about 30 ft (9.1 m). At this time the crop has attained its maximum canopy density and there is a maximum level of litter decomposition. With continued thinning after 30 ft, there is a gradual decrease in the level of annual littler fall and an increase in the level of radiation reaching the forest floor. The balance between the rate of litter deposition and litter decomposition is reached when the crop reaches a top height of 48 ft (15.6 m). As the accumulated litter decomposes, there are subsequent minima in soil pH and, due to the increase in soil organic matter, in bulk density.

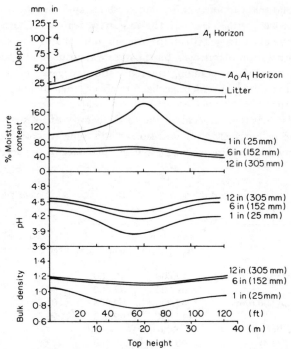

Fig. 11.5   The change in soil properties during a rotation of Sitka spruce; from Page [20].

Table 11.2
The response to nitrogen fertilizer, $(NH_4)_2SO_4$, of the Corsican Pine stand described by Table 11.1

Total annual application of N		Weight of litter fall after one season of fertilization		Growth response after two seasons of fertilization Quarter girth	
lb acre^{-1}	kg ha^{-1}	lb acre^{-1}	kg ha^{-1}	ft^2 acre	m^2 ha^{-1}
0	0	2450	2740	0.8	0.03
75	84	1950	2180	2.6	0.10
150	168	1810	2030	3.0	0.11
300	336	1840	2060	3.5	0.13
450	504	1730	1940	3.8	0.14

In general, attempts to alter the nutrient levels of established forests have been made by applications of fertilizer and without any attempt to cultivate the trees (see [18], however). In some instances straight-forward curvilinear relationships have been obtained between the level of nutrient applied and the growth response. Such an instance is illustrated by Table 11.2, which shows the result of applying increasing levels of nitrogenous fertilizer to the

Corsican pine stand described above. However, results from fertilizer experiments on forest crops are not always straightforward. Work conducted in Finland with Scots pine (*Pinus sylvestris*, L) and Norway spruce (*Picea abies* Karst.) has shown that there can be differences in response between species which interact with soil type [26]. In these experiments, Scots pine responded to nitrogen on both mor and moder soils but not on mull soils.

In Britain responses to both nitrogen and phosphorus have been obtained for a range of species, but there are instances where the crops have failed to respond, some of which have been attributed to waterlogging of the experimental site [4, 7].

Generally we are short of information on the response to fertilization of forest crops and particularly how this may vary at different stages in the life of the crop. One suggestion which has been made, [3] from an examination of the preliminary results of fertilization of established crops, is that crops respond well to phosphorous in their early years and well to nitrogen later. We need to know if this is a real effect and, if it is so, just which features of the crop growth system are involved. Are the different responses with increasing age due to differences in the plants or in the soil?

Interactions Between Crop Structure and Crop Nutrition

A major attribute of mathematical models is the ease with which they can express the interactions between the different processes in a system so that it is possible to examine in detail the consequence to the whole from altering one component. For an example of such use of models for biological processes see de Wit [28]. However, before a model can be used in such a way, it is essential that the basic processes be accurately understood and expressed. One process which is not fully understood in forestry is how an increase in nutrition increases growth. Does an increase in the level of nutrition increase the size of the photosynthetic machinery as it does in arable crops [27], or does it affect the rate at which photosynthesis takes place? The degree to which the size and efficiency of the photosynthetic machinery are influenced will, in turn, influence the relative performance of trees of different sizes within the crop and the operation of the overtopping mechanism described earlier. Millar [19] has demonstrated that application of nitrogen to the Corsican pine stand at Culbin increases the size of needles formed and also prolongs the retention of old needles, thereby increasing the size of the photosynthetic system (Table 11.2). Van den Driessche and Wareing [5] have suggested from work with seedlings of conifers that an increase in nutrient level increases photosynthetic rate.

This question 'By what process does an increase in nutrition increase growth?', is part of the general question 'How is the total production and distribution of photosynthate within trees controlled?' Sweet and Wareing [25] have demonstrated that growth and photosynthesis can be limited by a limitation of the sink size. The influence of sink size in controlling tree growth may be particularly important, because the canopy of forests differs from that of arable crops in that it is much more stable, e.g. Ford [8] for deciduous trees. Individual leaves or needles are functional throughout the time that they are attached to the tree [11,23], and although the photosynthetic machinery of trees appears stable, there is a phasic development of meristems during the growing season.

Conclusions

Some of the features of forest growth which are fundamental requirements for a model to answer questions about the potential production of forest crops have been examined. This model would permit an economic evaluation of how a specified production objective might be reached with a particular forest crop. A mathematical model is probably necessary, firstly because the clear-cut field experiment is difficult to achieve with forest crops and so information on their biology must be obtained from a range of sources including, for example, seedling experiments and controlled environment studies; the extrapolation of this sort of data to field situations must initially be made on a probability basis, and mathematical models are useful for doing this.

Secondly, a model would be useful to answer questions about the likely consequences of a whole range of different treatments which would be applied to forest crops. Even under seemingly intensive forestry conditions, foresters may not wish to achieve the full biological potential of their crop but may rather wish to optimise a whole series of investments.

REFERENCES
1. ASSMANN, E. 'The optimum utilization of growing space', Mitt. St. Forstverw. Bayerns No. 29, 1957.
2. ASSMANN, E. 'Den Fichten-Durchforstungversuch Bowmont', Allg. Forst-u. Jagtztg., 1964, 135.
3. BINNS, W.O. 'Current Fertilizer Research in the Forestry Commission', Forestry, 1966, 39, suppl. 60-4.
4. BINNS, W.O. and GREYSON, A.J. 'Fertilization of established crops: Prospects in Britain', Scott. For., 1967, 21, 81-98.
5. DRIESSCHE, R. VAN DEN and WAREING, P.F. 'Dry matter production and photosynthesis in pine seedlings', Ann. Bot. N.S., 1966, 30, 657-72.
6. FORESTRY COMMISSION. (1966). 'Forest Management Tables', Bookl. For Commn. No. 16, 1966.
7. FORESTRY COMMISSION, Rep. Forest Res., Lond., 1968.
8. FORD, E.D. 'Stand structure and production in the sweet chestnut coppice cycle', Ph.D. Thesis Univ. Lond., 1968.

9. FORD, E.D. and FRASER, A.I. 'The concept of actual and potential production as an aid to forest management', *Forestry*, 1968, **41**, 175-81.

10. FORD, E.D. and NEWBOULD, P.J. 'Stand structure and dry weight production through the sweet chestnut (*Castanea sativa*, Mill.) coppice cycle', *J. Ecol.*, 1970, **58**, 275-96.

11. FREELAND, R.C. 'Effect of age of leaves upon the rate of photosynthesis in some conifers', *Pl. Physiol. Lancaster*, 1956, **27**, 685-90.

12. HAMILTON, G.J. 'The relationship between increment and dominance in individual trees as a basis for thinning method', *MSc. Thesis Univ. Edinburgh*, 1966.

13. HANDLEY, W.R.C. 'Mull and mor formation in relation to forest soils', *Bull. For. Commn., Lond.*, 1954, 23.

14. HETHERINGTON, J.C. and PAGE, G. 'Forest site evaluation with particular reference to soil and physiographic factors', *Report of the Welsh Soils Discussion Group No. 6*, 1965, 58-70.

15. HILEY, W.E. *Conifers: South African methods of cultivation.* London: Faber and Faber, 1959

16. IVINS, J.D. The determination of production systems', in *Potential Crop Production*, Ed. J.P. Cooper and P.F. Wareing, London: Heinemann, 1970.

17. MALCOLM, D.C. 'Environmental Factors and the growth of Sitka spruce', *Rep. Forest Res., Lond.*, 1968.

18. MØLLER, C., SCHARFF, O. and DRAGSTED, J.R. '10 years' fertilizing experiments in Norway spruce and Beech representing the main variations in growth conditions in Denmark', *Forst. Forsøgsv. Danm.*, 1969, **31**, 85-278.

19. MILLAR, H.G. 'Current research into the nitrogen nutrition of Corsican pine', *Forestry*, 1966, **39**, suppl. 70-77.

20. PAGE, G. 'Some effects of conifer crops on soil properties', *Commnw. For. Rec.*, 1968, **47**, 52-62.

21. PIRIE, N.W. 'Leaf proteins', *A. Rev. Pl. Physiol.*, 1959, 10, 33-52.

22. RALSTON, C.W. 'Evaluation of forest site productivity', *International Rev. For. Res.*, 1964, **1**, 171-201.

23. SANDERSON, G.W., and SIVAPALAN, K. 'Effect of leaf age on photosynthetic assimilation of carbon dioxide in tea plants', *Tea A.*, 1966, **37**, 11-26.

24. SMITH, D.M. *The practice of silviculture*, New York: Wiley, 1962.

25. SWEET, G.B., and WAREING, P.F. 'Role of plant growth in regulating photosynthesis', *Nature*, 1966, **210**, 77-9.

26. VIRO, P.J. 'Forest manuring on mineral soils', *Medd. Norske. Skogsf.* No. 85, 1967.

27. WATSON, D.J. 'Some features of crop nutrition', in *The Growth of the Potato*, Eds. J.D. Ivins and F.L. Milthorpe, London: Butterworth, 1963.

28. WIT, C.T. de 'Photosynthesis of leaf canopies', *Versl. Landbouwk. Onderz.*, 1965, **663**, 1-57.

29. WIT, C.T. de 'A dynamic model of plant and crop growth', in *Potential Crop Production*, Ed. J.P. Cooper and P.F. Wareing, London: Heinemann, 1970.

30. ZAHNER, R. 'Site quality relationships of pine forests in southern Arkansas and northern Louisiana', *For. Sci.*, 1958, 4, 162-76.

12. Horticulture in 2000 A.D.

J.P. Hudson
Long Ashton Research Station University of Bristol

By contrast with the pattern of other chapters few data from work that has already been done will be presented in this, but instead it is proposed to concentrate on what seems likely to be needed in the future to ensure maximum productivity in the horticultural sector of the agricultural industry. However, since *potential* productivity is difficult to define, and presumably unrecognizable even if it was achieved, it has been assumed that the title of this book is an invitation to contributors to cast their nets widely and make a few outrageous suggestions.

Although it is proposed to look at the year 2000 A.D., the author has no special qualifications to speak on this subject — no private crystal ball. Indeed, it is not even clear whether we are trying to *predict* the future, as though it were something that is already settled and just waiting to unroll with the inevitability of fate or, more usefully, trying to identify different possible directions in which horticulture might develop, and their probable effects, so that we can *influence* the future by making conscious choices between various alternatives.

The scale of thinking is thirty-one years, i.e. from 1969 to 2000 A.D. Looking back over the same span of years, we have seen an astonishing list of changes since 1938, including, for instance:

Elucidation of the role of minor elements in plant nutrition.

The virtual elimination of the horse in farming.

Introduction of selective herbicides, with the practical possibility for the first time of growing plants in a 'weed-free environment'.

Emergence of a working knowledge of the whole spectrum of growth substances and the practical uses to which they can be put.

Introduction of all the modern range of insecticides, from D.D.T. onwards.

Development of dehydration and deep freezing as commercial methods of food preservation, and the supermarket based on self-service and pre-packing.

Introduction of mist propagation; aluminium glasshouses and the automation of glasshouse controls; growth rooms, growing rooms and other forms of environmental control; air blast and other low volume methods of spraying.

Use of photoperiodic control to produce all-year-round chrysanthemums, and growth retardants for dwarfed plants in pots.

Inactivation of viruses and production of virus-free clones, etc.

Horticulture is obviously in a state of flux, and some of these changes have very far-reaching consequences indeed. We could perhaps have forecast some of these changes thirty years ago, but certainly not all of them, and there will doubtless be as many exciting and unexpected developments in the future as in the past.

In addition to these technological developments, there have been changes in the plants themselves, based on a continuous flow of new and improved varieties. Some of these have a much greater potential for yielding well under good growing conditions than the older varieties, and it is safe to forecast that the results of plant breeding are going to be of the greatest importance in the next thirty years, especially in fruit, using new approaches based on a much better understanding of genetic principles. This could apply specially to the lesser known tropical fruits, many of which are still virtually unimproved species that should offer rewarding prospects to the plant breeder.

But despite the traditional interest in new *varieties,* there is little sign of the emergence of any new *crops* of importance. Yet it is not unreasonable to ask an audience that includes many botanists and geneticists, whether we are satisfied that we are growing the species which have the highest potential for yield. Crop production is now based on a few scores of species, many of which were selected in ancient times by our neolithic ancestors for reasons that are utterly irrelevant to modern methods of crop production. There must almost certainly be many other species that have a high potential for improvement and growth, and if one compares a crab apple with a Cox's Orange Pippin or a Lycopersicum species with a glasshouse tomato it is fair to ask how many of the other 300 000 plant species might, in the hands of a modern improver, develop into exciting new fruits or vegetables. For instance, fuchsia fruits appear to be edible and they are certainly luscious and tasty, unlike any other fruit at present available, and perhaps worthy of the attention of a plant breeder. And some of the British weeds, which seem to grow so fast under our conditions, might be worth considering as candidate crops for the extraction of leaf protein.

Future of the Horticulture Industry

Although the future of an industry is unpredictable, it will be assumed that by 2000 A.D. people will still want to eat natural fresh fruits and vegetables and pay an economic price for them (though one is not so sure about amorphous preparations such as pie fillings, that might by then be made from synthetic products). It is also assumed that the industry will be operating under the following restraints:

(a) There will be *less labour* and virtually no hand work — i.e. unless a job can be done by machine it will not be done at all.

(b) There will be *less land* devoted to horticulture, but growers will be much more highly selective in their choice of sites (latitudes, aspects, altitudes and slopes) for particular crops, and much more intensive use will be made of the land, to release areas for urban development and for recreational use by people who, by then, may spend much less time at work.

(c) There will be business men who are prepared to *invest heavily* in horticulture, provided they are assured of quick and adequate returns (i.e. no one will be planting orchards, or other slow-yielding crops, as a way of life).

(d) The consumer will be more perceptive regarding *real quality* (i.e. flavour rather than appearance) and will be prepared to pay high prices for high quality produce.

The theme of the forecast is, therefore, that horticulture will be producing *heavier yields* with *much greater reliability* but at *higher costs*, based on *better exploitation of the potentials of site, soil and climate*. This will be achieved by using much more sophisticated methods, which will largely stem from the results of research on the basic relations between plants and the weather.

Good Management and Good Luck — The Basis of Productivity

The basis of productivity for any crop can be shown schematically in the following way:

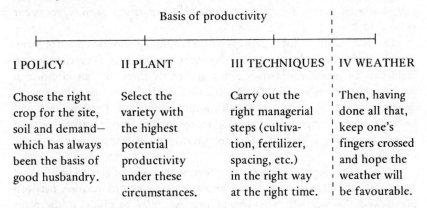

I POLICY	II PLANT	III TECHNIQUES	IV WEATHER
Chose the right crop for the site, soil and demand— which has always been the basis of good husbandry.	Select the variety with the highest potential productivity under these circumstances.	Carry out the right managerial steps (cultivation, fertilizer, spacing, etc.) in the right way at the right time.	Then, having done all that, keep one's fingers crossed and hope the weather will be favourable.

Items I, II and III are under managerial control but, as D.J. Watson said many years ago, climate determines what crop can be grown, but weather determines the yield we get. These weather effects are of extreme importance, as can be seen from a study of the yield data for any well-documented crop (Figure 12.1). The normal pattern is that, somewhere, there is a group of farmers who are getting much better yields than the

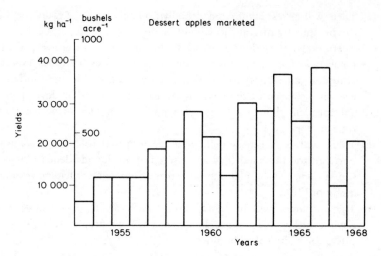

Fig. 12.1   *Output from one of the best managed orchards in the country,
showing the degree of unpredictable and uncontrollable variation
that occurs even in first-class orchards.*

national average, presumably because they are on better soils, have adequate
capital and, above all, are 'good farmers'. Within this group, one of the
farmers occasionally gets a 'record' crop, that is often nearly double his
normal yield, presumably because the weather is exceptionally favourable.
The farmers who get the record yields would no doubt always produce at that
level if they could, and the fact that they do not suggests that the
exceptionally favourable circumstances are not under their control. Thus
yield levels are partly due to good luck and only partly to good management
(Figure 12.2).

   This is a truism, but it is perhaps worth reminding ourselves that for many
crops the uncontrollable weather component can still have as much effect on
yields as all man's endeavours put together. Is there any significance in
Machiavelli's suggestion, in 'The Prince', that man's destiny and achievements
depend half on chance and only half on his own efforts? Perhaps we should
be less ready to congratulate the good grower on how much better he is than
others, but rather ask why he does not always get yields that are nearer to his
own records.

   If we are to attack this weather effect, in the hope of getting heavier and
more regular yields, we must first know more about the relation between
plants and the weather. The system that we refer to glibly as the plant
environment, the microclimate, or plant weather, as though it was a single
entity, is an extremely complex system of fourteen or so factors (Table 12.1),
some chemical but mostly physical, that vary continuously, largely independently, and even more unpredictably, but not chaotically. The system has
profound effects on all aspects of plant development and growth, and
somehow we must take its measure, both literally and metaphorically.

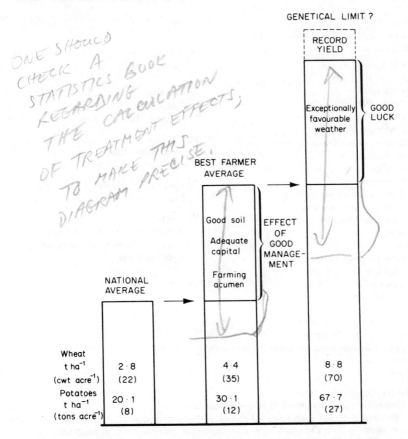

Fig. 12.2   Bonuses due to good luck and good management respectively, above the national average yield of a few typical crops.

Matching Crop and Site

The first necessity is to choose the right sites for the chosen crop. Horticulturalists have always been quite expert at this — from the local scale in selecting special sites for earliness or shelter to operations on the largest scale, such as the present move of the glasshouse industry to areas of better light and greater productivity, at a cost of millions of pounds. In the past these choices have been made empirically, by flair, experience and judgment, and often, no doubt, wrongly. Clearly we need much more information, so that sites can be characterized accurately for their crop potential. This is not an easy subject to study experimentally. Ideally, one would need a range of topographic sites, near to each other, providing various combinations of altitudes, aspects and slopes that produce a range of related climatological conditions, but research stations are rarely sited in such places. However, the Long Ashton estate fortunately offers a useful range of sites where preliminary studies of the relation between climate, weather, topography and

Table 12.1
Factors of the plant environment

Above ground	Below ground

Net radiation
    (heat + light etc.)
Light
    Daylength (duration)
    Spectral composition (quality)
    Intensity
    Integral (amount per unit time)
Temperature
    With special reference to the
    pattern of seasonal and daily
    fluctuations and the incidence
    of frost
Wind
    Average speed (wind run)
    Gustiness
    Direction
Cloud, mist and fog
Precipitation
    Dew, rain, sleet, snow, hail
Composition of the atmosphere
    Carbon dioxide concentration
    Pollution
    Ozone
	Temperature
	    With special reference to
	    gradients at different depths
	
	Soil moisture
	    Amount, availability to plants
	    and effects of salinity
	
	Composition of the soil atmosphere
	    (Especially concentration of CO_2)
	
	Nutrients
	    Concentration and availability of
	    each of a wide range of major and
	    minor nutrients
	
	Soil reaction (pH)
	
	Texture, as it affects the movement
	    of air and water and the growth
	    of roots.

Humidity (vapour pressure)
  Interactions at different levels of various factors
  Effects of change, i.e. direction of change and rate of change
  Variations in time and space in relation to the geometry and size of the plant

plant behaviour are now under way.

The future seems certain to see an increasing concentration of horticultural specialist crops in particularly suitable areas. Indeed, this is already happening, as in the recent spectacular concentration of cauliflowers in Lincolnshire, swedes in Devon, and the massive move of glasshouses to the high light areas on the south coast to which reference has already been made. In this connection we must not despair about the English climate. It is true that it does not reliably provide such good camping weather in July and August as the south of France, but our climate provides unusually high light-integrals in the long days of summer (Figure 12.3), that are probably more effective for growth than shorter, brighter days; a mild climate due to massive advection of energy from the Gulf stream; and relatively low evaporation rates that keep England the green and pleasant land it is, long after much of the nearby continent has dried out in the heat of summer. These are attributes of real horticultural significance, of which we are not perhaps taking the fullest possible advantage.

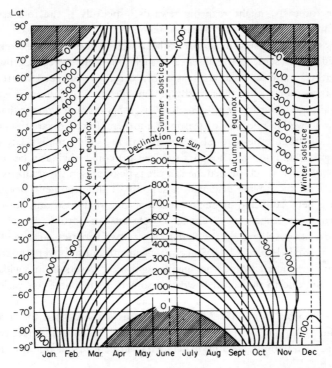

Fig. 12.3   Radiation energy (g cal cm⁻² day⁻¹) incident outside the earth's atmosphere, showing that areas at the latitude of Britain have as high a level of daily incident energy as the equatorial areas for a short period in summer; (from Smithsonian Tables, 4th reprint, 1968, p.419).

Exploiting the Weather

Having chosen the site, what can be done to make the best of it? There are four ways in which the effects of weather on yields might be affected, as shown in the scheme below:

Ways of altering the effects of weather on yields

(a) Plan according to weather	(b) Alter the weather	(c) Alter the microclimate	(d) Alter plant response to weather
Synoptic meteorology	Physics	Agricultural meteorology	Plant physiology

(a) *Planning according to probable weather,* based on short or long term weather forecasts, might reap big rewards, especially if the forecasts were sufficiently long-term, and accurate enough, to enable growers to sow varieties that were likely to do particularly well in the sort of season that is expected. At present, in the absence of such long-term forecasts, growers use 'all weather' varieties that are reasonably certain to succeed whatever the season turns out to be. Indeed, the present methods of testing varieties are specifically designed to identify such 'all weather' varieties rather than those likely to do well in one type of season or another. However, varieties *could* be selected that would be particularly suited for, say, hot summers, late springs, dry Augusts, and so on. Though a rich reward could obviously be reaped if the variety sown could be matched to the type of season we are likely to get, it is difficult to provide evidence in support of this argument, because few data have been collected on such a relation. One such case can, however, be cited from the results of a very large-scale trial of cotton varieties in the Gezira irrigation scheme, in the Sudan, where two varieties, Acala and Albar, were compared (Figure 12.4). Since management and soils were the same for both varieties in all years, the highly significant reversals in yields were, presumably, due to the fact that weather sometimes favoured one variety and sometimes the other. *If* the weather had been known ahead of sowing (admittedly a big 'if') and *if* Albar had been used throughout the scheme in 1960 and 1962, and Acala in 1961 and 1963, the Sudan would have reaped a very large cash bonus (*vide* a more detailed treatment of this point in Hudson, [3]).

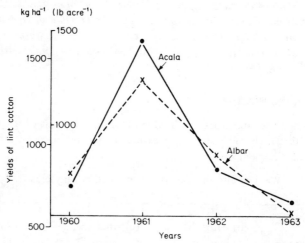

Fig. 12.4   Yields of two varieties of cotton in four different seasons in the Sudan; after Siddiq [4]. The trial was large-scale and well-replicated, and differences in yield were all significant at P = 0.01.

(b) *Altering the weather* appears to be a most unlikely possibility, partly because the amounts of energy involved are much too great to make the process economic, even if it were feasible, and partly because it would probably be impossible, anyway, to get everyone to agree to any particular change that it was proposed to make.

(c) *Altering the microclimate around the plants* is a real possibility, even in the open (it has, of course, been achieved long since by the glasshouse grower), and many methods are used already especially in harsher climates. For instance, overhead shade is in common use in the tropics to provide young plants with lower light intensities and milder evaporating conditions; thousands of acres of tobacco are grown under muslin tents in Connecticut for the production of cigar wrapper leaves; and the Japanese are past masters in the use of walls, shelters, flimsy film structures, and other devices to provide more favourable growing conditions. In Britain, late spring frosts are a particular bugbear to fruit growers, and the major effort in this country towards ameliorating the plant environment has been directed to preventing frost damage in orchards, though by relatively crude methods so far. On the Continent windbreaks are much more commonly used than here, though the climate in Britain is no less windy, and a programme of work has been started at Long Ashton with large portable windbreaks to find out whether it would be useful to provide more shelter here.

However, the big development in Britain may come from the use of what is now called *multi-purpose, solid-set irrigation,* which is a system that can be used to apply water for a great variety of purposes, namely for irrigation and frost protection; the application of insecticides, fungicides, herbicides, growth regulators and leaf nutrients; and to mist plants so that stomata can remain open throughout the middle of the day in hot, dry weather, even though there is an incipient shortage of soil water. The cost of this system is high, but apart from considerable savings in labour, it might enable good crops to be grown in relatively poor, shallow soil, so that its costs could be set off against the comparative cheapness of the land.

Horticulture, because of the high value of its produce, is certain to make full use of any methods that become available for ameliorating the bad effects of adverse weather conditions. Some of the methods, such as the use of mist in the open, would need far more perceptive control than we are now accustomed to give irrigation, and other methods will also have to be based on a much better understanding of the relation between plants and the weather.

(d) *To alter plant responses to weather* seems to be the most exciting prospect of all. A few experiments with raspberry plants some years ago showed that one could in fact do just that, e.g. makes shoots elongate under weather conditions where they would normally have rosetted, by the application of exogenous chemicals [2, 3]. Since then, many similar examples have been reported. The time seems ripe for a major effort to be applied to this field, to explore the possibilities of helping plants to keep growing if it is too dry, or too cold, or too cloudy for growth normally to continue; to help them to take greater advantage of higher light intensities (as with recent Australian work with clover and gibberellins); or to encourage the production of longer roots if there is a drought ahead, so that the moisture available in the soil can be exploited more efficiently.

Leaf Surfaces Hold the Key

Since the plant is affected so profoundly by environmental conditions it seems likely that, by the end of the century, we may be using plant responses as the basis of 'on-line control' for altering the setting of heating, cooling, lighting, CO_2 and ventilation controls in glasshouses and even, perhaps, to switch plant misting devices on and off in the open. The leaf surface is the major interface for the exchange of materials between plant and air, and this suggests that we should give much more thought to leaves, and the use of leaf phenomena, in plant management.

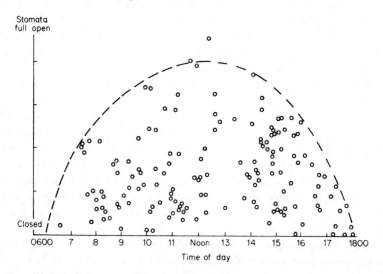

Fig. 12.5   Openness of stomata of sugar-cane leaves at different times on several different days, as measured by an Alvim-type porometer, showing that stomata can be closed, or nearly so, at any time of day according to weather, soil conditions, and other factors.

The leaf is an awkward structure to study because of its great area in relation to its mass, and also because its extreme mobility in most crops when the wind is blowing makes it difficult to study without altering the 'natural' conditions in which it operates. However, we can now see leaf surfaces very much better with the newly-available stereoscan electron microscope, and devices (porometers) are available for measuring the openness of stomata much more easily in the field. The use of porometers on crop plants sometimes shows that stomata are much more active than the classic 'open by day, closed by night' dogma used to suggest. This is shown, for instance, by data for sugar cane leaves (Figure 12.5), in which there seems to be a maximum degree of openness according to time of day, beyond which stomata rarely open, but the stomata are commonly much less open than that maximum, tending to close if a heavy cloud passes over the sun, if a leaf blows down into the canopy, if the soil dries out beyond a certain condition to produce a slight water stress, and for various other reasons.

However, it may be that leaf temperature will be an even more useful attribute to measure than stomatal openness. Leaves are commonly cooler than ambient when they are transpiring and warmer when stomata are closed by day, and a sensitive method of assessing leaf temperatures relative to ambient might give the first indication of day-time stomatal closure and, therefore, of the onset of water stress and the best time to irrigate. This might be done by taking the temperature of the leaf itself, by touching it with a very small thermometer [1] or more elegantly, by looking at the leaf and measuring its black-body radiation temperature, using infra-red or Schlieren effects, or in some other way.

Incidentally, though it seems unlikely that we shall be able to change the weather much, even by the end of the century, it may in fact change itself significantly in the foreseeable future. For the greater part of the evolutionary history of plants on earth, the atmosphere no doubt contained far more CO_2 than it does now. Colossal amounts of carbon were subsequently removed from the atmosphere and locked up in fossil fuels, chalk and limestone, since when plants have probably been chronically starved of sources of atmospheric carbon. There seems certain to be a steady increase in carbon dioxide in the air as we assiduously burn up the irreplaceable fossil fuels, and this *could* ultimately lead to a significant increase in growth and yield, since there is now a good deal of evidence that at least some glasshouse crops grow faster if the air is 'enriched' by up to three times its normal content of CO_2. It would be a curious quirk of fate if man's profligate waste of fossil fuels in the twentieth century increased the chances of his descendants feeding themselves in the twenty-first century! There is also, however, the possibility of a significant change in climatic conditions as a result of the effects of the higher CO_2 content on back radiation of energy from the earth, but that is not likely to have an effect on horticulture by 2000 A.D.

Use of Chemicals

By the end of the century, horticulturists are certain to be using growth regulators for a very wide range of purposes, some of which cannot yet be foreseen. Amongst the probable developments will be the use of growth substances to ensure that fruit hangs safely on the plant until it is ready to pick, and then other exogenous chemicals to loosen the fruit so that it will fall off at a touch. This will provide the basis for mechanical harvesting, and it is expected that *all* harvesting will be done by machine well before the end of the century.

Chemical pruning is likely to be used to stop all excessive shoot growth, so ending, not before time, the nonsense of allowing plants to produce unwanted shoot growth which then has to be pruned off to waste. Many other aspects of behaviour may also have come under chemical control including, no doubt, some aspects of the depressing effects of adverse weather on crop yields referred to earlier.

On the other hand, if we seem likely to use more chemicals for some purposes, these will all be completely innocuous, and it seems certain that there will be an increasing restriction on materials that are persistent or under the slightest suspicion of 'polluting the environment'. In recent years horticulturists have become chronic phytohypochondriacs, using as many potions to protect their plants as to dose themselves for their own imaginary ills. We have undoubtedly been far too brash in the past in using non-specific therapeutants, especially against pests, but there is now a noticeable revulsion against the present methods, and the tide of opinion may well run more strongly against the use of persistent and non-selective pesticides.

Already there are orchards advertizing that 'No sprays are used on this farm', which suggests that the public may be prepared to pay a premium for at least certain reassurances about the food they buy to eat. However, this introduces the whole concept of 'quality' on which horticulture basically depends, by attracting high prices for high-quality produce. The present situation is very odd, because the real attributes of quality, such as bouquet, flavour and texture of fruits and vegetables, on which the choice of varieties in private gardens used to be based, have on the whole given way to largely spurious conventions of quality such as colour, uniformity of size, and general 'market qualities'. As a result, the public now buys its horticultural products more on what they *look* like than on what they *taste* like, but there seems to be a good chance that this will right itself. There is no reason why good produce should not look well, but we perhaps ought to be giving more attention to the real attributes of quality, like aroma and flavour, that can now be characterised with precision using the modern sophisticated techniques of analytical chemistry.

Use of Space

However, important as some of the foregoing developments may be, the biggest real advance will probably come in the way we use *space*. Land can best be regarded as a place which receives incoming energy and provides an opportunity for it to be intercepted and 'fixed' by plants in a form that has a high saleable value. Light that falls on bare soil is wasted, and the time may even come when a grower or farmer who lets the sun shine on his soil will be regarded as profligate, wasting a valuable natural resource. Grass growers seem to be the most successful users of space, both on the score of density and continuity. Cereal growers cash in on the high light-integrals of May and June, but leave the ground bare for much of the year (and in any case, according to discussions elsewhere in this book, grow far too much straw). Row-crop producers, especially vegetable growers, are getting better at achieving full ground cover, though there is still a long way to go in some crops which are grown closely-spaced in wide rows, rather than equidistant.

Fruit growers are the worst offenders, leaving great swathes of space between their trees in the early years and wide alleys even when the trees are 'fully grown'. This has been a necessity in the past, because of the system of production on which fruit growing depended, but much thought has recently been given to more intensive systems of planting, such as, for instance, the hedgerow system that is now gaining momentum everywhere. Moreover, calculations suggest that there may be still more efficient ways of arranging trees on very dwarfing stocks, (e.g. [5] and S.K. Ries, Michigan State University, personal communication).

However, technology makes progress in two ways, by a steady improvement of old techniques and the sudden leap forward towards a brand new system, and it is the latter that is now being urgently sought for fruit production. The branching system that we call the fruit tree must necessarily be an inefficient structure for producing cropping units that are equally and precisely spaced, and various possibilities now being studied seek to by-pass the tree altogether, growing only the fruiting branches, evenly and closely spaced from the outset and then cut off when the fruit is ready to be harvested. This would involve planting very large numbers of trees per acre, which would only be practicable if much cheaper methods could be devised for raising the plants, and it will also require the solution of some other formidable problems. For instance, it will be necessary to induce growing shoots to form viable fruit buds freely in the first year, and it will also involve the perfection of the remote-control solid-set multi-purpose irrigation system referred to earlier, that would make it unnecessary to take men or machines through the orchard at all except for harvesting every second year. Although the difficulties are great, the evidence from comparable situations with other species suggests that none of the problems is insoluble. The production of fruit in this way is probably no more impossible than year-round pot chryanthemums would have seemed thirty years ago, and may enable fruit growers to produce yields that are at present completely unattainable.

This raises the difficult question of what *is* the potential of a crop, which is the central theme of this book. Mushroom growing is undoubtedly the biggest success story of the present century in horticulture, based on the incredible feat of increasing yields by more than threefold in less than twenty years by providing the crop with an ecological utopia. No one could have foreseen this development, and it seems most unlikely that a similar increase could be achieved with any other crop, but even so there still seems to be plenty of room for improvement before we approach the 'maximum' yield

Table 12.2
Levels of productivity for wheat

	cwt acre^{-1}	(t ha^{-1})
National average	22	(0.5)
'Good farmer' average	35	(7.1)
Record yield	70	(1.4)
Calculated possible (de Wit, 1966)	94	(1.9)

forecast by de Wit [6] from theoretical considerations (Table 12.2).

One of the problems, of course, is to know when crops have, in fact, reached their maximum size, i.e. achieved their potential. The only possible criterion, as a rule, is to assess how much better any particular crop is than others with which it can be compared, *because we normally have no yardstick by which to judge how far short it fell below the possible maximum.* For instance, it would be a great help, both in experimentation and in practical management, if the plant could indicate whether it is fully grown or not. It is difficult to see how this could be done for most crops, but colleagues at Long Ashton (A.J. Abbot and R.A. Webb, personal communication), working with strawberry, have recently found that the achenes on the fruit never draw further than a certain distance apart, i.e. when they are that far apart, the berry is as fully grown as is possible for that particular berry, which has thus by definition reached its potential. If the achenes on a ripe berry are closer than that potential distance, it is assumed that the berry could have grown bigger by a calculable amount but was prevented from doing so by adverse weather, inadequate soil water, or some other factor. It would be of great interest to know whether other crop plants have similar built-in markers to tell the grower whether his crop could have done better!

Conclusions

It seems likely that, by the end of the century, most of the world's food will still be coming from traditional plants, grown in more or less traditional ways, though horticulture may well by then have blazed a few new trails. Improvements in varieties, the much more sensitive use of irrigation and fertilizers, and better control of diseases and pests will all continue to pay off, but there will also have been some brand new thinking on the technologies concerned in crop production.

Since this book is devoted to crop potentials *in Britain*, it is perhaps permissible to hope that the result of research will give British growers a competitive advantage over their overseas rivals. This is most likely to stem from a better understanding and exploitation of those features of the British climate that are unique, and the introduction of new varieties that grow better here than anywhere else. What horticulture is like in 2000 A.D. will depend partly on what we do about it now, and the first step, if we wish to influence the future course of events, should be to define much more precisely the problems that we ought to be tackling in the next few years.

REFERENCES

1. ACOCK, B. 'Methods of measuring leaf temperatures', in Symposium on the Techniques of Experimentation in Greenhouses, *Technical Communication 7 of the International Society for Horticultural Science,* 1968, 74-80.

2. HUDSON, J.P. 'Effects of weather on plant behaviour', *Nature,* 1959, **182,** 1337-40.

3. HUDSON, J.P. 'Horticultural implications of long-term weather forecasts', *Proc. 17th International Horticultural Congress, IV,* 1967, 63-76.

4. SIDDIQ, M. 'Variation in performance of varieties of cotton in the Sudan Gezira', *The Empire Cotton Growing Review,* 1966, **43,** 98-106.

5. VERHEIJ, E. 'Mogelljkheden en grenzen van de rijenteelt. *De Fruitteelt,* 1968, **58, 528.**

6. WIT, C.T. de, 'Photosynthesis of crop surfaces', *Advancement of Science,* 1966, 159-162.

13. Novel Sources of Energy and Protein

Magnus Pyke
The Distillers Company Ltd., Glenochil Research Station, Menstrie,
Clackmannanshire

The main source of biological energy and protein, when considered in the context of crop production in Great Britain or in any other country, remain, as they always have been, the diverse plants capable of being grown in the environment of the British climate and the livestock which feed on them. There are, however, a few sources in use at present which might be considered to be novel. First, there are certain industrial by-products; second, there is the use of the chemical compound, urea, as a feedstuff. A third source of protein to which considerable attention has been given has been petroleum, on which yeast and certain other so-called 'single-cell protein' has been grown. Petroleum could, however, be used as a source of fat for human consumption. If this were successfully achieved, some proportion of the oil seeds now used as sources of fat would become available as a fifth source of animal feedstuff. Sixth and seventh sources of novel 'crops', which are possible but unlikely, would be the direct synthesis of sugar and protein. An eighth indirect source of energy and protein which would be novel to this country, though it has been adopted elsewhere, would be the consumption by human beings of what are customarily considered to be animal feeds. A final ninth category, from which again some minor supplies of feed could be put on the positive side of the balance sheet, would arise if, in the future, artificial foods were developed to allow over-nourished city dwellers to enjoy the pleasures of the table without at the same time absorbing any nutrients. The real food no longer eaten would, whether in Great Britain or elsewhere, release land for alternative crops. No attempt is made to estimate the magnitude of the supplies likely to become available from these novel sources; indeed, while each is, probably capable of being produced, some of the more speculative, may not in fact ever come into production at all.

Industrial By-Products

A good example of an industrial by-product from which energy, protein and accessory growth-promoting nutrients can be derived for animal feeding is that obtained from what was previously a discarded effluent liquor discharged from whisky distilleries. Malt whisky is made by extracting the sugars from ground, malted barley with hot water, cooling the 'worts' — that is, the liquor — thus produced and converting the sugars to ethanol by yeast fermentation. Grain whisky, which forms the substrate within which a number of malt whiskies are mixed in the preparation of blends, which are the form of whisky most commonly drunk, is made by combining a proportion of a non-malted grain, usually maize, with the malt, which contains sufficient enzyme activity to convert the maize starch as well as the starch initially present in the barley into soluble and largely fermentable sugars. When fermentation is complete, the alcoholic fraction of the fermented wash is separated by distillation. The aqueous portion contains husks and other outer layers of the grain, the fat originally present, the yeast which has multiplied about five-fold during the course of fermentation, and a proportion of oligesaccharides and so-called limit dextrins, which are starch residues from which all the disaccharide maltose units have been separated by the action of the alpha- and beta-amylase of the malt. In addition, there is a significant proportion of glycerol which occurs during the course of the alcoholic fermentation.

Table 13.1
Characteristic analysis of dried distiller's solubles

	Per cent		ug per g
Protein (N x 6.25)	27	Thiamine	3.5
Fat	9	Niacin	75.8
Fibre	5	Pantothenic acid	10.8
Ash	11	Riboflavin	11.9
Carbohydrate (by difference)	41	Choline	3080
Calories	353	Pyridoxin	1.0
	(per 100 g)	Biotin	0.3
		Inositol	7170

Traditionally, while a proportion of the yeast and other suspended solids present are recovered in settling ponds and sold wet to local farmers, the distillers disposed of the soluble solids as best they could, often by passing the spent wash through trickling biological filters. Partly due to the advance in technology and partly due to more stringent standards of effluent disposal, means have been developed to evaporate the liquor to a syrup and reduce the syrup to a powder by spray-drying or other means. The composition of the 'dried distiller's solubles', now obtained in quite significant tonnage, is shown in Table 13.1 [1, 18].

Such materials as dried distillery by-products, produced by the technical developments just described, constitute, together with brewers yeast, which can hardly be classed as a novel source of protein and energy, a modest contribution to the national supply of feedstuffs. A major change in chemical technology, however, affected to a major degree supplies of molasses, a traditional by-product of sugar manufacture, available as an animal feed. Molasses is accepted as a feed for dairy cows [12] and other livestock. Not many years ago, substantial quantities of molasses were used for the production of ethanol by fermentation. This means of production is no longer used, and the molasses distilleries are closed down. The magnitude and suddenness of the change are worth recording. In 1930, of the 102 million gallons of industrial alcohol manufactured in the United States, 96 million was made from molasses [21]. Ten years later in 1940, the total production was 128 million gallons, of which 88 million were made from molasses, while of the remainder 32 million gallons were synthesised from petroleum by esterification hydrolysis [2]. By 1960, of a total of 273 million gallons, 248 was synthesised. The change in Great Britain happened almost a generation later but has been equally complete. Between 1950 and 1960, the total production of industrial alcohol remained substantially steady at about 35 million gallons a year [3]. But whereas at the beginning of the decade 92 per cent was produced from molasses while 8 per cent was synthetic, by 1960 less than 30 per cent was still derived from molasses fermentation whole more than 70 per cent was produced synthetically as a petrochemical. It can reasonably be argued that the chemical procedure for making ethanol from petroleum provides, in effect, a novel source of energy for agricultural feeding in the form of the supplies of molasses not used in fermentation and available, at least in part, as an animal feedstuff.

The Manufacture and Use of Urea and Other Synthetic Nitrogen Sources

Urea is often claimed to have been the first biological product to have been produced by synthetic chemistry by Wohler in 1828. Today, it can be manufactured by several industrial processes. For example, calcium carbide heated with nitrogen is converted into calcium cyanamide. When an aqueous solution of calcium cyanamide is treated with carbon dioxide, the precipitated calcium carbonate removed and the solution of cyanamide acidified and warmed in the presence of a metallic catalyst, urea is formed. Alternatively, carbon dioxide and ammonia may be caused to combine directly at a pressure of 35 atmospheres and a temperature of $130\text{-}150^{\circ}C$ to form ammonium carbamate which decomposes to give urea.

Here, then, are two entirely non-biological industrial processes by which a chemical compound is produced which, as is now well known, [19], can be used in the nutrition of ruminants. Urea is now accepted as a supplementary source of available nitrogen convertible into protein by the flora of the rumen. In addition to numerous references to the exact procedure needed to obtain the best results from the use of urea in ruminant nutrition [4], a number of other purely synthetic nitrogen compounds have been employed in animal husbandry with at least some measure of success. A series of papers by Soviet workers published in 1967 [20] discuss in some detail the addition of ammonium bicarbonate, ammonium sulphate, ammonium chloride and diammonium phosphate, as well as urea, as novel sources of nutritionally available nitrogen.

A more direct and sophisticated approach to the application of industrial chemistry for the supply of alternative sources of synthetic or partly synthetic 'crops' for animal feeding is the manufacture of specific amino acids calculated to improve the biological value of natural feed protein either for growth or maintenance. Where vegetable protein constitutes the major proportion of the total protein supply of the ration, there is a likelihood that the amino acid, lysine, will be present in insufficient amount and that a supplementary supply of lysine, whether derived from a natural source, or as a synthetic chemical, will improve the biological effectiveness of the ration.

The practical usefulness of adding synthetic amino acids to animal feedstuff has already been demonstrated. Compounders of feed for pigs and poultry purchase a substantial amount of these substances, which must today be classified as industrial chemicals. Figures are most readily available for the United States, but they serve as an indication of what is feasible in Great Britain as well. It is, therefore, striking to note that a decade ago, in 1958, according to the records of the U.S. Tariff Commission, 121 000 lb (55 000 kg) of synthetic lysine was produced at an average cost of $9.08 a pound. By 1959, the quantity had increased to 273 000 lb (123 000 kg) and the cost fallen to $5.13 a pound; and by 1961, production exceeded 300 000 lb (136 000 kg) and the price averaged $4.33. At least two practicable synthetic processes have been described for the production of lysine, one using dihydropyran as a starting material [8] and the other based on caprolactam [5]. Furthermore, it has been found possible to produce synthetically the biologically acceptable laevo form of the amino acid to a degree of purity of 95 per cent [22].

Methionine was probably the first amino acid to be manufactured by chemical synthesis on a commercial scale and used as a feed supplement to increase the efficiency of meat conversion by livestock fed on predominantly cereal rations. In 1954, approximately 1 000 000 lb, that is 500 tons, was manufactured in the United States and marketed at an average cost of $2.91 per lb. By 1960, the total production had increased and the average price more than halved to $1.35 per lb [23].

Rather than discuss the synthesis of a series of amino acids one by one as novel sources of protein efficiency, it is probably more useful to consider the figures in Table 13.2 showing the proportion of the various amino acids required by chicks and pigs for growth, compared with the proportion present in the protein of a number of cereals and in that of egg, milk and meat. The comparatively low concentration of lysine and also of methionine and threonine can readily be observed.

The practical significance of these analytical determinations in animal husbandry is illustrated in the calculations made in the United States by the President's Science Advisory Committee [10]. These showed that, at the 1967 prices of synthetic amino acids, the addition of the appropriate amino acids as such was substantially more economical than adding either fish protein or soya. These figures are given in Table 13.3.

Similar though less explicit calculations have been made by D. Lewis at the University of Nottingham [14]. He reached the conclusion that a clear

Table 13.2
The requirements of amino acids by chicks and pigs compared with the
proportions present in certain feed proteins

Amino acids	Requirement (1% of diet)		Composition of protein (g./16 g.N)					
	Chicks	Pigs	Wheat	Maize	Sorghum	Egg	Milk	Meat
Histidine	0.3	0.3	2.1	2.5	1.8	2.4	2.6	3.4
Isoleucine	0.6	0.6	4.1	6.4	5.2	5.7	7.5	5.4
Leucine	1.4	1.2	6.8	15.0	13.2	8.8	11.0	5.1
Lysine	1.0	1.1	2.7	2.3	2.6	7.2	8.7	10.1
Methionine	0.4	0.4	2.0	3.1	0.5	3.8	3.2	2.6
Phenylalanine	0.8	0.7	5.0	5.0	4.6	5.7	4.4	4.4
Threonine	0.6	0.6	3.0	3.7	3.1	5.3	4.7	5.1
Tryptophane	0.2	0.2	1.3	0.6	1.0	1.0	1.9	1.1
Valine	0.8	0.6	4.3	5.3	4.7	8.8	7.0	7.0
Arginine	1.2	0.3	4.3	4.8	3.2	6.5	4.2	6.9

case could be made for encouraging a greater use of synthetic amino acids in poultry diets as well as in the diets of non-ruminant farm-animals. He suggested, indeed, that the time might not be too far distant when the laboratory might become a more effective site for the production of amino nitrogen than the farm.

Table 13.3
The relative cost of raising the protein value of a cereal ration to that of a ration containing casein as its protein either by synthetic amino acids or by the use of fish-protein concentrate or soya

Cereal	Amino acids (per cent)			Cost cents/lb (cents/kg)	Fish protein %	Cost cents/lb (cents/kg)	Soya protein %	Cost cents/lb (cents/kg)
	Lysine %	Threonine %	Tyrosine %					
Milled/ sorghum	0.45	0.18		0.72 (0.32)	4.65	1.16 (0.52)	7.0	1.05 (0.27)
Wheat	0.30	0.15		0.53 (0.24)	3.10	0.77 (0.35)	4.7	0.71 (0.32)
Maize	0.20		0.35	0.27 (0.12)	2.05	0.51 (0.23)	3.1	0.47 (0.21)
Barley	0.20	0.10		0.35 (0.15)	2.05	0.51 (0.23)	3.1	0.47 (0.21)

Petroleum as a Source of Protein

The attention which is at present attracted by the possibility of propagating yeast or other micro-organisms on petroleum hydrocarbons and using the dried yeast or bacteria as so-called 'single-cell protein' might give the impression that this is a new development. In truth, as is shown in Table 13.4, the fact that micro-organisms can be grown on a substrate of hydrocarbons has been known since 1895.

The papers referred to in Table 13.4 are, however, merely representative of more than 500 scientific reports which appeared in the decade from 1955 to 1965, while the micro-organisms, including yeasts, which are now known to be capable of living on hydrocarbons present in petroleum can be numbered in the thousands. It can be seen from all this that the production of 'single-cell protein' is technically feasible. And just as conventional feedstuffs can be produced with greater or with less efficiency, and consequently are economic or uneconomic depending on the skill of the producer and the environment in which he attempts to produce them, so also does the practibility of producing SCP from petroleum vary according to the capital cost of the equipment, the yield of product, the cost of purifying it for use and, finally, finding a market for it. Table 13.5 shows the comparative value, according to United States estimates, of SCP produced from yeast or from bacteria using the best available continuous-propagation systems, and the cost of other sources of protein with which it would need to compete.

Table 13.4
A selection of the published researches into the utilization of hydrocarbons by micro-organisms [11].

Date	Authors	Topic
1895	Miyoshi	Utilization of paraffin by *Botrytis cinerea*
1906	Sohngen	Utilization of methane by soil organisms
1913	Sohngen	Biological utilization by hydrocarbons
1928	Tausoon	Bacterial oxidation of crude oil
1940	Mogilevskii	Use of bacteria for oil prospecting
1942	Johnson *et al*	Studies of hydrocarbon metabolism
1942	Blau	Tests for microbes that metabolize hydro-carbons
1943	Hassler	First U.S. patent on the use of micro-organisms in oil prospecting
1943	Strawinski and Stone	Studies of hydrocarbon microbiology
1944	Novelli and ZoBell	Further development of hydrocarbon micro-biology
1947	Evans	Utilization of aromatic compounds by micro-organisms
1950	Hayaishi and Hashimoto	Studies of oxygenases
1952	Davis	Geomicrobiology of soil
1954	MacDonald, Stainier and Ingraham	Developments in aromatic breakdown
1959	Stewart and Kallio	Microbiological utilization of n-alkanes
1959	Leadbetter and Foster	Further studies with n-alkanes
1960	Raymond and Davis	Report of rapid metabolism of n-alkanes
1961	Senes and Azunlay	Mechanism of n-alkane utilization
1963	Champagnat	British patent for edible yeast from crude oil fractions
1964	Davis *et al*	Protein from methane-oxidising bacteria
1965	Takahashi *et al*	Production of glutamic acid

Several lines of research are being pursued in this field. On the one hand, the yeast or other micro-organism can be propagated on a crude petroleum fraction, and the SCP subsequently purified to free it from residues of unmetabolised hydrocarbons. An alternative approach is to purify the substrate carefully so as to ensure its complete metabolism by the organism.

Dried yeast recovered from both these approaches has been used successfully in feeding trials. Although full details are not at present very readily available, it would seem that the usefulness of SCP grown on a petroleum fraction will depend in the main on the price at which it can be produced.

Table 13.5
Comparative costs of protein produced by growing micro-organisms on petroleum compared with conventional protein sources

Product	Protein content	Price per lb	Price per lb protein
		(per kg)	(per kg)
	(%)	(U.S. $)	(U.S. $)
Peanut flour	59	0.07 (0.031)	0.12 (0.054)
Soya flour	43	0.05 (0.025)	0.12 (0.054)
Cottonseed	50	0.05 (0.026)	0.10 (0.045)
Skim milk powder	36	0.15 (0.068)	0.41 (0.019)
Food yeast (Torula)	48	0.17 (0.077)	0.36 (0.172)
Protein from petroleum (SCP)	—	—	0.35 (0.158) (estimate)

Petroleum as a Substitute for Oil Seeds

The production of dried yeast and other single-cell protein based on hydrocarbon as a raw material appears to be a practical proposition within reasonable reach of realisation. An alternative, although perhaps more speculative, possibility which might lead to the use of petroleum to provide a novel source of energy as well as protein would be the conversion of hydrocarbon oils into edible fats. During World War II this was done on a substantial scale in Germany. The aim of the work, however, was to produce fats for human consumption. An alternative possibility which does not appear to have been followed up would be to use such fat, in the same way as molasses is used, as an energy source for livestock. Although it is not possible to make any reasonable estimate of the economic feasibility of such an idea, the technical practibility of producing fat in this way is unquestionable.

The technological developments which German chemists, in the years between the wars, developed for converting coal into 'petroleum' by the Fischer Tropsch process, and then using the so-called 'Gatsch' fraction as the starting material for fat synthesis, were described by Kraut [13]. The whole operation represented a remarkable example of making use of a basic raw material, namely coal, to produce, as it were, both guns and butter. The use of a specially selected hydrocarbon fraction as the starting material for fat synthesis was essential for the production of a reasonably odourless product. In 1937, a German firm in Witten, using a Gatsch hydrocarbon fraction heated and aerated in the presence of a potassium-permanganate catalyst, produced fatty acids, subsequently esterified with glycerol and converted into fat on a commercial scale [24].

Some thousands of tons of synthetic fats were manufactured in Germany during World War II, converted into margarine and eaten. According to Williams, most people commented unfavourably about its taste but ate it nevertheless. On the other hand, it had a creamy consistency, was easy to spread and, due to the absence of traces of protein present in butter, it kept well. As shown in Table 13.6, the composition of synthetic fat differs from that of natural fat in containing fatty acids with odd numbers of carbon atoms. The only unfavourable physiological effect, an increased excretion of dicarboxylic acids and a tendency to cause diarrhoea in human beings, due, it was thought, not to the unnatural fatty acids but to the increased concentration of branched-chain fatty acids, though undesirable in human dietetics is probably of only minor significance in animal diets. The estimated price of £177 a ton (£3.6 /t) in 1939-45 is probably its most serious disadvantage. The fact remains, however, that it can be made if there is a sufficiently strong motive to make it, as there was in Germany between 1940 and 1945.

Table 13.6
The chemical composition of synthetic fat compared with that of butter fat and coconut oil (per cent)

Fatty acid	Synthetic fat	Butter fat	Coconut oil
C_8 and below	0	5.9	6.2
C_{10}	4.2	3.0	4.8
C_{11}	12.0	0	0
C_{12}	10.2	4.1	45.4
C_{13}	10.5	0	0
C_{14}	8.8	13.7	18.0
C_{15}	10.5	0	0
C_{16}	9.5	29.3	11.8
C_{17}	8.0	0	0
C_{18}	9.1	42.4	9.8
C_{19}	17.2	0	0
C_{20}	17.2	1.6	0.4

The Direct Utilization of Animal Feedstuffs in Human Diets

Clearly the potential crop production in Great Britain would be increased if human beings themselves ate some of the animal concentrates which are usually fed to livestock. The diversion of feed in this way could, therefore, be taken to fall within the area of a discussion on novel sources of energy and protein. In the main, a net increase of this sort in the nation's potential food production is as much a matter of sociology as it is one of food manufacture. For example, dried milk is an animal feed only because of the market for butter and a corresponding taste of a wealthy population for full-cream milk, thus leaving the skimmed milk to be used as an animal feed. During the war years, much of the liquid milk available in Germany for putting in coffee was so-called 'Magermilch', from which half the butter fat had been removed. Such a procedure was never accepted in Great Britain but there is no reason why it should not be. Indeed, such a step might actually benefit the nation's nutritional health.

Intense, although not very successful [16] efforts have been made to popularise so-called 'fish flour' as a human food. In effect, this commodity is fish meal from which the fat, and with it the fishy taste, has been extracted. Two difficulties have so far hampered the acceptance of fish flour as an ingredient of human diet: even when the taste has been removed, it is not particularly attractive to eat and tends to be gritty; and, secondly, it also tends to be expensive to prepare.

Table 13.7

Amino acids produced from simple gases (a) by heat in the presence of silica and (b) by electric discharge (per cent)

Amino acids	Fox and Harada's synthesis by heat			Miller's synthesis using electric discharge	
	Silica sand 950°C	Silica gel 950°C	Silica gel 1050°C	Spark discharge	Silent discharge
Aspartic acid	3.4	2.5	15.2	0.3	0.1
Threonine	0.9	0.6	3.0		
Serine	2.0	1.9	10.0		
Glutamic acid	4.8	3.1	10.2	0.5	0.3
Proline	2.3	1.5	2.3		
Glycine	60.3	68.8	24.4	50.8	41.4
Alanine	18.0	16.9	20.2	27.4	4.7
Valine	2.3	1.2	2.1		
Alloisoleucine	0.3	0.3	1.4		
Isoleucine	1.1	0.7	2.5		
Leucine	2.4	1.5	4.6		
Tyrosine	0.8	0.4	2.0		
Phenylalanine	0.8	0.6	2.2		
Alpha-aminobutyric acid	0.6			4.0	0.6
Beta alanine	?	?	?	12.1	2.3
Sarcosine				4.0	44.6
N-methylalanine				0.8	6.5

Various other proposals have been made, not so much in Great Britain as abroad where the level of nutrition is less satisfactory than our own, to compound mixtures to complement dietary deficiencies. For example, in Central America, INCAPARINA, a mixture incorporating cottonized meal as a source of protein, has had some limited success [7]. Here again is an example, which might perhaps develop in the future, of what is normally though to be animal feed used in human diet.

Speculative Possibilities

Individual amino acids are already manufactured as fine chemicals and marketed as ingredients of animal and poultry feed. This being so, it is worth referring to the discovery of Lob [15] in 1913, that when an electric discharge was passed through a mixture of CO, ammonia and water vapour, glycine was produced. Miller [17] in 1955 showed that not one but several amino acids were produced simultaneously. Later, Harada and Fox [9] showed that all the nutritionally necessary amino acids may be synthesized simultaneously from simple gases. These results are summarized in Table 13.7. Fox [6] has further shown that when such amino-acid mixtures are heated under appropriate conditions, polymerised 'proteinoids' are produced with molecular weights up to 8500. The possibility, therefore, exists of manufacturing something much nearer protein than urea as a novel animal feed.

REFERENCES

1. ANON, *Brewers Guardian,* June 1961, **49**.
2. CALDWELL, D.L. and LICHTENSTEIN, I. 'Ethanol', *Kirk-Othmer Encycl. Chem. Tech.,* 1965, **8**, 422.
3. CARLE, T.C. and STEWART, D.M., 'Synthetic Ethanol Production', *Chem. and Ind.,* 1962, **830**.
4. CHALUPA, W., 'Problems in feeding urea to ruminants', *J. Animal Sci.,* 1968, **27**, 207.
5. ECK, J.C. and MARVEL, C.S. 'A convenient synthesis of DL-Lysine', *J. biol. Chem.,* 1934, **106**, 387.
6. FOX, S.W. 'A Theory of Macromolecular and Cellular Origins', *Nature,* 1965, **205**, 328.
7. GALLIVER, G.B., 'Economic and production problems in the development of new protein sources', *Proc. Nutrition Soc.,* 1969, **28**, 97.
8. GAUDRY, R. 'The synthesis of D.L.α amino-ϵ-hydroxycaproic acid and a new synthesis of DL-Lysine', *Can. J. Res.,* 1948, **26B**, 387.
9. HARADA, K. and FOX, S.W. 'Thermal synthesis of natural amino-acids from a postulated primitive terrestrial atmosphere', *Nature,* 1964, **201**, 335.
10. HOWE, E.E., 'The World Food Problem', *Rept. President's Sci. Adv. Cttee.,* 1967, **2**, 319.
11. HUMPHREY, A.E. 'A critical review of hydrocarbon fermentations and their industrial utilization', *Biotechnol. and Bioeng.,* 1967, **9**, 3.
12. KOMBRIS, T., STANLEY, R.W. and MARITA, K., 'Effect of feeds containing molasses fed separately and together with roughage on digestibility of rations volatile fatty acids produced in the rumen, milk production and milk constituents', *J. Dairy Sci.,* 1965, **48**, 714.
13. KRAUT, H. 'The Physiological Value of Synthetic Fats', *Brit. J.*

Nutrition, 1949, **3**, 355.
14. LEWIS, D. 'Synthetic Amino-Acids in Poultry Diets', *J. Sci. Food Ag.*, 1966, **17**, 382.
15. LOB, W. 'Uber das verhaltes des formamibs unter ber wirkung derstillen ent-adung: ein beitrag zue frage der flictoff-assimilton', *Chem. Ber.*, 1913, **46**, 690.
16. LOVERN, J.A. 'Problems in the development of fish protein concentrates', *Proc. Nutrition Soc.*, 1969, **28**, 81.
17. MILLER, S.L. 'Production of some organic compounds under possible primitive earth conditions', 1955, **77**, 2351.
18. RAE, I.J. 'Distillery By-Product Recovery', *Process Biochem.*, 1966, 407.
19. STANGEL, H.J. *Urea and non-protein nitrogen in ruminant nutrition*, 2nd ed., New York: (Allied Chemical Corp.), 1963.
20. TOMME, M.F., ed., *Izdad*, Moscow: Kolos, 1967.
21. U.S. Bureau of Internal Revenue, 1930.
22. U.S. Patents 2,556,907; 2,657,230; 2,859,244.
23. WHITE, H.C., 'Practical synthetic routes to the essential amino acids', *Conf. on Protein Needs, Washington D.C.*, 1960.
24. WILLIAMS, P.M., *Chem. and Ind.*, 1947, **251**.

14. Efficiency of Food Production by the Animal Industries

W. Holmes
Wye College, University of London

Previous chapters have been concerned with the primary productivity of farm crops, but man and his animals can utilise only a proportion of this production. This chapter is concerned with the efficiency with which farm animals convert feedstuffs into food for man.

In supplying the human population with food and fibre the concern is not so much with the gross biological output as with the economic output, whether it be the proportion of the crop which is directly usable or the proportion of the crop which is converted by the animal into material for human consumption.

With the food crops only a proportion of the total photosynthate is utilized, e.g. 30 to 70 per cent for grain, pulses and root crops [11, 24]. Other forms of crop production, such as grass and forage crops, are generally considered to be unsuitable for human consumption, as are many of the by-products of crop production such as straws, haulms and brewing residues. These can be used by the animal. Moreover, many areas of land are inaccessible for cropping because of slope or wetness, or are unsuitable because of climatic or soil limitations. These lands again can be harvested only by the animal. The poorer lands receive no further consideration in this paper; their gross output is low and the proportion converted into animal product is governed by the same principles which apply to animal production on the better land.

Problems of Food Production on the Better Land

On the better land there are many alternative methods of exploitation.

(a) The production of crops for direct human consumption.
(b) The production of crops for animal feed.
(c) The production of forages for animal feed.

In a rational food policy the relative merits of these systems should be considered and the strong claims for direct use of vegetable foods in terms of output per hectare must be recognised [19].

Units

Much confusion is caused by the variety of units used in assessing conversion efficiency.

The botanist is concerned with total dry matter or total energy output, and he has demonstrated that up to 13 per cent of the usable light energy received may be converted into plant product [1, 11], or up to 5 per cent of total energy receipt, although 1 per cent of total energy is a more common figure.

The animal nutritionist is conscious that only a proportion of the total crop will be of potential use to the animal and that the energy concentration, and possibly the protein concentration, of the feed may limit animal output. For example the cow might digest 80 per cent of the dry matter of a young pasture, but only 45 per cent of a pasture which had been allowed to mature. Then there are urinary and gaseous losses from the animal body so that the metabolizable energy (M.E.) of a food may be only 40 to 85 per cent of its gross energy content. Similarly the digestible crude protein (D.C.P.) is only probably 50 to 90 per cent of the total crude protein content of a foodstuff.

To the livestock producer, therefore, it is not the total output of dry matter or gross energy but the production of metabolizable energy and digestible crude protein which is important. For simplicity, mineral balance and amino-acid balance (for non-ruminants) in the diets are ignored, not because they are unimportant, but because deficiencies in these nutrients can be more readily met by the addition of supplements to the main diet.

The human nutritionist considers it the function of agriculture to feed the people, and he is concerned with effective output of edible energy and edible protein. In addition to problems of the production of food crops and of the efficiency with which the animal converts feed energy and protein into animal product, the question of how much of the animal product is acceptable for human consumption is important. Blaxter [3], for example, points out that with beef animals, little over half of the protein is edible, and Davidson and Mathieson [8] have shown that only one third of the energy in a broiler chicken is eaten.

A diagrammatic breakdown of these aspects of food conversion is shown in Table 14.1. The efficiency with which gross energy or crude protein is converted into animal product thus depends on the digestibility of the feed and on the magnitude of the gaseous and urinary losses, as well as on the biochemical efficiency with which assimilated energy and protein is converted into milk, meat or eggs. However, efficiency also depends on the proportion of the total feed which is available for production, compared with that required to maintain the animal, and on the nature of the animal product, since with meat animals the relative proportion of fat and lean deposited influence the feed required per unit gain, and so the acceptability of the final product to the consumer.

The Efficiency of Farm Animals

The efficiency of farm animals for food production has fascinated many workers, and reference should be made to Middleton [23], Leitch and Godden [17], Brody [6], Kleiber [15], Duckham [10] and Blaxter [2, 3, 4]

Table 14.1
The conversion of gross energy or total protein into animal product

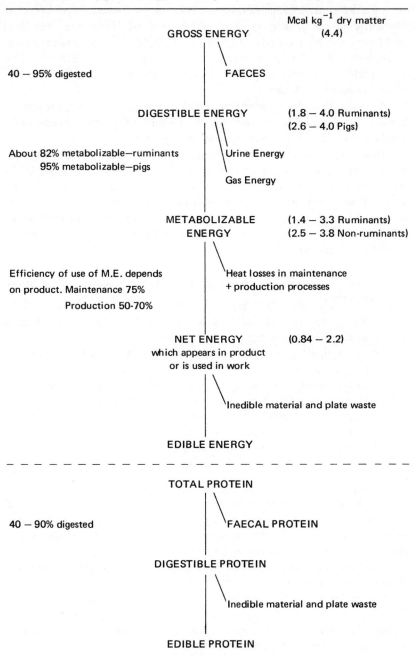

GROSS ENERGY — Mcal kg^{-1} dry matter (4.4)

40 – 95% digested — FAECES

DIGESTIBLE ENERGY — (1.8 – 4.0 Ruminants) (2.6 – 4.0 Pigs)

About 82% metabolizable–ruminants
95% metabolizable–pigs — Urine Energy / Gas Energy

METABOLIZABLE ENERGY — (1.4 – 3.3 Ruminants) (2.5 – 3.8 Non-ruminants)

Efficiency of use of M.E. depends on product. Maintenance 75% Production 50-70% — Heat losses in maintenance + production processes

NET ENERGY (0.84 – 2.2)
which appears in product or is used in work — Inedible material and plate waste

EDIBLE ENERGY

TOTAL PROTEIN — FAECAL PROTEIN

40 – 90% digested

DIGESTIBLE PROTEIN — Inedible material and plate waste

EDIBLE PROTEIN

for earlier surveys of the problem and for experimental studies on it.

A definition of feed conversion efficiency might be 'that proportion of the specified nutrient which in the specified time is converted into a product for consumption or use by man'. In agricultural circles the term feed conversion is often misused and applied to the weight of feed used per weight of animal product. The term *feed utilization* (as proposed by Blaxter [3]) is to be preferred for this more loose definition, which is in fact the reciprocal of feed conversion efficiency.

For meat animals, kg carcass per 100 kg DOM (digestible organic matter) has also been used [7, 26] but this can be misleading since carcasses may yield from 1.3 (broiler) to 5 Mcal (beef) energy per kg.

This chapter considers the following nutrients: gross energy, metabolizable energy and crude protein. The time scale is also of vital importance. To take only an extreme example, a cow at the peak of lactation may convert some 50 per cent of the M.E. consumed into milk energy, whereas when she is dry her efficiency of conversion to milk is zero, and over her lifetime efficiency will be between 10 and 30 per cent for M.E. and C.P., depending on yield and longevity.

The present survey will consider the influence of the productivity of the animal and the species on efficiency. Efficiency will be expressed in the following terms:

(a) The proportion of the G.E. and of the M.E. consumed which is available as food energy.

(b) The proportion of the crude protein consumed which is available as edible protein.

(c) The production of edible protein per unit of M.E. consumed. This criterion is justified because energy is usually the food source which limits animal production, while protein is the major nutrient of importance to human nutrition [4].

(d) The proportion of the crop harvested.

(e) The output of human food as energy and protein per unit area.

It cannot be too strongly emphasized that only the energy exchanges which take place at the tissue or cellular level are of constant efficiency. All other values depend on the management of the livestock and on the proportion of the total nutrient consumption devoted to the production of the desired nutrient, compared with that used for all purposes.

Schematically, efficiency can be expressed in the equation which is described in Table 14.2.

The estimates of efficiency can be considered in three stages:

(i) The range in performance which may be expected from individual animals over normal periods of life.

(ii) The comparative efficiency of normal breeding populations of farm animals.

(iii) The output per hectare which can be expected from these situations contrasted with that from other forms of food production.

Table 14.2

The generalized form for the overall efficiency of an animal product

Product in time t (gain and/or milk, wool, eggs)		
$E =$		
Total maintenance for time t (M)	Total, milk, eggs, wool in time t	Total gain in time t
+	+	
Efficiency for maintenance	Efficiency for milk Efficiency for eggs Efficiency for wool	Efficiency for gain

or

$$E = \frac{P}{\dfrac{M}{K_m} + \dfrac{milk}{K_l} + \dfrac{eggs}{K_e} + \dfrac{wool}{K_w} + \dfrac{total\ gain}{K_f} - \dfrac{total\ loss}{K_m}}$$

All measures relate to the same time period. In addition the food cost of producing the young animal must be considered.

P is expressed as product or energy or protein,

E is expressed as a decimal,

K_m is expressed as a decimal, and is efficiency of use of the nutrient for maintenance,

K_l is expressed as a decimal, and is efficiency of use of the nutrient for lactation,

K_w is expressed as a decimal, and is efficiency of use of the nutrient for wool production,

K_e is expressed as a decimal, and is efficiency of use of the nutrient for egg production,

K_f is expressed as a decimal, and is efficiency of use of the nutrient for fattening.

Factors which Influence Feed Utilization and Food Conversion Efficiency

(a) Blaxter [3] and Kleiber [15] have pointed out that the relative feed capacity (R.F.C.) i.e. Maximum intake: intake for maintenance, is of profound importance, since only the feed consumed above the maintenance requirement can be put to productive use. Within species, the animal which eats the greater amount of feed will be the more efficient. However, species also differ in relative feed capacity, and lactation and growth rate are associated with R.F.C.

(b) The animal whose output as milk, eggs or gain relative to maintenance is higher is the more efficient.

(c) Since the body tissues contain an increasing proportion of fat as the animal ages, the younger animal or the later-maturing animal is more efficient, both because the deposition of fat is a less efficient process than the deposition of muscle, and because above a certain level

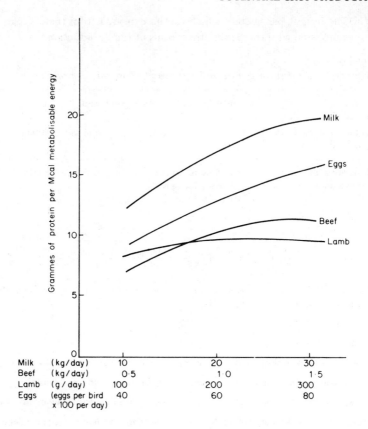

Fig. 14.1   Daily performance and efficiency of conversion of metabolizable energy.

fatness is undesirable to the consumer. With meat animals there is therefore an optimum age of slaughter which depends on the market demand [4].

(d) Since the early period of non-productive growth yields no immediate return, the animal which becomes sexually mature earlier is more efficient; this is of particular importance with chickens and dairy heifers but also affects sheep, cows and pigs. This generalization may be offset in economic terms where cheap feed supplies may justify later maturation.

(e) Since the maintenance requirement of the dam has to be charged to the production of young, prolificacy and regularity of breeding also influence feed utilization and feed efficiency.

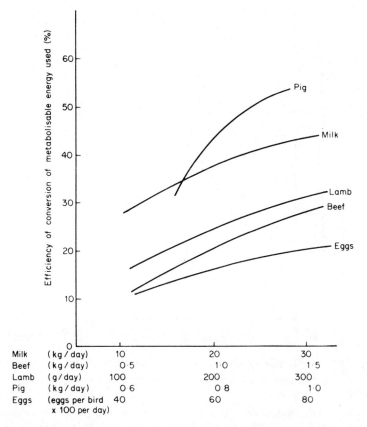

Milk	(kg / day)	10	20	30
Beef	(kg / day)	0·5	1·0	1·5
Lamb	(g / day)	100	200	300
Pig	(kg / day)	0·6	0·8	1·0
Eggs	(eggs per bird x 100 per day)	40	60	80

Fig. 14.2   Daily performance and efficiency of production of edible protein per unit of metabolizable energy consumed.

Efficiency in Simple Situations; the Individual Animal

For the cow, the chicken, and the growing fattening animal, the higher the rate of production, the greater the efficiency. An indication of normal levels is shown in Figures 14.1 and 14.2. These probably flatter the meat animals since not all the tissue deposited is edible.

In all farm animals, however, it should be noted that economic efficiency may fall off more rapidly than indicated where, with the cow or the laying hen, the animal's physiological state or the quality of the management does not encourage milk or egg production, and nutrients may be deposited as body fat. Similarly with the growing fattening animals, where the nutrient intake exceeds the capacity of the animal to deposit lean tissue, the additional nutrients may be converted to fat, which is converted with somewhat lower efficiency than lean meat and is liable to become an unacceptable product. The extreme example is the 'heavy hog' whose surplus fat may be a waste product.

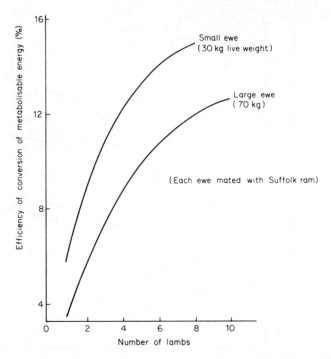

Fig. 14.3   Influence of number of lambs and size of ewe on efficiency of conversion of metabolizable energy; from Spedding [26].

Level of production can also refer to the output from reproducing animals. Clearly with the breeding cow or ewe, the whole food cost for the year must be charged to the calves or lambs produced. Spedding [26] has illustrated the potential increases in efficiency from sheep if lamb numbers can be increased, (Figure 14.3 based on Spedding [26]). This shows diminishing returns, and with the sow the additional advantage in feed efficiency is small when the number of piglets per year rises above ten.

Attention should also be paid to the size of the dam when it is maintained primarily to produce young. So long as the growth potential of the young is not impaired, the smaller the dam, the more efficient is the overall process [21, 26]. Cross breeding with a male of a larger breed may provide a greater growth potential in the young without increasing the maintenance cost of the dam.

With breeding animals, longevity is also important. Clearly the cow, sow or ewe which is reared and achieves only one or two pregnancies is much less efficient than the animal which continues to produce. As illustrated in Figure 14.4 for milk cows, however, little advantage in efficiency is gained beyond five lactations. Moreover, since modern methods of breeding allow some possibility of genetic improvement, undue lengthening of the generation interval is not desirable.

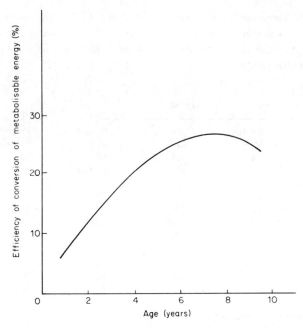

*Fig. 14.4   Effect of longevity on the efficiency of conversion of metaboliz-
able energy by the dairy cow.*

The data given in Figure 14.1 and 14.2 also may be applied to indicate
the efficiency of, for example, a hen over the laying period, a cow for a
lactation, or a growing fattening animal over its lifetime. The hen averaging
230 eggs (63 per cent) converts about 18 per cent of the M.E. consumed. A
cow in one lactation of 4000 kg milk converts 28 per cent of the M.E.
consumed, but if she is so managed that the yield is 5500 kg, efficiency of use
of M.E. rises to 35 per cent for that lactation. The beef animal raised to 400
kg liveweight in one year has converted 14 per cent of the M.E. consumed
into edible product. If it takes two years to reach a weight of 550 kg, the
increased cost of maintenance results in its energetic efficiency being reduced
to about 11 per cent.

The Efficiency of Conversion in Whole Farm Situations

While consideration of the individual aspects affecting feed efficiency in farm
animals is of value in understanding the problem, both the farmer and the
food planner are much more concerned with the overall performance of
representative flocks and herds.

It will be appreciated that level of crop production, intensity of stocking
and management, efficiency of administration of food, replacement rate of
breeding stock, success in the prevention or control of disease and the level of
performance of growing, milking or egg-yielding stock will affect these

figures. However, the data assembled in Table 14.3 indicate the levels of performance which may be reasonably expected under good conditions of management in the U.K., and allow for some comparison between the major forms of animal production.

Table 14.3
Efficiency in whole farm situations

	Energy M.E. (a) %	Energy G.E. (b) %	Protein M.E. (c) g/Mcal	Protein Protein (d) %
Dairy Farm (1)	21	12	10	23
Dairy + Beef (2)	20	11	9	20
Beef (3)	7	4.5	2.6	6
Sheep (4)	3	1.7	1.3	3
Pigs (5)	23	17	6	12
Broiler (6)	13	10	11	20
Eggs (7)	15	11	11	18

The efficiencies are expressed as:

(a) $\dfrac{\text{Edible energy}}{\text{Total metabolizable energy consumed}}$ (b) $\dfrac{\text{Edible energy}}{\text{Total gross energy consumed}}$

(c) $\dfrac{\text{Edible protein}}{\text{Total metabolizable energy consumed}}$ (d) $\dfrac{\text{Edible protein}}{\text{Total feed protein consumed}}$

The estimates are based on the following levels of physical performance

(1) 4100 kg milk per cow, 25% replacement rate, 0.6 ha per livestock unit, 1000 kg purchased concentrates per cow.
(2) As above, with 72 beef grazing cattle reared up to 450 kg liveweight, consuming 550 kg concentrates per head.
(3) 92% calves reared, 20% replacement rate, 0.6 ha per livestock unit, 250 kg concentrates per cow, 800 kg concentrates per suckled calf fattened.
(4) 150% lambs weaned, 25% replacement, 7.5 ewes per ha, 100 kg concentrates per ewe.
(5) 16 bacon pigs per sow per year, replacements = cast sows, 3.5 kg meal/kg gain.
(6) 2.5 kg meal per kg gain, broiler 1.6 kg liveweight at 56 days.
(7) 233 eggs per bird per year, 19.6 kg food per 100 eggs, 12 kg to rear chicken.

All concentrates balanced according to protein requirements from barley at 3200 kg grain per ha and beans at 2400 kg per ha.

Particular difficulty occurs in assessing the yield of edible product from meat animals. For the larger animals this analysis is based mainly on the data of Leitch and Godden [17], but for broiler chickens the data of Davidson and Mathieson [8] have been taken.

At the lowest level in all respects came the breeding ruminants used for meat production, with cattle somewhat superior to sheep because of the lower proportion of the total feed needed to maintain the breeding female and the lower replacement rate for cattle compared with sheep. Whether with sheep or cattle the limitation, indeed the almost insuperable handicap, is the need to maintain the dam for the year to produce one or two calves or one to three lambs. The considerable interest in achieving control over reproduction to increase the number or the frequency of births is stimulated by these facts. It should be realised, however, that while additional technical inputs may increase the feed efficiency of the process, this may be offset by other costs. It is for these reasons that Holmes and Jones [12] suggested that sheep and beef breeding-stock should be maintained on the cheaper land, and recent trends in the British sheep industry have agreed with this suggestion.

Another approach which is already widely practised, and which might be developed further, is for the breeding animals to be maintained on the land of lower productivity and for their progeny to be transported at weaning to better conditions. Thus only the more efficient process of growing and fattening takes place on the better land.

The much greater efficiency of lactation as an animal process is indicated by the much higher values in all respects calculated for the dairy herd. Surprising at first sight is the relatively small effect which rearing the progeny for beef has on overall efficiency. While the young cattle themselves convert only about 15 per cent of the M.E. and C.P. consumed into animal product, the overall depression on efficiency of the enterprise is small. Again these computations are in agreement with practice in the industry where, either within farms or between farms, a major proportion of British beef production is derived from the dairy herd.

With the pig enterprise, extremely high efficiency in use of energy occurs in growth and lactation and results in a high overall figure. At normal levels of feeding, however, efficiency of protein use is low.

With poultry there is a close similarity in estimates of efficiency of egg and broiler production, with relatively low efficiency of use of energy but a high efficiency of conversion of protein.

Output per Unit Area

When the efficiencies in Table 14.3 are applied to representative levels of crop yield and stocking rate, the outputs per hectare shown in Table 14.4 are derived. The ruminant animals assume a similar order to that in Table 14.3. With the non-ruminants, however, since the food is based on only some 50 − 60 per cent of the total energy of the cereal or bean crops (the grain), the outputs per hectare are reduced despite the high efficiency of the populations. Similarly, feeding of ruminants mainly on grain products reduces output per area used for food production.

The utilization of farm and industrial by-products cannot be considered

Table 14.4

Edible yields from animals and from crops

	Energy (Mcal ha^{-1})	Protein (kg ha^{-1})
Dairy	2500	115
Dairy & Beef	2400	102
Beef	750	27
Sheep	500	23
Pigs	1900	50
Broilers	1100	92
Eggs	1150	80
Wheat	14000	350
Peas	3000	280
Cabbage	8000	1100
Potatoes	24000	420

These yields of vegetables and farm crops are estimated on the following basis.

Crop	Yield harvested (D.M. kg ha^{-1})	Dry Matter % of crop harvested	Proportion of harvested crop eaten (%)	Nutritive value of edible portion Energy (Mcal kg^{-1})	Protein (%)	Yield of edible product Energy (Mcal ha^{-1})	Protein (kg ha^{-1})
Wheat	4140	85	85	3.46	8.6	14.300	360
Barley	3500	89	85	3.60	7.7	12.000	260
Vining peas	1050	21.5	100	0.64	5.8	3100	280
Brussels sprouts	3360	15.7	58	0.32	3.6	4000	450
Cabbage	6000	10.1	53	0.26	3.6	8100	1100
Potatoes	8400	24.2	86	0.80	1.4	24.000	420
Sugar beet	10.300	(6860 kg sugar per ha)		3.94	–	27.000	–

Data on yields from Milbourn [24] and on food values from McCance and Widdowson [20].

in detail here, but as an example the full use of straws could raise output per area from cereal crops by 20 to 30 per cent.

The ruminant animals are maintained largely on grass and its products. Although the efficiency with which this is harvested is commonly low (60 per cent), it has been demonstrated that substantial increases in efficiency of harvesting by the grazing animal, so that it approaches 100 per cent can be attained [16, 22]. Progress has been less rapid with beef cattle [14], although the potentiality is now realized [18]. The conservation of forage for winter results in from 40 to 80 per cent of the product being conserved [27].

Finally it is of interest to contrast the productivity from livestock enterprises with those attainable from direct crop production. The relevant values based on a good level of farm performance are included in Table 14.4. The values in Tables 14.3 and 14.4 are considered to be representative of several whole systems of animal farming as practised at the present time. If possible improvements are considered, it is clear that all the ruminant enterprises are capable of further increases (say 50 per cent) in output per hectare from grass: within the enterprises there is also scope for improvement from higher yields of milk, greater rates of gain and, particularly in the least productive enterprises, beef and sheep production, from increases in reproductive efficiency. However, if sheep are considered, and if, by the application of modern technology, litter size and litter frequency were increased to produce 450 lambs per 100 ewes per year, the efficiency measures would still be only 6 to 7 per cent of M.E. converted and 3 g protein per Mcal M.E. consumed, a doubling of normal values. These compare with the possibility from higher technical inputs of the production of 12500 kg milk or 1750 kg beef gain per hectare [14] with resulting efficiencies exceeding 20 per cent for M.E. and 10 g protein per Mcal.

In comparing animal and crop production, it is obvious that even when full allowance is made for the wastage which occurs in crop production, the non-use of straw, the harvesting of only a portion of the crop, the rejection by the housewife of a portion of the purchased vegetable crop (as indicated by McCance & Widdowson, [20]), the output both of energy and of protein from crop production normally considerably exceeds that from animal production; although the potential outputs from intensive milk and beef approach the levels of crop production. But animals and crop production should not be set in opposition. In the U.K. 18 M acres of hills and at least 16 M acres (50 per cent) of the lowlands are unfit for arable production; and even on much of the arable land, grass is still considered by many to be an essential break crop. Grass and arable production are complementary both in the maintenance of fertility and in the production of human food.

Conclusion

These observations are not new, but they confirm in more modern context the computations of Middleton [23], and the direct observations recorded by Duckham and Lloyd [9] and by Holmes [13], and may be compared with the estimates of Schuphan [25], Coop [7], Blaxter [5] and Spedding [26].

Although food usually accounts for 50 to 80 per cent of the total cost of an animal product, it should be appreciated that efficiency of food conversion is not the only criterion of efficiency in animal production. Efficient use of labour and, in the more intensive forms of animal production, efficient use of the capital in buildings and equipment are also vital to economic efficiency. Occasions may arise when food is saved only at a cost in labour or in capital. As a general rule, however, efficient animal production depends on attaining a high efficiency in food utilization.

'A detailed analysis of the determinants of the efficiency of animal production in terms of the way in which primary resources of land and labour are used is a Herculean task' [4]. The author is conscious of the many difficulties and risks of inaccuracies in a survey of this nature. However, it is hoped that it will give some guidance on the relative efficiency of crop and animal production and on the relative merits of various animal enterprises, and will indicate the areas in which further developments may most usefully occur.

REFERENCES

1. ALBERDA, T. and SIBMA, L. 'Dry matter production and light interception of crop surfaces. III. Actual herbage production in different years as compared with potential values', *J. Br. Grassld Soc.*, 1968, **23**, 206-215.

2. BLAXTER, K.L. 'Efficiency of feed conversion by different classes of livestock in relation to food production', *Federation Proc.*, 1961, **20**, 268-274.

3. BLAXTER, K.L. 'The efficiency of feed conversion by livestock', *Jl. R. agric. Soc.*, 1964, **125**, 87-99.

4. BLAXTER, K.L. 'Nutritional problems arising in intensive animal production – energy aspects', *Proc. 9 Int. Congr. Anim. Prod. Edinburgh*, 1967, **73-82**.

5. BLAXTER, K.L. 'The animal harvest', *Sci. J.*, 1968, 4, (No. 5) 53-59.

6. BRODY, S. *Bio-energetics and growth.* Reinhold. Publ. Corp. New York. U.S.A., 1945.

7. COOP, I.E. 'The efficiency of food utilisation', *Proc. N.Z. Soc. Anim. Prod.*, 1967, **27**, 154-165.

8. DAVIDSON, J. and MATHIESON, J. 'Conversion of the energy of the food into edible energy by two types of table poultry', *Br. J. Nutr.*, 1965, **19**, 353-359.

9. DUCKHAM, A.N. and LLOYD, D.H. 'Production of dietary energy and protein on University of Reading farms', *Fm Economist*, 1967, **11**, 1-3.

10. DUCKHAM, A.N. 'Biological efficiency of food producing systems in A.D. 2000', *Chem. Ind.*, 1968, 903-906.

11. HOLLIDAY, R. 'Solar energy consumption in relation to crop yield', *Agric. Prog.*, 1966, **41**, 24-34.

12. HOLMES, W. and JONES, J.G.W. 'The efficiency of utilisation of fresh grass', *Proc. Nutr. Soc.*, 1964, **23**, 88-99.

13. HOLMES, W. 'The University Farm – Practice with Science', *Agric. Prog.*, 1966, **41**, 60-69.

14. HOLMES, W. 'The use of nitrogen in the management of pasture for cattle', *Herb. Abstr.* 1968, **38**, 265-277.

15. KLEIBER, M. *The fire of life*, New York: John Wiley & Sons Inc., 1961.

16. LEAVER, J.D., CAMPLING, R.C. and HOLMES, W. 'The influence of flexible and rigid grazing management and of supplementary feed on output per hectare and per cow', *Anim. Prod.*, 1969, **11**, 161-172.

17. LEITCH, I. and GODDEN, W. 'The efficiency of farm animals in the conversion of feedingstuffs to food for man', *Tech. Commnw. Bur. Anim. Nutr.*, 1953, **14**.

18. LONSDALE, C.R. and TAYLER, J.C. 'The effect of stage of maturity of

artificially dried ryegrass and method of processing on the growth of young cattle (summary)', *Anim. Prod.,* 1969, 11, 273.

19. LUCAS, J.W. 'The role of plant foods in solving the world food problem 1. Energy requirements', *Pl Fds. hum. Nutr.,* 1968, 1, 13-21.

20. McCANCE, R.A. and WIDDOWSON, E.H. 'The composition of foods', *Spec. Rep. Ser. med. Res. Coun.,* 1960, 297.

21. MACDONALD, M.A. *Beef cattle production,* New Zealand: Massey Agric. Coll., 1958.

22. McMEEKAN, C.P. 'The effect of stocking rate and concentrate feeding on the conversion of pasture to milk', *Proc. N.Z. Soc. Anim. Prod.,* 1958, 18, 34-42.

23. MIDDLETON, T.H. *Food production in war.* Oxford: Clarendon Press, 1923.

24. MILBOURN, G.M. Internal report on work conducted at Wye College, 1969.

25. SCHUPHAN, W. *Nutritional values in crops and plants,* London: Faber and Faber, 1965.

26. SPEDDING, C.R.W. 'The agricultural ecology of grassland', *Agric. Prog.,* 1969, 44, 1-23.

27. WATSON, D.M.S. 'Beef cattle in peace and war', *Emp. J. Exp. Agric.,* 1943, 11, 191-228.

15. Comparative Production of Ecosystems

P.J. Newbould
The New University of Ulster, Coleraine, N. Ireland

Introduction

It is proposed to review some of the ideas and results derived from studying the productivity of natural vegetation in order to see if these are relevant and helpful to the study of agricultural and silvicultural systems. In the long term it is an article of faith that data, hypotheses and models of energy flow and mineral cycling in natural ecosystems will form the basis of much biological resource management, as for example in fisheries, grouse moors, nature reserves, recreational areas and so on. Their relevance to more intensively cropped systems may be less immediate. Methods of formulating, testing and refining such models have recently been discussed by Gates [4] . Such models, as they become more accurate, will allow discussion of the totality of natural and developed biological resources, all interacting with each other to make up the human environment.

Man has been manipulating agricultural systems for about 10,000 years. Natural ecosystems have evolved, more or less in equilibrium with changing climate, geomorphology and soil over much longer periods of time. They may therefore show greater balance or adaptation to environment. The objectives, arguing teleologically, of the two sorts of system are quite different. Natural selection operating on natural systems favours survival. This may be survival of genes, genotypes, gene pools or whole ecosystems. Survival may involve dispersal in space but ultimately it means persistence in time. Man on the whole has selected for high production, ease of harvest and ease of storage and consumption. More recently his selection has been more sophisticated, involving various ways of attaining these aims such as pest resistance, frost resistance, and characteristics aimed at increasing economic returns. The agricultural and natural systems were therefore designed for different objectives. It would be naive to assume, as some authors have done, that natural ecosystems are inherently more productive than their man-modified counterparts, because they utilize the environment more fully.

The Numbers Game

One approach to the comparative production of ecosystems is to tabulate as many estimates of production as possible, arrange them according to ecosystem type, or latitude, or any biological or environmental parameter, and attempt to establish correlations, hypothesis and conclusions.

Table 15.1

Production Estimates (after Westlake [25])

	Corrected, fairly maximal values $(t \, ha^{-1} \, year^{-1})$
Bracken, Scotland	26
Birch 0-24 yr, England	8.9
Alder 0-22 yr, England	> 16
Scots pine 0-23 yr, England	16
Grand Fir, 0-21 yr, England	> 35
Maize + rye, Holland	39
Sugar beet, Holland	18
Typha reedswamp, Minnesota	29
Good temperate grasslands	22-24
Maximum values for Wheat	21

Table 15.2

World Ecosystems (from Rodin and Basilevich [22])

		Net primary production $(t \, ha^{-1} \, year^{-1})$
Arctic tundra		1.0
Dwarf shrub tundra		2.5
	North taiga	4.5
Fir forests	Middle taiga	7.0
	South taiga	8.5
Oak forests		9
Beech forests		13
Sphagnum bogs		3.4
Subtropical forests		24.5
Tropical rain forest		32.5

This approach has been applied on a world scale, especially by Westlake [25] and Rodin and Basilevich [22]. Some of their data have been selected for Tables 15.1 and 15.2. Pearsall and Gorham [21] carried out a similar review for British vegetation (Table 15.3). Note that the authors referred to selected estimates and that the data in the table have been further selected from their papers. The estimates are derived by different methods and based on different concepts of production. Those of Pearsall and Gorham refer only to above-ground standing crop. In very few cases are standard errors presented, and they are extremely difficult to calculate in this type of work. Westlake in particular has attempted to bring all the estimates he presents to a common basis by applying carefully calculated correction factors to the original data. So although some of the differences are probably real and meaningful, it is difficult to use them as the basis for discussing the comparative production of ecosystems.

Table 15.3
Standing Crops in British Habitats (from Pearsall & Gorham [21])

	t ha^{-1} dry weight
Carex fens, various	4.2 – 6.3
Chalk grassland, Royston	8.2
Deschampsia caespitosa grassland	10.1
Juncus effusus flush	8.0
Molinia grassland, various	4.0
Phragmites reedswamp	7.5 – 13.0
Bracken	9.8 – 14.1
Schoenus nigricans fen	6.4
Sphagnum bog	2.3 – 9.6
Scirpus caespitosus blanket bog	4.5
Typha latifolia reedswamp	10.7

Table 15.4
Forestry and Agriculture in Holland (from Minderman [9])

	% total incoming solar radiation used in net primary production
Austrian Pine 19-22 yr	0.65
Austrian Pine 0-22 yr	0.43
Sugar beet	1 – 1.1
Potatoes	0.6
Onions	0.23

Table 15.5
Forestry and Agriculture in the English Breckland (Ovington [18])

	net primary production above-ground (t ha^{-1} year^{-1})
Scots Pine, maximum	
current production 23-31 yr	22
mean production 0-55	13
Wheat	5.2
Barley	3.5
Sugar beet	9.0
Carrots	6.5
Mangolds	6.0
Grassland (hay)	7.5

Several workers have presented comparative figures for natural vegetation and crops. In the case of Minderman [9] and Ovington [18], the crop production estimates appear to be based on local yield figures, with suitable conversion from crop yield to total biological production. Both authors (Table 15.4 and 15.5) demonstrate dry-matter production by even-aged stands of pine which is higher than, or close to, that by crops, although the latter have received added fertilizers. This may be attributable to the maintenance of a higher leaf area index for the whole of the year by the pine as compared with the rather low leaf area duration of the crops. The long functional life of a single leaf may also be an advantage.

Table 15.6
Cedar Creek, Minnesota (from Ovington et al [19, 20])

	Net primary production $t\ ha^{-1}\ year^{-1}$		Chlorophyll a + b $kg\ ha^{-1}$ August
	Above ground	Total	
Prairie	0.93		2.08
Savanna	5.26		10.23
Oakwood	8.19		26.50
Maize	9.46	10.67	13.25

In the study at Cedar Creek, Minnesota [19, 20] the production estimates (Table 15.6) were made on adjacent areas during the same growing season. The differences are attributed mainly to 'differences of form and structure of the vegetation'. Annual productivity was greater in the communities where the proportion of woody plants was greater. In the savanna, tree canopy covered just over a quarter of the area, whereas in the oakwood it was continuous. The actual vegetation distribution is at least partially attributable to soil conditions, since the prairie and savanna area were on dune sand and the oakwood on glacial outwash with a higher colloidal content.

The field of maize, however, with a shorter growing season, gave a higher production figure. During the part of the growing season when it was growing actively, it had a very high daily production rate. This may be related to its high proportion of photosynthetic tissue. The maize had received relatively heavy dressings of fertilizers which would stimulate the rapid build-up of photosynthetic tissue. The authors consider that the oakwood production figure may well be a considerable under-estimate, while that for maize is relatively accurate.

The figures for chlorophyll [20] serve as some indication of the photosynthetic potential at the height of the growing season. The value for oakwood and, to a lesser extent, that for savanna include a considerable contribution from stem tissue, and it is not clear to what extent this is active in photosynthesis. If this is ignored there is some correspondence between chlorophyll content and production, with the chlorophyll content of the maize field and the oakwood being reasonably similar and greater than that of the savanna, which is in turn greater than the prairie.

More such comparisons would be useful, and several of the IBP main site programmes do in fact involve comparisons of agricultural and natural systems; it is likely that the comparison of different ecosystems close to each other, during the same growing season, by the same group of workers, will in fact prove more valuable than global comparisons.

The Dangers of Comparisons

The 'numbers game' outlined above has numerous shortcomings. Firstly, there are difficulties inherent in the concept of productivity; related to these conceptual difficulties are practical difficulties of measurement.

The total carbon dioxide assimilated by a stand of vegetation, the gross photosynthesis, can be divided into net photosynthesis and plant respiration. The accumulation of net photosynthesis, with the addition of mineral ions in protein synthesis, represents net production. Similarly the accumulation of gross photosynthesis is gross production. Production, then, can be measured either as an increase in dry weight or as an uptake of carbon dioxide. All available methods involve substantial errors, attributable partly to the variability of natural ecosystems. Available resources seldom allow these errors to be reduced to acceptable limits [8, 12].

Carbon dioxide uptake can be measured either by the aerodynamic CO_2 flux method (e.g. [11]) which is satisfactory for an evenly grown crop in a flat field of large area but difficult to apply elsewhere, or by some sort of cuvette method (e.g. [1]) where corrections must be made for the artificial microclimate imposed. To obtain values for gross production, respiration must be measured, and this often involves the assumption that respiration rates are similar in the light and the dark, other factors being the same. There is good physiological evidence (discussed, for example, by Olson [16]) that this is not the case.

Increase in dry weight over a specified time interval can be estimated by harvesting replicate samples at the beginning and end of the interval. But to this simple figure for biomass change must be added the losses during the interval attributable to death or consumption; these are quite difficult to estimate. In woody communities the standing crop may be very large compared to the production, and an accurate estimate of biomass change correspondingly difficult to obtain.

No-one has yet found a satisfactory method of measuring root production [13]. The estimation of root biomass is tedious; partitioning roots into dead and alive categories can be difficult, but the real problem is the turnover of fine roots. Observation chambers show fine roots with a life as short as three weeks. Roots are eaten by soil animals; also they produce organic secretions, and both root cap and root hairs represent a loss of organic matter from the plant. The dry-matter production of mycorrhizal roots is impossible to determine at present. The situation may arise, therefore, where the above ground production of a forest is greater than that of a neighbouring grassland but one just does not know whether this difference is cancelled out or enhanced by differences in root production.

In addition to accuracy of measurement, other problems arise in comparing production. The production of an even-aged woodland changes with age [6, 10, 18], first increasing and then decreasing. The uneven-aged woodland with representatives of every age class is seldom found. One must distinguish, therefore, between the current annual production of a woodland (which will depend upon the main age-classes represented) and the mean annual production over some specified time interval, either the normal forestry rotation, or the natural life span, or the period from germination to the peak value for current annual production. High values are sometimes quoted for current annual production, from the most productive period of a rotation. However it is unlikely, even with careful and regular thinning, that these levels of production could be sustained for long. They probably represent a stage of optimal canopy development which pre-supposes an earlier suboptimal canopy and almost inevitably leads on to a supra-optimal canopy and decline of net production [2]. Thinning, an important element of silviculture, aims at least to prolong the period of optimal leaf area index.

Similar difficulties arise in estimating the production of a heather moorland, usually made up of even-aged stands related to the burning cycle [5].

Finally one further problem should be mentioned — that of the most meaningful quantities to compare when one is comparing production in two ecosystems. If one is interested in the efficiency of capture of solar radiation in photosynthesis, gross production might make a useful comparison. If one is interested in the accumulation of dry matter, then net production is more appropriate, but in forests net production is greatly influenced by stand age [6, 15]. In a particular region, forest may have a higher gross production and a lower net production than grassland. A tropical forest may have a higher gross production and lower net production than a temperate forest. One can distinguish four potentially separable components in ecosystem production — above-ground net production, above-ground respiration, root production, root respiration. Only the first of these can be estimated with any semblance of precision. But if comparison is based solely on above-ground net production it cannot really describe the important differences between different ecosystems.

Comparison of agricultural and natural systems (Tables 15.4 — 15.6) also poses difficulties. The crop production, or a large part of it, is harvestable, and can be more or less sustained under a regular harvesting regime. The natural ecosystem production is not harvestable since it is not all present at one time, and, if harvested, all the characteristics of the ecosystem would be altered. The systems differ qualitatively in a way not adequately expressed by simple production figures. The crop starts with a leaf area index of 0 which builds up fairly rapidly to a high value, at which time the daily rate of production is extremely high for a relatively short period. Most natural ecosystems show less of a peak of activity, often being composed of a succession of small peaks attributable to different species, giving the whole system a more consistent prolonged and lower daily rate of production.

The production of the two systems may also differ biochemically; thus in a forest:meadow comparison, the forest may have greater dry matter production, the meadow greater protein production. Within managed agricultural or silvicultural systems, production is greatly affected by management. This is presumably what farming and forestry are about. In these circumstances the measure of production most commonly used is the economic one, the net profit per unit of land, or of manpower or of capital. This cannot be properly assessed for natural ecosystems.

This discussion may seem negative and defeatist, but in the author's opinion ecologists are prone to wishful thinking and self deception. Considerable refinement of method is needed to allow meaningful comparison of quantities differing, say, by 10 per cent or less rather than by an order of magnitude; further, comparisons of natural and agricultural systems should be based on a whole range of criteria and not simply on net production. Meanwhile we should concentrate on the careful study of production processes attempting to isolate components of both the production system and environmental factors.

The Relevance of Ecosystem Studies to Agricultural Production

Despite all the difficulties discussed above, some of the major differences between production estimates may be real and significant. Other things being equal, reedswamp vegetation is highly productive; acid heath and bog have comparatively low rates of production. Conifer stands tend to be highly productive, more so than broadleaved deciduous woodland. It is simple to speculate about reasons for these differences but difficult to prove them. The major environmental factors affecting production are radiation, atmospheric CO_2, temperature, and the supply of water and mineral nutrients. Kira and Shidei [6] suggest that there is a correlation between gross primary production and leaf area duration. If this relationship proves to be fairly general (perhaps excluding from the leaf area duration figures periods when the mean daily temperature is below some defined threshold such as $6°C$) it implies that daily radiation totals do not vary sufficiently with latitude to be an important differential. Increases in daylength may be compensated by decreases in intensity ([3], Figure 2). In Britain, coniferous woodland probably has a greater leaf area duration than any other community.

Experimental addition of fertilizers to heath and bog communities appears to bring about greatly increased production (e.g. [7, 17, 23]). Odum [14] suggests that the residual fertilizers in abandoned agricultural land are responsible for the initial high production which tails off after a few years. So even uncropped ecosystems show increased production rates when fertilizers are added. Cropped systems are even more sensitive since the cropping itself represents removal of minerals from the mineral cycle.

The generally high production rate of reedswamp vegetation may be because it never suffers from water stress. Gates [4] shows clearly how high solar radiation intensity and low wind speed may bring about high leaf temperatures and lowering of photosynthetic rates. Aquatic plants, able to maintain high transpiration rates, may be less susceptible to this. Also reedswamp may represent an efficient shape for assimilation.

In order to elucidate further the relationship between environmental factors and production, it is necessary to divide production into its two major components, leaf area index (or, better, leaf area duration) and net assimilation rate. There seems general agreement that differences in leaf area duration contribute significantly to differences in production, whereas net assimilation rate is surprisingly invariable. Wild and cultivated varieties of sugar beet, for example, show no consistent difference in net assimilation rate [24]. However, agricultural crops as a whole are annuals and contain a high proportion of photosynthetic tissue; in this way they may attain high production rates during their short season of high leaf area index.

These and similar hypotheses are easier to state than to support, but they do indicate possible ways in which ecosystem studies are relevant to agricultural production. Agriculture has changed as much in the past 50 years as in the previous 5000. Even if we learn within the next 100 years (and we are unlikely to do it sooner) to stabilize human population, agricultural production still needs to increase at least threefold. The way to do this may be by increased mechanization, chemical fertilizers, plant breeding, mono-culture and pest control, in fact an acceleration of present trends, based as they are on comprehensive control of every aspect of an unstable and precarious system. Or these methods may turn sour on us. Chemical pesticides are creating a situation in which their use is bound to increase, and the chance of poisoning ourselves as well as the pests will also increase. Also the cost of pest control is increasing. It is not possible at present to predict whether or not the chemists will keep ahead of the pests. Also the widespread use of relatively heavy applications of inorganic fertilizers seems to be accelerating the eutrophication of fresh waters all over the world. We may need completely different techniques of cropping ecosystems.

The basis of the understanding of ecosystems is the energy flow model. Primary production is partitioned between the consumer food chain, where living plant material is eaten by herbivorous animals while still growing, and the detritus or decomposer food chain, where dead material is broken down both physically and chemically. Consumption usually acts directly by reducing the size of the photosynthetic system, and may therefore directly decrease the rate of primary production. In practice consumption is often less than 10 per cent of the primary production, and this may represent the result of adjustment between consumers and producers over long periods of time. This sets a limit to the possibilities of cropping natural ecosystems. Odum [15] demonstrates how ecosystems develop by the accumulation of organic matter, both living and dead. As they do so, they achieve increasing built-in stability, becoming more independent of environmental fluctuations. He contrasts many of the characteristics of young and developed or mature ecosystems. Agricultural systems correspond in general to young ecosystems. The stability of more developed ecosystems commends them as a basis for agriculture if only they could be cropped without, causing them to revert to immaturity, as Odum makes clear. The only way to do this would seem to be by tapping the detritus food chain. This would mean removing and processing the dead organic matter, replacing its mineral components as in normal agriculture if only they could be cropped without causing them to revert to processing, pest control may become quite negligible. We ought at least to develop this strategy as little further in case it becomes absolútely necessary at some future date.

Conclusions

Man's crops and natural ecosystems represent two radically different biological strategies. It is highly desirable that their properties should be compared in some detail, and not simply in terms of two net production figures. The basic agricultural strategy of monoculture, rapid growth and destructive harvest was inevitable as it evolved, but may not be so any longer. However at present ecosystem data in general are insufficiently precise for useful comparisons to be made. This is partly because such studies have lacked the necessary impetus and resources, and partly because they are dealing with much more complex and variable systems than are involved in agriculture. It is to be hoped that the International Biological Programme, currently in full swing, will provide useful data for such comparisons in the future. Indeed, this is precisely what the I.B.P. is about.

REFERENCES
1. ECKHARDT, F.E. 'Techniques de mesure de la photosynthèse sur le terrain basees sur l'emploi d'enceintes climatisées', in *Functioning of terrestrial ecosystems at the primary production level*, ed. Eckhardt, F.E. Paris: UNESCO, 1968, 289-319.
2. FORD, E.D. 'The potential production of forest crops', in *Potential Crop Production*, ed. J.P. Cooper & P.F. Wareing. London: Heinemann, 1970.
3. GATES, D.M. *Energy exchange in the Biosphere*. New York: Harper & Row, 1962.
4. GATES, D.M. 'Toward understanding ecosystems', *Adv. Ecol. Res.*, 1968, 5, 1-35.
5. GIMINGHAM, C.H. and MILLER, G.R. 'Measurement of the primary production of dwarf shrub heaths', in *IBP Handbook No. 6*, Oxford: Blackwell, 1968.

6. KIRA, T. and SHIDEI, T. 'Primary production and turnover of organic matter in different forest ecosystems of the western pacific', *Jap. J. Ecol.*, 1967, **17**, 70-87.

7. McVEAN, D.N. 'Ecology of *Alnus glutinosa* (L) Gaertn. VIII Establishment of alder by direct seeding on shallow blanket bog', *J. Ecol.*, 1959, **47**, 615-618.

8. MILNER, C. and HUGHES, R.E. 'Methods for the measurement of the primary production of grassland', *IBP Handbook No. 6*, Oxford: Blackwell, 1968.

9. MINDERMAN, G. 'The production of organic matter and the utilization of solar energy by a forest plantation of *Pinus nigra* var. *austriaca*', *Pedobiologia*, 1967, **7**, 11-22.

10. MOLLER, C.M., MULLER, D. and NIELSEN, J. 'Graphic presentation of dry matter production of European beech', *Forst. Forsvaes. Danm.*, 1954, **21**, 327-35.

11. MONTEITH, J.L. 'Analysis of the photosynthesis and respiration of field crops from vertical fluxes of carbon dioxide', in *Functioning of ecosystems at the primary production level*, ed. Eckhardt, F.E. Paris: UNESCO, 1968.

12. NEWBOULD, P.J. 'Methods for estimating the primary production of forests', in *IBP Handbook No. 2*, Oxford: Blackwell, 1967.

13. NEWBOULD, P.J. 'Methods of estimating root production', in *Functioning of terrestrial ecosystems at the primary production level*, ed. Eckhardt, F.E. Paris: UNESCO, 1968.

14. ODUM, E.P. 'Organic production and turnover in old field succession', *Ecology*, 1960, **41**, 34-49.

15. ODUM, E.P. 'The strategy of ecosystem development', *Science, N.Y.*, 1969, **164**, 262-70.

16. OLSON, J.S. 'Gross and net production of terrestrial vegetation', *J. Ecol.*, 1964, **52**, (Suppl.) 99-118.

17. O'TOOLE, M.A., O'HARE, P.J. and GRENNAN, E. *Renovation of peat and hill land pastures.* Dublin: An Foras Taluntais, (no date).

18. OVINGTON, J.D. 'Dry-matter production by *Pinus sylvestris* L.', *Ann. Bot.*, 1957, **21**, 287-314.

19. OVINGTON, J.D., HEITKAMP, D. and LAWRENCE, D.B. 'Plant biomass and productivity of prairie, savanna, oakwood and maize field ecosystems in central Minnesota', *Ecology*, 1963, **44**, 52-63.

20. OVINGTON, J.D. and LAWRENCE, D.B. 'Comparative chlorophyll and energy studies of prairie savanna, oakwood and maize field ecosystems', *Ecology*, 1967, **48**, 515-24.

21. PEARSALL, W.H. and GORHAM, E. 'Production ecology. I. Standing crops of natural vegetation', *Oikos*, 1956, **7**, 193-201.

22. RODIN, L.E. and BASILEVICH, N.I. 'World distribution of plant biomass', in *Functioning of terrestrial ecosystems at the primary production level*, ed. Eckhardt, F.E. Paris: UNESCO, 1968, 45-52.

23. TAMM, C.O. 'Some observations on the nutrient turnover in a bog community dominated by *Eriophorum vaginatum L.*', *Oikos*, 1954, 5, 189-94.

24. WATSON, D.J. 'Factors limiting production', in *The Biological Productivity of Britain*, eds. Yapp, W.B. and Watson D.J. London: Institute of Biology, 1958.

25. WESTLAKE, D.F. 'Comparisons of plant productivity', *Biol. Rev.*, 1963, 38, 385-425.

16. Efficiency of Hill Sheep Production Systems

J. Eadie and J.M.M. Cunningham
Hill Farming Research Organization, Edinburgh

It is widely recognized that sheep production per unit area on hill sheep farms is poor by lowland standards. Stocking rates per unit area are low, and Table 16.1 shows the distribution of stocking rates on hill sheep farms in Scotland.

Individual sheep performance is also poor. Weaning percentages range from around 60 per cent (at which point a self-replenishing flock is just possible) to over 100 per cent, but even this higher figure is well below the potential of the relevant breeds for reproductive performance. Lamb weaning weights range from under 40 lb (18 kg) to over 60 lb (27 kg) depending to some extent on breed but to a much greater extent on nutritional environment.

Table 16.1
Stocking rates of hill sheep in Scotland from [7].

Rough grazing per ewe and gimmer (acres)	(ha)	% of total hill sheep
0–1	0 – 0.40	0.6
1–2	0.40 – 0.81	6.2
2–3	0.81 – 1.21	34.7
3–4	1.21 – 1.62	20.6
4–5	1.62 – 2.02	11.6
5–6	2.02 – 2.43	10.2
6–7	2.43 – 2.83	5.8
7–8	2.83 – 3.24	1.8
8–9	3.24 – 3.64	3.6
9–10	3.64 – 4.05	1.1
10	>4.05	3.8

Thus output per unit area of saleable product in the form of lamb liveweight, ranges from under 3 lb acre^{-1} (3.4 kg ha^{-1}) in the poorer (but not the poorest) hill environments to over 30 lb acre^{-1} (34 kg ha^{-1}) in the better environments. These production figures compare with outputs per acre in the region of 400-500 lb acre^{-1} (450-560 kg ha^{-1}) in the more intensively managed lowland grassland flocks.

Pasture Production

One of the basic characteristics of hill pastures is their low level of primary production, a function of both climatic factors and low soil fertility.

Yields of hill pastures are poorly documented, but experience in the H.F.R.O., together with the studies of Milton [10] and Milton and Davies [11] would indicate that *Agrostis-Festuca* pastures yield some 2000 to 2500 lb dry matter acre $^{-1}$ annum $^{-1}$ (2240-2800 kg ha $^{-1}$) with some types approaching 3000 lb acre $^{-1}$ annum $^{-1}$ (3360 kg ha $^{-1}$). *Molinia* and *Nardus*-dominant grass heaths are less productive and what data exists suggests values of 1000-2000 lb acre $^{-1}$ annum $^{-1}$ (1120-2240 kg ha $^{-1}$). The annual production of the edible material of heather is in the region of 1000-2500 lb d.m. acre $^{-1}$ annum $^{-1}$ (1120-2800 kg ha $^{-1}$) [9].

These productivity figures compare with unfertilised lowland pasture yields of 2000-3000 lb d.m. acre $^{-1}$ (2240-3360 kg ha $^{-1}$) and lowland swards in which some clover is present, and to which some N fertiliser ($<$ 100 lb N acre $^{-1}$ annum $^{-1}$ (5600-8470 kg ha). Yields of 10 000-15 000 lb acre $^{-1}$ (11 200-16 800 kg ha $^{-1}$) have been recorded where 300-500 lb N acre $^{-1}$ annum $^{-1}$ (336-560 kg ha $^{-1}$) have been applied [6].

annum $^{-1}$ (336-560 kg ha $^{-1}$) have been applied [6].

Efficiency of Utilization

A few simple calculations will serve to place the problem of low pasture production in its proper context, i.e. within the context of a management system whose consequences are poor pasture utilization and poor animal nutrition.

Take, for instance, the example of a hill area whose stocking rate is one ewe to 3 acres, where the weaning per cent is 80 and the mean weight of a weaned lamb is 53 lb (24 kg). These production figures are likely to be associated with pasture production in the region of 1800 lb acre $^{-1}$ annum $^{-1}$ (2020 kg ha $^{-1}$) and efficiency, expressed as lbs (or kg) weaned lamb (produced, not sold) per 100 lb (or kg) pasture d.m. production, gives a value of 0.8 (approx.). A similar calculation for a lowland grassland sheep production system based on 4 ewes/acre on a year-long basis, a weaning per cent of 170 and a weaned lamb weight of 80 lb (36 kg) sustained by pasture production of 9000 lb acre $^{-1}$ annum $^{-1}$ (10 100 kg ha $^{-1}$) gives a similarly calculated figure of 6.0 (approx.). It is, of course, true that supplementary feed plays a more important role in lowland sheep production systems, but this accounts for only a very small part of the very considerable differences in the efficiency values.

This topic can perhaps best be pursued under two headings:

(a) the efficiency with which the pasture production is ingested by the sheep population, hereinafter referred to as the efficiency of utilization;

(b) the efficiency with which ingested pasture d.m. is converted to weaned lamb liveweight, hereinafter called the efficiency of conversion.

(a) The Efficiency of Utilization

From data on the annual cycle of nutrient intake of hill sheep in the hill environment [2], together with unpublished data on the nutrient intakes of lactating, grazing ewes we have calculated that a reasonable estimate of the total annual dry matter intake of a hill ewe, weighing some 110 lb (50 kg) at mating would be in the region of 1100 lb (500 kg). At the stocking rate, and on the basis of the level of pasture production cited above, the calculated efficiency of utilization is of the order of 20 per cent. Furthermore, since poorer hill environments are likely to be reflected to a much greater extent in lower stocking rates than in poorer levels of pasture production or lower levels of individual animal intake, utilization efficiencies below this level must be quite common.

Similar calculations under lowland pasture conditions and with lowland sheep suggest values in the region of 60–70 per cent.

(b) The Efficiency of Conversion of Ingested Pasture

This component of overall efficiency is greatly affected by individual sheep performance. As Spedding [14] pointed out, input is dominated by ewe maintenance requirements which often amount to some 75 per cent of the ewe's total food intake [1]. The extra requirement of the ewe which bears and rears twin lambs is small relative to that of the ewe which bears and rears a single lamb. Substantial improvements in the efficiency of food use therefore accompany increases in litter size in sheep.

Although poor lamb growth rates result in higher intakes of food per unit of lamb gain, the significance of this in the context of the ewe/lamb unit is small. But, where poor lamb growth rates require the disposal of the lamb at comparatively light weights, as is often the case in hill sheep farming, then, of course, efficiency is greatly affected.

Using the data previously cited for hill sheep, efficiency of conversion of ingested feed, expressed as lb (or kg) weaned lamb liveweight per 100 lb (or kg) pasture d.m. ingested would be of the order of 3.8. Similar calculations for lowland sheep suggest values in the region 8.5.

It is therefore clear that the efficiency with which ingested pasture d.m. is converted to animal product in hill sheep production is poor, relative to efficiency in lowland sheep, by virtue of much poorer levels of reproductive performance and much lower weights of lambs at disposal.

The Production Process

Progress in improving efficiency in hill sheep production can only be made if an adequate understanding of the production process is available. The relevant argument will be made in two parts, first under the heading of pasture utilization and secondly under nutrition and performance.

(a) Pasture Utilization

Hill sheep systems are, in the main, year-long, set-stocked, free-range pastoral systems which operate against a highly seasonal cycle of pasture growth. Stocking rates are maintained at levels which allow of a certain minimum level of winter nutrition, and this requirement inevitably produces stocking rates which are low in relation to summer pasture production.

Where utilization during the growing season is poor, ungrazed herbage accumulates and matures, and its nutritive value declines. For this reason, and because it has already been depleted of its higher quality fractions by grazing, the material conserved *in situ* as it were, and from which the sheep must select its winter diet is already, at the beginning of winter, of poor quality. The need to maintain a certain minimum diet quality ensures that this fund is poorly utilized, and despite the processes of plant death and decay, a considerable carry-over from one season to the next takes place.

Whilst it might be thought that low grazing pressure in summer ensures sufficient diet selection opportunity in early summer to produce good nutrition during lactation, this does not in fact take place. The reason is that selection opportunity is determined not only by grazing pressure, but by attributes of the pasture, and the evidence is that even at the quite low grazing pressures which exist in summer, the quantity of dead herbage present is of such a proportion as to set a moderate ceiling on ingested herbage quality.

Hunter [8] has shown that a pasture type tends to support a characteristic seasonal pattern and intensity of grazing. Hill pastures are vegetationally variable and it is quite obvious that some pastures, notably *Agrostis-Festuca* pastures and flush grassland, are much more closely grazed than others. But hill sheep range over a variety of pasture types in the course of a day's grazing, and are thus given ample opportunity to dilute diet quality.

This analysis is based on studies in a predominantly grassy hill environment, where it is contended that both set-stocking and free-range grazing are important factors in determining diet quality, and in limiting overall pasture utilization. The applicability of this analysis to other hill environments, because the necessary evidence is unavailable, is uncertain. There is, for example, the real possibility that the nature of the plant material in dwarf-shrub heath is a limiting factor to diet quality. Even so, the argument with respect to the processes by which year-long stocking rates are set, and that they lead to under-utilization and feed quality deterioration during the summer, is likely to be correct.

Regional variations in hill farming practices exist. These are particularly concerned with the amount of time during which sheep are removed from their hill pasture at tupping, during late winter, and at lambing. Manipulations of this kind, particularly removal during late winter, tend to be reflected in the relationship between overall stocking rate and summer pasture production, making the relationship a closer one and improving overall pasture utilization. But although the absolute amount of poor material carried over from one season to the next is reduced, any tendency for this to result in improved summer nutrition is counteracted by a higher grazing pressure. This hypothesis would explain the sensitivity of individual animal performance to stocking rate change in some environments.

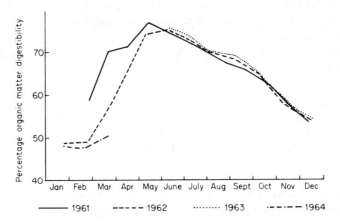

Fig. 16.1   Seasonal changes in digestibility of pasture consumed by sheep set-stocked on a Cheviot hill; from Eadie [2].

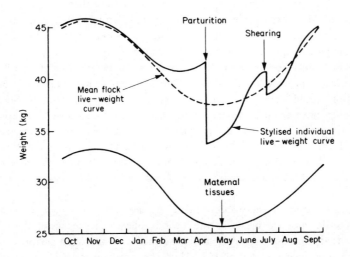

Fig. 16.2   Changes in ewe liveweight and in the weight of maternal tissues throughout the year; from Russell [12].

The major reason for the poor levels of pasture utilization in hill sheep farming is the management system. Better pasture utilization therefore requires a measure of grazing control.

(b) Nutrition and Performance

Year-long, free-range, set-stocked pastoral systems operating against the background of highly seasonal pasture growth, inevitably produce a cyclical pattern of nutrition. Cyclical patterns of nutrition are not, of course, unusual, but a major feature of that typical of hill sheep farming in the U.K. is the generally low level at which it operates. This is evidenced both by the data available on the energy intake cycle itself (Figure 16.1) [2] and by the generally low level of body weight and condition to which it gives rise (Figure 16.2) [12, 13].

A consideration of the available evidence on animal performance and its components under hill conditions, the available data on the annual cycle of nutrition, together with information on relations between nutrition and performance in the H.F.R.O., shows clearly that at each and every stage in the annual cycle of events, nutrition is a limiting factor to sheep performance.

Growth rates of single lambs in most hill environments are well below those of which hill lambs are capable. Nutrition during lactation is too poor to support reasonable growth rates of twin lambs. But early lamb growth can be markedly improved by better ewe nutrition during lactation. Lamb growth rates decline from marking at five to six weeks of age, and this is a function of declining pasture quality.

Current levels of reproductive performance are a function of nutrition and body condition at mating. Mating takes place at a time of sub-maintenance and declining nutrition. Body condition of hill sheep is quite poor by any standards other than perhaps those of hill farming, since recuperation of body condition after lactation is limited as a consequence of the decline in ingested pasture quality during the late summer.

Winter nutrition is poor, but this need not be inconsistent with good performance provided body reserves are adequate. Thus, improved summer nutrition could make an important contribution to winter nutrition by providing more adequate reserves on which the hill sheep is well able to draw.

Nutritional status in late pregnancy invariably leaves something to be desired, and there is little doubt that prepartum supplementation will improve lamb vigour at birth, and lamb survivability in most hill environments and, in some hill environments, lead to improved weaning weights in some years.

But, because of the overall poverty of the cycle, and in consequence of the interdependence between the various phases in the cycle, there is no doubt that, for really significant improvements in hill sheep performance, an overall improvement is required. Thus the problem is basically a pastoral problem, and of special importance are the periods of lactation and the recovery phase.

Improving Efficiency

It is now appropriate to consider the processes by which efficiency in hill sheep production may be improved. The implications of the foregoing analysis are that the root causes of the poor efficiency derive, in the main, from the management system itself, and it is clear that the development of improved systems of sheep production from hill land cannot be made within the existing framework. Capital injections are necessary, and at the end of the day these have to be shown to be financially sensible. Therefore distinction among the various possibilities will depend to a much greater extent on a cost/benefit analysis than on the contribution they make to improved biological efficiency.

It also must be recognized that capital availability in hill farming is limited, and that those improvements which successfully employ limited amounts of capital are likely to be of more immediate practical interest. Valid systems have to be ecologically sound, and this phrase usually implies the absence of any element which leads to deterioriation of the resource, or at least the knowledge and means to rehabilitate any such tendency. But in the context of limited capital investment, ecological soundness is a more positive requirement, implying that the initial investment should be made in such a way as to create a framework for a continuing improvement, if possible.

Perhaps the most obvious point which emerges from the analysis of pasture utilization is that the poor efficiency with which the pasture production is ingested owes much to the fact that hill systems are year-round systems. If they were to become only summer-grazing systems, considerable opportunities would be presented for substantial improvements in utilization efficiency. Off-wintering or in-wintering, therefore, have very attractive possibilities from the efficiency point of view, but even where the capital cost of housing is avoided, then because of the high recurrent costs of winter feeding, the increase in output necessary to recoup the extra costs, far less render them worthwhile, is considerable. In addition, the large part of these increases would have to come from increases in stocking rate, since the present limited experience of in-wintering has tended to fulfil the technical expectation that marked improvements in individual sheep performance do not accompany in-wintering alone. The improvement of individual sheep performance requires concomitant improvements in summer nutrition.

It is unlikely that in many instances the capital to meet in-wintering facilities and the cost of winter feeding, and that necessary to establish sufficient pasture improvement all at once, will be available, and it is much more likely that initial capital investment would be better made in land improvement. So that although from the efficiency point of view off-wintering appears to have much to offer, and although at the end of the day this may prove to be the case financially as well, initially at any rate it hardly seems a first priority.

Of perhaps more immediate interest is the less dramatic (from the efficiency standpoint) development of year-long grazing systems, requiring more modest capital injections, and with which much smaller recurrent cost increases are associated.

One implication of the argument advanced earlier in this chapter is that better pasture utilization and improved nutrition require a degree of grazing control. Precisely what is implied in this statement, and the extent to which other associated inputs are necessary, depends on the vegetational and soil characteristics of any given area. It is perhaps hardly necessary to point out that in the short term it is impossible to control the whole of a hill-grazing. In many situations this would be quite impossible even in the long term, and in any event is unlikely to be necessary.

Existing hill vegetation exists in balance with current levels and annual patterns of grazing intensity, as well as reflecting existing soil conditions and climate. Short-term changes in the vegetational morphology of bent-fescue pastures, largely reflected in a marked reduction of the amount of dead herbage induced by management change, have been shown in small-scale experiments to improve both utilization and the nutritive value of these pastures [3].

Many hill soils are capable of supporting alternative types of vegetation in response to changes in grazing management. Some will respond to combinations of grazing management and soils improvement. Others require not only a marked degree of soil upgrading, but also the provision of new plant material.

Thus on hill farms on which, say, 15—25 per cent of the area is of *Agrostis-Festuca* vegetation on reasonably good hill soils, the low cost approach would simply be to enclose a proportion of this vegetation with the object of changing pasture morphology by grazing control. On areas of poorer podsolized soils carrying *Nardus* and *Molinia* grass heath, desirable vegetational change, this time including a more important element of botanical change, will follow changes in grazing regime. There is little doubt, however, that in this case the pace of change would be greatly accelerated by improvements in soil base-status. On peat-covered areas, for example, there is little alternative to a substantial degree of soil improvement followed by reseeding.

But the major point to be made is that pasture improvement does not in all cases mean reseeding. In many situations there is a range of possibilities, and the best choice among them is not necessarily that which gives the most dramatic increase in production. On this point there is a clear need to evaluate the consequences to pasture production and nutritive value of a range of inputs over the spectrum of existing hill vegetation and soils. Work to this end has recently been started in H.F.R.O.

A second kind of problem is that which concerns the most effective way of integrating improved pasture into a production system. In many circumstances, the problem will be that of integrating limited areas of improved pasture, and the analysis of the problem of individual animal performance given earlier should enable this to be more efficiently done. Nutrition in the premating and mating period, together with nutrition during lactation, clearly have priority. The recognition of this fact, together with attention to the priorities so far as the sheep themselves are concerned, for instance, the preference during lactation for limited areas of improved pasture for twin-bearing ewes over singles, and gimmers with singles over older ewes, will ensure the maximum impact of improved pasture on sheep performance.

In the context of year-long systems, no mention has as yet been made of the winter situation. This matter is often discussed out of context, as if minimum winter nutritional requirements were independent of summer nutrition. This is not so. Hill sheep are well able to draw on their body reserves in winter, and one important aspect of winter nutrition is to ensure the adequacy of these reserves. It is in this respect that improved summer nutrition may make a very important contribution to winter nutrition.

The problem in many situations may well be the improvement of winter carrying capacity at existing levels of nutrition. On *Nardus*-dominant grass heath this can be accomplished by reducing the amount of dead herbage present on these pastures and so raising the proportion of the available feed which may be utilized above any given minimum acceptable level of ingested pasture quality. Similar possibilities may exist in other circumstances, but where appropriate pasture change cannot be made, the use of supplements to eliminate the nutritional penalty of higher grazing intensities is just as logical as, and probably even more valid than, using them simply to marginally improve nutritional status at existing grazing intensities.

In improved systems which result in superior levels of reproductive performance, nutrition during late pregnancy will naturally have to receive more attention. This introduces no new problem in principle, since a valid case can be made even now for better nutrition in most hill environments at this time. Late pregnancy requirements will increase as animal performance improves, but it is quite possible that feed inputs per unit of output will not rise, and may even fall.

The vital point, however, is that concern for late pregnancy nutrition alone will set a very limited ceiling on the improvement of individual animal performance, and a proper perspective requires that this issue be seen in the context of the problem as a whole.

Thus one foresees the development of pastoral systems on the hills in which selected areas are improved and utilized in the manner described, the improvement procedure depending very much on the nature of the resource. On the better grassy hills with fairly substantial proportions of bent-fescue pasture, the gains in efficiency will derive, in the main, from improved pasture utilization, although there are grounds for hoping that improved plant nutrient cycling may increase pasture production in time. It is also reasonable to expect some contribution to increased efficiency from better animal performance although, in the absence of larger inputs, it would be optimistic to expect too much.

At the other extreme, where quite small areas of substantially improved pasture 'service' a fairly large hinterland, the mainspring of the effect will derive from the increase in pasture production and greatly improved efficiency of utilization on the improved areas. The most important contribution to overall efficiency here is likely to come from improved animal performance.

To a large extent much of what has been said in this section is, in a sense, speculative. The value of the approach outlined will ultimately depend upon the extent to which it results in the development of improved systems of animal production from the hills. The integration of resources in improved systems must be tested, and the ultimate test is one of cost/benefit analysis.

Two projects have been started. One is in a grassy hill environment in which the initial inputs are largely concerned with enclosing areas of *Agrostis-Festuca* pasture. The second is in a much poorer high-rainfall environment, predominantly blanket bog, where small areas of improved reseeded pasture are being integrated with two much larger enclosures within which spot improvement has been made, and the open hill. Both of these projects are intended as year-round systems, and two further projects involving off-wintering are planned.

All of these projects are the result of a synthesis of a good deal of information of a variety of kinds — nutritional, botanical and agronomic, and new information is coming forward at an increasing rate. As this happens, the spectrum of possibilities continually widens. The extent of systems synthesis that can be carried out in the field with limited resources of land and people will clearly remain small, and since in any one of these, several interacting elements are integrated, the problem of ensuring that the systems tested are the best and most relevant that current knowledge can devise is difficult, and will become more difficult.

Looking to the future, therefore, the use of computer simulated models of grassland systems, for the normative purposes of excluding certain possibilities and predicting the better ones, has very great attractions. But the difficulties are considerable. Among other problems, the production process is a two-stage process involving the production of pasture, and its grazing for livestock production, with the two stages interacting over time. The problem of conservation of pasture *in situ* has to be handled, and within limits grazing animals themselves make decisions about how much they will eat. In the face of such complexity it would clearly be optimistic to expect early solutions.

In the meantime, using the approach devised by Harkins [5] it is possible to calculate the break-even point of any projected level of capital investment in terms of the various possible combinations of flock size increase and animal performance improvement necessary to service the investment. This procedure provides a background against which the financial implication of the technical arguments and possibilities can be evaluated.

REFERENCES

1. COOP, I.E. 'The energy requirements of sheep', *Proc. N.Z. Soc. Anim. Prod.* 1961, 21, 79-91.
2. EADIE, J. 'The nutrition of grazing hill sheep; utilization of hill pastures', *Rep. Hill Fmg. Res. Org.,* 1967, 4, 38-45.
3. EADIE, J. and BLACK, J.S. 'Herbage utilization on hill pastures', *Occ. Symp. Br. Grassld. Soc.,* 1968, 4, 191-195.
4. GRANT, S. (Unpublished data).
5. HARKINS, J. 'Assessing new capital investment on hill sheep farms', *Scott. Agric.,* 1968, 47, 196-200.
6. HOLMES, W. 'The use of nitrogen in the management of pasture for cattle', *Herb. Abstr.,* 1968, 38, 265-277.
7. HUNTER, R.F. 1952 (Unpublished data).
8. HUNTER, R.F. 'Hill sheep and their pasture: a study of sheep-grazing in south-east Scotland', *J. Ecol.,* 1962, 50, 651-680.
9. MILLER, G.R. 'Botanical studies', *Prog. Rep. Unit Grouse Moorld Ecol.,* 1966, 12, 20-26.
10. MILTON, W.E.J. 'The effect of manuring, grazing and cutting on the yield, botanical and chemical composition of natural hill pastures', *J. Ecol.,* 1940, 28, 326-356.
11. MILTON, W.E.J. and DAVIES, R.O. 'The yield, botanical and chemical composition of natural hill herbage under manuring, controlled grazing and hay conditions', *J. Ecol.,* 1947, 35, 65-95.
12. RUSSEL, A.J.F. 'Nutrition of the pregnant ewe', *Rep. Hill Fmg. Res. Org.,* 1967, 4, 54-68.
13. RUSSEL, A.J.F. and EADIE, J. 'Nutrition of the hill ewe', *Occ. Symp. Br. Grassld. Soc.,* 1968, 4, 185-190.
14. SPEDDING, C.R.W. 'The efficiency of meat production in sheep', *World Conf. Anim. Prod. Rome,* 1965, 2, 33-47.

17. Farming Systems Below 25 in (635 mm) Rainfall

E.R. Bullen
Ministry of Agriculture, Fisheries and Food, London

This chapter will consider the farming of certain counties in eastern England, each of which has less than 25 in (635 mm) annual rainfall over the majority of its area. These are the east-coast counties from Thames to Humber (Essex, Suffolk, Norfolk, Lincolnshire) plus Bedfordshire, Huntingdonshire and Cambridgeshire including the Isle of Ely. Unfortunately the location of the 25 in (635 mm) iso hyet in relation to county boundaries makes it difficult to include easily some other important agricultural areas, for example Holderness in the East Riding and much of the arable land of east Kent.

Table 17.1 summarizes the Ministry statistics for June 1968 for these counties, and expresses each figure as a percentage of the corresponding figure for England and Wales. In addition, some indication of recent trends in farmers' policy in the 1960s will be given by the figure which expresses each 1968 statistic as a percentage of a corresponding figure for 1960.

In 1968, about two-thirds of the total crop and grass area was accounted for by wheat, barley and grass. Almost another fifth was in cash row crops, mainly sugar beet, potatoes and vegetables. For a number of these commodities, the seven counties in this sample provide most of the national production. In the 1960s there has been a marked decline in the grassland area, particularly of leys; the extra tillage has largely gone into cereals, sugar beet, and vegetables with a notable expansion of 'vining' peas. Oats, roots for livestock, and even to some extent potatoes seem out of fashion.

The livestock figures provide an interesting contrast between the ruminants, which to some extent are matching the declining grass area, and the pigs and poultry, of which these sample counties now supply over a quarter of the national numbers, after a marked expansion in recent years.

In common with most farming areas, the labour force has been declining steadily, particularly the regular full-time male workers of whom over a third have left the land in the past nine years. So far, these counties have had a relatively low population density, and competition from industry has been less marked than in many other areas. In parts of the region, the development of new towns is having some impact on this situation.

One cannot hope in a brief review to discuss adequately the details of the farming systems being practised in this large area. It includes substantial areas of such specialized soils as the Fens, the Silts and the Breckland, each with very individual problems, and a number of highly specialised crops. It is, however, possible to discuss some aspects of the husbandry of a few of the main crops under the moisture-deficient conditions in the eastern counties, bearing in mind the probable developments of the early 1970s.

Before doing so, it is perhaps appropriate to indicate something of the nature of the climate where rainfall is below 25 in (635 mm). The figures for Boxworth E.H.F. will serve as an example. Here the average rainfall amounts to 22 in. (560 mm) a year; of this about 12 in. (305 mm) falls on average in the six summer months (April to September inclusive) with August

Table 17.1
Agricultural statistics for the eastern counties* of England, June 1968

	Total (thousand acres)	(thousand hectares)	as % England and Wales	% change since 1960
Crops				
Total crops and grass:	4806	1944	20	− 1
Permanent grass	676	273	7	− 26
Lucerne and Temporary grass	298	121	8	− 40
Tillage	3831	1550	36	+ 12
Wheat	1015	411	44	+ 12
Barley	1284	519	25	+ 10
Oats	94	38	18	− 51
Total Cereals	2393	968	30	+ 7
Sugar Beet	359	145	78	+ 14
Potatoes	250	101	48	− 8
Mangolds	10	4	33	− 74
Peas (for canning, freezing or dehydration)	86	35	82	+ 76
for harvesting dry	44	18	88	+ 10
for market	5	2	30	− 50
Carrots	27	11	84	+ 3
Brussels Sprouts	27	11	56	+ 4
Total Vegetables	253	102	60	+ 14
Livestock	(thousands)			
Dairy cows (in milk or calf)	147		5	− 45
Total cattle	673		8	− 27
Total sheep	662		3	− 26
Total pigs	1610		28	+ 55
Total poultry	25 687		25	+ 38
Labour	(thousands)			
Regular full-time male workers	66		27	− 35
Total workers	101		27	− 19

Source: M.A.F.F. June Returns

*Bedford, Cambridge (with Isle of Ely), Essex, Huntingdon, Lincolnshire, Norfolk and Suffolk.

statistically the wettest month of the year. However, potential transpiration
(on a full ground cover basis) in the same months has averaged over 18 in. (457
mm) with consequently, on average, a moisture deficit of 4 in. (102 mm) at
the end of June, rising at the end of July and thereafter to over 6 in. (152
mm). These average records conceal the fact that a dry year (i.e. with less
than 19 in. (478 mm) total rainfall) occurs on average about once every four
years.

Cereals

About one-third of the national cereal acreage is grown in these seven counties,
and it is reasonable to assume that for practical purposes none of this area is
irrigated. A dry climate, at least in the British sense, has some clear
advantages for the cereal grower and Figure 17.1 (reproduced from Colman's
data summarised in the Britton Report) suggests that wheat yields over the
years 1954 to 1966 have shown a yield pattern varying inversely with the

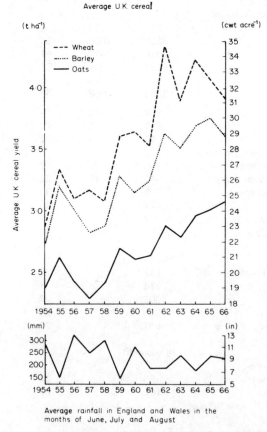

*Fig. 17.1   Average United Kingdom cereals yields, and rainfall during
June-August, 1954-66.*

total rainfall for June to August inclusive. The 1968 data will certainly support this. However, with both barley and oats the yields do not follow this pattern quite so closely.

Despite considerable talk about intensive cereals, and a number of fields in these counties have been in barley for fifteen years or more, the actual proportion of the tillage devoted to cereal crops in the counties as a whole fell slightly between 1960 and 1968. It is difficult to be confident of future rotational trends, but the eastern counties have always tended to have more wheat relative to barley than the counties of the midlands and the west. With increasing encouragement to wheat in terms of price, the probable introduction of a number of promising new winter wheats in the next few years, and the growing disillusion of many farmers with their returns from barley, it seems likely that the traditional importance of wheat in the eastern counties will not diminish.

Prices of land, if viewed realistically, mean that, if cereals are to maintain their position, reasonably good yields are essential. Our average yields are so far below the potential of modern varieties that serious consideration of the efficacy of our husbandry appears desirable. Despite many attempts to short-circuit seed-bed preparation, a reasonable tilth is important in getting cereal crops established if one is hoping for good yields. Conversely, a poor tilth where brairding is slow, root development is retarded, and hence the uptake of nutrients reduced, is likely to give backward crops more vulnerable to the attacks of soil-borne disease and nematodes which are likely to occur when cereals are being grown in many modern 'rotations'.

One cannot define at all precisely what is meant by 'reasonable tilth', but it is possible to suggest conditions which will make this desirable condition difficult to obtain. For example, there is a marked difference between land which has been ploughed when wet — especially after it has been rutted during harvesting — as compared with dry; hence perhaps the heavy-land tradition that the best spring seed-beds result from ploughing when the land is too hard to plough. Further, in the dry, almost continental climate of eastern England one is much more likely to have suitable spells of frost to improve the soil conditions for spring cereals. Almost half the area of the counties mentioned here is on heavy soils; late ploughing may well create problems, but it is likely to be inevitable where the farming is so dominated by cash roots.

Easy spring seed-bed preparation, of course, would give a yield bonus for farmers in a dry area, since the fewer cultivations which are required, the smaller the loss of moisture in seed-bed preparation and consequently the more moisture left for the crop. Moisture is, very frequently, one of the main limiting factors for yield in spring-sown crops in this sample area. The development of paraquat has enabled its integration into conventional systems of tillage, simplifying the destruction of weeds or volunteer cereals, especially in a catchy spring. This technique, instead of relying on cultivations in dry weather, permits further conservation of moisture. So far, however, replacing all tillage by paraquat in the direct drilling technique, has had little effect on cereal husbandry. One cannot generalize about cereal diseases in relation to climate. In a dry climate, crops will tend to be relatively free of the 'splash-spread' diseases, and experience in the eastern counties suggest that both *Rhynchosporium* and *Septoria* are much less troublesome than in wetter areas, despite the fact that close rotations are often being followed. Rainfall does not directly affect yellow rust (*Puccinia spriiformis*) but there is, in theory, a greater chance, under eastern counties conditions, of the combination of dry weather with high air temperatures which can clearly check a yellow rust epidemic. On the other hand, mildew (*Erysiphe graminis*) is frequently worse, partly because one has less chance of heavy rain checking mildew, as it certainly can do; in practice the reduced risks of lodging in a dry climate mean that farmers may tend to be over-generous with nitrogen and hence accentuate their mildew problems.

It is difficult to distinguish between the effects of climate, soil, and husbandry on the cereal root diseases such as take-all (*Ophiobolus graminis*). Our E.H.F. intensive cereal trials demonstrate that centres in the west consistently have a higher incidence of take-all at a given point in the rotation than those in the east or north-east. However take-all damaged plants might be expected to suffer more serious yield reductions where the plant is suffering from moisture stress in a drier climate. On the whole one would expect eyespot to be less serious in the east than in damper climates, where winter cereals are often sown earlier and where the crop is more likely to develop winter-proudness through mild temperatures persisting through the winter.

Cereal weeds are likely to be particularly important where the crop is vulnerable to competition for moisture. It is not proposed to discuss the broad-leaved weeds, because their control is relatively straightforward with the herbicides now available. The grass weeds are much more important in terms of crop damage and cost of control. In terms of area infested, couch (*Agropyron repens* and *Agrostis* species) is our most widespread cereal weed, but the seven counties mentioned here probably contribute less than their proportionate share to the national couch problem. Despite a number of chemical methods, which clearly have their place in appropriate circumstances, the desiccation of couch under drying conditions by appropriate cultivations often gives better results, given some luck with the weather and sufficient manpower to follow up the job thoroughly before the weather breaks. The control of couch by cultural methods is most easily achieved in late summer, preferably after early ripening winter cereals, such as winter barley, or crops such as peas for drying, which ripen at a similar time of year. The East Anglian winter sometimes gives a second chance to cultivate, so that the rhizomes can be exposed in hard frost, and finally there may be some chance to tackle couch in the spring, if conditions are sufficiently dry. While the latter can check couch, it will rarely control it effectively, and the danger of sowing cereals into seed-beds which have lost their moisture as a result of couch control cultivations is sometimes not recognized. Recent work at the Weed Research Organisation has shown that delayed sowing of cereals much reduces their competitive effect against couch. The grass weeds — wild oats (*Avena fatua* and *A. ludoviciana*) and black grass (*Alopecurus myosuroides*) — are probably more troublesome in the eastern counties than couch. Cultural methods of control of wild oats, such as the Boxworth spring fallow technique are now generally less economic than the use of herbicides. Both Barban (used after the emergence of crop and wild oats) and Triallate, (used either before drilling or before emergence) are effective techniques provided that the spraying is done properly and, in the case of Triallate, that the material is worked in promptly to avoid volatilization. Such application techniques are clearly most effective in a climate where spraying is not likely to be interfered with by spells of wet weather, and this is one of the advantages usually unrecognised of the eastern counties cereal-grower.

Black grass is a traditional weed where winter cereals are grown too frequently. Nevertheless winter cereals are highly desirable on a large part of the area under discussion because of their greater tolerance of drought conditions, and there may well be further expansion of the winter barley acreage, despite the fears of some plant pathologists.

Black grass can be controlled effectively by several chemicals but the economics of their use demands careful thought. If one has to increase the chemical-spray bill by, say, £5 per acre to permit a winter cereal being grown, this sum may absorb most of the increased return which that cereal could be expected to give relative to a spring crop, Further evidence is accumulating that black grass competion is unlikely to affect seriously well-manured, vigorous cereals with a potential yield exceeding two tons per acre (5000 kg ha). While black grass can be a cause of a poor wheat crop, it is equally true that poor wheat crops are often largely responsible for the blackgrass problems in heavy land farming. Much of the black grass problem could be overcome if our husbandry standards for winter cereals could be improved.

Row Crops

Apart from fodder roots, because of the relatively small number of ruminants, and potatoes, most of the national production of row crops occurs in these seven sample counties.

Although it is advantageous to have irrigation available, if one considers the year as a whole, relatively dry climates have some advantages for row-crop cultivation. Where the row crop is a root crop, a dry climate is particularly important for harvesting, as the autumns of 1967 and 1968 so clearly stressed. Indeed it is doubtful whether many of the heavier soils are really economic propositions for sugar-beet and potato cultivation despite the dry climate, although, because of contract acreages and potato quotas, these crops are likely to be grown for some years, particularly on the medium-sized farm.

The eastern climate, apart from its dryness, has relatively severe winters compared to most of Great Britain, and this assists spring seed-bed production. Seed-bed requirements for many row crops have become increasingly important with modern methods of husbandry. For example, sugar-beet cultivation, with the introduction of monogerm seed, the tendency towards drilling-to-a-stand and the use of soil-acting herbicides to control weeds, demands better seed-bed preparation than traditional husbandry. Even on favourable soils, such techniques can be difficult for the early sowings, but a reasonably dry spring is clearly important in achieving the desirable results. These problems have not been solved on the stronger soils but, in view of their doubtful suitability for potatoes and sugar beet, this may not be a very important problem in the long term.

For potato husbandry, seed-bed conditions are also important, particularly if mechanical harvesting is being attempted, in view of the importance of avoiding clod production.

Many farmers are now working towards potato-growing techniques based to a greater or lesser extent on Dutch ideas. After ploughing, provided this is well done in dry conditions, shallow working in the spring with conventional or powered harrows, or in extreme circumstances a rotary cultivator, suffices to prepare a suitable tilth for planting. Before emergence, one application of herbicide is all that is given to control weed growth until the tops meet in the row; to achieve this the tilth must be fairly fine.

It would be optimistic to claim that a low rainfall is a major factor in controlling potato blight, but protective sprays are far more likely to be successful in a climate where the crop is less susceptible to blight than it would be in the west.

A number of crops, other than those such as potatoes and sugar beet, which produce their economic yield under the surface, present serious harvesting problems in a wet climate. Among these are horticultural crops like onions and bulbs; the bulk of the British production of onions and bulbs for planting takes place in the counties under discussion. The same applies, though for different reasons, to the strawberry crop which demands a fairly dry summer climate if serious losses from *Botrytis* are to be prevented.

Peas for harvesting dry have, for climatic reasons, long been an eastern counties speciality, but the vining pea is a comparative newcomer. The occurrence of over 80 per cent of the vining pea area in these counties in probably in spite of the climate rather than because of it. Although what has been said about seed-bed preparation is important, the high temperatures and low humidities which often occur in July make it difficult to harvest peas at the optimum stage of maturity. It is arguable that vining peas are grown in the coastal counties because of the presence of factory facilities originally provided for processing fish, rather than for agronomic reasons.

The use of irrigation has been more widespread on row crops than on any other part of our agricultural production, but even so it is possible to over-emphasize its importance nationally. Relating that October 1967 survey of irrigation to the crop areas returned in 1968, the potential use of irrigation amounted to about 12 per cent of the potatoes, 10 per cent of the vegetables, and 7 per cent of the beet crop. Clearly, the husbandry of non-irrigated crops under moisture deficit conditions will continue to be important, and the great strides in techniques achieved in the past ten years has enabled us to make much better use of such natural moisture resources as are available to our crops. Techniques such as reduced spring cultivations and chemical weed control are important means of conserving moisture, and this may be part of the reason why, so far, the irrigation responses at Gleadthorpe E.H.F. have been conspicuously lower in the 1960s than in the early years of the irrigation experiment in the late 1950s.

Grassland

It may seem unnecessary to spend any time in reviewing the agriculture of an important arable area to refer to grassland, but in fact about one-fifth of these sample counties is returned as grass by farmers in their June returns; of this grass, about two-thirds is described by them as permanent. If one relates livestock units to the grassland area, on average, these counties devote 2¼ acres (0.9 ha) to each grazing livestock unit. This is a fairly modest achievement, but it must be remembered that much of this grass is somewhat unpromising material. There are substantial areas of land adjoining the East Anglian rivers which would certainly have been ploughed in the last thirty years if this had been practicable; some fields remain in grass to permit access to adjoining arable fields; some grass consists of 'safety valve' land like the Fenland Washes; some no doubt only exists to make the area of the farm add up. Nevertheless, there are many arable farms with a substantial area of grass which has not really had an effective use since the horses which used to graze it disappeared.

It should be noted that grass as a break is unimportant. Temporary grass amounts to only one-third of the land returned as grass and about 7 per cent of the tillage. A substantial proportion of this temporary grass is not, of course, ley farming as this would be understood in wetter climates; one-year clover leys still exist, although they are hardly fashionable or profitable by comparison with other break crops; a high proportion of the herbage seed in the country is grown in the eastern counties, often on stockless farms where its by-products are not of much use. But clearly the eastern counties farmer has little interest in ley farming, partly because of the substantial technical difficulties which this involves in fencing and water supply, but also because of economic and social factors like return on capital and ability of farm labour to do livestock work. Ley fertility trails have been carried out at two experimental husbandry farms, Boxworth and Gleadthorpe, with rainfall in each case below 25 inches (635 mm); the results at Boxworth seem to indicate that the benefit from the ley by comparison with a good arable rotation is largely attributable to the nitrogen residues which it leaves behind. Lucerne leys and grazed leys have given higher crop yields than conserved leys. It should be emphasized, of course, that the arable rotation in the ley fertility trials is hardly typical of the present practice of many farms in the area, in that it has been designed to minimize the risks of intensive cereal cropping. At Gleadthorpe, on very light soil, the results suggest that there is something more than a nitrogen residue effect but, taken together, the results of these centres over the first eighteen years do not supply the adviser with very much ammunition to combat the strong reluctance of arable farmers to practice ley farming.

In view of the much greater area of permanent grass, and its slower rate of decline relative to temporary grass in the 1960s, the author believes that more of our efforts should be devoted to the improvement of permanent grass systems in dry areas. In this context it is unfortunate that, of our grazing animals, dairy-cow numbers are falling fastest. The autumn-calving cow, which has been traditional in the eastern counties, offers a good method of blending the demands of the animal with the growth curve in a dry area. As grass growth declines during June and July, an increasing proportion of the herd will become dry and their demand for food will only increase in September, when grass production is usually tending to increase again. The dairy cow, of course, is much more resistent than young animals to the parasite problems which are likely to arise when intensive stocking is practised on permanent grass.

It is difficult to be enthusiastic about the traditional method of beef production where forward stores are put out to grass in the spring and sold fat from June onwards. Store cattle prices in recent years have been discouraging to enterprises of this kind, but it is fair to say that a few farmers who are skilled cattle buyers have achieved gross margins from their beef enterprise at least comparable with those from cereals in recent years. This system again makes reduced demands on grass in July and August if it is being operated efficiently, since many of the cattle will have been marketed in a fat condition before serious droughts take place. By contrast, eighteen-month beef from autumn calves presents a particular challenge. As the animals are increasing in size during the summer their appetite naturally increases, and maintaining good liveweight gains in August and September taxes management. Supplementary feeding, beloved by many traditionalists, tends to reduce grass intake and is probably uneconomic if adequate grass can be produced. Sheep do not appear to be of great importance in this area, since the eastern counties supply only 3 per cent of the national flock, and the sheep flock only provides about 6 per cent of the grazing livestock units in these seven counties. It is doubtful whether gross margins consistantly exceeding £40 per acre can be achieved from sheep, but with beef cattle such a return can often be obtained on an eighteen month system, and rearing of dairy heifers may well give comparable returns if the stocking rate is high and management is good.

Good management must involve control of the grazing in some way, taking advantage of the flexibility which the electric fence permits, and a much higher use of nitrogen than has been traditional. According to the 1966 survey of fertilizer practice grassland in arable areas received on average 42 lb/N/acre (47 kg ha). Adequate use of nitrogen can be a major factor in reducing the severity of drought, and there is something in the belief of one eastern farmer that dry summers only happen to people who do not put enough nitrogen on. At Boxworth E.H.F., techniques are being investigated of putting a large part of the nitrogen on in spring or early summer when moisture is available, in the hope that some of this nitrogen may be taken down the profile to a depth at which some moisture is available when the deficits becomes serious, thus enhancing grass growth in the summer. This may well be a promising field for further work, particularly for classes of livestock where one can achieve a high rate of growth in the early summer and a measure of compensatory growth thereafter. With the eighteen-month beef animal, there may be risk of them becoming 'leggy' if the plane of nutrition declines too drastically, although cattle often do best on the high dry-matter grass, available in a dry season provided that reasonable growth is taking place.

Despite continual exhortations towards silage, the majority of the grass crop is still conserved as hay, although silage is, at the moment, making one of its periodic come-backs on those farms which have become converted to the tower. One cannot see much likelihood of silage being of any real significance on the arable farm until the sugar-beet crop has been fully mechanised in the spring. Barn-drying of hay is a useful technique in permitting grass to be cut earlier, and hence achieving a more certain aftermath growth. Nevertheless, the solution to the problem of aftermath in a dry year probably lies in changing our concepts of grass; the re-growth of the legumes — both clover and lucerne — is so much more predictable that we may well be neglecting opportunities in not making wider use of our leguminous species, particularly lucerne. At Boxworth E.H.F. lucerne mixtures have given appreciably higher hay-yields than grass without any expenditure on nitrogen; one can be sure of aftermath to graze, or for a second cut if necessary, and judging from the ley fertility work, lucerne is very much the best preparation for subsequent wheat crops.

18. Farming Systems with more than 30 in (760 mm) Rainfall

P.J. Jones
Bridget's Experimental Husbandry Farm, Winchester.

Introduction

A study of a rainfall map of Britain shows that a line drawn from Berwick-on-Tweed due south to Oxford, and then south-east to Hastings would divide the country into two, with the area receiving less than 30 in. (760 mm) of rain annually to the east of this line. It is, however, summer rainfall which has the greatest influence on farming systems, and a summer rainfall of more than 14 in. (350 mm) during the six months of April to September provides an appropriate dividing line. This line starts on the east coast near the Northumberland/Durham border, bulges into north Yorkshire and then runs mainly due south to Derbyshire in the midlands, swings due west to the Welsh border counties, and then south and south-easterly, so that parts of Sussex, Hampshire and the south western counties are included in the wetter areas. Most of the area to the east of this line has an average summer potential transpiration in excess of the summer rainfall, and so benefits from irrigation, while in most years the area to the west has sufficient summer rain to balance the potential transpiration. Averages can sometimes be misleading, but a map of the frequency of irrigation need shows that almost the whole of this western area would rarely benefit from irrigation — the exceptions being the southern chalkland counties of Sussex, Hampshire, Wiltshire and Dorset.

But summer rainfall alone does not determine farming systems. Height above sea level and both winter and summer temperatures are equally important. However, it is more difficult to determine their direct effect on farming systems, except for such special crops as early potatoes and broccoli which will be mentioned later. Factors other than climatic and geographic, of course, also determine farming systems, and perhaps the most important of these are economic. These economic factors include the influence which local markets have on farming and, in particular, the siting of processing works, such as vegetable canning factories, beet sugar factories and potato processing works. These processing factories have obviously been sited to exploit the farming areas best suited to the crops they serve, but at the same time this siting does deny the advantages of growing these crops in other areas where they could be grown. There was, for instance, a struggle for many years to establish a beet factory in the south of England. Had such a factory been established, possibly in the Chichester area, then the crop would have been encouraged in the south and the knowledge and expertise to grow the crop acquired by both farmers and workers. In the event, no such factory was built, and although the crop lingered in the south until a few years ago, real expertise was never obtained, and the high transport costs to the beet factory at Kidderminster, a distance of more than 100 miles, virtually killed the crop. Similarly, one can speculate what would have happened to farming systems in the south of England if a firm such as Birds Eye Foods had established itself south of the Thames.

Patterns of Cropping

A study of the statistics produced annually by the Ministry of Agriculture, Fisheries and Food shows that the line of 14 in. (350 mm) of summer rainfall roughly divides England and Wales into two equal areas, if rough grazing is excluded (Table 18.1). The vast area of rough grazing in the high rainfall area is mainly devoted to sheep or forestry, the potential of which has been discussed in earlier chapters.

Table 18.1
Distribution of grass and crops in high and low summer rainfall areas

	Grass & Crops	Rough Grazing	Total
High summer rainfall (>350 mm)	12 750 000 ac (5 164 000 ha)	4 500 000 ac (1 822 000 ha)	17 150 000 ac (6 986 000 ha)
Low summer rainfall (<350 mm)	11 500 000 ac (4 658 000 ha)	250 000 ac (101 000 ha)	11 750 000 ac (4 759 000 ha)

These statistics show a wide difference of land use between the two areas. In the high rainfall area, 9.5 million acres (3.8 million ha) (67 per cent) are in grass and only 3.25 million acres (1.3 million ha) (33 per cent) in crops while in the low rainfall area the proportions are reversed, 4.7 million acres (1.9 million ha) (33 per cent) in grass and 6.8 million acres (2.8 million ha) (67 per cent) in crops.

Nearly 7 million acres (2.8 million ha) of the grass in the high rainfall area is classified as permanent compared with about 3.5 million acres (1.4 million ha) in the low rainfall area. These figures show a higher area of permanent grass than expected in the drier area, but much of this grass occurs in the marginal counties between the two main areas.

Of course, grass and livestock go naturally together, and this difference in cropping is reflected in the wide difference which occurs in the cattle and sheep populations of the two areas. 67 per cent of the cattle (5.8 million) and 73 per cent of the sheep (14.7 million) are to be found in the high rainfall areas of England and Wales.

These figures show the preponderance of livestock in the grassland areas of the country. They include 68 600 milk producers (77 per cent) compared with only 20 500 in the east. But because the size of herd is larger in the eastern areas, the difference in milk production is not quite of the same order – the wet areas producing 1500 million gallons (6810 million kg) annually (69 per cent) out of a total of approximately 2000 million gallons (9080 million kg).

The statistics in Table 18.2 emphasize the differences which exist between the farming in the two areas of the country.

Table 18.2
Comparison of farming systems in wetter (W and N) and drier areas (S and E)

83% of the farms in W and N have cattle or sheep or both	

	10 of the farms in W and N have arable crops
26%	5 of the farms in W and N have horti. crops
	11 of the farms in W and N have mixed

33% of the farms in S and E have cattle or sheep or both	

	33 of the farms in S and E have arable crops
59%	17 of the farms in S and E have horti. crops
	9 of the farms in S and E have mixed

Within the wetter area there are, of course, local pockets of intensive cropping of both agricultural and horticultural crops, and this area as defined here includes parts of Yorkshire and most of the southern chalk downland, all of which are areas of intensive cereal production. It also includes the Cotswolds and the cereal areas around Bridgewater in Somerset, the early-potato growing areas of south Wales, the strawberries of Cheddar, and, of course, the early potatoes and broccoli of the Cornish peninsula.

Attempts have been made from time to time to extend arable crops to the wetter areas not normally considered suitable for them, but usually without complete success. A good example has been the move to extend cereal growing, particularly spring barley, westwards into the wetter parts of the country to replace the oat crop. Cornwall and Devon, for example, have increased the acreage devoted to this crop quite considerably since 1963, but yields have been disappointing, partly because of difficult weather conditions at planting and harvest times, and also because of cereal diseases such as *Rhynchosporium* which is much more severe in those areas than elsewhere.

It is true that plant breeders have helped considerably in producing varieties showing some degree of resistance to such diseases, and the exceptionally early-ripening barley, Akka, may help to maintain the present acreage in these areas.

Grassland Systems

Apart from the above exceptions, however, farming systems in the wetter areas mainly revolve round the grass crop and are likely to do so for some years ahead.

As mentioned earlier, much of this grass is of a permanent nature, so farming systems depend less on crop rotations and more on stockmanship.

The so-called temporary grass often consists of direct reseeding to perennial ryegrass/white-clover type leys, although some farmers do take a cereal crop, often oats, as a cover crop, and the occasional root crop also appears. The shorter Italian ryegrass type ley, usually down only for one to two years, features more widely in the fringe areas, where it is used for intensive animal output, mainly milk, before the land is returned to cereals — thus acting as a break from cereals and often providing a re-entry point for winter wheat into the rotation.

But much of the grass is permanent, much has never seen the plough, and some is of extremely poor quality. Frequently topography is such that cultivations, including ploughing and fertilizer application, are extremely difficult, and poor drainage is often a limiting factor to improvement. Fertilizer usage is too low, and grazing intensity is too lax, so that weeds and the poorer types of grass predominate. Silage is rarely made and, in spite of the weather risks, conservation usually takes the form of field-dried hay, made usually in July from mature grass low in digestibility and low in protein.

These are general remarks and may not be completely true in specific cases. Some farmers are very good managers of their grass, but these are the leaders in the industry, and on most farms appreciable improvements in grazing techniques can be made. Surveys have shown that utilized starch equivalent (U.S.E.) averages under 2500 lb acre^{-1} (2800 kg ha^{-1}) but as described in other chapters, dry-matter yields of well over 5 tons acre^{-1} (12 500 kg ha^{-1}) are possible with good management, correct fertilizer use and adequate stocking rates, resulting in yields of U.S.E. in excess of 60 cwt acre^{-1} (7500 kg ha^{-1}).

These conclusions are based on the work of the six experimental husbandry farms in the region under discussion, as well as that of Fison's Experimental Station at North Wyke and that of I.C.I. at Henley Manor, all of which have had an impact on farming systems. At these centres all classes of livestock are represented.

Farmers are now showing considerable interest in the eighteen months-old beef system. Usually the calves are born in autumn, spending the first six months of their lives indoors. They are then turned out to grass for the summer before being finished in yards the following winter. Both at North Wyke and Liscombe E.H.F., liveweight gains of around 1000 lb acre^{-1} (1120 kg ha^{-1}) have been obtained under good and intensive grassland management. This figure is for total gain per acre and is not necessarily combined with finish, but it does indicate the potential of the grass. Even so, animals can be both fattened and finished ready for the butcher with gains of over 500 lb liveweight per acre (560 kg ha^{-1}), leaving gross margins of well over £50 per acre. However, this is possible only where good management can be combined with good grazing conditions. Because of factors such as drainage, slope and altitude, lower stocking rates and liveweight gains per acre have often to be accepted, with gross margins falling to £35 to £40 an acre, a figure which still compares well with gross margins from cereal growing.

In these wetter areas, however, many farmers find it more profitable to concentrate on the rearing stage only and pass the animals on to others for the finishing process. This was the traditional method of beef production in the arable districts. Store cattle from the north and west of the country and from Ireland, aged between eighteen and twenty-four months, moved to the eastern side of the country for finishing in yards on arable by-products. Under this system, the true potential of the grass is often not achieved because less grazing pressure is exerted. However, with the aid of lower rents and land values, and calf and hill farming subsidies, it can prove attractive financially to the rearer, reducing his need for winter fodder, and allowing him to carry more stock on his farm. It still appeals to many arable farmers who find it a profitable enterprise complementary to their other farming activities, and we may well see a return to this method of beef production.

Rearing heifer replacements is also attracting more attention on those farms which are looking for an alternative livestock enterprise which requires little capital for fixed equipment. Here again, where standards of management are high, liveweight gains approaching 100 lb $acre^{-1}$ (1120 kg ha^{-1}) can be achieved, giving gross margins of about £50 an acre. Usually, however, less intensive grazing methods are employed, requiring in all more than one acre (0.4 ha) per animal; the heifers do not calve until over two years of age and gross margins are only around £30 an acre.

Work at Henley Manor and at Trawscoed and Bridget's E.H.F.'s has shown that well-managed grass can make a major contribution to summer milk-production. The results from Bridget's E.H.F. show that by the correct use of nitrogen and paddock grazing, with a high stocking rate per acre and with adequate rest periods for the grass, spring-calving cows can achieve yields of milk in excess of 1500 gallons per acre (> 17 000 kg ha) without the need for expensive concentrates. The influence of stocking rate per acre can be seen from the results from Bridget's E.H.F. given in Table 18.3.

Table 18.3
Influence of stocking rate on milk production at Bridget's E.H.F.

	per acre	(per ha)	per acre	(per ha)	per acre	(per ha)	per acre	(per ha)
Cows	1.75	(4.3)	2	(4.9)	2.25	(5.6)	3	(7.4)
Cow days	287	(709)	308	(761)	367	(906)	488	(1205)
Milk (gallons)	1109	–	1272	–	1327	–	1622	–
(l)	–	(12 780)	–	(14 60)	–	(15 290)	–	(18 680)
Value of milk	£157	–	£182	–	£190	–	£234	–
Margin over food and fertilizer	£137	–	£134	–	£164	–	£182	–

Even at these extremely high stocking rates, the use of concentrates has not proved beneficial. At Trawscoed with its better climate for grass, no benefit has been obtained from the feeding of additional barley. At Bridget's, barley has helped to maintain milk yields in very dry periods, but economically this has proved of doubtful value.

These results illustrate that under good management, when the true potential of grass can be realised, it is capable of giving gross margins in excess of £90 per acre. Obviously under less favourable conditions slightly lower returns might be expected, but of all the livestock systems, milk remains the most profitable. This is true even with an autumn-calving herd. An overall stocking rate of 1 cow per acre (2.5 cows per ha) to supply both summer grazing and winter fodder is frequently found on the best managed farms.

Warnings of overproduction of liquid milk are frequently heard, but many farmers in the wetter areas of the country have little alternative but to continue in milk. Summer milk seems the obvious answer because there is no crop other than grass where production can be so easily raised, in many cases three-fold, simply by better management. This can usually be done without the need for additional capital, other than for the animals themselves, and possibly for improved drainage. Furthermore, creameries already exist in these areas to process the milk.

Finally, systems involving sheep must be considered, since there are 14.7 million sheep in the area under review. Many of these are for breeding, traditionally moving lower down the hill and eventually reaching the lower grassland areas. Here again, intensification has taken over, and 1000 lb of fat lamb per acre (1120 kg/ha) is being achieved under the best systems of management. Such systems are extremely attractive to those arable farmers who require a grass break for their cereals, particularly those in the traditional sheep and corn areas of England. The grass is cashed through the ewe and lamb to leave a gross margin per acre often better than can be obtained from cereals themselves.

The above account of farming systems in those areas with more than 30 in. (760 mm) of rainfall is admittedly a general one, and obviously there are many deviations from the systems outlined. In only a few cases is the output from the farms at its maximum and the true potential of grass achieved. There is still a need for advice and encouragement to the farmers in these areas to allow them to raise their standard of living in line with their colleagues in the arable parts of the country.

19. The Determination of Production Systems

J.D. Ivins
School of Agriculture, University of Nottingham

The purpose of this chapter is to look at systems of crop production enterprises in Britain, to assess the factors which determine them, and from that standpoint to see what is practicable. Land is much more than space for photosynthesis; if it were not then it would be necessary only to simply give an account of the traditions and economic factors which determine systems of crop production. These factors are involved, of course, particularly the economic ones, for crop production is a business and it must be profitable for those who engage in it. Profitability is a major determinant, and a few successive annual price reviews can swing the emphasis of cropping in one direction or another depending on changes in the guaranteed prices for agricultural products. It would not be unreasonable to guess that a deduction of two shillings per hundredweight off the price of barley and an increase of fourpence a gallon on the guaranteed price of milk would probably mean that at least two million acres (800 thousand hectares) of land now in cereals would be sown down to grass. This is not a prediction of what might happen at future price reviews but merely an illustration of the manner in which production systems are determined.

Several estimates have been made of potential photosynthesis and potential yields of dry matter, and it is clear that the crop yields and food production at present achieved is but a small fraction of the potential. There is no doubt that some of the poorer grassland, as far as food production for man is concerned, is biologically grossly inefficient; in fact most grassland is of low efficiency if judged in terms of efficiency of energy fixation for man's food. Nevertheless three-quarters of the farmed area of Britain is covered with grass of one sort or another if rough grazings are included, and there are many reasons why it will stay that way despite its relative inefficiency. Most of the remaining quarter of Britain is growing cereal crops with barley predominating. Some of the factors involved in the determination of systems can be illustrated by discussing first the changes which have taken place in the last decade in Britain, and then the factors which determine crop yields, with particular emphasis on the limiting factors.

The changes in systems are taking place within certain background trends. There is less land available for agriculture each year. Ellison [2] likened the loss of land for urban development to the loss of a county almost the size of Nottinghamshire every eight years, and nearly the same area is being planted with forests. More and more capital is being invested in farming, and the purchase price and rent of land have risen steeply. As farms fall vacant many are amalgamated to form bigger units, and it is claimed that the larger units are more viable economically and that they justify the higher degree of mechanization, specialized management and specialized labour which characterizes them. For many years the labour force in agriculture has decreased annually and the extent of mechanization has increased. There has been more specialization with fewer but larger productive units — the Milk Marketing Board reports an appreciable fall in the number of dairy farmers (some 28 per cent in the period 1954-64) but an increase in the size of the average herd; the Potato Marketing Board reports a fall in the number of registered growers from 87 000 in 1955 to just over 57 000 in 1965. This specialization is often accompanied by intensification, particularly with some livestock enterprises. Even so a large area of Britain, between 16 and 17 million acres, (about 6½ million hectares) is classified as rough grazing, involving very extensive livestock production and a comparatively low output per unit area of food for man. This rough grazing has hardly changed in area or productivity, but the area of permanent grass has declined from 12¼ million acres (about 5 million hectares) in 1958 to slightly less than 11 million acres (less than 4½ million hectares) in 1968, and the area of leys has also fallen, both to make way for more cereals.

The advantages of ley farming proclaimed so well by Robert Elliot and Stapledon and Davies still hold good today. Few will dispute that a ryegrass/white-clover sward is more productive than an Agrostis/fescue sward. There are more of the latter than the former, and a sown ley is more likely to consist of the better grasses, which is the argument for re-seeding. Technically there are several advantages from incorporating the ley into crop rotations, in particular those with a predominance of cereal crops. The break under grass reduces some soil-borne pests and diseases of wheat and barley, the accumulation of organic matter may be beneficial on some soils, and the grazed ley results in increased soil fertility. But technical reasons are not always economic ones, and the realisation that in many cases the fertility accumulation under the ley can be replaced by an additional fifty or sixty units of nitrogen in fertilizer form has led to the abandonment of ley farming on some farms, particularly in the eastern half of Britain, where there are great economic advantages in specialized arable farming rather than mixed ley farming. An exception is the arable and dairying farm big enough to allow specialization in both enterprises but, as indicated earlier, the number of dairy herds is declining.

Again, in the eastern counties barley grain, with or without the straw, is tending to replace grass as a feed for cattle, either for beef production or even for milk production, where it may replace conserved grass in the winter. Barley now dominates the cereal acreage at not far short of 6 million acres (2½ million hectares), oats have declined to less than one million acres (less than half a million hectares) and wheat has remained reasonably constant at between 2¼ and 2½ million acres (about 1 million hectares). Ten or twelve years ago there were approximately 2 million acres (about 800 thousand hectares) of each of these three cereals, but the introduction of high-yielding, short strawed varieties of barley responsive to high levels of nitrogen fertilizers, and the realization of the higher energy value of barley compared with oats, and its equal suitability for ruminant feeding, have all contributed to higher returns from barley and have led to the big increase in barley production at the expense of oats.

The need for crops to break up the frequency of cereals in a rotation has already been mentioned. Potatoes and sugar beet do this very well, but all arable soils are not suitable for these crops and the area is limited, not by any biological problem, but in the case of potatoes by a quota system which aims to limit production to what the market will absorb at a price which gives a reasonable return to the grower, with penalties for exceeding the quota, while in the case of sugar beet the area contracted is limited to the capacity of the factories to process the crop. So over the last decade we have seen a decrease in the area of potatoes from 722 000 to 640 000 acres (292 000 to 258 000 hectares) and only a slight increase in sugar beet, which is still short of half a million acres (less than 200 000 hectares). Root crops for stockfeeding now stand at less than 300 000 acres (120 000 hectares) — less than half the area of ten years ago. These crops, mangolds, fodder beet, swedes and turnips, can give high yields of animal food, often higher than cereals when compared in terms of digestible dry-matter per unit area, but they have a much higher labour requirement and so have given way to barley which is a highly mechanized crop.

One important cause of the gap between potential yields and actual yields, is the fact that very few of our crops have an active closed leaf-canopy from April to September. There are however, some ways in which the period of crop growth can be extended. For instance, raising sugar beet seedlings under cover and transplanting them in the field in early spring will bring forward the development of the leaf canopy, and a leaf area index of 3 or above can be obtained early in June, compared with mid-July in a normal field-sown crop. This results in increased yields but costs of production are also increased, possibly to an extent which precludes the technique on a farm scale, illustrating that in farming the highest yield may not always be the target. Similarly, the producer is not interested in gaining the highest total yields of dry matter, but only high yields of that part of the dry matter which has the highest value, e.g. grain or tubers rather than straw or haulm. Hence the partition of assimilates within the plant is most important, and situations can occur where particular treatments may lead to increased crop growth rates and increased yields of dry matter per unit area, but no extra or even less economic yield. For example, irrigation of sugar beet at Sutton Bonington in most years results in more dry matter per unit area but no more sugar, for the extra dry matter is contained within increased leaf and petiole weight.

Sometimes yield is sacrificed in order to obtain a product of a particular quality, if there is a premium to encourage this. For malting barley, the highest yielding varieties may not be ideal, and much lower levels of nitrogen fertiliser are used than when a crop is grown for livestock feeding, resulting in a lower dry-matter yield. The extent to which King Edward potatoes are grown is a reflection of the demand for quality for, apart from the premium, this variety has most of the possible disadvantages as far as the grower is concerned, including low yield. With grassland too, quality is as important as quantity, and the composition of the dry matter is important rather than the yields of dry matter alone. Here also high quality can in some cases mean less quantity.

The limitations to yield vary with each individual crop. In most years in Britain the limit to potato yields is blight, while sugar-beet yields are low because of limited early growth and leaf development. Grassland productivity is limited by the species and the nitrogen supply, except on a few farms where excessive quantities of fertilizer are given, while cereal yields are limited by wet weather, which can cause serious lodging and losses at harvest as in 1968, or late sowing and waterlogging as in 1969. Low temperatures limit the growth of maize in Britain, while a higher price, say at the European level, would stimulate a big increase in the area of oilseed rape.

Future developments in plant breeding are considered in later chapters, but plant-breeding achievements have already permitted the evolution and, more readily, the modification of some systems of production. Because of the introduction of new varieties, cereal yields have increased greatly over the last twenty years; but some problems remain, particularly diseases, such as take-all, rusts and mildews, where the interesting question now arises whether the chemist, by producing systemic fungicides, will achieve the objectives which have always been regarded as those of the plant breeder. With some crops very little progress has been made in developing new varieties, the main example here being potatoes where, although there are some younger challengers, the varieties which still dominate the area of maincrops are Majestic and King Edward, which were introduced in 1911 and 1902 respectively, and with grassland the plant breeder is rarely given an opportunity to demonstrate his products, for much grassland is permanent and is not re-sown.

Soil-type and climate together determine the time when any treatment is given to a crop. Such timing is usually critical and so these are the two main physical factors which determine systems of crop production. This point has been emphasised in earlier chapters; for example, when soil type is difficult from the point of view of cultivations and total annual rainfall is appreciably higher than 30 in. or so, attempts to grow arable crops are made only in times of national emergency and the normal system is grass farming. Heavy capital investment in machinery may enable cultivations to be carried out in a short time — a point of some importance with difficult soils — but there are limits to such investment when the return on capital becomes important. To a small extent the farmer can overcome the limitations of climate, for instance, extra capacity driers may alleviate a wet harvest, but the wet May of 1969, with several thousands of acres unsown and many thousands of acres of spring cereals looking very poor, illustrates very clearly how puny man's efforts are when he is faced with extreme weather conditions in a particular year. Similarly, in a very dry year, the water supplies in our rivers, lakes and reservoirs are inadequate to meet the demands of industry let alone the needs for irrigation, even though economic responses to irrigation can be shown in the majority of years with crops such as potatoes and grass in eastern England. The fact that water supplies for irrigation are strictly limited and often expensive has encouraged research on the effects of the time of irrigation and the quantities of water on crop growth and yields, and work with sugar beet has already been mentioned in which increased yields of dry matter resulted from irrigation but no extra yield of sugar was obtained. With potatoes the response depends on the time of application of water, as shown by Llewelyn [3] in experiments at Sutton Bonington. Irrigation at the time of initiation and early growth of tubers led to an increase in leaf area without depressing rates of tuber growth; later rates of tuber bulking were increased and so was the final yield. Earlier irrigation, at the time when stolons were being formed, resulted in more early leaf growth and a delay in the initiation of tubers and, although tuber bulking rates were higher than in the case of non-irrigated treatments, the earlier-formed leaves senesced earlier, and the period of tuber bulking was shorter, resulting in a decrease in yield when compared with no irrigation.

For generations the need for rotation of crops has set the pattern of cropping systems. The underlying principles have been firmly held, and deviation from a fixed rotation was deemed to be against the tenets of good husbandry. Now, however, the emphasis is rightly on specialization rather than diversification. Mechanization has eased the problem of peaks of labour demand, herbicides have solved many weed problems, and fertility is becoming almost synonymous with fertilizers, so that the only remaining and apparently real necessity for crop rotations is to control certain soil-borne pests and diseases. This is where the need for a break crop from cereals becomes important. Except on fine sands and fine silts, both of which have a soil structure problem, which may be remedied by heavy dressings of organic matter, farmyard manure is no longer highly valued, and very rarely are systems of animal production operated with one eye on this by-product. Most of the experimental evidence shows that, except on the fine sands and fine silts, any effects of farmyard manure can be reproduced by the application of nitrogen, phorphorus and potassium, and extra fertilisers plus burned straw have replaced the traditional systems of fattening yarded cattle on the predominently arable farm in eastern England. There is some interest in fattening cattle mainly on home-grown barley, but this arises from the attempt to utilise barley more profitably, rather than to make farmyard manure for the benefit of arable crops.

Increased use of fertilizers over the years has, without doubt, resulted in increased yields, particularly when more responsive varieties have been available, as in wheat and barley. On some arable farms in the east, the use of phosphates and potash fertilizers is now merely a topping-up operation, and it is difficult to measure or even detect a response to P and K. In this case levels of nitrogen usage are also high and there is no doubt that the limit has been reached, or even on some occasions overstepped, and that yields have suffered in consequence.

It is interesting to examine what happens when high levels of nitrogen are used. With cereals the effect can be dramatic, resulting in lodged crops, reduced yields and poorly filled grain. The usual nitrogen application in spring often proves to be too high if the following summer is wet, and hardly enough if the summer is dry, so there is need for reliable weather forecasts six months ahead. Less spectacular are the effects on potatoes and sugar beet where high nitrogen acts in a similar way to irrigation. For many reasons, exact figures in terms of fertiliser input per unit area would have little meaning, but at reasonable levels with maincrop potatoes there is a stimulus to stem and leaf growth from nitrogen and a delay in tuber initiation; but as a result of the extra leaf area, tuber bulking rates are higher and yields are usually higher. Additional nitrogen stimulates haulm growth still further and yield reductions then occur by the adverse partition of assimilates within the plant, giving lower tuber bulking rates and possibly a shorter bulking period as a consequence of the susceptibility of the luxuriant foliage to blight. Sugar beet manured with heavy applications of nitrogenous fertilizers may look extremely vigorous but, as in the potato crop, the extra dry-matter may be contained in the foliage; this is found to be the case following irrigation of sugar beet at Sutton Bonington. Nitrogen is a key factor in crop yields, and in grassland there is every justification for the use of increased quantities provided the herbage is fully utilized, but in arable crops there are cases where in farm practice the limit to response has been reached until new model varieties can be developed. These may take the form of varieties with much sparser leaf growth, so that the levels of N can be pushed still higher to give longer leaf area duration rather than above-optimum values of leaf area index. Certainly it appears impossible to push the leaf growth of many early varieties of potatoes to the point where tuber bulking rate is affected, for they have innately sparse foliage; unfortunately this sparse foliage is accompanied by early senescence which is only slightly delayed by high N, resulting in lower yields than maincrops if left to mature.

The use of C.C.C. (chlormequat) on wheat crops, to reduce straw length and hence lodging, does in effect attempt to gain more precise control of the partition of assimilates within the crop and at the same time to gain the advantages of high levels of N. Bodlaender and Algra [1] achieved some success along these lines by using B995 on potato crops, for they estimated that if further growth of foliage at high nitrogen levels could be prevented after the optimum leaf area index had been achieved, a larger percentage of the total dry-matter might be diverted to the tubers. Recent work at Sutton

Bonington [4] has tested the effect of B995 on potatoes, and of both B995 and C.C.C. on sugar beet, in field experiments. There was a marked interaction between nitrogen, B995 and tuber yields of Majestic, but tuber yields were increased more by B995 at the lower nitrogen level (112 lb N acre $^{-1}$ = 125 kg ha $^{-1}$) rather than at the higher level (224 lb N acre^{-1} = 250 kg ha^{-1}). C.C.C. increased the net assimilation rate of the sugar-beet crop and stimulated the storage of a higher percentage of assimilates in the roots, but B995 was ineffective. When more is known about their effects, growth regulators may supplement the efforts of the plant breeders and fertiliser companies which have been so successful in giving higher yields. In fact, C.C.C. is already being used to increase the yield of wheat.

To summarize, soil type, climate and profitability are the main factors which determine cropping systems. Technical developments such as new varieties, fertilizers, pesticides and herbicides have led to increased yields, often allowing profitable crops to be grown under far from ideal conditions. It is possible that other technical developments such as systemic fungicides, growth regulators or soil sterilants will go further in helping to reduce the limitations imposed by the environment, and thus will increase the potential for crop production in Britain. Even so, there will still remain an art of crop production, for, using the same variety and the same fertilizers and sprays, one farmer will grow good crops while his neighbour will grow poor ones, even with identical weather and soil type. The best crops will result from the correct judgement of when to carry out operations on the land and the crop in relation to soil and weather conditions, and, of course from the capacity in machinery to carry them out at the right time. Operations will usually be carried out too late on the poorer crops, either through the inability to judge the right time or the lack of equipment to do the right job at the right time. Poor drainage may also prevent the right timing of operations, for on well drained land the crop is less at the mercy of high rainfall; May 1969 for instance, highlighted widespread drainage problems on arable crops. In most years in Britain, there is only one right time for a particular farming operation, and the art of crop production is in judging when this time has arrived; no technical developments can replace such experienced judgement.

REFERENCES

1. BODLAENDER, K.B.A. and ALGRA, S. 'Influence of growth retardant B995 on growth and yield of potatoes', *Eur. Potato J.*, 1966, 9, 242-58.
2. ELLISON, W. 'Agriculture and Changes in land uses', *Advmt. Sci.*, 1966, 23, 287.
3. LLEWELYN, J.C. 'The influence of water regimes on the growth and development of the potato crop', *Ph.D. Thesis, Univ. Nottingham*, 1967.
4. SCOTT, R.K. Unpublished data.

20. Plant Breeding: Arable Crops

J. Bingham
Plant Breeding Institute, Trumpington, Cambridge.

The objective of this chapter is to assess the prospects of breeding more productive varieties of the principal arable crops, cereals, sugar beet, potatoes and field beans. This will be done by considering the genetic variability available to the breeders and how it might be exploited, either by traditional or by new plant breeding techniques. In these crops it is useful to look back at the national records of productivity per acre (Table 20.1) and decide what proportion of the increases in yield can be ascribed to plant breeding. This can give a good indication of the value of the traditional breeding techniques and help in the prediction of future developments.

Table 20.1
Yield of agricultural crops in Great Britain

	Wheat		Sugar beet		Potatoes		Beans	
	Cwt acre^{-1}	(t ha^{-1})	Tons sugar acre^{-1}	(t ha^{-1})	Tons acre^{-1}	(t ha^{-1})	Cwt acre^{-1}	(t ha^{-1})
1896	18.6	(2.32)	–		6.3	(15.75)	–	
1906	18.9	(2.36)	–		6.1	(15.25)	–	
1916	15.8	(1.97)	–		5.4	(13.50)	–	
1926	16.5	(2.06)	1.49	(3.72)	5.7	(14.25)	15.7	(1.96)
1936	16.4	(2.05)	–		6.5	(16.25)	15.3	(1.91)
1946	19.1	(2.39)	1.44	(3.60)	7.0	(17.50)	13.5	(1.69)
1956	24.8	(3.10)	2.04	(5.10)	8.4	(21.00)	17.3	(2.16)
1957	25.4	(3.17)	1.71	(4.27)	7.1	(17.75)	17.7	(2.21)
1958	24.6	(3.07)	2.09	(5.22)	6.9	(17.25)	16.1	(2.01)
1959	28.9	(3.61)	2.27	(5.67)	8.6	(21.50)	17.2	(2.15)
1960	28.5	(3.56)	2.60	(6.50)	8.7	(21.75)	19.4	(2.42)
1961	28.2	(3.52)	2.24	(5.60)	9.0	(22.50)	18.3	(2.29)
1962	34.7	(4.34)	2.18	(5.45)	9.1	(22.75)	22.2	(2.77)
1963	31.1	(3.89)	2.14	(5.30)	8.6	(21.50)	21.2	(2.65)
1964	33.8	(4.22)	2.58	(6.45)	9.1	(22.75)	22.4	(2.80)
1965	32.4	(4.05)	2.39	(5.97)	10.2	(25.50)	21.0	(2.62)
1966	30.6	(3.82)	2.39	(5.97)	9.8	(24.50)	23.5	(2.94)
1967	33.3	(4.16)	2.45	(6.12)	10.1	(25.25)	24.4	(3.05)
1968	28.9	(3.61)	2.42	(6.05)	10.0	(25.00)	19.3	(2.41)

Cereals

In cereals it is clear that genetic improvements in new varieties have made a major contribution. This is easy to demonstrate because, due to their inbreeding system, cereal varieties are largely homozygous and when carefully maintained do not change genetically, so that direct comparisons can be made of many old and new varieties. For example, in winter wheat, Cappelle-Desprez (marketed in 1953) outyields Holdfast (marketed in 1938) by about 20 per cent, even in the absence of lodging or severe disease. The latest additions to the N.I.A.B. recommended list, Cama, Joss Cambier and Maris Ranger are at least 10 per cent higher yielding than Cappelle-Desprez. Therefore it is reasonable to conclude that the increase in yield of winter wheat attributable to breeding alone has averaged 1 per cent per annum over the last 30 years. In addition, the increase in yield due to increased use of fertilisers has been largely dependent on the greatly improved standing ability of the newer varieties. Genetic improvements in the other cereals have been on a similar scale. The achievements in winter barley, winter oats and spring wheat are especially notable because they have made possible large increases in acreage, virtually as new crops for this country. Results with varieties currently in trials show that this pace is being maintained, indicating that the principal breeding technique, of selecting true-breeding recombinants in intervarietal crosses, still has considerable potential and has not exhausted the genetic variability.

Consequently, there is little doubt that in cereal breeding the emphasis will continue to be on improving the choice of parents with desired characters and on using more efficient selection techniques to identify the best genetic recombinants [2, 42].

Exploitation of Physiological Characters

Easily the best prospect in breeding for potential yield is offered by the insight into the physiological basis of grain yield which has been obtained in recent years and discussed by Thorne [40] in an earlier chapter. From the relationship of the physiological characters shown in Figure 20.1 and considered by Bingham [3] it is possible to draw up a plant breeder's specification of the ideal variety in physiological terms. There is now general agreement that the sink characteristics of the grain can limit yield in many environmental situations, though there is insufficient evidence to be sure of the mechanisms involved. The photosynthetic capacity of the crop after anthesis is also important, and it seems probable that these characters interact in such a way that frequently neither is fully exploited. This situation is analogous to blowing up an elastic bladder with an inefficient air pump for a limited period; increase in final size can be obtained by using either a more efficient pump or a bladder with less resistance to inflation.

Although yield is directly determined during the post-anthesis period, the potential of the crop is largely dependent on earlier events. During this early

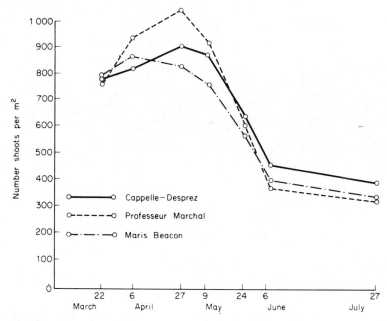

Fig. 20.1 *Shoot production and survival in three winter wheat varieties in a field trial in 1966. The differences in this pattern between Professeur Marchal and Maris Beacon are probably responsible for the higher yielding ability of Maris Beacon; from Bingham [3].*

period vegetative growth, is very inefficient in terms of subsequent grain production. The L.A.I. needed for maximum vegetative growth could be reached earlier by husbandry methods, but present varieties are unable to convert this strategic advantage in potential assimilation into yield of grain. The greatest opportunity for improvement by breeding in the pre-anthesis period is to breed varieties in which a higher proportion of the assimilates is used for development of the ear, upper leaves and perhaps also roots which have a direct effect on grain filling. This can be done most effectively by reducing tillering, increasing the proportion of shoots which survive to ear, reducing stem weight and increasing the period of rapid ear development.

The breeding of Maris Beacon is a good example of the importance of tillering pattern. This winter wheat variety was selected from the following cross:

$$\{(\text{CI } 12633 \text{ x Cappelle-Desprez}^5 \text{) x } (F_1 \text{ Cappelle-Desprez x Hybrid } 46)\}$$
$$\text{x Professeur Marchal}^2$$

The segregating generations were selected mainly for production of fewer tillers and better shoot survival than Professeur Marchal, which is rather poor in this respect (Figure 20.2). Grain yield of Maris Beacon has been consistently above Professeur Marchal (Table 20.2). This is probably

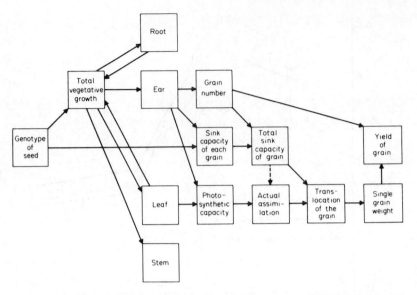

Fig. 20.2   Relationship of the principal heritable characters which determine yield of grain in wheat. This relationship may also apply to a considerable extent to barley and oats; from Bingham [3].

Table 20.2
Harvest analysis of components of yield and vegetative characters in wheat 1966

	Straw length (cm)	Grain yield (g m^{-2})	Straw wt (g m^{-2})	Grain straw	No. grains per m^2 x 10^{-3}	1000 grain wt (g)	No. grains per spikelet
*Holdfast	97	351	800	0.44	10.3	35.5	1.65
Cappelle-Desprez	87	481	797	0.61	9.2	52.3	1.59
Prof. Marchal	88	507	732	0.69	10.3	49.5	2.00
Maris Beacon	85	587	783	0.75	11.4	51.6	2.04
Marne X VG 9144	58	543	642	0.84	13.6	40.1	2.09

*Data for Holdfast derived from a 1963 trial (by comparison with Cappelle-Desprez) and included as an example of an older variety.

attributable to the improvement in tillering pattern because several other selections of similar performance were obtained from this cross and, due to the backcross to Professeur Marchal, the chance of significant improvement without selection was restricted. This indicates that the use of main-shoot assimilates in early tiller growth may have more far-reaching effects than is generally supposed. Loss of even a small amount of assimilate from the main shoot at this stage could have a direct effect on meristematic activity, possibly restricting growth of the primordia of the ear and upper leaves more than that of the earlier differentiated leaves and stem. This might permanently affect the distribution of assimilates, and account for the improved grain:straw ratio characteristic of newer varieties (Table 20.2).

From the onset of stem elongation to anthesis the stems and ears are growing rapidly [3] and are in direct competition for the available carbohydrate. Many floret primordia are aborted, but probably only because their carbohydrate supply is inadequate for complete development. The most logical way to increase the carbohydrate supply to the ear and flag leaf is to reduce the demand of the stem by breeding dwarf varieties. In wheat there is an excellent prospect that genes for dwarfness, present in the Japanese variety Norin 10, will be exploited in varieties for this country as successfully as they have been in the Mexican semi-dwarf varieties [9].

A more favourable partition of assimilates before anthesis might also be obtained by alterations in the timing and duration of the developmental stages. Earlier spring growth would facilitate earlier ear initiation and allow a longer period of ear development. Provided the growth rate of the ear was not reduced, this would result in an increase in ear size at anthesis, and possibly also of sink capacity by increasing grain number or improving the growth characteristics of each grain. In wheat, grain number per spikelet is probably the easiest component of grain number to increase because it is the last to be determined and requires the least vegetative change. For this reason considerable emphasis is given to grain number per spikelet in the breeding work, and in this connection it is interesting that lines carrying the Norin 10 genes for dwarfness are usually good in this character. Similar reasoning can be applied to oats, but in barley, owing to the determinate spikelet, the emphasis should be on grain number per ear.

After anthesis the principal breeding objective should be to increase the longevity of the leaves, with the objective of increasing the growth rate of the grain and extending its period of growth. There are small varietal differences in N.A.R. of the flag and penultimate leaves in wheat, but these have to be considered with caution because they may be a secondary effect of the demand of the grain for assimilate. Selection for more erect leaves is more promising, as there is considerable genetic variation in this respect, and in wheat another possibility is to add awns. Almost all varieties are awned in areas where the growing period is curtailed by drought. However, awns rarely increase yield in wheat in cool humid climates. It is feasible that the developing awns use a significant amount of the carbohydrate available at that time so that more floret initials are aborted. If this is the case, awns might be more useful in dwarf varieties, because in them the supply of carbohydrate available for ear development is probably greater.

Resistance to Disease

Introduction into cultivation of varieties with new major genetic factors for seedling (or race-specific) resistance to disease is frequently followed by the appearance of races of the pathogen capable of attacking them. Moreover, when a variety with such major gene resistance is overcome, it is usually more susceptible to the disease than its parents. For example, in yellow rust (*Puccinia striiformis*) of wheat, at least four new races, 8b, 3/55, 60 and 58, have appeared since 1955 and the first three of these caused serious epidemics on varieties considered resistant when introduced (Table 20.3). At least ten major factors for race-specific resistance have been identified [29]. They are specific in action against particular races of the pathogen and give complete resistance throughout the life of the plant. It seems probable that there are equivalent genes for virulence in the pathogen, so that development of a new race requires a change in only one or two genetic factors. This might be expected to occur by mutation or, in fungi with a sexual stage, by genetic recombination. In yellow rust no sexual stage has been found but the hyphal cells are binucleate, and Little and Manners [27] have very good evidence that recombination, resulting in new races, can occur by nuclear exchange between cells in hyphal fusions. Once this has occurred, transfer of chromosomal material between nuclei might also be expected. Surveys of races of mildew on oats [20] and mildew on barley [44] indicate that these pathogens have a similar ability to produce new races.

It might be possible to make more effective use of major genetic factors for race-specific resistance by combining several non-allelic factors in one variety. This should greatly reduce the chance of new races appearing because all the corresponding virulence genes would have to occur together to have a selective advantage. Unfortunately, it is difficult to devise a breeding technique which can be used to identify the segregates with all the required resistance factors. The most obvious method is to make test crosses on a very large scale, but this is too tedious and time-consuming. Alternatively it is possible to recognise some genetic factors by specific resistance reactions, particularly when testing for resistance can be carried out in contrasting environments. However, if combining major genes is to have long-lasting value, it is essential that they should not be used individually in other breeding programmes, and this cannot be expected.

A much better prospect is to exploit non race-specific (or general) resistance [10 and 14]. This differs from race-specific resistance in that it is not expressed in the seedling stage but becomes effective in adult plants in field conditions. Although never complete it is sufficient to prevent epidermis occurring, it is equally effective against all races of a particular pathogen and not readily overcome by new races. There are good sources of resistance of this type to all the major airborne cereal pathogens, particularly in older varieties, e.g. to yellow rust in Holdfast (Table 20.3). It has been lost in many new varieties because it is frequently masked in breeding material by complete resistance of the specific type. However, breeders recognise its value and there is every reason to expect that it will be successfully used.

Table 20.3
Reaction to yellow rust in wheat in seedling tests and as mature plants in the field

Seedling reaction — R resistant, S susceptible
Field reaction — 1-5, 5 most susceptible

(all varieties resistant as seedlings are also resistant in the field)

	Yr. Resistance factors	Race and year identified in the U.K.					
		2B (1954)	8	8B (1955)	3/55 (1965)	60 (1966)	58 (1969)
Chinese 166	1	R	R	R	R	S4	S?
Heine VII	2	R	R	S5	R	S5	S?
Cappelle-Desprez	3a, 4a	S1	R	R	S3	R	S1-2
Hybrid 46	3b, 4b	R	R	R	S3	R	R
Peko	6	R	R	R	R	S2	R
Professeur Marchal	(3c)	R	R	R	R	R	S1-2
Holdfast	—	S2	S2	S2	S2	S2	S2
Maris Widgeon	(3a, 4a)	S1	R	R	S1	R	S1
Maris Ranger	(6, 3a, 4a)	R	R	R	R	R	R
Maris Beacon	(3a,3b,3c,4a,4b)	R	R	R	R	R	R
Maris Envoy	(1, 3a, 4a)	R	R	R	R	R	S5

Little is known about the inheritance and mode of action of general resistance. There are indications that it may be inherited polygenically or simply and that the essential difference from race-specific resistance is probably in mode of action rather than in the number of genetic factors involved.

Improvement of disease resistance has been an important objective in cereals because the use of fungicides has not been practicable except for the limited possibilities of seed dressings. However, the rapid progress in developing systemic fungicides such as Milstem (PP 149) may radically alter this situation and must be taken into account. Such fungicides are often effective only against a small group of closely related pathogens. This indicates that their mode of action relates to biochemical processes specific to each pathogen and that the pathogens may be able to circumvent them by developing new races. Resistance to one of these systemic fungicides, Benomyl, has already been reported in powdery mildew of *Cucurbita* [37].

Hybrid Varieties
In hybrid varieties the commercial crop consists entirely of an F_1 hybrid between two parents which are often inbred of lines but may themselves also

be F₁ hybrids. The objective is to increase vigour and yield by exploiting heterosis, and its success in many crops, including maize, sorghum, kale, onions and tomatoes, is well-known. In wheat and barley, techniques for producing hybrid varieties have been developed [19, 43], but it is not yet known if they will be practicable. To operate the simplest system (Figure 20.3) three lines have to be developed and crossed in two stages. Line 'A' is male sterile, due to cytoplasmic factors, and has to be maintained by pollinating with line 'B' which has normal cytoplasm. The commercial hybrid seed is produced by pollinating the 'A' line with line 'R', which is homozygous for a dominant nuclear genetic factor which restores male fertility to the F₁ hybrid. In cereals the lines have to be grown in strips so that they can be harvested separately.

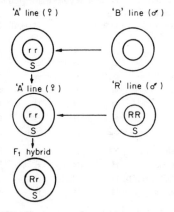

Fig. 20.3   Production of hybrid varieties, using cytoplasmically determined male-sterility. This method, which is being developed in wheat and field beans, has already been used to produce commercial varieties of sugar beet.
S = a cytoplasmic factor for male sterility.
R = a nuclear gene dominant to S and restoring male fertility.
r = the recessive allele which does not restore male fertility.

Now that the basic genetic material has been discovered, the main problems will be to obtain sufficient pollination of the 'A' line and a sufficient increase in yield of the hybrid crop to offset the extra seed cost. Adequate pollination can be obtained in warm, dry areas but is unreliable in this country, so the seed might have to be produced elsewhere. Theoretically, in cereals, it should be possible to fix most, if not all, of the vigour of any F₁ hybrid in a homozygous line. Therefore, it will be very interesting to see if the exponents of hybrid varieties are able to get ahead and stay there.

Chromosome Manipulation
In wheat, there is an excellent prospect of exploiting cytological techniques in the near future. Riley, Chapman and Johnson [32] have already

transferred the yellow rust resistance of *Aegilops comosa* into wheat by a technique in which normal meiotic pairing was genetically suppressed. This allowed some pairing between the *Aegilops* and wheat chromosomes, which otherwise does not occur, so that the required translocation could take place. Genetic analyses of polygenically controlled characters by chromosome substitution may also have a practical application [26]. Polygenes controlling complex characters such as yield and grain quality are often concentrated in relatively few linkage groups. It should be possible to transfer them between varieties by chromosome substitution, which has the advantage of leaving the rest of the genetic complement intact.

Sugar Beet

Sugar beet is naturally outbreeding and the maintenance of varieties involves reselection, often accompanied by elimination or addition of constituent lines, so that the current stocks of a variety can differ considerably in genetic constitution and yield from the original of the same name. Consequently the contribution of variety is much more difficult to determine than in cereals or potatoes. Campbell (unpublished) has assessed the contribution of variety by calculating the multiple regression of sugar yield on plant population, virus yellow occurrence and nitrogen usage, from factory returns over the last twenty years. He concluded that most of the upward trend in sugar production could be accounted for by an increase in the number of roots per acre reaching the factory, improved control of the aphid vectors of virus yellow and increased use of nitrogen fertilisers. The increase in sugar yield due to varietal improvement has probably been relatively small. Nevertheless, Willey has estimated this improvement at not less than 0.6 per cent per year by an alternative method of comparing the mean yield of all varieties in N.I.A.B. trials with varieties considered by their breeders to have remained constant.

Results for new varieties now on trial indicate that there is unlikely to be a major breakthrough in productivity in the next few years. Moreover, as national yields have not increased significantly over the last five years, it is possible that the present varieties frequently reach their potential yield in the U.K. climate and are now restricting increases in yield which might be expected from further improvements in husbandry. This may well be a temporary pause due to major changes in emphasis in breeding programmes to other characters which can substantially reduce the costs of growing and processing the crop. During recent years, breeders have concentrated on meeting the more exacting requirements for precision drilling, monogermness, mechanical harvesting and more economic sugar extraction at the factories. It is apparent from the rapid changeover in the type of variety grown during the last four years (Table 20.4) that some important improvements have been obtained.

In 1966 the most commonly grown varieties were diploid multigerm synthetics. Such varieties consist of a number of lines (usually at least ten) which have been chosen for good general combining ability and maintained separately. The lines are mixed during the final stages of multiplication to give highly heterozygous commercial seed.

Table 20.4

Percentage of the total sugar-beet acreage sown to the main types of variety

	1965	1966	1967	1968	1969
Diploid Multigerm	93	93	80	66	38
Polyploid Multigerm (mainly anisoploid)	7	7	(8)	(10)	15
Monogerm (mainly triploid)	—	Experi- mental	12	24	47

Anisoploid multigerm varieties are produced from a mixture of diploid and tetraploid lines which interpollinate to give mainly triploid commercial seed. They were little grown in the United Kingdom until the last year or two, although they had been available since 1955 and appeared to have raised productivity in other European countries, where it was considered that triploids were higher yielding than diploids or tetraploids. This was probably because they rarely outyielded the diploids and their seed was more irregular in size, making it difficult to drill evenly. The irregularity resulted from the naturally greater size of the tetraploid fruit clusters, and frequent floret sterility due to meiotic irregularities. This effect has since been turned to advantage by improved mechanical processing and pelleting of the seed — enabling anisoploids to give a braird of 80 per cent or more single plants compared to about 60 per cent in the diploids. They are therefore now proving more popular, possibly as an interim measure, in the quest for monogermness. They are at least as productive as the best diploids and the seed is cheaper than monogerm varieties.

Genetical monogerm varieties have been developed rapidly, mainly from American monogerm material which is very low yielding and susceptible to bolting in this country. The best monogerm varieties are currently only about 3 to 4 per cent lower in sugar production than the best multigerm varieties, and this is a considerable achievement. However, the emphasis on monogerm breeding may have resulted in a neglect of the possibilities of breeding more productive multigerm varieties, and sugar production may have suffered in consequence. It seems certain that monogerm varieties will be further improved and occupy most of the acreage within a few years. This is in line with the N.I.A.B. recommended list which, considerably revised, now comprises four monogerm varieties and seven multigerm varieties, of which two are anisoploid.

There is still insufficient information to be certain of the relative merits of the diploid, triploid, anisoploid and tetraploid states in sugar beet varieties. However, it seems to be commonly accepted, at least in this country, that polyploidy has little effect on productivity. Probably the most valuable use of polyploidy to date has been as an aid to the rapid development of monogerm varieties. This has been achieved in some varieties by pollinating relatively poorly-adapted diploid monogerm lines with well-adapted multigerm tetraploids. Multigerm seed resulting from intercrossing of the tetraploid lines can be removed by sieving so that the commercial seed is mainly triploid monogerm and dominated by the genotype of the tetraploid material.

In sugar beet it must be admitted that the way ahead in breeding for increased productivity is not clear. However, the breeders seem to be satisfied with the genetic variability available to them and expect to make progress by closer control of the breeding system. Easily the most important possibility is the development of hybrid varieties through the use of male sterility. By the close control of crossing obtained, it should be possible to exploit specific combining ability and increase hybrid vigour. At present, in multiline synthetics, it is possible only to utilise general combining ability. Incorporation of polyploidy may also have a greater advantage in hybrid varieties but it is significant that in the United States almost the whole crop is produced from diploid monogerm hybrid varieties. In the American system, which is similar to that proposed for wheat, the cytoplasmic male sterile and equivalent non-restoring 'O-type' lines are monogerm. The commercial seed is produced from a mixed population of the cytoplasmic male sterile and a diploid multigerm fertility restoring line. The seed resulting from selfing of the restoring line is sieved out, thereby overcoming one of the main difficulties in exploiting this system in wheat and beans. An interesting recent development has been the discovery [13] that cytoplasmic male-sterility can be transmitted by grafting into 'O-type' scions. If this can be established as a practical technique, it will permit easier identification of 'O-types' and production of their male-sterile equivalents.

Physiological Characters

Progress may also be made by looking more closely at physiological characters, principally with the objective of reaching the optimum leaf area

Table 20.5
Improvement of resistance to bolting in sugar beet

Number of varieties on N.I.A.B. recommended lists in categories of less than twice to more than five times as susceptible as Camkilt

	<2X	3X	4X	>5X
1958	1 (Cambro)	–	–	15
1960	–	–	–	15
1962	–	1	7	7
1964	4	5	4	2
1966	5	5	1	1
1968	12	2	–	–

index earlier. A considerable improvement has already been obtained in all the commonly grown varieties in resistance to bolting. This development, which was stimulated by the breeding of Cambro and Camkilt (Table 20.5), has contributed to productivity by making earlier sowing more reliable and mechanical harvesting more efficient [1, 11]. Another possibility is to select for more rapid and reliable germination, establishment and growth at low temperatures, but the available variability is very limiting in this respect. However, even small improvements will be very useful, so that greater advantage can be taken of the very high levels of resistance to bolting already obtained to make drilling to a stand from early sowings more reliable.

Quality

The proportion of sugar in the beet which can be extracted by the factory processes is largely dependent on the concentration of sugar in the beet and on the purity of the juice. These quality components are affected adversely by increased use of fertilizers, especially nitrogen, so that breeding for improvements in them is an important aspect of productivity. Sugar percentage has already been increased considerably by breeding, and further increases can be expected. Concentrations of the principal juice impurities, Na, K, amino-nitrogen and betaine, are to a large extent independently inherited and amenable to selection, so that improvements can also be expected in this respect.

Disease Resistance

The incidence of virus yellow has been considerably reduced by the control measures advocated by the Broom's Barn Experimental Station [24]. These include elimination, as far as practicable, of courses of virus in spring, mainly mangold clamps and volunteer overwintered sugar-beet plants, and use of systemic insecticides in conjunction with the spray warning system to control the aphid vectors. However, annual surveys of virus yellow show that the disease is still a serious hazard in Essex, Suffolk and south Cambridgeshire, causing an average loss in sugar production of 5 to 10 per cent in these areas [36].

The virus yellow syndrome is due principally to beet yellow virus (BYV) and beet mild yellowing virus (BMYV). In addition BMYV predisposes plants to attack by *Alternaria spp.* so that the older leaves of BMYV are invariably attacked by *Alternaria*. The combined effect of BMYV and *Alternaria* on yield is similar to that of BYV. The losses in sugar production can be reduced by breeding varieties with various forms of resistance. Tolerance to both viruses has been obtained in the multigerm diploid variety, Maris Vanguard [33, 34], which is recommended by the N.I.A.B. [30] for use in those factory areas where virus yellow is prevalent. Maris Vanguard was not resistant to infection but, when infected, the loss in sugar production is only about half that in normal susceptible varieties. This form of tolerance is polygenically inherited and effective against all isolates of the viruses, so that it is unlikely to break down to new strains.

Breeding of monogerm varieties with tolerance to virus yellows is now well advanced and the best of these may be marketed in about four years time (Table 20.6). A considerable effort has also been made to improve on the rather low sugar percentage and juice purity of Maris Vanguard. This has proved possible except in the case of K content of the juice, which appears to be linked with tolerance. During this second phase of the work, inherited variation has been demonstrated in resistance to virus infection [35] and also in resistance to attack by the aphid vectors *Myzus persicae* Sulz. and *Aphis fabae* Scop. [28]. Resistance to aphid attack is of three kinds, namely: resistance to settling, resistance to multiplication and tolerance of attack. The mechanisms involved are not understood, but the inheritance of each type of resistance is probably polygenic and can be improved by selection. The ultimate objective is to combine virus tolerance with resistance to virus infection and resistance to aphids. The use of such varieties would reduce the need to control aphids in the field by insecticides.

Table 20.6
Performance of monogerm stocks of sugar beet under conditions of severe virus-yellow infection in 1968

	Sugar yield (cwt acre^{-1})	(t ha^{-1})	Sugar content (per cent)	Sodium content (mg per 100g)	Potassium content (mg per 100 g)
Commercial Monogerm Varieties					
A	39.4	4.92	13.5	30.4	141
B	42.4	5.30	13.6	29.0	146
C	41.2	5.15	13.4	31.4	149
Experimental Monogerms					
VT 90	47.7	5.96	13.7	31.2	160
VT 91	48.2	6.02	13.6	34.5	166
VT 99	43.1	5.39	13.8	27.7	156
L.S.D. (P=0.05)	7.9	0.99	N.S.	2.7	6.4

Potatoes

Potatoes are naturally outbreeding and all varieties are genetically highly heterozygous, but, due to clonal propagation and the rigorous culling of off-types to meet the standards of the seed certification schemes, the varieties do not change materially. Therefore, as in cereals, increases in yield due to breeding can be determined by comparing new varieties with the old. However, in spite of a considerable effort in breeding new varieties, the greater part of the acreage is still of varieties such as Majestic, King Edward

VII and Arran Pilot, which have been in cultivation for 35 to 60 years (Table 20.7). This is partly due to the reluctance of the consumer to change to a new variety; for example it is difficult to convince the housewife that a new variety cooks as well as King Edward VII, but also because, until recently, varietal improvements in yield have been small. Some varieties bred in the last ten years are at least 10 per cent higher yielding, especially the main crop varieties Pentland Dell, Pentland Crown and Maris Piper and the second earlies Maris Peer and Maris Page. The paracrinkle-free stock of King Edward VII [25] should also be included in this group, though it is an achievement of plant pathology rather than plant breeding. These varieties are rapidly gaining favour and can claim a large part of the recent increase in yield from 9 to 10 ton acre^{-1} (22.6 to 24.9 t ha^{-1}).

Table 20.7
Popularity of potato varieties in Gt. Britain, 1968
(As percentage of maturity group)

Variety	%	Date Introduction
Earlies (119,680 acres)		
(48.410 ha)		
Home Guard	18	1942
Red Craigs Royal	17	1957 Bud sport of Craigs Royal
Arran Pilot	14	1930
Maris Peer	11	1962
Ulster Prince	10	1947
Craigs Royal	5	1948
Epicure	5	1897
Maincrop (488.670 acres)		
(197.67 ha)		
Majestic	35	1911
King Edward VII	20	1902 Paracrinkle free 1964
Pentland Dell	14	1961
Pentland Crown	11	1959
Record	6	1932

Techniques and prospects in potato breeding have been considered in detail by Howard [21, 22]. The breeders in general agree that the traditional technique of selecting within intervarietal crosses cannot be expected to give a much greater productivity. The genetic variability of the European potato (*Solanum tuberosum* group *Tuberosum*) is probably too limited due to historical accident [38]. *Tuberosum* varieties were selected from cultivated potatoes of the group *Andigena* introduced in the late sixteenth century from tropical latitudes, but temperate altitudes, of S. America. Both groups are tetraploid and differ essentially only in adaption of tuber initiation to daylength. The number of original introductions is unknown, but certainly few. Moreover, much of the original variability may have been lost because very few varieties survived the blight epidemics of 1845 and 1846. Therefore, it should be possible to breed higher yielding varieties by using new introductions of *Andigena*. Such work has been hampered because tuber initiation is polygenically controlled so that it has been necessary to backcross to *Tuberosum* with consequent dilution of the *Andigena* genotype. Nevertheless, high yielding lines can be selected from such backcrosses [21] and it is quite likely that the high yielding ability of Maris Piper is in part due to *Andigena* genes incorporated from the *Andigena* parent used as a source of resistance to stem eelworm. Simmonds [39] is carrying out a programme of mass selection in *Andigena* for long day tuber initiation, and it appears that a full conversion to the *Tuberosum* type can be obtained. Glendinning [17] crossed selections from this experiment with cultivated *Tuberosum* varieties and found that unselected F_1 progenies of the selected *Andigena* x *Tuberosum* outyielded *Tuberosum* x *Tuberosum* by an average of 13 per cent. It would be reasonable to expect a yield increase of at least 20 per cent in selections of such crosses.

Disease Resistance

Breeding for resistance to blight (*Phytophthora infestans*) using the wild species *Solanum demissum* as the source of resistance, is a very good example of the danger of using race-specific resistance to combat a prolific airborne pathogen. Thirty years ago many breeders thought that derivatives of *S. demissum* would be the final answer to the blight problem. At least six major factors conferring a hypersensitive type of resistance have been transferred to *Tuberosum*, but races of blight are now known which can overcome them all. In addition, when such material does break down it is often more susceptible to attack than its *Tuberosum* parents. For example Pentland Dell, which carried the resistance factors R1, 3 and 4 of *S. demissum*, was resistant when first introduced but a resistance-breaking race appeared in 1967, and the variety now has to be treated as a susceptible which is particularly prone to blight in the tubers.

Consequently all potato breeders are now concentrating on polygenic field resistance. It is possible that such resistance may be gradually eroded away by the pathogen building up a complementary polygene system [10], but in potatoes there is already good evidence that this is not necessarily an inescapable corollary. Compared to the most susceptible varieties, Majestic has a moderate degree of resistance to late blight (*Phytophthora infestans*) in the foliage and good resistance in the tubers. This resistance has been maintained since the variety was first cultivated in 1911, and its derivation dates even further back to varieties which survived the epidemics of the 1840's. Therefore it is reasonable to conclude that polygenic field resistance can be stable. The most difficult problem will be to improve field resistance in *Andigena* derivatives, which are usually extremely susceptible, especially in the tubers. The mechanisms of field resistance are not well understood, but probably depend on such characters as microclimate, resistance to infection, incubation period and spore productivity. Tuber resistance is to a considerable extent independent of foliage resistance and will probably be given more attention in the future with the objective of improving storage and marketability.

Presumably new varieties will continue to be resistant to wart disease (*Synchytrium endobioticum*) and more emphasis will be given to the principal virus diseases [23]. Resistance to the viruses X (mild mosaic) and S is especially useful because they are transmitted by leaf contact and therefore not controlled by the usual seed production schemes unless these involve serological testing. Immunity to X, due to necrosis controlled by the gene Nx, is easily obtained from a number of varieties of Tuberosum (e.g. Maris Piper) and the gene Ns, available in *Andigena*, gives similar resistance to S. Varying degrees of resistance to the aphid transmitted viruses Leaf roll and Y (severe mosaic or leaf drop streak) can also be expected. Immunity to Y is available in *S. stoloniferum*. The variety Pentland Crown has a degree of polygenic resistance to both these viruses which makes it relatively easy to maintain a good standard in 'once grown' seed.

Resistance to pathotype A of potato cyst nematode (*Heterodera rostochiensis*) has already been obtained in the commercial varieties Maris Piper, Ulster Glade, Pentland Javelin and Pentland Lustre. This is the most successful case of utilization of material outside the *Tuberosum* group [12]. There is no resistance to this pest in *Tuberosum*; the gene H_1 conferring resistance was derived from *Andigena*, and in Maris Piper has been combined with acceptable field resistance to blight. Resistance to other pathotypes, of which E is the most important, is known in some wild species (including *S. vernii*) and considerable progress has been made in transferring the resistance genes to *Tuberosum*. It would be easier for the breeder if resistance to pathotypes other than A could also be found in *Andigena*, and there is now some indication that they do exist there.

Tuber Quality

Potato breeders are now having to pay more attention to tuber quality to meet specialised consumer requirements. For example, there is at present a shortage of varieties with the high dry matter and low content of reducing sugars favoured for the manufacture of crisps, chips and instant mashed potatoes; there is also a small but growing demand for varieties suitable for canning. With the considerable increase in sale of washed and prepacked potatoes for household use, appearance is now of greater commercial value, making resistance to common scab (*Streptomyces scabies*) a more desirable breeding objective.

New Techniques

Perhaps the most interesting recent development in potato genetics has been the discovery that it is possible to produce large numbers of dihaploids by pollinating *Tuberosum* and *Andigena* with certain clones of the diploid specie

S. phureja [31]. The plants obtained, comprise a mixture of tetraploid ($2n$ = 48) and triploid ($2n$ = 36) hybrids and dihaploids ($2n$ = 24) of the *Tuberosum* or *Andigena* parent. The dihaploids probably arise from pollinators in which *S. phureja* contributes two 12-chromosome gametes to the endosperm and none to the egg-nucleus. The dihaploids are recognised first by lack of a purple hypocotyl marker present in the *S. phureja* clones used, and then by counting chloroplast numbers in the guard cells.

There are several possible ways of using dihaploids in practical breeding. The most immediately attractive is to produce tetraploids, by colchicine treatment, which are duplex for major genes conferring disease resistance. When used in crosses with multiplex varieties, these will give a ratio of 5 resistant to 1 susceptible as compared with only 1 : 1 for multiplex x simplex. The duplex parents are even more useful where two or three dominant genes are involved, considerably increasing the volume of material that can be selected for agronomic characters in any particular breeding programme.

It should also be possible to use this technique to produce inbreds with a high concentration of polygenes for desired characters. These could be tested for specific and general combining ability and then used to synthesise high-yielding heterozygous tetraploids. However, more investigations are needed to show whether or not this is a practical technique.

Field Bean (*Vicia faba* Linn.)

The national average yield of field beans showed no consistent trend for many years but has increased steadily since about 1961, though to a lesser extent than in cereals, sugar beet and potatoes. There is no doubt that this increase in productivity is mainly due to improvements in husbandry, chiefly the use of insecticides to control black fly (*Aphis fabae*) and selective herbicides based on simazine, though favourable seasons may have had some effect, judging by the yields in 1968. For field beans to be as remunerative as cereals, and to encourage more widespread cultivation of the crop as a break from cereals, varieties are needed which can consistently give considerably higher yields.

The natural breeding system in field beans results in an average of 30 per cent cross and 70 per cent self-fertilization [14, 16]. All the plants are self-compatible but automatic selfing is mechanically restricted, though not precluded, because the pollen cannot easily come into contact with the stigma unless the keel is tripped. Presumably the selective and agricultural advantage of this system is that a degree of automatic self-fertilization is useful when the bee population is too small or inactive due to weather conditions.

Inbreeding results in a depression in vegetative vigour and yield, though this is less than in completely cross-fertilized crops, so that the breeding system tends to maintain an intermediate level of vigour. This is the case in varieties in which pollination is not controlled. These include local stocks which have been maintained without selection, or with mass selection only, and also varieties such as Maris Beaver and Maris Bead which are based on a number of lines selected by progency testing, but then grown as a population for several years during seed multiplication.

It might be possible to obtain steady but slight progress in maximum yield by selection of improved open-pollinated varieties, but a far more promising prospect is to develop breeding techniques which can exploit hybrid vigour. This has been achieved to a limited extent in the winter bean Throws M.S., which is a synthetic of four components which are not inbred and perform relatively well on their own. These are maintained individually and mixed in the generation producing the commercial seed. There appears to be a small advantage in yield due to hybrid vigour, but even so, this variety only outyields the best of the old open-pollinated varieties, such as Garton's S.Q., by about 8 per cent.

At the Plant Breeding Institute, considerable progress has been made in developing F_1 hybrid varieties by a system very similar to that already discussed for wheat and sugar beet [4, 7]. The investigations have included the discovery and exploitation of cytoplasmic male-sterility and both types of male-fertile line. Increases in yield of up to 20 per cent have been consistently obtained in breeder's trials with these F_1 hybrids and some are now in N.I.A.B. trials. It is hoped that an increase in yield of this order will more than offset the higher cost of seed, but investigations are also being made into production methods which might reduce the cost of the commercial seed. The seed is expensive due to the extra work in drilling and combining alternate blocks of the lines, and also because more seed of the male-fertile lines is produced than required for further seed production.

One possibility is to grow the parents in mixtures, as in sugar beet, instead of in separate blocks. This might also improve pollination of the male-sterile lines, which is sometimes unsatisfactory when the lines are grown in blocks because some bees collect pollen only and tend to stay on the male-fertile lines [8]. The method will be practicable if the F_1 seed can be separated by an automatic method from seed set on the male-fertile pollinator. This has been done experimentally by seed colour but a future development might be to ulitlise the considerable variation in seed size and shape which exists in the species. Alternatively it may be possible to obtain good pollination with a much smaller proportion of the male-fertile parent in a mixture. In this case, especially if the male-fertile parent is not inbred, it may be feasible to market commercial seed consisting of a mixture of F_1 hybrid and the pollinator without a significant reduction in yield.

One of the principal factors limiting yield in commercial bean crops is inadequate pollination [15]. The number of bumble-bees is thought to be declining, particularly in arable areas, and only a small proportion of hive bee colonies are in these areas. This has stimulated work at the Welsh Plant Breeding Station to develop a variety with complete automatic self-fertility [18]. Some Mediterranean varieties have this character, but it will take a long while to transfer it into varieties suitable for this country. Also, it will be necessary to select varieties which do not suffer from inbreeding depression, with the ultimate objective a homozygous true-breeding variety independent of bee pollination.

At the Plant Breeding Institute it has been shown that F_1 hybrids have much greater automatic self-fertility than open-pollinated varieties, which gives them a considerable advantage in yield when pollination is restricted (Table 20.8) [5]. This is an extension of the deduction [14] that under open-pollination, inbreds have a greater tendency to cross than the crossbreds; the greater self-fertility of the crossbreds probably depends on the amount of pollen produced. It is certain that increased self-fertility will be an important breeding objective by whichever method it is sought.

Table 20.8
Yield of hybrid winter beans in the presence and absence of bees: from Bond [5]

	Open-field				Cage			
	1965		1967		1966		1967	
	cwt acre^{-1}	t ha^{-1}	cwt acre^{-1}	t ha^{-1}	cwt acre^{-1}	t ha^{-1}	cwt acre^{-1}	t ha^{-1}
Hybrid varieties	44.0	5.5	28.6	3.6	41.3	5.2	50.7	6.3
Open pollinated varieties	35.2	4.4	22.8	2.85	22.4	2.8	28.6	3.6
Difference	8.8	1.1	5.8	0.75	18.9	2.4	22.1	2.7
L.S.D. (P = 5%)	5.2	0.65	3.6	0.45	13.4	1.7	16.2	2.0

Very little is known about the physiology of yield in field beans, and further investigations in this respect could be of considerable help to the breeder in defining his objectives. The plant normally has at least ten times as many flowers as the final number of pods, and in the field pollination may be more or less than adequate to set this pod number. If too few flowers at the lower nodes are fertilized, stem growth is prolonged and more flowers and leaves are produced. However, if there are still too few pods, yield is affected in spite of the additional leaf area, indicating that the sink characteristics of the grain are important in determining yield. If too many flowers are fertilized, many young pods may be aborted; clearly the mechanism which controls pod number is of great interest in attempts to improve yield. A change to greater self-fertility might allow the development of a plant which produced only as many flowers as it could carry pods. Such a plant should be physiologically more economical than present varieties.

Resistance to Diseases and Pests
It has not been possible to cross *Vicia faba* with any other species, so that breeding for yield and disease resistance has to rely on variation within the species [6]. There is some possibility of breeding varieties with improved polygenic field resistance to chocolate spot (*Botrytis fabae*), particularly by

avoiding the conditions which predispose the crop to the aggressive phase — such as lodging and early senescence of the lower leaves. There is also some prospect of exploiting the useful degree of resistance to black fly existing in the German variety Rastatt. This variety is too low-yielding for our conditions, but there is good evidence that its form of resistance can be transferred to high-yielding British material.

ACKNOWLEDGEMENTS

I am most grateful to my colleagues at the Plant Breeding Institute for their interest and advice in the writing of this chapter.

REFERENCES

1. BELL, G.D.H. 'Developments in sugar beet breeding', *J. natn. Inst. Agric. Bot.*, 1963, 9, 435-444.
2. BELL, G.D.H. 'Plant breeding for crop improvement in Britain; methods, achievements and objectives', *Proc. R. Soc. B.*, 1968, **171**, 145-173.
3. BINGHAM, J. 'The physiological determinents of grain yield in cereals', *Agric. Prog.*, 1969, 44, 30-42.
4. BOND, D.A. 'Combining ability of winter bean (*Vicia faba* L.) inbreds', *J. agric. Sci. Camb.*, 1967, **68**, 179-185.
5. BOND, D.A. *Field and broad beans — a manual for the farmer and adviser. Botany of the crop, breeding and varieties.* Cambridge: Fisons Ltd., 1969.
6. BOND, D.A. (1970) The development of field beans as a crop in Britain *Proc. Nutr. Soc.* 29 (in the press)
7. BOND, D.A., FYFE, J.L. and TOYNBEE-CLARKE, G. 'Male sterility in field beans (*Vicia faba* L.), IV. Use of cytoplasmic male sterility in the production of F_1 hybrids and their performance in trials', *J. agric. Sci. Camb.*, 1966, **66**, 369-377.
8. BOND, D.A. and HAWKINS, R.P. 'Behaviour of bees visiting male-sterile field beans (*Vicia faba*)', *J. agric. Sci., Camb.*, 1967, **68**, 243-247.
9. BORLAUG, N.E. 'Wheat breeding and its impact on world food supply', *Proc. 3rd Int. Wheat Genet. Symp.*, Canberra 1968, ed. K.W. Finaly and K.W. Shepherd, 1969, 1-36.
10. CALDWELL, R.M. 'Breeding for general and/or specific plant disease resistance', *Proc. 3rd Int. Wheat Genet. Symp.*, Canberra 1968, ed. K.W. Finlay and K.W. Shepherd, 1969, 263-272.
11. CAMPBELL, G.K.G. and RUSSELL, G.E. 'Breeding sugar beet', *Annu. Rep. Plant Breeding Inst. 1963-64*, 1964, 7-32.
12. COLE, C.S. and HOWARD, H.W. 'The effect of growing resistant potatoes on a potato-root eelworm population — a microplot experiment', *Ann. Appl. Biol.*, 1962, **50**, 121-7.
13. CURTIS, G.J. 'Graft-transmission of male sterility in sugar beet (*Beta vulgaris* L.)', *Euphytica*, 1967, **16**, 417-422.

14. DRAYNER, Jean, M. 'Self- and cross-fertility in field bean (*Vicia faba* Linn.)', *J. agric. Sci., Camb.*, 1959, **53**, 387-403.

15. FREE, J.B. 'The pollination requirements of broad beans and field beans (*Vicia faba*)', *J. agric. Sci., Camb.*, 1966, **66**, 395-398.

16. FYFE, J.L. 'Plant breeding studies in leguminous forage crops. II Further observations on natural cross-breeding in winter beans', *J. agric. Sci., Camb.*, 1954, **45**, 141-147.

17. GLENDINNING, D.R. 'The performance of progenies obtained by crossing Groups *Andigena* and *Tuberosum* of *Solanum tuberosum*', *Eur. Potato J.*, 1969, **12**, 13-19.

18. HANNA, A.S. and LAWES, D.A. 'Studies on pollination and fertilisation in the field bean (*Vicia faba* L.)', *Ann. appl. Biol.*, 1967, **59**, 289-296.

19. HAYES, J.D. 'The genetic basis of hybrid barley production and its application in Western Europe', *Euphytica Suppl. No. 1*, 1968, 87-102.

20. HAYES, J.D. and JONES, I.T. 'Variation in the pathogenicity of *Erysiphe graminis* D.C. F. Sp. *Avenae*, and its relation to the development of mildew-resistant oat cultivars', *Euphytica*, 1966, **15**, 80-86.

21. HOWARD, H.W. 'Some potato breeding problems', *Annu. Rep. Pl. Breed. Inst. Cambridge, 1961-1962*, 1963, 5-21.

22. HOWARD, H.W. The genetic of the potato, *Solanum tuberosum*. London: Logos Press Ltd., 1970.

23. HOWARD, H.W. and FULLER, J.M. 'The inheritance of top-necrosis to viruses X, A, B and C in *Solanum tuberosum*', *Euphytica*, 1965, **14**, 189-195.

24. HULL, R. 'The spray warning scheme for control of virus yellows', *Br. Sug. Beet Rev.*, 1969, **37**, 169-172.

25. KASSANIS, B. 'Therapy of virus-infected plants', *Jl. Ry. agric. Soc.*, 1965, **126**, 105-114.

26. LAW, C.N. 'Biometrical analysis using chromosome substitutions within a species', in *Chromosome manipulations and plant genetics*, ed. R. Riley and K.R. Lewis, London: Oliver and Boyd, 1966, 59-85.

27. LITTLE, R. and MANNERS, J.G. 'Somatic recombination in yellow rust of wheat (*Poccinia striiformis*) I. The production and possible origin of two new physiologic races', *Trans. Br. mycol. Soc.*, 1969, **53**, 251-8.

28. LOWE, H.J.B. and RUSSELL, G.E. 'Inherited resistance of sugar beet to aphid colonization', *Ann. appl. Bio.*, 1969, **63**, 337-343.

29. MACER, R.C.F. 'The inheritance of resistance to yellow rust in wheat', *Cereal Rust Conference, Cambridge, 1964*, 1966, **19-26.**

30. Nat. Inst. Agric. Bot. Recommended lists for cereals, sugar beet, potatoes and field beans, 1969.

31. PELOQUIN, S.J., HOUGAS, R.W. and GABERT, A.C. 'Haploidy as a new approach to the cytogenetics and breeding of *Solanum tuberosum*', in *Chromosome Manipulations and Plant Genetics*, ed. R. Riley and K.R. Lewis, Edinburgh and London: Oliver and Boyd, 1966, 21-28.

32. RILEY, R., CHAPMAN, V. and JOHNSON, R. 'The incorporation of

alien disease resistance in wheat by genetic interference with the regulations of meiotic chromosome synopsis', *Genet. Res. Camb.*, 1968, **12**, 199-219.

33. RUSSELL, G.E. 'Breeding for tolerance to beet yellow virus and beet mild yellowing virus in sugar beet. I Selection and breeding methods', *Ann. appl. Biol.*, 1964, **53**, 363-376.

34. RUSSELL, G.E. 'Breeding for tolerance to beet yellow virus and beet mild yellowing virus in sugar beet. II. The response of breeding material to infection with difference virus strain', *Ann. appl. Biol.*, 1964, **53**, 377-388.

35. RUSSELL, G.E. 'Breeding for resistance to infection with yellowing viruses in sugar beet. I. Resistance in virus-tolerant breeding material', *Ann. appl. Biol.*, 1966, **57**, 311-320.

36. RUSSELL, G.E. 'The distribution of sugar beet yellowing viruses in East Anglia from 1965-1968', *Br. Sug. Beet Rev.*, 1968, **37**, 77-84.

37. SCHROEDER, W.T. and PROVVIDENTI, R. 'Resistance to Benomyl in powdery mildew of cucurbits', *Pl. Dis. Reptr.*, 1969, **53**, 271-275.

38. SIMMONDS, N.W. 'Variability in crop plants, its use and conservation', *Biol. Rev.*, 1962, **37**, 422-465.

39. SIMMONDS, N.W. 'Studies of the tetraploid potatoes. III. Progress in the experimental recreation of the *Tuberosum* group', *J. Linn. Soc. (Bot.)*, 1966, **59**, 269-288.

40. THORNE, G.N. 'Physiological factors limiting the yield of arable crops', *in Potential Crop Production* London: Heinemann, 1970.

41. WATSON, I.A. and LUIG, N.H. 'The Ecology and genetics of host-pathogen relationships in wheat rusts in Australia', *Proc. 3rd. Int. Wheat Genet. Symp.*, Canberra 1968, ed. K.W. Finlay and K.W. Shepherd, 1969, 227-238

42. WHITEHOUSE, R.N.H. 'Barley breeding at Cambridge', *Annu. Rep. Pl. Breed. Inst. Cambridge, 1968*, 1969, 6-29.

43. WILSON, J.A. 'Problems in hybrid wheat breeding', *Euphytica Suppl. No. 1.*, 1968, 13-33.

44. WOLFE, M.S. 'Physiologic race changes in barley mildew 1964-67', *Pl. Path.*, 1968, **17**, 82-87.

21. Plant Breeding: Forage Grasses and Legumes

J.P. Cooper and E.L. Breese
Welsh Plant Breeding Station, Aberystwyth

Introduction

Forage crops, both annual and perennial, are grown to provide digestible energy and other nutrients, including protein and minerals, for the ruminant. The basic climatic limit to production is set by the seasonal input of solar radiation, but the use of this energy by the crop can be limited by two other important climatic factors, low temperature and water stress, or by the shortage of soil nutrients, particularly nitrogen. The plant breeder is basically concerned with the efficiency of the crop in converting these inputs of energy and nutrients into a form most suitable for the animal, and the possibility of increasing this efficiency by selection and breeding.

This chapter examines the potential production of present forage species and varieties, discusses the characteristics of the crop through which this production could be improved, and the sources of variation available, and finally outlines the breeding methods by which this variation could be used in the synthesis of new and improved varieties.

Potential Production of Existing Varieties

In assessing the scope for improvement in any crop, it is important to know (i) the environmental limitation to production, both climatic and edaphic, and (ii) the extent to which existing varieties are already adapted to these environmental limitations. This in its turn must be followed by an assessment of how far such adaptation and potential production can be improved by the introduction of new genetic material.

In Britain, the primary climatic limits to production are set by the seasonal distribution of solar energy, but the use of this energy by the crop can also be influenced by winter cold or summer drought. In the British Isles the input of solar energy shows a tenfold variation from below 50 cal cm^{-2} day $^{-1}$ in December to over 400 cal in June (Figure 21.1). In fact, more than 75 per cent of the total annual energy is received in the six months from April to September.

The distribution of temperature follows closely that of solar energy, but with a time lag of one to two months. In Aberystwyth, for instance, the coldest month is January with a mean temperature of 5 °C, and the warmest is August with a mean temperature of 16 °C. Since the optimum temperature for both assimilation and leaf growth in many of our temperate grasses and legumes is 20 to 25 °C, outdoor temperatures are usually below the optimum for much of the summer. Similarly, in most of these forage species, the minimum temperature for active leaf growth is around 5 °C, although photosynthesis can continue below this value. Winter production can, therefore, be limited by both low light-energy input and low temperature.

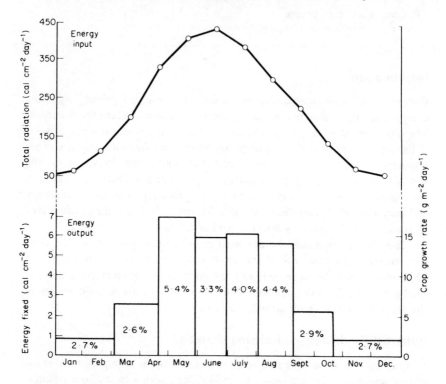

Fig. 21.1   Seasonal production and energy conversion in simulated sward plots of perennial ryegrass (Lolium perenne). Aberystwyth 1967; from Cooper [20].

The other important climatic limitation to grassland production is water stress in the summer, resulting from an excess of evapotranspiration over precipitation. Potential evapotranspiration is influenced mainly by the seasonal energy input, and in the British Isles varies from below 2 cm month^{-1} in the winter to over 10 cm month $^{-1}$ in the summer. Calculations of seasonal water balance, allowing for soil storage, show that for much of the south and east of England, water deficits in the summer can markedly affect crop growth in most years.

Even so, in practice, the major limitation to the total annual production of most British grasslands is set by the input of soil nutrients, particularly nitrogen. Most grassland responds steadily to increased nitrogen application, up to over 500 kg N ha $^{-1}$ annum $^{-1}$, while the average nitrogen input in

Britain is well below 100 kg ha^{-1}.

Most limitations of water and soil nutrients can be remedied by the farmer, either by irrigation or increasing fertilizer input, though it is not always economic to do so, but the seasonal climatic limitations of light energy and temperature cannot be changed, and can be dealt with only by the development of better adapted varieties.

The efficiency of existing forage varieties in converting the seasonal input of light energy, and hence their potential production, can be assessed from sward plots grown without limitations of water or soil nutrients, and under a system of harvesting which maintains adequate light interception, but minimises senescence and decay at the base of the sward [20].

In the maritime regions of western Europe, such a system usually involves five to eight harvests during the growing season, a fertilizer input of up to 600 kg N ha^{-1} and corresponding amounts of phosphate and potassium, and the maintenance of an adequate water supply during the summer. With this type of management, highly tillering varieties of perennial ryegrass have revealed a potential of over 25.000 kg ha^{-1} at Aberystwyth [20] and up to 20 000 kg ha^{-1} annum^{-1} at Cambridge [48] and in the Netherlands [1] (Table 21.1). Such yields at Aberystwyth (Figure 21.1) were equivalent to the conversion of 3 to 4 per cent of the incoming light energy over the whole year. During the summer period, April-September, higher conversion figures of 4 to 5 per cent were obtained, but during October-March only about 2.5 per cent of the light energy was fixed, probably due to low temperature limitations. The corresponding crop growth rates ranged from 140 to 170 kg ha^{-1} day^{-1} in the summer period (April-September) to less than 20 kg ha^{-1} day^{-1} for October-March, the digestibility (DOMD) of the herbage was maintained above 66 per cent and the crude protein content above 12 per cent (Table 12.1). Under this frequency of cutting, at five to seven-week intervals, Italian ryegrass and the less persistent Irish perennial give appreciably lower yields than the more highly tillering persistent varieties, such as S.23 and Ba 6280. Under a conservation management, however, dry matter yields of over 20 000 kg ha^{-1} have also been obtained from Italian ryegrass.

Table 21.1
Biological potential of perennial ryegrass

Location and year	Variety	Harvestable dry matter (kg ha^{-1} annum^{-1})	Conversion of light energy (%)	Digestibility (%)	Digestible energy (Mcal ha^{-1})	Crude protein (%)	Harvestable protein (kg ha^{-1} annum^{-1})	Reference
Aberystwyth 1967	Ba 6280	29 000	3.7	67-75	99 000	12-23	4500	20
	S. 23	25 000	3.2	66-75	85 000	14-28	4300	20
Wageningen 1967	Barenza Hay	22 250	–	–	–	15-23	4500	1
	Sceempter pasture	21 270	–	–	–	17-24	4200	1
Cambridge 1962	S. 24	19 500	–	–	–	–	–	37,48

*calculated from analysis for total nitrogen

These annual dry-matter yields approach the values of 30 000 kg ha^{-1} quoted by Westlake [55] for the maximum productivity of temperate perennial crops, while the levels of summer production (150 to 200 kg ha^{-1} day^{-1}) are similar to those reported by Sibma [51] for many crop canopies in the Netherlands. It would be most useful to have comparable estimates for the biological potential of other grasses and legumes, and for other forage crops, such as brassicas and forage cereals.

These potential dry-matter yields are much greater than the average production from grassland in Britain which is probably 6 to 7000 kg ha^{-1} annum^{-1} of dry matter, but values of around 15 000 kg ha^{-1} annum^{-1} are already being obtained by a number of intensive grassland farmers using high fertilizer inputs and/or high stocking rates [2, 33].

In discussing production targets from the grass crop on a farm scale, Holmes [33] suggests that with a nitrogen input of 450 kg ha^{-1} annum^{-1}, 13 200 kg ha^{-1} dry matter should be available to the grazing animal during a 180-day grazing season. At a stocking rate of 5.2 dairy cows ha^{-1} this should provide 14 100 kg milk ha^{-1}, a level of production already achieved on a number of farms. In terms of beef production, this amount of herbage could theoretically carry 10.9 beef cattle ha^{-1} giving 1970 kg ha^{-1} live weight gain but few values greater than about 1000 kg ha^{-1} have been reported in Britain.

In terms of both digestible energy and protein, these potential yields from the grass crop compare favourably with those from other farm crops [19, 32]. Under British conditions, a good cereal crop, with a grain yield of about 5000 kg ha^{-1} (about 40 cwt acre^{-1}) converts only about 0.5% of the annual input of light energy into grain, and provides a protein yield of below 600 kg ha^{-1}. This is partly because the crop occupies the land for only a portion of the year, most of the dry matter in the grain being fixed during the five to six weeks shortly before and after ear emergence, and partly because the economic yield includes only part of the total dry-matter.

Although the energy and protein yield from grass is considerably higher than from other field crops, the grass crop requires serial harvesting, either by grazing or regular cutting, consists of fresh material with a high water content which is difficult to conserve, store and transport, and must, of course, be processed through the animal. Even so, the biological margin between grass and a cereal crop as an energy source for the ruminant is considerable; and as shown by Rogers [48], even a combination of a winter-growing forage crop, such as winter rye, with a potential of 5000 kg ha^{-1} and a summer-growing crop such as maize with a potential of 15 000 kg ha^{-1} gives yields no greater than those of a well-fertilized and irrigated perennial sward.

Breeding Objectives

The high potential production of present varieties, which provides the baseline for any further improvement, has been achieved by comparatively simple breeding techniques, largely by selection and progeny-testing within locally adapted varieties or semi-natural populations [36]. There have, so far, been few attempts to deliberately synthesize varieties containing particular morphological or physiological characteristics.

Future breeding objectives can be grouped as follows:

(i) to improve the growth and production of the crop through the year including the summer months of high light intensity and high temperature, and also the period from late autumn to early spring when production is limited by low energy input and low temperature;

(ii) to improve the utilization of the crop once it is produced, ensuring efficient adaptation to methods of harvesting, either by grazing or cutting, and to techniques of conservation, whether as dried grass, hay or silage;

(iii) to improve the nutritive value of the herbage to the animal in terms of digestibility, the content of protein and appropriate minerals, and those characteristics of the herbage which determine intake.

Having outlined the future breeding objectives, the next step is to examine which physiological and morphological features of the crop can contribute to these objectives, and how much genetic variation for these characteristics is available for the breeder.

Production Characters

The effective utilization by the crop of the seasonal input of light energy will depend on (i) the photosynthetic rate of the individual leaves, (ii) the pattern of light interception by the canopy, and (iii) the distribution of assimilates in relation to active expansion of the leaf surface and/or accumulation of reserves, and to seasonal cycles of flowering and dormancy [18, 58].

(i) Photosynthetic Activity of the Individual Leaf

The photosynthetic response of the individual grass leaf to increasing light intensity is well-known [21, 31]. At low intensities of about 2000 lux, the leaf can fix about 12 to 15 per cent of the incoming light energy, but as the light intensity increases, the photosynthetic rate becomes limited by other factors such as the availability of CO_2, and eventually a saturation level is reached beyond which further increase in light intensity has no effect on the rate of net photosynthesis. In many temperate forage species, including perennial and Italian ryegrass, cocksfoot, and red and white clover the individual leaf reaches light saturation at about 20 000 to 30 000 lux. Consequently in the high light intensities of summer, which may exceed 90 000 lux at midday, it is able to fix less than 2 to 3 per cent of the incoming light energy. In contrast, many sub-tropical grasses, such as *Paspalum dilatatum* and *Cynodon dactylon*, like sugar cane and maize, which possess the Hatch-Slack pathway of carbon fixation and lack photorespiration [21, 26], continue to increase their photosynthetic rates up to light intensities of over 60 000 lux, and can therefore achieve conversion rates of 5 to 6 per cent of the incoming light energy.

Even within temperate species, however, differences in light saturation level, and hence in maximum photosynthesis, can occur. In *Lolium perenne*, for instance, variation of more than 50 per cent in maximum photosynthetic rate occurs between individual genotypes from different climatic origins (Figure 21.2), associated with differences in the mesophyll structure of the leaf [22, 57]. Such variation may contribute usefully to increased production during the high light intensities of summer.

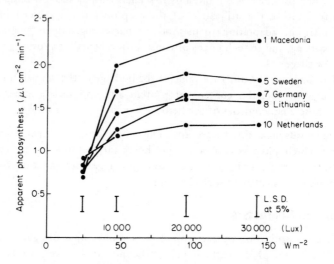

Fig. 21.2   Variation in photosynthetic rate between genotypes of perennial ryegrass (Lolium perenne); from Cooper and Wilson [22].

The photosynthetic activity of the leaf can, however, also be limited by low temperature. Most temperate forage grasses have an optimum temperature for photosynthesis of 20 to 25 °C, and photosynthesis decreases considerably below 10 °C. In many tropical species, however, such as *Cenchrus ciliaris* and *Paspalum dilatatum*, the optimum temperature is over 30 °C, and at 15 °C, corresponding to British summer temperatures, photosynthesis is no greater than in the temperate species [21].

The response of photosynthesis to temperature can also vary within the species. In both *Dactylis glomerata* [52] and *Lolium perenne* [27], marked population differences in photosynthetic rates at low temperatures (5°C) have been reported, and it should be possible to select material which can carry on photosynthesis more effectively during the low temperatures of the British winter.

These forage-grass species evidently contain useful genetic variation for maximum photosynthesis at light saturation, which may be important in determining summer potential, and for the ability to carry out photosynthesis actively during the lower temperatures of winter. It remains to be seen how far such variation can be used to improve seasonal production in the crop canopy.

(ii) Light Interception by the Canopy

The grass crop does not, however, consist of individual leaves fully exposed to the incoming light, but of a more or less closed canopy, in which light falls on the surface and is reflected or transmitted down the crop. This dilution of the incoming light over a greater leaf area results in more efficient energy conversion and a greater potential production per unit area of ground.

The relationship between the growth of the crop and the size and distribution of its leaf area has been extensively studied [10, 25]. Following germination or defoliation, the amount of assimilation, and hence the crop growth rate, are limited by the small amount of leaf surface exposed to light. As the crop grows, the assimilation per unit area of leaf is reduced through mutual shading, although the crop growth rate continues to increase. Eventually a stage is reached where the canopy is large enough to intercept all the light falling on it, and the maximum crop growth rate is achieved, though this may decrease again at greater leaf areas because of a greater respiratory load at the base of the sward.

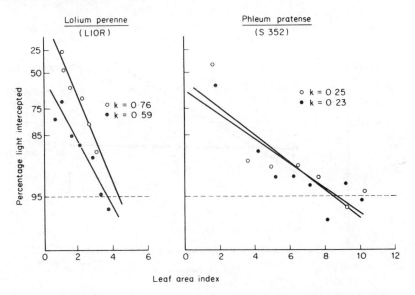

Fig. 21.3   Differences in light interception and critical leaf area index between prostrate (LIOR) and erect (S.352) grass canopies; from Sheeby [50].

In general, light interception declines logarithmically with the distance from the top of the canopy, but the rate of decline, and hence the amount of leaf area needed to intercept all the incoming light will differ according to the arrangement of leaves in the canopy (Figure 21.3). In white clover, for instance, which has flat, horizontal leaflets, all the light will be intercepted by the comparatively small leaf area index of 3 to 4, but in a grass sward the same amount of light can be spread over a leaf area index of 6 to 10 or more,

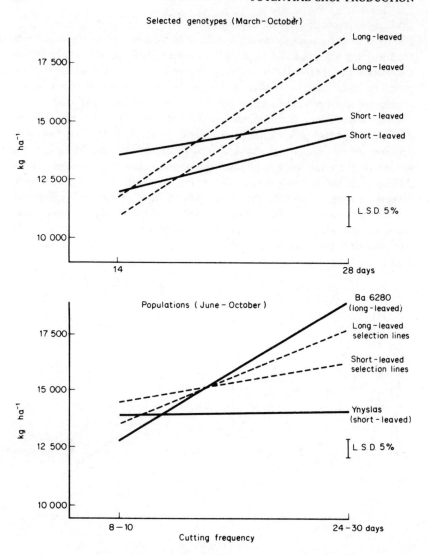

Fig. 21.4   *Response of populations, selection lines, and individual genotypes of perennial ryegrass (Lolium perenne) to frequency of cutting; from Rhodes [45].*

depending on the habit of growth and arrangement of the leaves (Figure 21.3) [9]. Even within a single species, *Lolium perenne* an erect-leaved variety, such as Ba 6280, will spread the incoming light over a greater leaf area than a prostrate variety, such as S.23, and consequently will have a greater maximum crop growth rate during undisturbed growth or infrequent cutting (Table 21.2) [44]. More recent work has shown that it is even possible to select individual genotypes from within a single ryegrass variety which differ

Table 21.2

Variation in light interception, critical leaf area index and crop growth rate between two ryegrass varieties of contrasting leaf arrangement: from Rhodes (unpublished)

Variety	Extinction coefficient of visible radiation down the canopy	Critical leaf area index*	Crop growth rate $(g\ m^{-2}\ day^{-1})$	Conversion of light energy (%)
Ba 6280 (erect)	0.31	10.7	15.5	3.7
S. 23 (prostrate)	0.43	7.1	10.8	2.6

*i.e. that which intercepts 95% of the incoming light energy

in their habit of growth and hence maximum crop growth rate (Figure 21.4). The most productive individual genotype, in fact, showed an increase of 26 per cent in dry-matter yield under sward conditions over the variety from which it was derived [45].

The most efficient leaf arrangement for a grass variety will, however, depend on the system of harvesting which is to be used. In general terms, the greater the leaf area over which the incoming light can be spread, the more efficiently is it converted, and the most efficient canopy during uninterrupted growth or under infrequent cutting, say, for conservation, would have an erect growth habit with leaves well spaced out on the stem. The grass sward may, on the other hand, be harvested by regular and frequent grazing or cutting, and under such a management, a more prosptrate growth habit can be more efficient in intercepting the light, particularly during the early regrowth period [17].

(iii) Distribution and Use of Assimilates

The seasonal production of the grass crop will also be influenced by the pattern of distribution of assimilates once they are formed, particularly their use for new leaf growth and/or their accumulation in the roots or shoot bases.

The optimum temperature for leaf growth of most temperate grasses, including perennial ryegrass, cocksfoot and tall fescue, is about 20 to 25 °C, although for many sub-tropical grasses, such as Paspalum dilatatum, it is much higher, 30 to 35 °C [21]. Even in temperate grasses, however, species and varieties differ greatly in their lower temperature limits for active growth [16, 28, 46, 47]. Many ecotypes of perennial ryegrass, cocksfoot and tall fescue from Mediterranean environments, where winter is the active growing season, can expand leaves quite actively at 5 °C, compared to northern and continental varieties which often become dormant or semi-dormant (Table 21.3). Assimilation may, however, continue in the northern material at that temperature and the assimilates accumulate as stored carbohydrates in the base of the shoot, becoming remobilized at the higher temperatures of the spring [52]. The active leaf growth of the Mediterranean material at low temperatures is often associated with lack of frost resistance (Table 21.3) and the breeder needs to select for the most appropriate balance between these two characters for his own winter conditions [15]. It might well be valuable under British conditions to select material which remains green and actively photosynthetic during the winter, but diverts most of its assimilates to storage in the shoot bases rather than to continued leaf expansion.

Table 21.3
Leaf growth at low temperatures and cold hardiness in ryegrass and cocksfoot populations; from Cooper [16].

Origin	Mean temp. of coldest month ($^{\circ}$C)	Leaf growth at 5°C (as % of growth at 25°/12°C	Survival at -5°C (%)
Ryegrass			
Algiers	12	25	0
New Zealand	7	14	20
N. Ireland	6	13	47
Belgium	2	10	20
Denmark	0	8	73
Lithuania	-4	8	92
Cocksfoot			
Israel	9	29	0
Portugal	8	24	0
Wales	6	26	0
Denmark	0	17	14
Lithuania	-4	16	33
Norway	-6	7	88

Conversely, many northern varieties of cocksfoot and perennial ryegrass can expand their leaf area very rapidly during the long photoperiods and high light intensities of summer, while under these conditions leaf expansion is reduced in much of the Mediterranean material, and a degree of summer dormancy sets in [28].

The onset of flowering and seed production also influences the distribution and use of assimilates within the plant, and in such temperate grasses as perennial ryegrass and cocksfoot, the season of flowering is often related to past climatic or agronomic selection [15]. In a Mediterranean environment, where summer drought is the limiting climatic factor, locally adapted varieties grow actively through the winter, and flowering and seed production must take place in spring before the summer drought begins. By contrast, in a northern or continental environment, where winter cold is the limiting factor, local varieties do not produce heads until late spring or early summer, and seed development occurs during the long days of mid-summer.

In the maritime climate of the British Isles, where neither summer drought nor winter cold are severely limiting, a range of early, medium and late-flowering varieties have been developed in response to different systems of management. These differences in the date of flowering are based on developmental responses to temperature and photoperiod, which can be easily measured and selected by the plant breeder [15].

Adaptation to Management Techniques

The grass crop is normally utilized by a series of harvests through the year. This may be done by grazing, with associated treading and dunging by the animal, or by cutting either for feeding direct or for conservation. The optimum structure of the crop canopy and distribution of assimilates will therefore depend on the method of harvesting envisaged. As already mentioned, with the increase in leaf area following defoliation the crop growth rate of the sward also increases, but eventually a leaf area is reached at which all the light is intercepted and the crop growth rate becomes stabilized. This maximum crop growth rate, which varies with the variety and the season, can often be maintained for some time, but a further increase in leaf area may result in excessive respiratory losses at the base of the canopy, and hence in a reduction in the growth rate. In theory, the optimum method of harvesting would maintain the sward at this maximum crop growth rate for as long as possible. In practice, it is usually necessary to defoliate to well below complete light interception, and then allow the crop to grow to full interception again [10, 25].

The frequency of cutting, and hence optimum leaf arrangement, will differ with the system of management [33]. Most systems of rotational grazing involve frequent defoliation at intervals of three to five weeks, resulting in a fairly low leaf area index, and the most efficient light interception is therefore obtained from a flat, prostrate habit of growth, as in the highly tillering pasture varieties of perennial ryegrass. In conservation managements, however, where the crop is often allowed to grow up to its maximum leaf area index, a taller, more erect habit of growth, as in Italian ryegrass or the hay varieties of timothy, is more efficient and provides a greater crop growth rate. Even within a single species, perennial ryegrass, Rhodes [45] has shown marked differences between prostrate and erect varieties in relative production under different frequencies of cutting, and has been able to select within a single variety for such differences in response to defoliation (Figure 21.4). The greater production of the short-leaved prostrate forms under frequent cutting appeared to be based on a greater amount of leaf tissue remaining after defoliation, while the better performance of the erect, long-leaved types under less frequent cutting was due to their higher optimum leaf area index.

In all systems of management, the ability to regrow actively after defoliation is important, and is often related to the balance struck between the storage of assimilates as energy reserves in the shoot bases on the one hand, and their use in continued leaf expansion on the other. This balance is under genotypic control but is also markedly influenced by management. Thus in Italian ryegrass and the less persistent forms of perennial ryegrass, a high proportion of the assimilates is used in continued leaf expansion; frequent defoliation together with high nitrogen input further depletes the carbohydrate reserves in the shoot bases, so leading to severe damage. By contrast, the highly tillering persistent forms maintain adequate reserves under these conditions and can sustain regular high production [20].

In varieties which are to be used for grazing, adequate resistance to treading by the animal is also essential. Such resistance is usually associated with a prostrate growth habit, and with the survival of a large number of tiller buds below the level of grazing as in pasture varieties of ryegrass, or of axillary buds on the stolons, as in pasture types of white clover [12].

Many of these characteristics have in fact already been developed in existing varieties as a result of past agronomic managements. In Britain, for instance, intensive grazing has selected a prostrate growth habit with rather small leaves and tillers, but a high tiller number per unit area. Late-flowering types are favoured [15], and species such as *Arrhenatherum elatius* and *Phleum pratense* with extensive internode elongation above ground level are eliminated. In other words, the crop structure adapted to these conditions maintains a useful leaf area and population of tiller buds below the level of grazing, but may be limited in the amount of light it can intercept [25, 40].

Management for hay or for seed production, on the other hand, has selected a taller and more open crop structure, with deeper light penetration and freer air exchange. A greater critical leaf area index and maximum crop growth rate should therefore be possible [25]. In fact, Mitchell [40] has suggested that for maximum light interception and conversion under a cutting management, one needs a crop with small leaves, well distributed over a wide zone of height, perferably a perennial with a vigorous root system, and the ability to recover rapidly from defoliation.

Finally, although the fertilizer input to the crop, unlike climatic factors, can be controlled by the farmer, the efficient use of applied fertilizers is likely to be of increasing importance to forage varieties [53]. In perennial ryegrass, for instance, varieties and individual genotypes have been shown to differ in their response to nitrogen [37, 54]. Similarly, in the herbage legumes, genetic variation in both the host and the *Rhisobium* is important in determining the nitrogen-fixing ability of the legume/*Rhizobium* association [24].

Nutritive Value

Forage crops are processed through the ruminant. Thus the content of digestible energy and other nutrients and their availability to the animal are important features in the breeding programme [17, 43].

The metabolizable energy content of forage species depends largely on their digestibility, which is strongly influenced by the stage of development of the plant. In most temperate grasses, including ryegrass and cocksfoot, digestibility remains at a plateau through the spring, but declines rapidly and regularly after ear emergence [43]. Red clover and lucerne show a similar decline with maturity, but white clover maintains a high digestibility for most of the year, as it is only the leaves and petioles which are grazed or harvested [24]. Variation in the time of flowering will thus influence the relative digestibility at any particular time of the year, but even so, definite specific and varietal differences at comparable growth stages have been reported. Cocksfoot, for instance, usually has a lower digestibility then perennial ryegrass, although some cocksfoot varieties fall within the ryegrass range. The development of the *in vitro* technique, using rumen liquor, has made it possible to assess the digestibility of individual plants and hence, for example, to select for improved digestibility within cocksfoot varieties [14, 43].

In temperate grasslands, intake is often more important than the metabolizable energy of the feed in determining animal production, but little is yet known of the intrinsic properties of the crop which affect voluntary intake. In dry conserved feeds, digestibility has a marked effect on intake, but it does not appear to be so significant in fresh grass or silage. It has been claimed that in cocksfoot and *Sorghum* voluntary intake and the content of soluble carbohydrates are highly correlated [43] and more recently Patil and Jones [42] have shown that the reduced intake of timothy by lambs, compared to ryegrass and cocksfoot, is related to a higher content of cell wall material, with a slower rate of digestion *in vitro*, and a slower rate of passage *in vivo*. Similarly, in New Zealand, the great voluntary intake of Italian compared to perennial ryegrass is found to be associated with a higher content of soluble carbohydrate and lower content of cellulose in the Italian ryegrass [3].

The composition of the digested part of the herbage may also be important, since the relative proportions of structural and soluble carbohydrates in the feed may influence the pattern of rumen fermentation, and hence the efficiency of energy conversion by the animal. Differences between species and varieties in soluble carbohydrate content have been reported; cocksfoot usually has a lower content than ryegrass at the same growth stage, while tetraploids of Italian and perennial ryegrasses often have a higher soluble carbohydrate content than the corresponding diploids [43]. Varietal differences occur within perennial ryegrass, timothy and cocksfoot. In perennial ryegrass it has been shown that individual genotypes within a single variety differ [14], and high and low carbohydrate lines can be selected.

Similarly, the content and availability of protein and of various important mineral elements such as calcium, sodium, magnesium, copper and cobalt vary between species and varieties [29, 35, 43, 56]. Timothy for instance, has a much lower sodium content than perennial ryegrass, cocksfoot and tall fescue, while the sodium content of red clover is very low compared to that of white clover. Legumes, in general, have a much higher content of calcium, magnesium and potassium than most forage grasses and are richer in trace elements (S, Fe, Zn, Cu and Co). Both grasses and legumes, however, have a low content of phosphorus in relation to the requirements of the dairy cow. (Table 21.4).

Table 21.4
Mineral content of grasses and legumes in relation to livestock requirements

	Ca (%)	P (%)	Mg (%)	Na (%)	Cu (ppm)	Co (ppm)
Grasses						
Perennial ryegrass	0.25	0.23	0.10	0.60	4.5	0.11
Cocksfoot	0.25	0.30	0.11	0.69	6.6	0.08
Timothy	0.27	0.17	0.08	0.03	5.5	0.08
Legumes						
Red clover	1.18	0.29	0.19	0.10	10.0	0.27
White clover	1.14	0.21	0.19	0.27	8.0	—
Livestock requirements						
Dairy cow						
(20 kg milk/day)	0.52	0.42	0.15	0.15	10.0	0.10
Beef cattle						
(0.75 kg live weight/day)	0.47	0.38	0.11	0.11	10.0	0.10
Sheep						
(0.20 kg live weight/day)	0.50	0.25	0.06	0.07	5.0	0.10

(based on Patil and Jones [42])

Considerable variation in the uptake or content of particular nutrients can be found within a single species, or even within a single variety. In perennial ryegrass, for instance, varietal differences occur in the uptake of potassium and calcium [53], often associated with differences in cation exchange capacity, and also in the K/(Ca + Mg) ratio, which has been implicated in hypomagnesemia in dairy cows. Similar varietal differences in the content of sodium and potassium have been reported in tall fescue, ryegrass and cocksfoot [39].

Within a single variety, long-rotation ryegrass, significant differences have been found in the content of phosphate, nitrate, sulphate, sodium, iron, titanium, aluminium, manganese, copper and zinc, none of which were correlated with dry-matter production, while a fifteen-fold difference in iodine content between different ryegrass clones has also been reported [11].

Deficiencies in some of these mineral elements may prevent the full utilization of otherwise highly digestible herbage. For instance, Patil and Jones [42] found that lambs fed only on timothy showed reduced live weight gain, and lack of crimp and colour in the wool, when compared with lambs fed on perennial ryegrass and cocksfoot of the same high digestibility. These symptoms could be rapidly alleviated by supplementation with cobalt and copper.

The mineral content of the herbage is likely to become increasingly important under intensive systems of management with high nitrogen inputs and high dry-matter yields. Under such conditions, for instance, the levels of calcium and magnesium in many ryegrass varieties can fall well below those regarded as necessary for a highly-producing dairy cow (Table 21.4). In practice, however, it may be preferable to provide the necessary level of certain minerals, such as sodium and magnesium, by supplementation, rather than by developing varieties with a higher mineral content.

Useful variation thus exists for many of the chemical and physical properties of the herbage which determine its nutritive value to the animal, but the breeder needs guidance from the animal nutritionist as to which of these characteristics are most important in limiting animal production.

An understanding of those physiological, morphological and biochemical features of the crop which contribute to its efficient conversion of energy and nutrients enables the breeder to set up appropriate models of the combination of characters required in improved varieties for specific management systems. The model required will of course, depend on the proposed method of utilization, whether for grazing or for conservation or both, and also on the type of livestock enterprise, whether for meat, milk or wool production. It is becoming clear that ample genetic variation is available, both within and between forage species, for many of the physiological and morphological features required in these models. The next step is to examine the genetic techniques of selection and recombination available to the breeder for synthesizing such models in practice.

Breeding Techniques

(i) Introduction and Selection

In the pioneering phases of herbage crop improvement, the use of material climatically adapted to the regions of utilization was of primary importance. In Britain, such adaptation was provided by indigenous material, and further adaptations to specific grassland systems could be recognised. These were exploited at an early stage by the use of local varieties such as 'Kent' perennial ryegrass, wild white clover, and 'Montgomery' or 'Cornish Marl' red clover. In Australia and New Zealand, most of the important grasses and legumes had to be introduced from similar climates elsewhere, coincidentally with the development of livestock farming. Thus in Australia, subterranean clover, Wimmera ryegrass and *Phalaris tuberosa* were introduced directly from Mediterranean environments, while in New Zealand the two most important forage species (perennial ryegrass and white clover) were derived from the corresponding maritime environment of the British Isles [30]. More recently, the collection and introduction of a wider range of Mediterranean material has been carried out for the winter rainfall areas of south and west Australia, whilst in sub-tropical regions of Australia such collection at the species and ecotype level forms the basis of most present-day forage improvement [34].

Even in Britain, which already has a wide range of productive varieties, some of the recent collections of forage grasses and legumes from Mediterranean regions, with increased winter production, have appeared sufficiently useful for direct multiplication [5, 8, 41].

The direct use of such locally adapted populations, however, is only the first step in an improvement programme. The next stage in most forage breeding programmes has involved deliberate selection for uniformity and for other desirable characteristics from within these indigenous and introduced populations. Most of the existing forage varieties in Britain and in western Europe have been produced in this way [36]; S.23 perennial ryegrass and S.184 white clover, for instance, having been selected from indigenous material from old pastures. This stage in the programme, involving the selection of a small number of desirable parents, makes it possible to increase the uniformity of locally adapted material, and to provide a regular and uniform supply of seed.

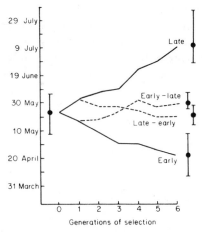

Fig. 21.5   Response to selection for flowering date in one local population (Kent) of perennial ryegrass (Lolium perenne); from Cooper [13].

Most perennial grasses and legumes are cross-fertilizing with a high degree of self incompatibility. Individuals are therefore, heterozygous, and release appreciable genetic variation by segregation following recombination. Even well-adapted local populations and selected varieties can contain considerable genetic variation and may show useful response to selection for particular important characteristics [13, 15] (Figure 21.5). Increased digestibility in cocksfoot, reduced seed-shedding in tall fescue, rust resistance in timothy, and winter hardiness in Italian ryegrass have already received the attention of the breeder [8], and similar selection within existing varieties is now in progress for such important physiological features as photosynthetic rate, leaf expansion at low temperature, leaf arrangement in relation to light interception and a number of nutritional characteristics.

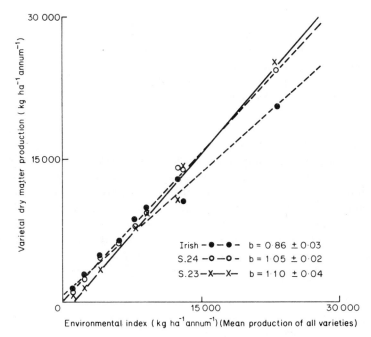

Fig. 21.6   Analysis of genotype-environment interaction for dry matter production among varieties of perennial ryegrass (Lolium perenne); from Samuel et al [49].

More recently, appropriate statistical techniques have been developed for selecting families or potential varieties for adaptability to a range of environments, even when the limiting environmental factors cannot be specified [7, 49] (Figure 21.6).

The outbreeding nature of the species, although conferring considerable advantages in the amount of genetic variability available for selection, presents problems in the stable reproduction of varieties during multiplication. Continued reproduction by seed from closely related plants leads to inbreeding depression. Following selection, therefore, heterozygosity has to be maintained, or even restored where selection procedures involve a degree of inbreeding. At present it is not considered a practical or necessary proposition to maximize heterozygosity by the production of commercial quantities of F_1 hybrids; instead a high average heterozygosity is achieved and maintained by the construction of the synthetic variety. This involves selecting unrelated plants or lines for desired characteristics, followed by progeny-testing for good general combining ability using appropriate mating designs, such as the polycross. A small number of plants are then chosen to form the basic parents of the variety. The number chosen is a compromise between having too many parents, and consequently too wide a spread in combining abilities, or too few parents which would lead to inbreeding depression. Experiments indicate that the optimum number is of the order of four to eight [8] . These basic parents are where possible propagated clonally by the breeder and multiplied through a limited number of generations (three or four) to provide certified seed for the farmer. The multiplication generations are grown under carefully controlled managements to avoid possible shifts in type under selection, and are isolated to prevent contamination by cross pollination from other plants of the same species [36] .

(ii) Combination of Characters

So far, most breeding programmes have concentrated on using the variation and combination of characters which already exist in natural ecotypes or cultivated varieties, but a more long-term approach lies in deliberately combining characteristics from different climatic or agronomic populations, in accordance with a well defined physiological or morphological model. This can be attempted either *within* a genetic species at the same ploidy level or, more ambitiously, *between* related species, involving interspecific hybridization often accompanied by induced polyploidy.

Table 21.5
Use of Mediterranean collections of white clover to introduce improved autumn production: based on Davies [24].

	Summer production (cut 19 July 66)	Late Summer production 13 Sept. 66)	Autumn production (cut 9 Oct. 6)	Winter damage score (1965-6)*
Original populations				
		(green wt, g/plant)		
Kersey, Suffolk	910	333	48	4.5
Israel	351	276	71	6.9
Turkey	485	323	78	5.1
Selected F_2 families (range)				
Kersey x Israel	829-1104	400-600	103-195	3.6-4.7
(Kersey x Israel)				
x (Kersey x Turkey)	941-1241	533-868	99-177	3.3-4.2

*1 = least damage   9 = most damage

An early example of such combination of characters from within the same genetic species was the development in New Zealand of Manawa (short-rotation) and Ariki (long-rotation ryegrass) from the hybridization of *Lolium perenne* and *L. multiflorum*, followed by back-crossing to the *multiflorum* or *perenne* parent respectively [23] . Similar hybrids between *L. perenne* and *multiflorum* have been developed elsewhere and, more recently, the introduction of more active winter growth from Mediterranean collections of ryegrass, cocksfoot and tall fescue into productive British varieties is being attempted [5, 8] , although in cocksfoot and tall fescue the programme is complicated by the existence of different levels of ploidy, or even by hybrid sterility between forms of the same chromosome number, as between some British and North African populations of tall fescue ($2n = 42$). Similarly, Mediterranean varieties of white clover are being used as a source of more active autumn and winter growth in breeding programmes in both Britain and New Zealand [4, 24] (Table 21.5).

One difficulty often encountered in this approach is the existance of undesirable correlated characters which may be difficult to separate from the more useful features. The active winter growth of Mediterranean populations of grasses and legumes, for instance, is often associated with a lack of winter hardiness. A further difficulty is that of stabilizing the new combinations of characters in these outbreeding and heterozygous species [8] .

The difficulty of stablisation may be overcome by more complex breeding programmes which involve the combination of characters from different genetic species, often of different polyploid levels, although even within a single genetic species, the segregating hybrid at the diploid level between *Lolium perenne* and *L. multiflorum* can be stabilised by induced polyploidy [8] . In cocksfoot, for instance, most of the cultivated varieties from north-west Europe are tetraploid ($2n = 28$), but a series of natural diploid ($2n = 14$) populations occurs, ranging from the Canary Isles through the Mediterranean region to northern Europe. These diploids often contain desirable characteristics, such as the active winter growth of the Portuguese *D. lusitanica*, or increased digestibility, and their combination with the cultivated tetraploids by induced polyploidy, followed by hybridization, shows considerable promise [6] .

Table 21.6
Combination of desirable characteristics of Lolium multiflorum and Festuca arundinacea in a new fertile hybrid
Objectives: *To produce a winter-hardy variety with rapid establishment and early spring growth, capable of high production over 4-5 years*

Source of desirable characteristics	*L. multiflorum*	*F. arundinacea*
Rapid establishment from seed	+	—
Good production in seeding year and spring of first harvest year	+	—
Palatability	+	—
Winter hardiness	—	+
Early spring growth	+	+
Persistency	—	+
Continued high production after first and second harvest years	—	+

Similarly, the development of interspecific hybrids between *Lolium perenne* or *L. multiflorum*, both of which are diploid ($2n = 14$), and members of the polyploid series ($2n = 14$ to 70) of the broad-leaved fescue has already produced a wide range of forms with quite novel combinations of characters (Table 21.6). These forms can be stabilized at higher polyploid levels, either by crossing autopolyploid forms of the parents, or by doubling the chromosome number of the hybrids [38] (Table 21.7). The amphiploids between *Lolium multiflorum* ($2n = 14$) and *Festuca arundinacea* ($2n = 42$), aimed at improving the establishment vigour, seasonal yield and palatability of the tall fescue, are particularly attractive [8].

Table 21.7
Two alternative methods of producing fertile hybrids of Lolium multiflorum
x Festuca arundinacea

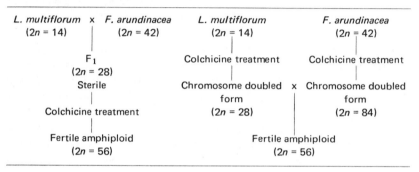

It is evidently possible, by this kind of interspecific hybridisation associated with induced polyploidy, to produce in effect new species of forage plants often with quite unusual combinations of characters, genetically stabilized at higher polyploid levels. These new species can then form the raw material for further intensive selection and breeding.

Conclusions

Up to the present time, most improved varieties of forage grasses and legumes in Britain have been derived by mass selection and subsequent progeny testing from indigenous local varieties or natural populations. These techniques have produced a range of good general-purpose varieties, whose potential is in fact greater than that achieved by most grassland systems in Britain. Future improvement is likely to involve varieties specifically tailored to particular intensive management systems and, as pointed out by Rogers [48], a potential production of 20 000 kg dry matter ha/annum (i.e. about 60 000 Mcal digestible energy/ha) and an adequate protein and mineral content, should be regarded as the baseline from which to start. The development of such specialized varieties, possibly derived from new species combinations, may well be based on specific physiological and morphological models, derived from an increased understanding of the physiological, morphological and biochemical features which contribute to the conversion of energy and nutrients by the crop, under specific managements and environmental inputs [17].

REFERENCES

1. ALBERDA, Th. 'Dry matter production and light interception of crop surfaces. IV. Maximum herbage production as compared with predicted values', *Neth. J. agric. Sci.*, 1968, **16**, 142-53.

2. ARMITAGE, E.R. and TEMPLEMAN, W.G. 'Response of grassland to nitrogenous fertilizer in the west of England', *J. Br. Grassld Soc.*, 1964, **19**, 291-7.

3. BAILEY, R.W. 'Pasture quality and ruminant nutrition. I. Carbohydrate composition of ryegrass varieties grown as sheep pastures', *N.Z. Jl agric. Res.*, 1964, **7**, 496-507.

4. BARCLAY, P.C. 'Breeding for improved winter pasture production in New Zealand', *Proc. 8th Int. Grassld. Congr. 1960*, 1961, 326-30.

5. BORRILL, M. 'Grass resources for out-of-season production', *Rep. Welsh Pl. Breed. Stn for 1960*, 1961, 107-13.

6. BORRILL, M. 'Chromosomal status, gene exchange and evolution in *Dactylis*. I. Gene exchange in diploids and tetraploids', *Genetics, Princeton*, 1961, **32**, 94-117.

7. BREESE, E.L. 'The measurement and significance of genotype-environment interaction in grasses', *Heredity, Lond.* 1969, **24**, 27-44.

8. BREESE, E.L. and LEWIS, E.J. 'Grasses-species and hybrids', *Occ. Sym. Br. Grassld Soc.*, 1969, **5**, 15-20.

9. BROUGHAM, R. 'The relationship between the critical leaf area, total chlorophyll content, and maximum growth rate of some pasture and crop plants', *Ann. Bot.*, 1960, N.S., **24**, 463-74.

10. BROWN, R.H. and BLASER, R.E. 'Leaf area index in pasture growth', *Herb. Abstr.* 1968, **38**, 1-9.

11. BUTLER, G.W., BARCLAY, P.C. and GLENDAY, A.C. 'Genetic and environmental differences in the mineral composition of ryegrass herbage', *Pl. Soil*, 1962, **16**, 214-28.

12. CHARLES, A.H. 'Differential survival of plant types in swards', *J. Br. Grassld Soc.*, 1964, **19**, 198-204.

13. COOPER, J.P. 'Selection and population structure in *Lolium*. V. Continued response and associated changes in fertility and vigour', *Heredity, Lond.*, 1961, **16**, 435-53.

14. COOPER, J.P. 'Selection for nutritive value', *Rep. Welsh Pl. Breed. Stn for 1961*, 1962, 145-56.

15. COOPER, J.P. 'Species and population differences in climatic response', in *Environmental Control of Plant Growth*, London: Academic Press, 1963, 381-403.

16. COOPER, J.P. 'Climatic variation in forage grasses. I. Leaf development in climatic races of *Lolium* and *Dactylis*', *J. appl. Ecol.*, 1964, **1**, 45-62.

17. COOPER, J.P. 'The use of physiological variation in forage grass breeding', *Proc. 12th Easter Sch. Agric. Sci., Univ. Nottingham*, 165, 293-307.

18. COOPER, J.P. 'The significance of genetic variation in light interception

and conversion for forage plant breeding', *Proc. X Int. Grassld Congr.*, 1966, 715-20.

19. COOPER, J.P. 'Energy conversion in crops', *J. Inst. Corn agric. Merch.*, 1967, **15**, 100-5.

20. COOPER, J.P. 'Potential forage production', *Occ. Symp. Br. Grassld. Soc.*, 1969, **5**, 5-13.

21. COOPER, J.P. and TAINTON, N.M. 'Light and temperature requirements for the growth of tropical and temperate grasses', *Herb. Abstr.*, 1968, **38**, 167-76.

22. COOPER, J.P. and WILSON, D. 'Variation in photosynthetic rate in *Lolium*', *Proc. 11th Inst. Grassld Congr.* 1970, 522-527

23. CORKILL, L. 'Pasture plant breeding in New Zealand', *Agric. Rev. Lond.*, 1957, **3**, (6), 31-7.

24. DAVIES, W.E. 'Herbage legumes − special considerations', *Occ. Symp. Br. Grassld Soc.*, 1969, **5**, 21-7.

25. DONALD, C.M. 'Competition among crop and pasture plants', *Adv. Agron.*, 1963, **15**, 1-118.

26. DOWNTON, W.J.S. and TREGUNNA, E.B. 'Carbon dioxide compensation − its relation to photosynthetic carboxylation reactions, systematics of the Gramineae and leaf anatomy', *Can. J. Bot.*, 1968, **46**, 207-15.

27. EAGLES, C.F. 'Apparent photosynthesis and respiration in populations of *Lolium perenne* from contrasting climatic regions', *Nature, Lond.*, 1967, **215**, 100-1.

28. EAGLES, C.F. 'The effect of temperature on vegetative growth in climatic races of *Dactylis glomerata* in controlled environments', *Ann. Bot*, 1967, N.S. **31**, 31-39.

29. FLEMING, G.A. 'Trace elements in plants with particular reference to pasture species', *Outl. Agric.*, 1965, **4**, 270-85.

30. FRANKEL, O.H. 'Invasion and evolution of plants in Australia and New Zealand', *Caryologia*, 1954, **6**, Suppl. 600-19.

31. GAASTRA, P. 'Photosynthesis of leaves and field crops', *Neth. J. agric. Sci.*, 1962, **10**, 311-24.

32. HOLLIDAY, R. 'Solar energy consumption in relation to crop yield', *Agric. Prog.*, 1966, **41**, 24-34.

33. HOLMES, W. 'The use of nitrogen in the management of pasture for cattle', *Herb. Abstr.*, 1968, **38**, 265-78.

34. HUTTON, E.M. 'Breeding tropical pasture plants', *Span.*, 1968, **11**, 72-5.

35. JONES, D.I.H. and WALTERS, R.J.K. 'Varietal variation in nutritive characteristics', *Occ. Symp. Br. Grassld Soc.*, 1969, **5**, 37-43.

36. LAZENBY, A. and ROGERS, H.H. 'Grass breeding in the United Kingdom', *Herb. Abstr.*, 1963, **33**, 73-80.

37. LAZENBY, A. and ROGERS, H.H. 'Selection criteria in grass breeding. V. Performance of *Lolium perenne*, genotypes grown at different nitrogen levels and spacings', *J agric. Sci., Camb.*, 1965, **65**, 79-90.

38. LEWIS, E.J. 'The production and manipulation of new breeding material

in *Lolium-Festuca'*, *Proc. X Int. Grassld Congr.*, 1966, 688-92.

39. MILES, D.G., GRIFFITH, G and WALTERS, R.J.K. 'Variation in the chemical composition of four grasses', *Rep. Welsh Pl. Breed. Stn for 1963*, 1964, 110-4.

40. MITCHELL, K.J. 'Production potential of New Zealand pasture land', *Proc. N.Z. Inst. agric. Sci.*, 1963, **9**, 80-96.

41. MORGAN, D.G. 'The eco-physiology of Mediterranean and north temperate varieties of tall fescue', *Outl. Agric.*, 1964, **4**, 171-6.

42. PATIL, B.D. and JONES, D.I.H. 'The mineral status of some temperate herbage varieties in relation to animal performance', *Proc. 11th Int. Grassld Congr.* 1970, 726-730.

43. RAYMOND, W.F. 'The nutritive value of forage crops', *Adv. Agron.*, 1969, **21**, 1-108.

44. RHODES, I. 'The yield, canopy structure and light interception of two ryegrass varieties in mixed culture and mono-culture', *J. Br. Grassld Soc.*, 1969, **24**, 123-7.

45. RHODES, I. 'The relationship between productivity and some components of canopy structure in ryegrass (*Lolium* spp.). I. Leaf length', *J. agric. Sci., Camb.*, 1969, **73**, 315-9.

46. ROBSON, M.J. 'A comparison of British and north African varieties of tall fescue (*Festuca arundinacea*). I. Leaf growth during winter and the effects on it of temperature and daylength', *J. appl. Ecol.*, 1967, **4**, 475-84.

47. ROBSON, M.J. and JEWISS, O.R. 'A comparison of British and north African varieties of tall fescue (*Festuca arundinacea*). II. Growth during winter and survival at low temperatures', *J. appl. Ecol.*, 1968, **5**, 179-90.

48. ROGERS, H.H. 'Breeding for maximum production', *Occ. Symp. Br. Grassld Soc.*, 1967, **3**, 66-73.

49. SAMUEL, C.J.A., HILL, J., BREESE, E.L. and DAVIES, ALISON, G. 'Assessing and predicting environmental response in *Lolium perenne*', J. *agric. Sci., Camb.*, 1970, **75**, 1-9.

50. SHEEHY, J.E. 'Studies in light interception in herbage canopies', *Ph. D. Thesis, Univ. Wales*, 1970.

51. SIBMA, L. 'Growth of closed green crop surfaces in the Netherlands', *Neth. J. agric. Sci.*, 1968, **16**, 211-6.

52. TREHARNE, K.J. and EAGLES, C.F. 'Effect of temperature on photosynthetic activity of climatic races of *Dactyles glomerata*', *Photosynthetica*, 1970, **4**, 107-117.

53. VOSE, P.B. 'Varietal differences in plant nutrition', *Herb. Abstr.*, 1963, **33**, 1-13.

54. VOSE, P.B. and BREESE, E.L. 'Genetic variation in the utilization of nitrogen by ryegrass species *Lolium perenne* and *L. multiflorum*', *Ann. Bot.*, 1964, N.S., **28**, 251-70.

55. WESTLAKE, D.F. 'Comparisons of plant productivity', *Biol. Rev.*, 1963, **38**, 385-425.

56. WHITEHEAD, D.C. 'Nutrient minerals in grassland herbage', *Commonw. Bur. Past. Fld. Crops. Mimeo. Publs.* 1966, **1**, 1-83.
57. WILSON, D. and COOPER, J.P. 'Diallel analysis of photosynthetic rate and related leaf characters among contrasting genotypes of *Lolium perenne'*, *Heredity, Lond.,* 1969, **24**, 633-49.
58. WIT, C.T. de 'Photosynthesis of leaf canopies', *Versl. landbouwk. Onderz.* 1965, **663**, 1-57.

22. Control of Pests and Diseases

S.H. Crowdy
Department of Botany, University of Southampton.

Introduction

The control of pests and diseases is a wide subject, and consideration here will be limited to the general areas in which developments are likely to have the greatest impact on total production, the major problems within these areas and some of the technical advances which may help in their solution.

In the period between the world wars, the United Kindom assumed that all the bulk food it required could be imported cheaply. In these circumstances, our resources were concentrated on maximising the output of high-value horticultural crops, particularly those which did not travel well. In contrast, the present situation calls for a shift of emphasis to the production of bulk foods. The initial justification for this is to reduce imports, but in the long run, rising populations and standards of living all over the world will force Britain to rely on its own resources. An involvement in bulk food production demands the efficient use of every acre of land rather than high production on a limited acreage under expensive crops, and priorities must be assessed on the basis of land wasted in supporting pests and diseases, the 'untaken acres' [24]. Table 22.1 shows the general distribution of agricultural land use in Britain and the wastage in each category, arbitrarily assuming a uniform loss of 10 per cent due to pests and diseases.

Table 22.1
Land use in Great Britain

Crops	Area in acres x 10^5 (hectares x 10^5)		
	Total	Producing crops	Untaken (10% loss assumed)
Horticulture	10 (4.04)	9 (3.64)	1 (0.4)
Agriculture	100 (40.4)	90 (36.4)	10 (4.0)
Grassland	180 (72.8)	162 (65.6)	18 (7.2)
Rough Grazing	170 (68.6)	153 (61.9)	17 (6.9)

The bulk of the acreage of the agricultural crops is devoted to cereals, wheat 2.5 million acres (1 million hectares), barley 4.7 million acres (1.9 million hectares), temporary grass about 2 million acres (0.8 million hectares) and oats about half a million acres (0.2 million hectares). In very crude terms, research leading to a doubling of the yields per acre in the horticultural sector

would only release 500 000 acres of land for bulk food production; this area
would be released by an increase in yield of only 5 per cent in the agricultural
sector of 3 per cent in grassland. Major increases in production might be
sought in these latter sectors.

Losses due to Pests and Diseases

Planning research directed towards increasing productivity must be based on a
calculation of the potential return; this in turn depends on estimates of losses,
which are currently being assessed. Estimates of losses caused by pests and
disease are notoriously unreliable and difficult to make, but any estimate
gives better guidance than none. Earlier assessments were often based on data
derived from experiments designed to control a particular condition; these
tended to over-estimate overall losses, since the experiments were usually
located in areas where trouble was likely; however, they did demonstrate the
advantages of control where the disease was serious. Reliable estimates of
overall losses should be based on randomly distributed observations spread
over a wide area; for this control experiments are too cumbersome and must
be replaced by methods specially suited to surveys. Suitable methods are
being developed which depend essentially on comparing yields of infected
and uninfected plots and relating the yield losses recorded to estimates of the
intensity of disease. These records can usually be converted to give a linear
regression of yield on symptoms, and the relationship is expressed as this
linear regression. Commonly the uninfected plots are maintained free of
disease by spraying, or suitably weighed comparisons between susceptible and
resistant varieties may be made. Regressions of this type have been reported
for cereal mildews [18, 19] sharp eyespot [25] yellow rust [8], take-all [28,
32], barley yellow-dwarf virus [39] and frit-fly on oats [34]. There are
obvious errors inherent in this approach, since there is no certainty that the
spray is completely without phytotoxicity or that it is controlling only the
disease or pest under investigation; one must also assume that all the varieties
in all the locations examined react in the same way at a given level of
symptoms. However, in spite of all the uncertainties, estimates like this do
provide a quantitative basis for comparing different diseases and estimating
their overall effect on the crop.

A number of estimates of losses due to pests and diseases of cereals have
been made. The potential losses from insect attack are serious [35] and could
amount to about 4 per cent of the acreage under these crops, about 250 000
acres. Most of the pests can be controlled with pesticides, and the actual
losses need not be serious. However, the most effective chemicals used for
control are the more persistent chlorinated hydrocarbon insecticides and
adequate replacements must be found as these are withdrawn. There is also
the possibility that insecticide resistance will develop. Probably the most
serious pest, for which there is no adequate chemical control, is the cereal
root eelworm, *Heterodera avenae* Woll.; this is a widely distributed pest [33]
which is usually controlled adequately by crop rotation. It can cause losses of

CONTROL OF PESTS AND DISEASES

the order of 30 per cent in susceptible varieties in heavily infested soils [5]. Strickland [36] estimates the overall losses due to this pest as about 60 000 untaken acres, about 1 per cent of the cereal acreage. Several species of slug, notably *Agriolimax reticulatus*, are widely distributed and may cause serious damage locally, especially in heavy soils; Strickland [36] estimates that they cause an overall loss of about 40 000 acres.

The control of fungal diseases is much less satisfactory. Most of the seed-borne diseases are adequately controlled with mercurial seed dressings. Seed dressing has virtually eliminated the seedling infection smuts, e.g. *Tilletia caries* and *Ustilago bordei*, and provides a useful control of a number of fusaria and *Gibberella zeae*. However, there is evidence that mercury-resistant strains of the fungus causing leaf stripe of oats, *Pyreophora avenae*, have developed [22, 23], and if other fungi develop resistance, the position could well become serious. The blossom infection smuts, *Ustilago nuda*, are a group of seed-borne diseases which are at present controlled by using resistant varieties; the pathogen is known to develop new races and so presents a potential threat to cereal production: the current losses due to these diseases are negligible, but losses up to 20 per cent have been recorded in the past [7].

Cereals are also subject to attack by a number of soil-borne pathogens, of which the most important are *Ophiobolus graminis*, *Corticium solani* and *Cercosporella herpotrichoides* causing respectively take-all, sharp eyespot and eye-spot; the losses caused by these diseases are commonly maintained at an acceptable level by crop rotation. Slope [32] quotes the results of an experiment in which the yield of a wheat crop following wheat-oats-wheat was 28.4 cwt acre^{-1} (398 kg ha^{-1}), as compared with 51.5 cwt acre^{-1} (567 kg ha^{-1}) when the wheat followed wheat-oats-beans; if the potential yield is estimated from the intensity of take-all recorded, the first rotation gave a loss of 50 per cent and the second a loss of 4 per cent. It is extremely difficult to estimate the damage caused by root pathogens, since the pests and diseases interact and their effects are markedly influenced by the previous history of the land and the level of fertilizers, particularly nitrogen, used.

Leaf diseases are probably the most serious cause of yield loss in cereals in Britain at present. James [17] collated the results of a survey of leaf diseases of spring barley carried out in 1967 by the National Agricultural Advisory Service on farm crops. Yield loss was estimated from records of disease intensity. He concluded that in this year losses amounted to 20-25 per cent of the crop in England and Wales. This estimate is considerably higher than the 4 per cent losses quoted by Doling [6] and Strickland [36], but it is based on a larger population and is probably a better estimate of the position in this year. Since 1967 was not recorded as abnormal, there is reason to accept the higher estimate as the more accurate. James' figures suggest that about a million acres (400 000 ha) were devoted to cultivating barley leaf diseases, of which 600 000 to 800 000 acres (200 000 − 300 000 ha) were devoted to mildew. In 1967, the cost to the country of these lost acres of barley was £40 to £50 million.

James estimated a loss of about 6 per cent for other leaf diseases the most important of which were the rusts, accounting for a loss of 4 per cent. The present status of rust disease of wheat has been reviewed recently by Manners [20]. In Britain yellow rust, *Puccinia striiformis*, is the most serious; a severe attack in the field, which Doling [6] estimates may occur at intervals of eight to nine years, may cause losses of about 20 per cent. Losses up to 50 per cent may occur with very susceptible varieties and prolonged attacks. Black rust, *P. graminis*, and brown rust, *P. recondita*, are important locally, but less widely distributed. Rust diseases are controlled by growing resistant varieties and provide the plant breeder with a continuing problem, since they are notoriously prone to develop new physiologic races by hybridisation and mutation in the fungus.

Table 22.2
Losses attributable to leaf diseases in wheat and barley

Crop	Yield [1] cwt ac^{-1} (t ha^{-1})	Mildew (t ha^{-1})	Rust (t ha^{-1})	Others (t ha^{-1})	grown [1]	Acres x 1000 (hectare x 1000) untaken due to Mildew Rust Others
Barley	28.2 (3.54)	18 (2.26)	4 (0.50)	2 (0.25)	5287 (2140)	809 (327) 201 (81) 111 (45)
Wheat	30.5 (3.82)	9 (1.13)	4 (0.50)	2 (0.25)	2171 (878)	176 (71) 82 (33) 41 (17)

(1) Ministry of Agriculture Fisheries and Food, Annual estimates of crop production 1967/68 England and Wales (revised data)

Estimates of the losses caused by cereal leaf diseases are presented in Table 22.2. For barley these are based on James' estimates; the losses due to mildew in wheat have been assessed as half those in barley, a factor which was used by Doling [6]. The losses due to rusts and other leaf diseases in wheat have been assessed as the same as those occurring in barley; this is probably an under-estimate in the case of the rusts. In all, cereal leaf diseases probably account for a loss of 1.3 million acres (0.5 million ha).

The diseases caused by viruses are even less well known than those caused by fungi. Watson [38] described four virus diseases, cereal, or barley yellow dwarf, European wheat striate mosaic, both of which are persistent in their insect vectors, ryegrass mosaic, which is transmitted in sap, and barley false stripe, which is transmitted in seed and pollen. Barley yellow dwarf infects barley, wheat and oats, and seems to be the most serious of these diseases. Watson noted that the history of this virus recalled that of beet yellows, which developed from a curiosity in 1940-42 to a menace by the 1950s. Barley yellow dwarf also infects perennial ryegrass and is widely distributed in that host in England and Wales; of the 112 samples tested by Doodson [9] 104 (93 per cent) were infected and 80 per cent of the infected samples carried a virulent strain. The yield losses that can be caused in barley by a virulent strain depend on the interval between drilling and infection: 37 per cent loss was recorded when infection followed 25 days after drilling, and 19 per cent when the interval was 32 days; the straw was reduced by 40-50 per cent [39]. Strickland estimated the losses at about 7000 acres (2800 ha) [35]; this seems a low estimate for a virus disease which can cause over 30 per cent loss, is widely distributed and can over-winter in a perennial host. There seems every prospect that the disease will intensify and the position worsen, as Watson forecasts.

Our knowledge of the losses caused by insect and fungal attack in pasture is very limited indeed, and practically no attempt is made to control pests and diseases. Strickland [35] estimates that pest control would lead to an increase in yield of 5 to 10 per cent; this would represent about a million untaken acres. Virulent strains of barley yellow dwarf can reduce barley straw by 50 per cent and may well cause a serious reduction in yield of the sward. Grass seed is known to carry pathogenic fungi, and trials with seed dressed with a fungicide in Scotland have shown that establishment can be improved significantly by this treatment [30]. If the importance of disease in grass relative to the pests is comparable to this importance in cereals, an additional 10 to 20 per cent would be a conservative estimate.

Pest and Disease Control

In current practice, the control of diseases which are not carried on the seed rests on the provision of resistant crops or crop varieties, crop rotation and other adjustments of the agricultural system. These, on the whole, are effective, but they impose restrictions on farming which may well contribute to a loss in productivity. In the case of rotations, it should be possible to quantify the loss, but the need to maintain resistance to a number of diseases must also restrict the plant breeder, and it would be interesting to speculate on the possible improvements in yield and quality if these restrictions were removed. Bell [2] has recently reviewed the situation. In present circumstances, reducing the dependence on resistant varieties will involve bringing the use of fungicides for disease control to the same pitch of efficiency as has been achieved with insecticides for pest control. Protectant fungicides have been rejected in cereals on account of the expense of maintaining a protective cover during the growing season of the crop, since this involves repeated spraying to cover new growth. In the small areas under cultivation in Britain, aerial spraying is expensive, and ground spraying in the later stages is unpopular because of the damage caused to the crop.

However, there seems now to be a real prospect of effective systemic fungicides, and two are emerging into the development stage. In this country the most hopeful development is 5-butyl-2-ethylamino-4-hydroxy-6-methyl-pryimidine which is being tested under the code PP149 or the trade name 'Milstem'; this is particularly effective against mildew of barley, and will also control mildew of wheat, oats and various grasses [1]. The second group of chemicals are derivatives of oxathiin, particularly 2,3-dihydro-5-carboxyanilido-6-methyl-1,4-oxathiin, D 735, or 'vitavax' [31] which appear to be particularly effective against basidiomycetes and have given control of a number of rusts and smuts in cereals [3, 12, 21, 26, 29]. This chemical has also given control of smut diseases in a number of grasses [13] and of a seedling disease of cotton [4] caused by *Corticium solani*.

Both these chemicals can be used as conventional eradicant fungicides, but they are most effective when applied either as seed dressings or directly to the soil and taken up by the roots. D 735 has an effective life of only ten to twenty days in the soil [11]; PP 149 is more persistent and may remain effective for twice this time; it is stable and not readily mobile in the soil, possibly because it is bound loosely in the base exchange system. In a series of large scale trials, PP149 gave an average yield increase of over 10 per cent, and increases of over 20 per cent have been recorded; these figures do not conflict with James' estimates of losses. The results offer the encouraging prospect that serious mildew losses may soon be a thing of the past, unless the fungus develops tolerance to the fungicide, which is a possibility with a highly specific chemical like PP 149. D 735 offers some prospect of controlling rusts, the other major leaf diseases, and smuts, particularly the latter, which can be controlled early in the life of the plant.

The prospects for the control of soil borne diseases with chemicals are much less promising, though even in this area there are some leads. D 725 would probably be worth testing against sharp eye-spot. The herbicide diuron appears to have some effect against the foot rot caused by *Cercosporella herpotrichoides*; treatment has resulted in yield increases of 160 per cent in conditions where foot rot was bad [15]; this treatment could well be useful against eyespot, which is caused by the same species.

There is little prospect at the present time of providing a direct control of virus diseases, and control should depend on avoiding infection and reducing the spread of the disease in the crop. Useful control of sugar-beet yellows has been achieved by using insecticides to reduce the spread of the vectors [16]; some of these, such as menazon, can be applied as seed dressings [14]. Similar treatments should certainly be tried for the control of cereal and grass viruses.

There are a variety of very effective insecticides, and it is safe to forecast that the range will increase in the future. Their use, however, is causing some concern probably for four main reasons:

(a) Too many have a broad spectrum of activity and kill predators as readily as they kill pests, and in the absence of predators minor pests can become serious; or a failure of the insecticide may lead to an explosive increase of the major pest.

(b) A few insecticides have proved so persistent that they become a threat to the environment.

(c) The emergence of resistance in the insect populations makes a constant succession of new insecticides essential, and a failure in this succession may be disastrous, especially if natural predators have been killed.

(d) The last cause for worry, which may in fact be the most important, is that the insecticides have allowed agriculturalists to control pests without any deep knowledge of the reasons for their occurrence; in effect, they allow the treatment of symptoms without any enquiry into causes.

The first two of these difficulties can be met within the present framework by allowing the distribution of only the new insecticides that do not accumulate in food chains, and by ensuring that they are specific in their action, either by selecting chemicals that show a narrow spectrum of activity, by using selective methods of application such as seed dressings, or by using systemic chemicals that are only accessible to phytophagous insects.

Developments in chemicals to control diseases of cereals and grass must be supported by a parallel development in the methods of application. The new chemicals are taken from the soil and can be applied either directly to the soil or as seed dressings. Seed dressings have many advantages since the chemical is applied exactly where it is needed and a minimum dose can be used; further, this method of use reduces contamination of the environment to a minimum. An alternative to seed dressing is application of the pesticide in the furrow with the seed, which retains some of the advantages of the seed dressing, but uses rather more material. Either of these methods of application avoids an independent spraying operation and the damage which may accompany it. Seed dressing with a mercury derivative to control seedling infection smuts and a variety of root rots, and an insecticide to control wire worm and bulb fly, are already routine; this type of treatment could in principle, be extended to include an aphicide such as menazon, to reduce the vector spread of virus disease, PP 149 to control mildew and D 725 to control loose smut and rusts. The seed would not carry a conventional dressing which contained all these chemicals in adequate quantities, and alternative methods of treatment such as pelleted seed and applications in the furrow will be required.

To meet all four of the objections listed above, the dependence on chemicals must be reduced to a minimum, possibly by devising systems of integrated control for specific problems. Integrated control of insects is an old concept which is being given a modern dress; its scope has been surveyed recently by Price Jones [27]. It can be defined as pest control which combines and integrates biological and chemical methods, and it must be based on a thorough knowledge of the pest and its interactions with the crop. The use of insecticidal chemicals must be reduced to a minimum, which means the substitution of prophylactic and routine spraying with sprays timed to coincide with the development of epizootics. Parasites and predators must be encouraged or introduced and cultivated. This will preclude the use of blanket sprays with broad spectrum insecticides, and may also involve accepting the damage caused by the small pool of the pest which will be necessary to maintain the predator population. The more specifically insecticidal measures will also be combined with the use of resistant varieties and cultural practices designed to discourage the pests. The novelty here is in the approach to insect control rather than in the introduction of new methods; however, research is also developing new methods whose full potential has yet to be explored, but which will certainly have their part to play. These include chemicals and other stimuli which interfere in various ways with insect behaviour, such as feeding, mating and egg-laying. Induced sterility and genetic manipulation, designed to make the insect populations uncompetitive, also offer a promising line of attack. The release of sterile screw-worm flies has been strikingly successful in eliminating this pest from Curacao and areas of the southern and south-western parts of the United States, but has called for the production of sterile insects on a factory scale and a concerted effort over a large area. These new methods all require a very thorough knowledge of the insect involved and, if total elimination is aimed at, integrated efforts covering ecological units without regard to political boundaries.

Discussion

It seems clear that while the pathologists who are interested in controlling plant diseases are looking forward to a future of more and better fungicides, those who have been concerned with controlling pests and who have had excellent insecticides at their disposal for many years are becoming disillusioned with their dependence on chemicals. It seems fairly safe to forecast that history will repeat itself and that too great a dependence on fungicides will eventually lead to difficulties. The appearance of a mercury-resistant strain of *Pyrenophora avenae* is one indication of this. These difficulties can probably be avoided if the studies on crops and their diseases and pests keep in step with the development of insecticides and fungicides. It should then be possible to evolve systems of integrated control which develop with the available knowledge and avoid the dangers inherent in too great a reliance on any single control measure, whether it be rotation, a resistant variety or an effective chemical. The chemical industry can be relied on to provide new insecticides and fungicides as long as there are worthwhile problems which require solution, but it will probably fall to the Government to sponsor the supporting biological work.

If overall productivity is to become a national aim, research must be concentrated on problems which account for the largest number of 'untaken acres'. These can be defined by surveys and assessments of disease losses, and will probably be found in the crops which occupy the greatest areas of land, the arable crops and grassland. The extent to which the present distribution of research effort meets this requirement is indicated in Table 22.3. The figures in this table cannot be taken too seriously. They were compiled from lists of the staffs of the institutes, and assume that all the plant pathologists were listed as such and that their interests were identical with the advertised interests of the research institute. Further, they cover only a limited sector of the research field. However, these figures probably give a reasonable indication of the balance of effort and suggest a need for a considerable increase in support for agriculture and grassland.

Table 22.3
Distribution of plant pathologists (working with pests and diseases) in State Aided Research Institutes

Crop group	Cultivated area ac x 10^6	(ha x 10^6)	Number of pathologists
Horticulture	1	(0.40)	74
Agriculture	10	(4.0)	
Grassland	18	(7.3)	60
Rough grazing	17	(6.9)	

Research effort is only of economic value when it is translated into practice. This will not simply involve providing support from development and extension services, it will also involve ensuring that the farmer does not have to pay more for treatment than he is likely to gain from increased yield. One difficulty in controlling plant disease in relatively low-priced crops is that the returns will seldom reward the effort and expense laid out by the farmers. However, this should not obscure the cumulative losses to the country in terms of unproductive land, the potential yield of which is now replaced by imports.

Summary

Consideration of area under cultivation and our present information on crop losses lead to the conclusion that major increases in productivity will arise from the control of pests and diseases in arable crops, particularly cereals, cultivated grassland and rough grazing. There is some information on the magnitude of losses suffered by cereals; the most important are probably due to leaf diseases, particularly mildew; soil-borne diseases are controlled reasonably effectively by crop rotation and other agricultural practices, and virus diseases appear to have a restricted distribution. Pests are well controlled at present by insecticides. There is almost no information on the losses suffered in grassland. Two new systemic fungicides offer some prospect of control of cereal leaf diseases; both are taken up by the roots and distributed in the transpiration stream.

The effectiveness of current insecticides has led to an almost complete dependence on chemicals for pest control, and the advent of more efficient and specific fungicides may encourage the same tendency in the control of diseases. This dependence is dangerous, since any breakdown in the chemical treatment renders the crops vulnerable to attack; the risk of a total breakdown in protection is best avoided by developing systems of integrated control, reducing the use of chemicals to a minimum, and taking full advantage of biological factors to reduce pests and diseases. These systems of integrated control will require an intensive study of the biology of crops and their diseases and pests, and of the effect of chemicals on the whole biological system.

REFERENCES

1. ANON, 'pp. 149, A new systemic fungicide for the control of cereal powdery mildew', *Plant Protection Ltd. Bracknell, Berks.*, 1969.
2. BELL, G.D.H. 'Plant breeding for crop improvement in Britain: methods, achievements and objectives', *Proc. R. Soc.*, 1968, B 171, 145-173.
3. BORUM, D.E. and SINCLAIR, J.B. 'Systemic activity of 2,3-dihydro-5-carboxanilido-6-methy-4-oxathiin (Vitavax) against *Rhizoctonia solani* in cotton seedlings', *Phytopathology*, 1967, 57, 805.
4. BORUM, D.E. and SINCLAIR, J.B. 'Evidence of systemic protection against *Rhizoctonia solani* with 'Vitavax' in cotton seedlings', *Phytopathology*, 1968, 58, 976-980.
5. COTTEN, J. 'A comparison of cereal root eelworm resistant and susceptible genotypes at two sites', *Ann. appl. Biol.*, 1967, 59, 407-413.
6. DOLING, D.A. 'The incidence and economic importance of cereal disease', *Proc. Brit. Insecticide and Fungicide Conf.*, 1963, 2, 27-34.
7. DOLING, D.A. 'Loose smut in wheat and barley', *Agriculture*, 1966, 73, 523-527.
8. DOLING, D.A. and DOODSON, J.K. 'The effect of yellow rust on the yield of spring and winter wheat', *Trans. Br. mycol. Soc.*, 1968, 51, 427-434.
9. DOODSON, J.K. 'A survey of barley yellow-dwarf virus in S 24 perennial ryegrass in England and Wales, 1966', *Pl. Path.*, 1967, 16, 42-45.
10. DOODSON, J.K., MANNERS, J.G. and MYERS, A. 'Some effects of yellow rust (*Puccinia striiformis*) on the growth and yield of a spring wheat', *Ann. Bot. N.S.*, 1964, 28, 459-472.
11. EDGINGTON, L.V. and CORKE, C. 'Biological decomposition of an oxathiin fungicide', *Phytopathology*, 1967, 57, 810.
12. EDGINGTON, L.V. and KEINBERGS, E. 'Control of loose smut in Barley with systemic fungicides', *Can. J. Pl. Sci.*, 1966, 46, 336.
13. HARDISON, J.R. 'Chemotherapeutic control of stripe smut (*Ustilago striiformis*) in grasses by two derivatives of 1,4-oxathiin', *Phytopathology*, 1967, 57, 242-245.
14. HEATHCOTE, G.D. 'The use of menazon seed dressing to decrease spread of virus yellow in sugar-beet root crops', *Ann. appl. Biol.*, 1968, 62, 113-118.
15. HUBER, D.M., SEELY, C.I. and WATSON, R.D. 'Non-fungicidal control of root rot of winter wheat with the herbicide diuron', *Phytopathology*, 1968, 58, 1054.

16. HULL, R. and HEATHCOTE, G.D. 'Experiments on the time of application of insecticide to decrease the spread of yellowing viruses of sugar-beet, 1954-66', *Ann. appl. Biol.*, 1967, **60**, 469-478.

17. JAMES, W.C. 'Survey of foliar diseases of spring barley in England and Wales in 1967', *Ann. appl. Biol.*, 1969, **63**, 253-263.

18. LARGE, E.C. and DOLING, D.A. 'The measurement of cereal mildew and its effect on yield', *Pl. Path.*, 1962, **11**, 47-57.

19. LARGE, E.C. and DOLING, D.A. 'Effect of mildew on yield of winter wheat', *Pl. Path.*, 1963, **12**, 128-130.

20. MANNERS, J.G. 'The rust diseases of wheat and their control', *Trans. Br. mycol. Soc.*, 1969, **52**, 177-186.

21. MAUDE, R. and SHURING, C.G. 'Preliminary studies on the use of new seed treatments for the control of loose smut of barley', *Pl. Path.*, 1968, **17**, 155-157.

22. NOBLE, M., MACGARVIE, Q.D., HAMS, A.F. and LEAFE, E.L. 'Resistance to mercury of *Pyrenophora avenae* in Scottish seed oats', *Pl. Path.*, 1966, **15**, 23-28.

23. OLD, K.M. 'Mercury tolerant *Pyrenophora avenae* in seed oats', *Trans. Br. mycol. Soc.*, 1968, **51**, 525-534.

24. ORDISH, G. *Untaken Harvest*, Constable, 1952.

25. PITT, D. 'Studies on sharp eyespot disease of cereals. III, Effects of disease on the wheat host and the incidence of disease in the field', *Ann. appl. Biol.*, 1966, **58**, 229-308.

26. POWELSON, R.L. and SHANER, G.E. 'An effective seed treatment for systemic control of seedling infection of wheat by stripe rust (*Puccinia striiformis*)', *Plant. Dis. Reptr.*, 1966, **50**, 806-807.

27. PRICE JONES, D. 'New horizons in insect control', *Chemy. Ind.*, 1967, 770-774.

28. ROSSER, W.R. and CHADBURN, B.L. 'Cereal diseases and their effects on intensive wheat cropping in the East Midland Region, 1963-65', *Pl. Path.*, 1968, **17**, 51-60.

29. ROWELL, J.B. 'Control of leaf and stem rust of wheat by an 1,4-oxathiin derivative', *Plant Dis. Reptr.*, 1967, **51**, 336-339.

30. SANGSTER, H.M. 'Disease and herbage seeds', *Farming Review*, 1967, **31**, (Scottish Agricultural Ind.) 26-28.

31. SCHMELING, B. von and KULKA, M. 'Systemic fungicide activity of 1,4-oxathiin derivatives', *Science, N.Y.*, 1966, **152**, 659-660.

32. SLOPE, B.D. 'Disease problems of intensive cereal growing', *Ann. appl. Biol.*, 1967, **59**, 317-319.

33. SOUTHNEY, J.F. 'Survey of cereal root eelworm in England and Wales', *Pl. Path.*, 1954, **4**, 98-102.

34. STRICKLAND, A.H. 'Frit-fly attack and yield of oats', *Ann. appl. Biol.*, 1958, **46**, 486-493.

35. STRICKLAND, A.H. 'Pest control and productivity in British Agriculture', *J.R. Soc. Arts.*, 1965, **113**, 5102.

36. STRICKLAND, A.H. 'Some costs of insect damage and crop protection', *Proc. F.A.O. Symposium on Integrated Pest Control,* 1966, 1, 75-88.
37. STRICKLAND, A.H. 'Some problems in the economic integration of crop loss control', *Proc. Br. Insecticide and Fungicide Conf.,* 1967, 2, 478-491.
38. WATSON, M.A. 'Cereal viruses in Britain', *N.A.A.S. Quart. Rev.,* 1959, 43, 93-102.
39. WATSON, M.A. and MULLIGAN, T.E. 'Comparison of two barley yellow-dwarf viruses in glasshouse and field experiments', *Ann. appl. Biol.,* 1960, 48, 559-574.

23. Mechanization

K.E. Morgan
Department of Agriculture, University of Reading.

Introduction

Mechanization as such can make little contribution to increasing potential crop yields — indeed, the usual effects are often smaller yields than those which can be obtained by careful handwork. However, mechanization can increase the scale of crop production and can make cropping economically and physically possible in conditions which would otherwise be prohibitive for example in high-wage industrialized economies or in thinly populated areas. Mechanization can also reduce the physical effort involved in crop production, and can increase crop utilization by reducing losses in harvested stored products.

The mechanization of crop production is dependent on and is part of agricultural engineering, which can in fact contribute directly to the increase of crop yields, for example by the on-line optimization of plant environments. Mechanization is merely the substitution of machines for human labour; agricultural engineering includes this substitution but is also concerned with facilities, equipment and techniques which are beyond the replacement of human effort, which are outside the range of human capabilities and for which there are no non-engineering substitutes. The distinction should be obvious, but experience shows that it is often not recognized, any more than is the difference between a mechanic and an engineer. However, having established this distinction, it can be seen that, in the context of realizing the potential production of a crop, agricultural engineering may be very important. The emphasis in the present chapter will be on British agricultural engineering, which will naturally align itself to the requirements of British agriculture. Thus there are two main sections in this chapter — the first is concerned with some specific developments and research projects in agricultural engineering, while the second is concerned with the present and future state of research, development and production in this country.

Current Research and Development

The need for agricultural physics (as opposed to physics for agriculturists) as one of the sciences underlying agricultural engineering has been emphasized [8]. It was suggested that agricultural physics was a proper subject for research and could develop into a coherent teaching discipline. Today a great deal of work is going on in the U.S.A., for example, at the University of Purdue, and it is hoped that the idea will become accepted in this country.

A case has also been made for instrumentation [10], automatic tractors [7], ergonomics [11, 12, 13], automation [9, 15], systems [16], and so on. All these ideas have now become respectable. The National Institute of Agricultural Engineering has an instrumentation department and the Scientific Instrument Manufacturers Association Agricultural Instrument Group has been in existence for five years. It is accepted that we can monitor machine performance, e.g. the grain loss monitor on combine harvesters [14, 17], that we can build decision-making logic equipment, and that we can monitor some aspects of animal health and some aspects of plant growth. We have not gone as far nor as fast as was hoped — indeed in some ways we have still not generally appreciated Gilmour's paper [3] on the subject. Nevertheless if the biologists and husbandrymen can define what they want to measure and how accurately they need to measure, suitable instruments can and will be devised.

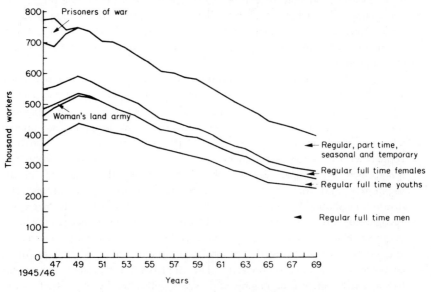

Fig. 23.1   Change in the size of the agricultural labour force, 1945-67. (M.A.F.F. June Censuses, England and Wales.)

Automatic tractors are more than respectable, they are commercial. Leader-cable guidance systems are in operation in the U.S.S.R. and the U.S.A., and many people will have read about the Autotrack Systems Ltd. system which was demonstrated at the Royal Show (1919). Opinions expressed in various papers dating from 1958 remain unchanged. Automatic tractors are economically justifiable and technically feasible. Even without the economic advantages they offer, automatic tractors will be forced on us by the unavailability of labour (Figure 23.1). Leader-cable systems still seem ideal for carting and transport and for operations in orchards and vineyards.

Doubts have been expressed about the suitability of leader-cable guidance for fieldwork, and these doubts remain even though the systems have gained commercial acceptance.

The Autotrack system, in which the sensing head is positioned directly above the guiding wire, needs wires laid at 18 ft (550 cm) centres; the programme must be synthesized and the tractor can only work parallel to the wires. Brooke [1] has described the system developed at Reading in which the sensing head works between wires, where wires spaced at 120 ft (36.5 m) centres are 'embarrassingly close', where the tractor can work in any direction and can either 'learn' its job from a human operator or can accept a synthesized programme. This system has a lead over those of the other universities, research institutes and commercial organizations now working on automatic tractor control. Nevertheless it is felt that the Reading University/ International Harvester Company of Great Britain Ltd. system is only an intermediate stage in the automation of field world, and that by the end of the century it will have been superseded by some form of beacon system.

Now that the ergonomics of agricultural machinery has been fashionable, tractor design appears to be open to change. It is ironic that design teams in the U.S.A., in the U.S.S.R. and in this country are suggesting 'tractors of the future' which have such a strong resemblance to the toolcarrier described in 1958 [6, 11, 12]. In practice, however, the situation is not so fluid. Most of our tractor production capacity is owned by foreign firms, most of the design comes from abroad and, even given the ideal 'tractor of the future', any British firm will find it very difficult either to bring about radical changes in a design which has congealed or to break into a market which is monopolized by two organizations.

With housed animals and intensively-grown plants, we now have the ability to pre-determine and maintain temperature, humidity, radiation levels, oxygen and carbon dioxide concentration, air speed and day length. The chief difficulties are to discover from the biologists the exact values required, and commercially to justify the present costs of the equipments involved. In some circumstances, e.g. where input parameters are uncertain but where outputs can be readily measured, it should be technically possible to arrange on-line optimization of environments. In other cases it may be necessary to write mathematical models of animals or plants before we can optimize their environments.

This line of thought leads to the Systems approach. The validity of a Systems approach has already been accepted in many industrial activities. However, in spite of several papers [2, 4, 19] on the subject, it is doubtful whether the Systems philosophy is wholly accepted — or indeed wholly understood — in agriculture and agricultural engineering in this country. A vast amount of work is being published in America and is being taken up elsewhere, though it seems that the only countries at present able to benefit from a Systems approach would be the U.S.A. and Canada, Australia and possibly New Zealand, Israel, Denmark and Great Britain.

'Systems' can be mis-interpreted in several ways. Manufacturers of farm machinery use the term as a synonym of 'machine compatibility', which it is not. Machine compatibility, e.g. the fact that a tractor, a forage harvester and a self-unloading trailer may be easily connected to form an efficient, integrated harvesting unit, is only one very small part of a system. Farm mechanization specialists regard 'Systems' as meaning the use of computers to select machines for farms to provide integrated equipment to carry out some

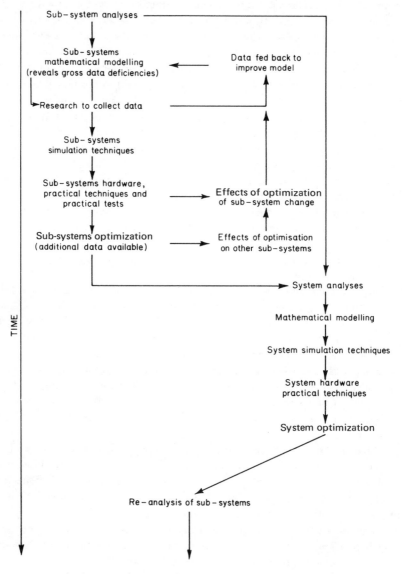

Fig. 23.2   The 'Systems' approach.

particular enterprise. This again is only one very small part of a Systems approach. Many agricultural engineers seem to think that the use of computers is Systems-thinking, though the truth is that the computer is a tool in Systems-thinking in much the same way as a slide-rule is a tool in machine design. Figure 23.2, taken from a previous paper [16] is an attempt to illustrate the author's interpretation of Systems thinking in agricultural engineering. The main stages are shown as a progression which is set out alongside some implied time-scale.

Properly carried out, this exercise would not lead to the isolated development of harvesting equipment, for example for oranges. It would lead to a series of models, beginning, perhaps, with the genetic potential of orange trees, with intermediate models of planting distances, irrigation regimes and harvesting requirements and ending with a study of whether the oranges should be sold in London in their skins, or pulped and packed in polyethylene containers — or indeed whether it would be 'better' to market orange-flavoured coloured water with added ascorbic acid. 'Better' might mean 'more profitable', 'yielding more energy', 'yielding more protein' or 'making the most work for the unemployed' — but it is clearly necessary to define the objective before running the model.

This approach would lead to requirement specifications being written for the machines involved in the system — performance criteria, bracketed costs and so on. Given this specification, any competent engineer could design the machine, confident that it would have a genuinely useful role, in contrast to the present situation where machines are often designed to do unnecessary jobs more efficiently. Similarly a Systems approach could do a great deal to rationalize research.

Many people are reluctant to construct mathematical models because complete data is unavailable. A rough model full of approximations and assumptions is better than none. Even writing the flow diagram is a useful exercise and may make it unnecessary to proceed with the subsequent computation. The rough model can easily be tested against the real-life situation and its deficiencies will be revealed, though many approximate models have been found to work better in practice than could have been presupposed. The deficiencies in the model will indicate where more data is required. To collect this data, new instruments and new techniques will be needed.

Examples of this can be seen in the animal 'tagging' project. At present pigs are weighed weekly, each pig is identified by its ear tag, its number and weight are manually recorded, and the records are brought together for analysis. Unfortunately some tags are lost, others become indecipherable. This is time-consuming and expensive, weighing is slow, the pigs are disturbed by the procedure, some records are mislaid and the results are never analysed because of the time it would take. Anyone with experience of field research will recognise these problems.

Of course, automatic weighing machines are available which record as a punched code on paper tape. This can then be fed into the computer for analysis. For recording other essential data, e.g. the pig's number or its feeding regime, a portable general-purpose tape punch has been designed. This is an interim measure which at least produces computer-compatible information direct, eliminating the mistakes of manual entries in a record book and the subsequent work of translation into punched tape.

Work is now in progress aimed at producing a small transponder which can be injected into the skin of the pig or clipped inside its ear, so that when the pig steps onto the weighing machine the transponder is automatically interrogated. It then identifies the animal, whose number is punched on the tape at the same time as its weight. This has obvious implications for the automatic feeding and recording of dairy cows, and so on, but another development is likely to intervene. Techniques have been devised for recording data on ¼ in. magnetic tape on a cheap domestic tape recorder, with accuracies better than 1 in 1×10^4, by measuring parameters directly as frequency modulation, rather than using voltage-to-frequency conversions. The tape recorder has been interfaced with a PDP 8 computer, a small 4K-store digital machine, and for many reasons this is preferred to a punched tape system.

This example of new instruments and techniques flowing from an attempt to model pigs is a real-life case. There is no reason why the techniques — and indeed some of the hardware — should not be used to collect and analyse data from crops.

Modelling and simulation techniques are proving indispensable in another project. It is intended to build an improved Stirling [18] engine, but neither sufficient money nor time is available to run a development programme, building a series of progressively improved versions. A Stirling engine simulation programme has been written to run on a large digital computer, which makes it possible to alter design parameters instantaneously and at will. Much of the initial information in the programme was merely informed guesswork, but an instrumented scale-model of the engine has now been built. A PDP 8 has been bought to run on-line with the scale model, collecting and analysing the data it produces. These results can be incorporated in the simulation programme, replacing the guesswork with facts and allowing the design of a full-scale engine to be optimised before construction begins. It is unnecessary to emphasize how much time and money can be saved by these methods.

It is believed that this engine will replace the internal combustion engine in many applications, especially in view of the difficulties inherent in reviving steam engines for automative applications and the apparent lack of commercial future for the fuel cell.

The Stirling is a multi-fuel design, running on any source of heat. It is an external combustion engine, producing $\frac{1}{10} - \frac{1}{100}$ part of the atmospheric pollution produced by internal combustion engines. It is silent, self-starting and can be free from electrics. It is more efficient than a comparable diesel and has excellent power/weight and power/volume ratios. The power density is high and the speed/torque characteristics are reminiscent of steam engines, with maximum torque occurring at very low speeds. For this reason it may be possible to dispense with clutches and gearboxes in automative applications. Figures have been published [5] showing that the full-scale engines can run for 10 000 hours at full power between services, but these figures can easily be doubled. This would be equivalent to driving a car flat out for about 1¼ million miles (2 million km) between services. The Stirling cycle is reversible, and one machine can act as a prime mover, a cryogenerator or a heat pump. It must be part of the future of mechanization.

From computer-designed engines to tape seeding machines seems a long step down to earth, but this is another development which appears to have a future. Tape seeding techniques are useful in under-developed areas because the peasant farmer can have the benefits of precision seeding without incurring the cost of a drill, and the authorities can control seed type and variety. In advanced countries, the technique enables one machine to handle any type of seed, and the tape-laying machines lend themselves to automatic control and monitoring. The system also has considerable advantages for some research purposes.

It may also help another pipe-dream to come true — the construction of a machine which can identify crop plants and distinguish them from weeds — though as yet there are only the vaguest ideas as to how this may be done. However, there is no great point in thinking enthusiastically about the future unless one feels that there is a future. In the past, technological progress depended on invention and demonstrable economic benefits. Today ideas are the cheapest commodity on the market, advertising is often more important than research and development, the 'not invented here' complex appears more widespread and the economics of industrial progress can be the plaything of politics.

The Future

It seems that there are several situations which encourage rapid technological advance. One is to be at war, when technological development is demanded whatever the cost. The second situation is that which obtains in the Soviet Union. There a strongly structured technocracy controls a system where technological advance is not subordinated to short-term profit. A third situation can be found typically in the U.S.A. where in general profits are not subservient to politics, and where technical advance can earn financial reward.

Similarly there are situations which inhibit technological advance, many of which can be found in Britain today. First, our economic system seems to fall between the two extreme systems operating in Russia and America. The structure of our present taxation system neither allows wholly state-financed research, development and production nor encourages adventurous capital. British industry is slow to adopt new ideas because development is expensive, it reduces short-term profits and no shareholder can afford to remain faithfull to a company during the lean years if he knows that he will be heavily taxed if and when the fat years come. Furthermore, at present interest rates, few companies can afford to tie up funds in a development project unless it can be shown in advance that the project will 'break even' in less than five years. Few really new departures are likely to become profitable in this period. Consequently there is almost no industrial research and development in agricultural engineering in this country, and very little non-industrial research.

The future of farming depends on internal and external politics. Agriculture is becoming a politically unimportant industry. In any case, the State already holds most of the effective controls, through Price Reviews, subsidies, marketing boards, acreage quotas, through pressures exerted on banks, through company taxation, death duties and an increasing number of quasi-governmental commissions and committee. The decision whether, for instance, to turn the whole country into a national park and to subsidize farming in order to keep rural areas neat and presentable, or at the other extreme to let agriculture become more efficient by using asbestos-cement buildings, pylons and factory-farming methods, is basically a political one; as are the decisions whether or not to exclude farms from the proposed Wealth Tax, and whether to increase or decrease imports and foodstuffs. There is a danger that we may be protecting our out-worn, non-competitive heavy industries at the same time as we are opting out of the higher technologies, so that agricultural engineering will no longer benefit from the spin-off we might have obtained from a space project or a thriving aircraft industry. We are providing aid for underdeveloped countries, while we starve our own technological developments.

In the Department of Applied Physical Sciences at Reading, for instance, there are many exciting projects. One of these is concerned with graphical communication with digital computers, another is concerned with punched-tape control of machine tools. It requires little imagination to visualize these two projects being linked together, so that the creative designer could produce engineering components, sub-assemblies or even complete machines, with little need for draughtsmen, model shops, personnel officers or men on the shop floor. If this project ever came to fruition, the rise in productivity would be enormous, and the reduction in costs would make exports not merely competitive but positively aggressive; however, it would pose considerable social problems. Similarly if agricultural engineering produced a device which displaced most paid farm-workers – a really major technological advance – it would stand little chance of going into service because of its profound social repercussions. It is somewhat ironic that, in an age of automation, the Selective Employment Tax was deliberately devised to drive people out of the leisure and service industries, which are often impossible to automate, into the manufacturing industries, which could and should be automated.

The innate conservatism of farmers may well hinder the adoption of new techniques and equipment, and in the present economic climate, unless a quick sales build-up seems likely, this new equipment will never be produced. The structure of British agriculture makes rapid changes unlikely; the structure of the agricultural engineering industry accentuates the problem. We have a few very large manufacturing organizations, all of whom have too much money invested in their assembly lines to be willing to change their product. Most of the remainder of the industry consists of small companies which cannot employ the specialists necessary to keep abreast of modern technology. The large companies are American or Canadian and prefer to carry out research and development in their home countries. The small British companies cannot finance research programmes and would find it difficult to exploit state-financed research. The N.A.A.S. machinery officers have only an advisory function, the N.I.A.E. has a somewhat restricted area of influence and activity, and in all our universities we have but one department of agricultural engineering. Unless conditions undergo some radical change, it is doubtful whether agricultural engineering has any long-term future in Britain — as an industry, as a profession, as a research study or as a teaching discipline. The social and political environment has changed since the promising, expansionist years in the mid-1950s, and the rate of deterioration has accelerated during the past five years. Our export sales continue to break records, partly because of earlier developments, partly through devaluation, partly because of our relatively cheap labour. However, export figures should not be allowed to mask the increasing level of imports, the foreign ownership of some of the biggest exporting companies and the dearth of new developments coming forward for manufacture in the 1970s. We are now at the point where it seems we shall become increasingly dependent on American hardware — tailored to North American requirements and not necessarily suited to our conditions. Techniques and software will continue to be produced for a longer period, because they involve less investment and we are still an inventive people. Inputs from peripheral industries — fertilizers, instruments, oil and fuel — will continue longer still. But in the end, if we continue on our present course, there is little to stop us becoming a cheap labour pool for some technically advanced country.

Nationally, we have lost one of the basic indentification marks of an industrially pre-eminent country — we no longer have cheap power. We have lost one of the main advantages of industrial pre-eminence — we no longer have a particularly high standard of living. We find more and more things which we, as a nation, can no longer afford to do. Our production is stagnating and our comparative rate of invention is declining.

Clearly other industries are finding themselves in similar difficulties, where the solution lies for these other industries is outside the scope of the present chapter and the competence of the author to discuss. However, it is pertinent to suggest measures which would help to arrest, and maybe reverse, the present decline in agricultural engineering in this country.

The main hope for the industry must lie in a series of mergers and takeovers. If some of the many small companies could be combined into half-a-dozen middle-sized organizations in the £15 to £25 million range production could be rationalised, markets could be consolidated, selling could be made more effective and spares and servicing could be made economic. Such companies could employ better managements, could justify more qualified engineers and specialists able to keep the organization up-to-date, could make more impact on overseas markets, might fund modest research and development programmes and could certainly exploit state-financed development.

It would be essential to support this re-structured industry with state-financed research and development. Projects would need to have commercial potential as well as scientific validity and would have to be sufficiently advanced to ensure sales of licences, export sales and sales in this country against foreign competition. Licensing and consultancy fees from *one* steel-making process, for instance, earns more foreign currency for Austria than any other single activity, including the tourist industry. Export sales must be made in advanced countries, (a) because advanced countries can buy sophisticated equipment with high know-how/materials ratios and which incur low proportional freight charges, and (b) because markets in emergent countries are not developing. This slow market expansion is a fundamental problem in the tractor industry, which is already suffering from excess production capacity. Clearly, the research complex producing this research and development should be efficient and should cost as little as possible to set up. Finally, since research and development must come before production, the establishment of a suitable research complex should not wait for the re-structuring of the industry — indeed, its establishment might well be the catalyst required to bring about the industrial change.

Some of the ingredients for a really effective research complex are already in existence. The Department of Agricultural Engineering in the University of Newcastle is justifiably world-famous for its work on, for example, terrain/vehicle systems. Much of the basic research in the more traditional areas of agricultural engineering could be carried out at Newcastle, though this would imply some expansion of that department. A second university department would be necessary to cover the newer areas of agricultural engineering research — for example, Automation, Systems and Control. Allowing for possible bias on the part of the author, a logical location for this department would seem to be in the University of Reading. There it could provide a link between the existing Faculty of Agriculture and the rapidly developing Department of Applied Physical Sciences, which already includes Chairs for Engineering Science, Cybernetics and Instrument Physics and Materials Technology, and has commercially-funded research units in Instrument Physics and Tribology, and diverse research interests in automation and control.

Two university departments could cover much of the area of basic research — including the more speculative projects — in agricultural engineering. Some basic research, most of the development of projects showing commercial promise, and all product testing, could be left to the N.I.A.E., though this should be moved to a university with a strong agricultural faculty and close links with other relevant research institutes. This would give the N.I.A.E. ready access to specialist academic and research staff in a wide range of disciplines, from animal physiology through geology and applied statistics to plant genetics, and from 'whisker' reinforced metals through gas turbine design to aerodynamics. It would also provide the N.I.A.E. with land, crops and livestock necessary for research, and would ensure adequate computing facilities.

Finally, it might help to relax the somewhat rigid organization and terms of reference under which the N.I.A.E. now operates, facilitating staff movements into and out of the Institute, allowing closer liaison with industry and re-establishing interests in foreign agricultures.

Behind this re-organization it would be desirable to have a strengthened National Research Development Corporation, having closer connections with the Ministry of Technology. The N.R.D.C. ought to control National Inventions Workshops along the lines suggested by Professor Thring [20], and it would be relatively simple to ensure liaison between the N.I.W. and the N.I.A.E. where new developments appeared to have implications for agricultural engineering.

Of course, these proposals are grossly over-simplified and are necessarily brief and generalized. No criticism of the personnel in any existing company or establishment is intended or implied. It is the present system — or perhaps the lack of system — which is at fault. Certainly difficulties would arise before these measures could be implemented, but these difficulties are largely political and organizational, rather than technical, and many of them are artificial. Certainly there would be side-effects arising from these measures; several small research establishments would gravitate towards one or other of the universities as would the National College of Agricultural Engineering. But the difficulties and sacrifices involved would be small compared with the benefits which would be obtained if the future agricultural engineering in Britain, with all its implications for British agriculture, could be guaranteed.

REFERENCES

1. BROOKE, D.W.I. 'Off-the-wire guidance for leader-cable vehicles', *Winter Meeting, Am. Soc. Agric. Engrs., Chicago,* 1968, paper 68, 619.
2. COALES, J.F. 'An outline of systems engineering', *J. Proc. Instn. Agric. Engrs.* 1969, 24, 13-24.
3. GILMOUR, W.D. 'Some applications of electronic equipment to agriculture', *Agric. Hort. Engng Abstr.,* 1960, 11, 2.
4. HUNT, D.R. 'A systems approach to farm machinery selection', *J. Proc. Instn. Agric. Engrs.,* 1969, 24, 25-30.

5. MEIJER, R.J. *The Philips Stirling Engine* Philips Research Laboratories, N.V. Philips, Eindhoven, 1967.

6. MORGAN, K.E. 'The steering of wheeled tractors', *J. Proc. Instn. Br. Agric. Engrs.*, 1958, 14, 1, 38-40.

7. MORGAN, K.E. 'The automatic tractor — its background and future', *Fm. Mechanics.*, 1959, 11, 164-166.

8. MORGAN, K.E. 'Electronics in agriculture', Unpubl. paper presented to Oxford Farming Conference, Oxford, 1960.

9. MORGAN, K.E. 'The future of farm automation', *New Scient.*, 1961, 11, 581-583.

10. MORGAN, K.E. 'Instruments for agriculture', Unpubl. paper presented to S.I.M.A., London, 1962.

11. MORGAN, K.E. 'The agricultural tractor — some unorthodox concepts', *J. Proc. Instn. Agric. Engrs.*, 1964, 20, 102-112.

12. MORGAN, K.E. 'Unorthodoxy in tractor design', *New Scient.*, 1965, 28, 668-671.

13. MORGAN, K.E. 'Design and function of the agricultural tractor', *Wld. Crops*, 1965, 17, 68-71.

14. MORGAN, K.E. 'Improvements in combine harvesters', British Patent Application 38280/5, filed 8 Sept. 1965.

15. MORGAN, K.E. 'Automation in agriculture', *Outl. Agric.*, 1965, 4, 295-301.

16. MORGAN, K.E. 'Future fields of research for agricultural engineers', Paper presented to International Colloquium, V.U.Z.T., Prague, 1968.

17. MORGAN, K.E. 'Aids to efficient combining', *Pwr. Fmg.*, 1968, 41, 21.

18. MORGAN, K.E. 'Patent 4081 of 1816', *Esso Fmr.*, 1969, 21, 18-22.

19. O'CALLAGHAN, 'The systems approach to engineering design', *J. Proc. Instn. agric. Engrs.*, 1969, 24, 31-6.

20. THRING, M.W. 'A workshop for inventions', *New Scient.*, 1969, 32, 576-577.

24. Chemical Control of Plant Growth

B.J. Heywood
May and Baker Ltd., Dagenham.

This chapter will consider the chemical control of plant growth, including both herbicides and plant growth regulators, from the point of view of a commercial organisation wishing to discover and sell a particular chemical at a profit. The detailed comments do not however, necessarily represent the views of the pesticide industry in general, nor those of one company in particular.

Herbicides

The farmer or grower in Britain has the choice of fifty-eight chemically different herbicides given in the 1969 Ministry of Agriculture list of officially approved products [7]. In a particular crop, his choice is more restricted, often to only a few chemicals. For example, in a major crop such as wheat, he has a choice of nineteen herbicides, while in less extensive crops, such as celery, there are only two herbicides on the approved list. In a particular crop situation there will usually be one or two dominant weeds which cause serious damage to the crop, and the grower must select the herbicide appropriately, so that now his choice becomes very limited. For example, there are only two approved herbicides to control the very serious weed problem of wild oats in cereals. Of course, by the use of mixtures of herbicides, usually provided by the manufacturer as a 'cocktail', a wider range of weeds can be controlled. The choice of such products, usually under a brand name, is naturally greater.

The range of herbicides can, however, be increased if the farmer relies on the manufacturer's recommendations, for not all herbicides which have been registered — that is, cleared as being safe for use from the point of view of the operator, and the consumer of the treated foodstuff, either man or domestic animals or wildlife — have reached the status of being placed on the approved list. Obtaining approval takes time — perhaps two or more seasons of commercial use — so there are, of necessity, some herbicides in the pipeline pending the accumulation of evidence of satisfactory performance. In certain cases a manufacturer may not wish to apply for approval. Even with these registered, but unapproved herbicides [8], the total number available for use in Britain is still quite small — about eighty.

This figure can be compared with the 139 different chemicals listed as herbicides and plant growth regulators in the current issue of 'Weed Abstracts', or with over 250 chemically new herbicides described by manufacturers in the technical literature over the past ten years throughout the world. It may be pointed out that it is rare to find a chemical so specific in its action in a weed/crop situation that it only has value in one limited temperate or tropical territory. We have, therefore, the situation in Britain that less than half of the chemicals used as herbicides in some part of the world are available for use by our farmers and growers, in fact, probably less than thirty are used in substantial amounts.

At the Weed Research Organization (W.R.O.) at Oxford some twenty-five chemicals are received each year for further evaluation [1]. These are chemicals which have already been shown by the manufacturer to be active as herbicides. Nearly 200 new herbicides have been received from industry by the W.R.O. during the period 1960 to 1968; and since the W.R.O. is probably the largest single, non-commercial organisation in the world specialising in weed control, it is more than likely that the great majority of all new herbicides are sent to them. The success in the search for new herbicides on a global basis is therefore about twenty-five commercially interesting compounds per year. Of course, not all of these chemicals submitted to the W.R.O. will emerge as marketed products. It is the experience of those engaged in the search for new pesticides that only one compound in about 5000 merits commercial development; this figure varies from 1 in 2000 for the more successful, or perhaps lucky, research teams to 1 in over 10 000 for the less fortunate teams, but 1 in about 5000 is generally accepted as an average figure. Thus, each year, not less than 125 000 compounds are prepared and screened for herbicidal activity throughout the world, or over one million compounds since 1960.

The non-chemist may be dismayed to realize that there is virtually no limit to the number of compounds which the chemist can prepare; many more millions can be made before the chemist's output is restricted. The cost of making and testing so many compounds is enormous. For example, it is estimated that the average cost of finding a potentially interesting herbicide is about £500 000. By and large, this expenditure must be recouped from the sale of herbicides, and so the research item is a very appreciable cost-factor to be included when the selling price of a new herbicide is being calculated. The cost of making and discarding the 4999 other compounds must be borne by the one commercialized product.

With the increased emphasis on safety studies, it may now take four to eight years before a new product is launched, so that the £½ million employed to find the new herbicide becomes £¾ million before the product is on the market. With the cost of the safety studies, the cost of development of a new pesticide is, therefore, likely to be over £1 million. If the manufacturer considers that he must recover his research and development expenditure at the rate of 10 per cent on the selling price, he must therefore look for a total market of not less than £10 000 000. Further, if the commercial life of the new herbicide is seven years, then the manufacturer can only consider markets in which the potential sales are over £1.5 million per year. By any standards this represents a substantial market for a herbicide, and so the manufacturer is forced to the conclusion that only very serious and widespread weed problems justify a programme for the research and development staff having a planned specific objective. This is perhaps a blessing in disguise for the research man, as at the present state of our knowledge, we just do not know how to tackle a specific objective in a logical way with any real guarantee of success. We cannot, for example, devise from our fundamental knowledge a compound which will control blackgrass in cereals. The best the research man can do is to note what compounds or, more properly, what class of compounds possess activity in a particular weed/crop situation and then use his experience, and perhaps his intuition, to make chemical modifications to the structure within this group of compounds in the hope of discovering a chemical with higher activity, greater selectivity, lower animal and wildlife toxicity or some similar objective. It must be obvious that no single weed problem peculiar to Britain justifies a team working on a specific objective. There are just not enough acres of cultivated land in Britain. However, as weeds and crops are unrestricted by international boundaries, a serious weed problem in Britain is usually also a serious problem in Europe and other temperate areas. For example, blackgrass in cereals is a serious problem in most European countries besides Britain. The rewards, therefore, for an extensive research programme to solve this specific problem may be commensurate with the expenditure. It is for this reason that practically all industrial concerns engaged in the search for new agricultural chemicals are internationally-based, usually with well over 50 per cent of their production going to overseas countries. From the herbicide manufacturer's point of view, problems of controlling plant growth in Britain are of limited interest to agricultural chemical manufacturers unless it is also demonstrated that these problems are encountered in many other countries.

In many cases the situation is not as difficult as described above, for at least two reasons. First, compounds are sometimes discovered with high herbicidal activity as 'fall-outs' from other studies, perhaps arising from the so-called random screening of chemical compounds. In this way the high cost of preparation of the 5000 compounds is reduced, and it becomes possible to consider less extensive crop areas. The other reason is that the main use of a herbicide has already carried the heavy research and development expenses, so that to extend the use of the compound to other not so crucial crop/weed situations may not involve large additional safety studies, and in fact often only trial and residue work is involved. Here the manufacturer is very pleased to increase the range and sale of his herbicides. The difficult situation is where a new compound is discovered which is extremely effective and safe but on a small acreage crop. In this situation the manufacturer cannot hope to make a commercial success of marketing the product. To recover the cost of the development studies may put the price of the product to the grower so high as to be uneconomic for him. During the next few years, ways and means must be found to enable the specialist grower to take advantage of the discovery of a useful product even though the total volume of use is not large. Perhaps a consortium between the manufacturer, or a patent holder, the growers' association and a government research institute may be a means to sponsor the development of new chemical with limited outlets. By such an arrangement all three participants have something to gain — the essence of a workable agreement. May and Baker, for instance, jointly with a growers' association, successfully sponsored the development of a new use for a herbicide where individually the expenditure was considered as unjustifiable by either party.

During the past fifteen years the search for new weed killers has been intense, and many valuable new groups of chemicals have been discovered, for example the considerable number of triazine herbicides, over thirty new ureas, many amides and aniline derivatives, and benzonitrile derivatives. As mentioned earlier, only a small proportion of the new herbicides are available to the British farmer. Why? One reason is that, with a few important exceptions, the farmer and the grower have enough herbicides to deal with their most serious weed problems. An obvious example is the control of annual broad-leaved weeds in cereals. In Britain the farmer has a choice of 14 different approved chemicals for general use and over 180 approved commercial products, usually in the form of mixtures, to obtain general weed control. Certain products will naturally be more suited to his particular conditions than others, but the addition of a new chemical or a new product is no longer of great interest to the cereal farmer, unless it offers a considerable price advantage — you can only kill a weed once. This target, therefore, does not justify the efforts of a research team to find a new herbicide for control of broad-leaved annual weeds in cereals.

Table 24.1
Herbicides introduced for sugar beet

Year of Introduction	Chemical
1954	Pentachlorophenol
1958	Trichloroacetic acid
1958	Diquat
1961	Endothal + propham
1962	Propham
1963	Dimexan + cycluron + chlorbufam
1963	Di-allate
1964	Pyrazon
1965	Chlorpropham + propham + fenuron
1966	Lenacil
1967	Medinoterb + propham + endothal
1968	Phenmedipham

Control of weeds in sugar beet has been another objective, but thanks to detailed studies, a new product has been introduced almost annually. Table

24.1 lists twelve chemicals, or combinations of chemicals which have been introduced in the last fourteen years [3].

Turner pointed out that in 1966 the damage to the crop arising from the use of these herbicides was sufficiently great in 0.9 per cent of the acreage to necessitate ploughing up the crop. It is most likely that by the mid 1970s these difficulties in less than 1 per cent of the present acreage will have been surmounted, and that entirely acceptable chemicals will be available to the grower. Weed control in second early and main-crop potatoes is a third example where the use of weed killers has grown very rapidly, as follows [1].

Table 24.2

Year	% Acreage of potatoes treated with a herbicide
1963	1
1965	16
1966	20
1967	34

Clearly the need for a herbicide in potatoes is being met and the grower is unlikely to press for the development of a new herbicide.

There is a clear distinction between the farmer's requirements and the chemical manufacturer's requirements. A limited but adequate choice of herbicide may be perfectly acceptable to the farmer, but to the commercial organization without access to one of these herbicides, there may be a very compelling need for their research and development team to find a new herbicide with similar or improved properties, so that they can continue in a particular sector of their business. Therefore, quite apart from the farmer's requirements, active research may be undertaken by industry.

It seems possible that we are now approaching the point where most of the weed/crop problem in Britain can be controlled with herbicides already in commercial use or herbicides which are already under development. In short, there may now be enough herbicides, but what the farmer lacks is information regarding the best method of use and the value of particular mixtures. Unlike insecticides, resistance is no problem with herbicides; a minor change in the weed pattern can be countered by the appropriate addition to the herbicide cocktail.

Most of the losses in crop yields arising from weed competition can be brought to acceptable levels in Britain by the use of the appropriate herbicides at the right time and in the right way. A new herbicide is no longer going to be responsible for dramatic increases in yield just by eliminating weed competition. During the last few years, several papers have appeared analysing the reasons why the cereal grower buys a herbicide. The control of weeds is taken for granted, and the farmer assesses other benefits derived from the use of the herbicide. Stanley Evans [4] has pointed out that, at least in the east and south-east of England, the cereal growers are losing little if any, of their yield by omitting a spray treatment for one season at least. New priorities have been put forward by Hughes [5] for spraying cereals, and one of the main reasons for spraying is to facilitate harvest by having a crop free of weeds, particularly of the climbing weeds such as bindweed and cleavers at harvest. He points out that the weeds which affect yields by competition in the growing crops are not necessarily those same weeds which cause difficulty in the combine at harvest. This may, therefore, be a worthwhile target for a search for a new chemical — a chemical which will control the harvest weeds in cereals.

Plant Growth Regulators

Losses in grain from the combine can be serious, amounting to as much as 10 per cent in severe cases. Cereals which have lodged have a greater tendency to shed the grain. The rapid growth of the use of plant-growth regulators such as chlormequat (C.C.C.), which shorten and thicken the stem of the cereal and so reduce the tendency to lodge, reflects the cereal grower's concern with problems at the time of harvest.

The use of various chemicals to control the type of plant growth of a crop is becoming very much more important in Britain and, for that matter, in all highly developed countries with relatively advanced agricultural techniques; these are the same countries which have high labour costs, and strenuous efforts are made to reduce this item of expense in growing the crop. Also in these countries, the marketing of foodstuffs to the consumer is becoming increasingly in a pre-packed form, often with transparent containers. The housewife and the packer are, therefore, going to demand food products which are uniform in size and quality, particularly in appearance. The packer, with his expensive packaging line, is going to require delivery of farm crops at a particular date, with an abrupt start and finish, so that the line can be dismantled or readjusted for the next product he has to pack. To meet this increasing demand, the grower will need special plant-growth regulators which will give uniform crops in size and quality; he will require regulators which will accelerate, delay, or extend harvest to meet the demand of the public or the packer. Until very recently plant growth regulators have been considered as ancillary agents to the main insecticide, fungicide and herbicide products. Often the use of the plant-growth regulator was a matter of preference to the grower, and he was not compelled to use these agents by economic considerations. Such regulators included the well-known agents to set fruit, to control pre-harvest drop, to thin the fruit crop when an excessive fruit set has occurred, and to assist the rooting of cuttings. That plant-growth regulators can do very much more than this has been largely overlooked until recently. The new generation of plant-growth regulators now being studied offer the grower the opportunity to increase the crop potential. For example, the plant-growth regulator dimas, 'Alar', can induce flowering buds in fruit trees for the following season. Therefore, not only can yields be increased but, more important, trees can be brought into bearing on an annual basis whereas hitherto they may have been giving commercial crops in alternate years. A new product, 2-chloroethanephosphonic acid, or C.E.P., is under intensive study; this compound is also known under the trade name 'Ethrel' [2], C.E.P. can bring about a variety of changes in the habit and form of plant growth. It can initiate flowering in pineapples. It can cause tomatoes to ripen earlier or to be picked green and after a dipping treatment to ripen into typical red fruit. In certain plants it can inhibit side-branch formation, in others remove apical dominance. In cucumbers and melons it controls sex expression and so increases the number of female flowers. Sprayed on to apples, cherries or blackcurrants five days before harvest, C.E.P. can cause the formation of an abscission layer in a fruit stalk, so that harvesting by mechanical means by simply shaking the tree and catching the fruit in nets is possible. Thus, this compound C.E.P. has a very wide variety of properties which need detailed study for full evaluation.

Unlike most agricultural chemicals, the biochemical mode of action of this compound was appreciated at the outset; 2-chloroethane phosphonic acid at pH of over 6.5 rapidly breaks down in the presence of absence of the plant to give an almost quantitative yield of ethylene [2, 6].

$$Cl\,CH_2\,CH_2\,\underset{\overset{\|}{O}}{\overset{\overset{O^-}{|}}{P}} - OH \rightarrow CH_2 = CH_2 + Cl^- + H_2PO_4^-$$

All the plant-growth regulator properties of C.E.P. observed in plants so far described can be interpreted in the terms of liberation of ethylene at the appropriate site. We have here, therefore, the unusual situation of a new agricultural chemical based on original fundamental work carried out by a plant physiologist, a plant biochemist and a chemist. They may serve as a pointer to further searches for useful compounds. The chemistry of many of the plant-growth regulators is understood, for example, the chemical identity of many auxins, the gibberellins, the kinetins, and compounds like ethylene and abscisic acid are all well established.

There are now two features which should greatly assist those concerned with the search for new agricultural chemicals. Firstly, there is already a need for special plant-growth regulators, and this requirement is going to increase markedly with the years. By the mid-seventies the need will be very great. The other factor is that much of the fundamental chemistry associated with the natural plant-growth regulators is understood, so the search for new compounds to control growth can be less random and more directed towards specific compounds or groups of compounds than was the search for herbicides.

REFERENCES

1. AGRICULTURAL RESEARCH COUNCIL, Report for 1967-8.
2. COOKE, A.R. and RANDALL, D.I. '2-haloethanephosphonic acids as ethylene releasing agents for the induction of flowering in pineapples', *Nature*, 1968, **218**, 974.
3. EVANS, S.A. 'Herbicides', *J. Roy. Agr. Soc. Eng.*, 1968, **129**, 149-168.
4. EVANS, S.A. 'Spraying of cereals for the control of weeds', *Exp. Husbandry*, 1969, **18**, 102-109.
5. HUGHES, R.G. 'New priorities for profitable spraying', *Farmer and Stockbreeder*, 1968, **82**, (4022), 29.
6. MAYNARD, J.A. and SWAN, J.M. 'Organ phosphorus compounds. II. Chloroalkylphosphonic acids as phosphorylating agents', *Austr. J. Chem.*, 1963, **16**, 596-608.
7. MINISTRY OF AGRICULTURE, FISHERIES AND FOOD, 'Approved Products for Farmers and Growers', 1969.
8. MINISTRY OF AGRICULTURE, FISHERIES AND FOOD, 'Chemical Compounds used in Agriculture and Food Storage in Great Britain',

25. Environmental Limitations in Crop Production for the Quick-Freezing Industry

J.W. Bundy
Birds Eye Foods Ltd., Walton-on-Thames.

Introduction

Vegetable processing is essentially marketing-orientated, aimed at satisfying consumer demand, and the success of the industry depends on the ability of the grower and processor to provide the finished product which meets the standards required by the consumer.

Improved crop productivity, to be successful, must be accomplished within quality and cost standards which meet consumer demand and which can only be interpreted to the grower through the processor. Such consumer requirements are therefore imposed on crop production methods, and traditional crop priorities become amplified by marketing ones which are essentially competitive in cost and consistent in quality.

Environmental limitations to crop production, and their effects on different crops and systems of production, are therefore important issues to the industry, since they largely determine the extent to which the cost and quality of increasing product demand can be controlled. Any limitations on these controls assume major economic importance, and so justify considerable time and effort to resolve them.

This chapter will therefore discuss the crop production systems used in the quick-freezing industry, the restrictions imposed by environmental limitations and the effort which must be directed to help overcome these restrictions against the future needs of the industry.

Marketing Requirements

This industry is making an increasing impact on national vegetable production, and although this discussion relates primarily to quick-freezing, it has important implications for vegetable processing and pre-packing generally.

How then does the quick-freezing industry meet its vegetable marketing needs, and what are these needs in terms of quantity and proportion of national output?

The U.K. frozen food market has shown an average growth rate of 9 per cent per annum in the past ten years, and in 1968 shot up a further 16 per cent to the £141 000 000 mark, so that by 1968 frozen foods were 2 per cent of all food sales, and this is expected to rise 4 per cent within the next five years.

Table 25.1
U.K. consumers' expenditure on food, 1956—1968

	All food (£m)	Quick-frozen foods (£m)	% Q.F.F. to all food
1956	4274	16	0.37
1962	5174	72	1.39
1968	6446	141.5	2.20

Table 25.2
U.K. sales of quick-frozen fruits and vegetables, 1964—1968

	1964 (tons)	1965 (tons)	1966 (tons)	1967 (tons)	1968 (tons)
Green peas	53 300	51 300	63 300	69 400	74 600
Green beans	11 000	12 900	15 900	16 600	21 000
Brussels sprouts	5300	5800	7800	8100	9300
Broad beans	1800	2000	2200	2300	2000
Other varieties	10 900	13 300	18 900	23 200	45 300
Totals	82 300	85 300	108 100	119 600	152 200
U.K. market	81 400	84 600	106 700	118 600	151 600
Export	900	700	1400	1000	600
Fruit (U.K. and Export)	1300	1600	200	2100	

(1 ton = 1016 kg)

Table 25.3
U.K. production of quick-frozen fruit and vegetables, 1956—1968

	Vegetables (tons)	Fruit (tons)
1956	23 936	1215
1957	30 054	1029
1958	31 568	1455
1959	41 991	1022
1960	57 600	900
1961	68 000	1200
1962	79 800	1300
1963	79 700	1200
1964	85 800	1000
1965	79 700	1000
1966	97 600	1300
1967	133 800	1000
1968	118 900	700

(1 ton = 1016 kg)

Table 25.4

The main vegetables frozen in the United Kingdom, 1964—1968

	1964 (100 tons)	1965 (100 tons)	1966 (100 tons)	1967 (100 tons)	1968 (100 tons)
Green peas	549	505	610	821	649
Green beans	139	125	172	233	157
Brussels sprouts	62	39	50	95	63
Broad beans	17	19	14	20	(320)
Other varieties	91	109	130	169	
Totals	858	797	976	1338	1189
Retail packs	394	270	270	202	74
Catering packs and bulk	509	527	706	1136	1115

(1 ton = 1016 kg)

Table 25.5

Consumer expenditure on peas, 1963—1968

	1963	1964	1965	1966	1967	1968
Quick-frozen	26%	28%	29%	30%	33%	36%
Canned garden	23%	21%	20%	20%	19%	18%
Canned processed	25%	25%	25%	25%	25%	24%
Market and other types	26%	26%	26%	25%	23%	22%

Sales of quick-frozen fruit and vegetables account for about 45 per cent of the total frozen-food market, and have increased 200 per cent in the last ten years. Table 25.2 shows U.K. sales in different vegetables since 1964. Table 25.3 the U.K. quick-frozen fruit and vegetable production during 1956—1968. The fluctuation in production against increasing acreage and demand is significant, and indicates the effect of climate on crop performance. Table 25.4 shows the breakdown of the main vegetables frozen in the U.K. during 1964-68. Green peas are the major vegetable to be quick frozen, but green beans and, to a lesser extent, brussel sprouts, contribute substantially to the overall tonnages. 'Other varieties' include spinach, carrots, cauliflower and potato products. Since 1964, more money has been spent on peas bought from the frozen-food cabinet than from any other source as shown in Table 25.5. By 1975, the frozen peas' 36 per cent share of consumer expenditure on all peas is likely to rise well above 50 per cent. Table 25.6 shows the significant changes in the pea acreage grown in this country during 1956—1968. There has been a marked increase in the acreage of peas grown for vining, i.e. for quick freezing, canning green and de-hydration, and they have replaced peas for market and those for harvesting dry.

Table 25.6
Changes in the British pea harvest, 1956—68

| | Thousands of acres (Thousands of hectares) | | | | | | | | | | | | |
	1956	1957	1958	1959	1960	1961	1962	1963	1964	1965	1966	1967	1968
Peas, green, for quick-freezing	51.5 (20.8)	55.9 (22.6)	59.2 (24.0)	66.6 (27.0)	73.6 (29.8)	36.3 (14.7)	38.2 (15.5)	45.7 (18.5)	48.3 (19.6)	42.5 (17.2)	87.0 (35.2)	101.4 (41.1)	108.6 (44.0)
Peas, green, for canning						35.8 (14.5)	31.7 (12.8)	37.1 (15.0)	38.3 (15.5)	33.2 (13.4)			
Peas, green, for dehydration					—	—		—	—	7.4 (3.0)			
Peas, green, for market	36.7 (14.9)	31.1 (12.6)	34.7 (14.0)	29.2 (12.2)	33.1 (13.4)	27.7 (11.2)	30.3 (12.3)	25.6 (10.4)	20.6 (8.3)	18.4 (7.4)	15.5 (6.3)	17.3 (7.0)	17.7 (7.1)
Peas, harvested dry	104.9 (42.5)	78.1 (31.6)	72.5 (29.4)	55.4 (22.4)	46.7 (18.9)	26.3 (10.6)	22.6 (9.1)	33.8 (13.7)	32.0 (13.0)	34.0 (13.8)	35.2 (14.2)	40.0 (16.2)	49.5 (20.0)

Similarly, well over two-thirds of the green-bean acreage grown in this country is now processed, mostly for quick freezing, and probably about 10 per cent of the national acreage of brussels sprouts will be quick-frozen in 1969.

A similar trend occurs in the consumption of potatoes, namely an eightfold increase between 1955 and 1970 in potato utilization for processing, at the expense of ware potato usage. At present, frozen and dehydrated potatoes represent about 3 per cent of all the potatoes we eat in Britain. Between them, the companies producing frozen chips, instant potatoes and potato crisps account for about 10 per cent of the national potato crop and perhaps this has been one of the most startling developments in the vegetable sector recently. It is now estimated that by 1972, 20 per cent of all our potatoes will be bought processed, at least a quarter of this coming in frozen form.

Obtainment of Vegetables for Quick-Freezing

We should, therefore, briefly consider how the quick-frozen industry obtains its vegetables in terms of tonnage, quality and cost.

The crop acreage is contracted with farmers in the local vicinity of the processing factories. Seed is supplied by the processor, and the growers are advised and supervised on all aspects of crop production and harvesting.

A large-sized quick-freezing factory will be contracting 15 to 20 000 acres (6750-8100 ha) with 200 to 300 farmers within a 30 mile (48 km) radius. The factory site would preferably have easy access to the farms with suitable topography and land spread for maximum use of mechanization, and a favourable fertility and climate for the crops required, in particular a low harvest-season rainfall. It is, of course, no coincidence that the factories are sited mainly in the eastern arable regions of the country, and in particular on the sea coasts, in order to obtain adequate fish supplies. Thus it is no surprise that East Anglian farmers are now growing over 40 per cent of all field vegetables grown in Britain, and the Eastern Counties nearly 70 per cent of all vegetables grown for quick freezing.

Within the last ten years, the traditional hand-harvesting methods have rapidly given way to mechanical harvest and bulk transport systems, which allow high volume throughput and quick despatch from field to factory to retain optimum quality in the produce. These involve a large unit size of farm operation, which now must be handled through an increasing use of machine and farm labour syndicates.

Quality is maintained by the processor through specific varietal choice and optimum maturity determination. On the Bird's Eye Foods research station alone well over 1000 varieties have been tested in the last ten years, and currently about two dozen varieties are being used in the commercial cropping programme, 50 per cent of these having been introduced within the last five years.

Optimum maturity determination is more a matter of hours than days, and can of course be adversely affected by climatic changes.

Climatic environment, however, has its greatest effect in the control of cost. The heavy investment in capital, processing and cold-storage facilities can only be justified by round-the-clock production over the longest possible harvest season, and by dove-tailing in sequence the variety of crops to be frozen throughout the summer, autumn and winter. Thus the plans finalized in the spring already lay down the starting and finishing dates for peas, beans, sprouts and potatoes etc., including the daily planned raw-material intake over the total period to establish farm and factory facility requirements, labour load and cost.

Lack of available raw material at this time through climatic intervention during growing period or at harvest is, of course, a deciding factor in the success or failure of the plan or business.

The price paid to the farmer for raw material is a vital factor in the industry cost breakdown, and the aim of the processor, namely, a low price per ton, and that of the grower, namely, a high return per acre, are not incompatible if yields can be high and cost of production low, that is, if productivity is improved. The industry has therefore aimed its crop research at maximizing usable field yield and minimizing grower crops. In the last ten years, average yields of peas and green and broad beans have increased by more than 40 per cent and spinach by 80 per cent. Within this time all the major vegetables have become mechanically harvestable. The improved productivity of all contracted crops by the introduction of better varieties and improved growing systems, and by the introduction of mechanization and farmer syndicates to reduce growing costs, are largely responsible for the present growth of the industry, and help to explain why the cost of frozen-food products to the consumer has moved only 5 per cent up in the last ten years, against the national food increase of 30 per cent over that same period.

Effect of the Quick-Freezing Industry on Vegetable Production

Let us now consider how the introduction and extension of quick-freezing has affected British vegetable-production generally.

Undoubtedly the biggest change is in the type of crop grown over the last ten years. During this period traditional crops have been increasingly replaced by those suited to processing, and these crops are understandably grown in the location of the factories which process them, at the expense of similar crops in other areas, e.g. sprouts in the west midlands, market peas and broad beans in the south-west, and carrots in the northern region. The acreage shift is being determined by the market and an ability to produce extensively on a large mechanical scale.

Thus we see a change not only in the type of vegetable grown but in the area and size of farm-holding where it is produced. More than two-thirds by value are now grown on farms as opposed to small-holdings.

This shift has been made easier by a labour drift from the land affecting the market gardener, by the increasing use of land for building in the vicinity of towns, and by the desire of arable farmers to introduce break cash crops into the farming rotation, with their ability to operate on a large commercial scale with mechanization and bulk transport.

The next major effect has been the increase in crop specialization with those growers who are increasingly becoming involved with vegetable contract farming. This has come about partly from increased acreage requirement, but mostly from introduction of mechanization which has allowed full exploitation of group machinery operations in the field to minimize production costs, and has resulted in a dramatic increase in the acreage contracted per grower for these specialized crops over the last ten years.

Parallel with the move towards mechanization has been the breeding of new varieties suitable for mechanical harvesting and determinate in nature to allow maximum yields from once-over harvests. The change in the harvesting system from hand-picking to mechanization has, in itself, certain implications, in that the non-discrimination of harvesting machines has emphasized the changes in relative importance of diseases.

We now find that diseases which occurred in low incidence, and were not considered economically important when crops were hand-picked, have now assumed new significance. These include particularly the pod- or leaf-spotting diseases or blemishes which affect the physical appearance of the finished product. Infected produce previously left in the field by hand pickers now presents a major problem, even at low incidence, when harvested by machine, because their presence in factory intakes can seriously affect factory throughput costs. The presence in green beans of botrytis rot, for instance, which occurs annually to varying extent, needs only to build up to 5 to 6 per cent in the crop delivered to the factory to present a major problem in production. Even at 3 per cent level, 25 per cent of factory inspection labour is occupied solely in removal of botrytis-infected beans. The presence of such disease in a crop is not helped by the fact that bulk-handling transport is on the increase, and disease spread in boxes or bulk can be rapid.

Environmental Limitations to Raw Materials for Quick Freezing

Having briefly mentioned the size of the quick-freezing market, its systems of production and the effect on the general agricultural pattern, it is now necessary to consider the limitations which exist, particularly with respect to environment.

Perhaps the prime economic need of the processor and producer who have invested in capital and labour to meet market requirement is to ensure that they do, in fact, produce the tonnage required at the quality needed. This will apply to several different vegetables being processed in one or more factories. Within one factory site, several different crops requiring different optimum growing conditions need to be grown. With peas, the eastern counties are suitable, although the climatic effect on existing varieties can be disastrous, particularly in the latter part of the season, if conditions are cold or wet. The varieties in commercial use, whilst being the best available, do not perform consistently under adverse conditions, which results in low yields, and hence shortage of raw material and underpacks at factories. The further north the factory site, the shorter tends to be the season, and the more limiting are these factors. In the case of dwarf green beans, crop production risk increases substantially the further north they are grown, not only in yield, but also in quality shown up as mishapen or poorly-coloured pods.

The inability of suitable dwarf green-bean varieties to produce satisfactorily under temperate conditions which average less than 15 °C is a major restriction to the potential production of this rapidly increasing market-product.

Stability of crop yield throughout the harvest season and over different seasons decides the success of a vegetable operation in terms of quantity required for marketing, and the extreme variation in yield performance in commercial varieties under varying environmental conditions is probably the most serious problem on the production site of the industry. One of the main causes of the substantial quick-frozen annual imports into this country lies in the fact that field yields have failed to meet their plan, largely through adverse climatic effects, as in 1965, 1966 and 1968, and the raw product has not been available to the factories in sufficient quantity to meet market demands.

The character which is lacking and needs to be bred into varieties used for processing is stability of yield under stress conditions. The character is far more important than breeding for maximum potential yield, which can vary by 50 per cent under varying environments, and is an issue which is taking up much time with our own breeders and physiologists.

Environmental limitations also express themselves in terms of crop quality through the presence of pests, diseases or weeds. Numerous examples exist of pests and disease for which there is no control, where their presence adversely affects the economy of production. Such problems include botrytis or sclerotinia rot in green beans, which is prevalent in wet seasons such as 1968, 1966 and 1965, or internal browning in brussels sprouts which can cause substantial crop rejection annually. This is attributed to wide fluctuation in day and night temperature prior to harvest, and is one reason why the sprout processing cannot be extended into January. Cabbage root-fly maggot infestation in sprouts where the levels of field control have been inadequate under adverse climatic conditions to allow the processor to use many crops, is the main contributor to crop rejection in September/October which restricts the start of sprout processing. Stain in broad beans is a factor which restricts the use of over-wintered beans for freezing. It is significant that many of these disorders have little or no effect on the field yield of the crop at optimum maturity but do, nevertheless prevent their use for processing.

In considering the need to control pests and diseases in raw material for processing or prepacking, it is important to recall that we are dealing with produce which will ultimately be made available to the consumer under a brand name. The consumer is well aware that her own garden and market produce can, and frequently does, contain aphis, caterpillars, or slugs, and these she removes during preparation in the kitchen. Any prepared food is expected to be completely clear of such animals. This gives manufacturers or packers a very live problem in more ways than one. There are numerous systems used to help remove these pests at the factory, but here we are concerned with preventing them being present in the crop.

On a branded product, every consumer complaint must be of great concern to the processor. Indeed, it is an offence against the Food Hygiene Regulations. We would consider one complaint in, say, every 10 000 packets as being a seriously high level, but if only one in ten of the consumers were complaining, the content would in fact be one in every thousand packets. In terms of crop infestation this would mean, say, five slugs or caterpillars per acre, or if we are removing 99 per cent in the factory, 500 slugs or 500 caterpillars per acre. One can therefore imagine the tremendous shortcomings of any control procedure which eliminates say 65 per cent or 70 per cent of the pest or damage. This is nothing like the level of control required to make any impression on the processors' problem, and failure to resolve such consistent problems in any specific area must lead to the decision to stop production of that crop. It is therefore evidence that the levels of field control to which we have been accustomed can no longer be tenable for processed crops. It is no longer sufficient to control a pest or disease in the field to a level where crop yields are no longer reduced. We must meet a level of control which allows the processor to handle large quantities of raw material on a mechanical field and factory scale, and ensure that his product is completely acceptable to the consumer on both quality and cost terms.

Future Development of the Frozen-Food Industry

What then, are the future trends in the industry, and what must the industry do to resolve many of its present limitations? We can all speculate, but the consumer is not going to change overnight from one type of food to something quite different. In fact, our food today consists basically of the same ingredients as it did thirty years ago. But what the housewife of the future will be able to do will be to try the same thing in rather a different form. Food habits change very slowly, but the rapid changes will be in the way the housewife buys and prepares the food, and there is no doubt that the present trend will accelerate.

By the 1980s, half of all Britain's food is likely to be in prepared or convenience form, compared with 20 per cent today. By this time, the frozen-food market itself will be three times its present size.

The shift in vegetable production from the traditional areas to sites adjoining the processing factories or prepacking stations will continue. These sites may not necessarily, however, be in the most obvious farming areas, since choice of factory site is largely determined by non-agricultural issues such as power, water, labour, effluent disposal and, not the least, government policy through the control of Industrial Development Certificates and encouragement to operate in Development Grant areas. Geographic environment will be less of a deciding factor in controlling geographic crop distribution than industry or government decisions. If these sites are not in the best farming areas, it becomes even more important to control the effects of environment on crop performance to ensure economic factory-thoughput and farm-production.

Farmer co-operation through the formation of labour and machinery syndicates will increase, and is being helped, of course, by Ministry grant and in the form of co-operative or development grants. Farm production will specialise even more in these areas to meet the need of even larger scale economy.

Above all, research and development is and will be aimed at overcoming present limitations in crop productivity. Plant breeders will seek to establish varieties which have stability of yield performance under stress conditions, improved quality, suitability to mechanical harvesting and extension of harvest season. If the processing industry, with its rapidly changing techniques, is to achieve the full benefit of these varieties, then such varieties must be commercially introduced as quickly as possible, and reconsideration of the present Varietal Index procedures and limitations are now justified.

To meet the levels of consistently high quality required by the consumer, it is likely that, as chemical manufacturers produce the chemicals which increasingly meet the specification of pest and disease elimination in the field, the decision on which chemical to use will pass from the grower to the processor. This is inevitable because it is the processor and not the grower who can distinguish at this level which pest or disease poses the greatest cost or problem during factory production, and who can best emphasise the choice of control measure which eliminates the process problem as well as the field problem.

It is relevant, too, that the high levels of control needed in the field will have to be achieved under conditions which will have to conform to legal tolerance limits of chemical residues present on harvested crops.

Despite the dramatic changes in farm mechanization for harvesting vegetables within the last ten years, even greater changes will come in the next five. Emphasis will be placed on machines which can eliminate waste in the field, reduce field bulk to minimise transport and disposal costs, but minimise damage to the usable product to prevent post-harvest deterioration and retain its quality and appearance.

Thus we are now seeking such machines as the pea-pod picker, which takes the pod off the plant on the field, and allows transit of the pods for freezing immediately after shelling at the factory; the multi-row bean harvester with a higher capacity rate for harvesting closer row crops and suitable for bulk handling; sprout stripping combines, which work on the field and allow transport of the stripped sprouts only into the factory; or such things as seed drills which drill the seed in soluble tapes to minimise use of high-cost hybrid seed and allow better direct plant spacing. Impregnation of the tape with growth regulator, bird scarer, fertilizer, herbicide and pesticide will surely complete the requirement.

Use of growth regulators to control the development of plants is still in its infancy, and the use of cell-tissue culture to improve the purity of stock of outcrossing crops and their rapid propagation will be an exciting area of investigation over the next few years.

All this will call for as close a working relationship between the research worker and the processor as there currently exists between the grower and the processor. The problems which face the processor today are those which will involve the bulk of the vegetable industry ten years hence, and it is important that these problems be communicated to the research worker at the earliest opportunity.

Equally, the chemical manufacturer and agricultural engineer must appreciate that the industry's needs are extensive enough to warrant their increasing investment and effort.

As the proportion of vegetables sold under brand names increases, the greater will be the influence of the brand name in deciding the variety grown, the chemical sprayed and the harvest machine used.

Seed will be bought from the breeders, who can give better quality and consistent yield under stress in preference to that with higher potential, but extremely variable, yield.

The chemicals used will be those which control field pest and disease levels to an extent which reduces not only field but also factory problems, and still maintain processor quality standards. The harvest machines purchased will be those which can separate waste effectively in the field and minimise damage to the product as much as improving field performance.

The existing limitations must be resolved if growers and processors are to satisfy the people that matter most of all, namely, the consumers.

26. Potential Crop Production in Britain — Some Conclusions

P.F. Wareing
Department of Botany, University College of Wales, Aberystwyth.

The chapters at the beginning of this book were concerned with the basic biological principles determining productivity, which were followed by chapters on the problems of specific types of crop and of different systems of production in contrasting environments. Finally, various approaches to the problems of increasing production were discussed, i.e. breeding, control of pests and diseases, and chemical control of growth. It is proposed in this chapter to draw attention to some of the main conclusions and to examine certain aspects of crop production in Britain from the standpoint of the plant physiologist.

We start from the premise that there is a need to produce as much of our own food as is possible and expedient on economic, social and political grounds. There are two aspects of this problem, one short-term and the other more long-term. Within the present world monetary and economic situation, the national 'balance of payments' problem renders it desirable that we should keep food imports to a minimum. Apart from this immediate problem, however, there is the further possibility that a world food crisis will arise by the year 2000 or earlier, because of the 'population explosion', which may render it necessary for Britain to be as self-supporting in food production as possible.

Clearly, a densely-populated country such as Britain cannot hope to supply all its food requirements, although it would be possible to supply all our needs for temperate foods if this were desirable, and we therefore need to consider how best to deploy our resources of land and labour in the light of a wide variety of economic and other factors, and in relation to other demands on the land. Thus, it becomes a problem of what balance to strike between different types of farming system (i.e. as between arable and grassland, and between dairy farming and meat production) and what types of crop to grow, to give us the best return from our resources. In arriving at decisions on these matters, economic and political factors will occupy an important and often over-riding place, but clearly any such decisions must be based upon sound biological principles, in relation to the special features of the British climate. For example, national strategy in relation to the balance between crops for direct human consumption, dairy farming and meat production ought to be examined from the standpoint of biological productivity, as has been done in several papers in the Symposium. However, apart from the question of the balance between different production systems, there is a need to improve productivity in all these systems, and here the contributions of the biologist, as well as of the agriculturalist, are of prime importance. Thus, there is a need to identify and study the major limiting factors for different crops and farming systems, for each of the main climatic regions within Britain. The principles involved are very clearly stated by Watson [38] and are worth repeating here:

'The yield of a field crop depends on all that happens to it during its previous growth, so if our aim is to understand how, and by how much, yield can be increased, we need information on the changes that occur throughout the growth period, on how they depend on properties of the plant and are affected by environmental factors, and to what extent the state of the crop at any stage influences the final yield. From such information, rational judgements should become possible on how to alter the form or development of the plant by breeding, or how to change the environment by husbandry procedures or adjust the relation of plant development to seasonal climatic change to increase yield.'

Climatic Factors

The special features of the British climate are, on the one hand, its cool summers, with ample rain in many regions and associated low sunshine totals, and on the other hand, its relatively mild winters, giving a fairly long 'growing season'. However, within the British Isles there are considerable variations with respect to these climatic factors, which have a profound effect upon the distribution of different farming systems [12]. As is well-known, the variation in rainfall over the country is primarily responsible for the predominance of grass in the north and west, and of arable in the east and south. Low summer rainfall can be identified as a major limiting factor in crop production over a wide area of the south east [6]. On the other hand, the wetter summers in the north and west tend to militate against cereal production, because of the high incidence of fungal diseases and the greater risk of wet conditions during harvest in these regions [23].

The extent to which crop growth in Britain is limited by temperature and light conditions is a much more complex problem. There is no doubt, of course, that the marked seasonal variation in production of grass is closely correlated with the annual cycle in the intensity of solar radiation [2, 10] and similar effects can be demonstrated for other crops [34, 38]. Clearly, low light-intensity constitutes a major limiting factor during the winter – a conclusion which would be fully supported by growers of glasshouse crops.

There is also the question of how far crop growth in Britain is limited by radiation intensity in the peak growing period of May-August. For many crop plants, the radiation intensity of full sunlight in the summer is well above that required to give maximum photosynthetic rate *in individual leaves*, but because of the mutual shading of leaves in a crop with a closed canopy, the maximum photosynthetic rate for the crop is not reached even in full sunlight

[4]. Moreover, in cloudy weather the light intensities are frequently about only one-fifth those in bright sunlight. It is not surprising, therefore, that the variation in yields of cereals from year to year can be closely correlated with sunshine data [33]. Thus, it is not difficult to understand that even in summer, radiation intensity is frequently one of the major factors limiting production in Britain. However, the lower light intensities are partly compensated for by the longer summer days in Britain than at lower latitudes [21]. When one considers the poor sunshine records of much of upland Britain in the north and west, low radiation intensities would seem to be even more important in these areas than in the lowland regions of the south and east.

Although there seems to be little doubt that deficiency in solar radiation is a major factor limiting production in Britain compared with more sunny countries, there are, in fact, few accurate data on this matter for specific crop plants, but it is to be hoped that the International Biological Programme may provide useful information.

Temperature is also a factor of the utmost importance in determining crop production in Britain [26]. As we have seen, many parts of Britain enjoy a relatively long growing season, with fairly mild winters due to the maritime influences. But these same influences tend to delay the rise of temperature in the spring, owing to the higher specific heat of the sea compared with that of the land, and lead to a less rapid fall in temperature in the autumn, again due to the buffering effect of the sea. As a result of this buffering effect, there is a marked 'phase-shift' in the seasonal temperature variation in relation to the annual radiation cycle, so that the temperature maximum is not reached until July or August, whereas radiation reaches its maximum at midsummer, i.e. the temperature cycle lags one to two months behind the radiation cycle. The result of this lag is that temperatures still remain relatively low during the period mid-March to mid-May, when light conditions are improving rapidly. One consequence of this effect is that although in many temperate crop plants the photosynthetic rate is relatively insensitive to temperature changes over the range $15°-25°C$, nevertheless at lower temperatures it is adversely affected, and hence, photosynthesis will be reduced by cool spring temperatures.

However, a more important effect of low spring temperatures is on the rate of leaf growth in both grass and arable crops. The temperature requirements for growth are not the same as for photosynthesis, and in many plants there is a steep rise in growth rate as temperatures rise above the minimum (i.e. the temperature coefficient for growth is high). In arable crops, the limitation of growth by low spring temperatures has more serious implications than in grass, since until a closed leaf canopy has been attained, only a small proportion of the incident radiation will be intercepted by the leaves and used in photosynthesis, so that the efficiency of dry-matter production will be greatly below the full potential [34, 38].

Leaf growth will be directly affected by the ambient air temperatures, but

Brouwer [5] and Monteith and Elston [26] have drawn attention to the important effects of root temperature on leaf growth, no doubt partly due to the effects of uptake of water and mineral nutrients, but possibly also due to the effects of temperature on the biosynthesis of hormones such as cytokinins, which are produced in the roots but have a marked effect upon leaf growth.

In addition to the limiting effects of low temperatures on growth in the spring, the cool summers prevailing in many areas of Britain, especially in the uplands, render it probable that crop production in these areas is limited by the effects of low summer temperature, as well as by low light intensities. Thus, studies on ryegrass in controlled environment rooms have indicated that the optimum temperature for relative growth rate is about $20^{\circ}C$ [11], whereas the mean July temperatures in many areas are well below this. Certainly, the much shorter length of the growing season in upland areas [19] is a direct indication of the importance of temperature in these areas.

Clearly, except for glasshouse crops, we cannot improve the light and temperature conditions, as we can with water and mineral nutrient defficiencies, but we can take several other measures to improve the situation, namely:

(a) Select appropriate crops and varieties for the conditions prevailing in a given region.

(b) Select the best climatic regions for growing a particular crop. The smaller areas required for horticulture make it possible to be fairly specific in choosing the best regions for a particular crop, such as top fruit, but the same principle clearly operates on a larger scale in agriculture.

(c) Endeavour to take maximum advantage of the optimum light conditions, particularly in the spring, by adopting appropriate cropping procedures. This problem is discussed at some length in the articles by Watson [38] and Thorne [34] who point out, for example, the necessity for developing an adequate leaf area index sufficiently early in the spring to take advantage of the improving light conditions in April and May. To achieve this, some sugar-beet growers now raise seedlings under glass and later transplant them to the field. Similarly, Cooper and Breese [10] point out the importance of adopting a grazing regime which will allow an optimum interception of incoming radiation.

(d) Breed varieties which are adapted to the prevailing conditions of light and temperature in Britain. Intra-specific differences in photosynthetic rate are found in both grasses [p. 1] and maize [34] and there is, therefore, the possibility of producing varieties with increased photosynthetic rates at lower light intensities, i.e. under cloudy conditions. Dry-matter production might also be increased by reducing the losses arising from respiration, which may amount to as much as 50 per cent of the material produced in photosynthesis in some species.

The possibility of breeding varieties which are adapted to the relatively cool conditions of the British climate has received relatively little attention, and hence it will be now discussed in some detail.

Breeding for Growth at Low Temperatures

There are really two aspects of this problem, since the development of the crop may be limited either (a) by low photosynthetic rates, or (b) by low growth rates. To put it another way, overall growth may be limited either (i) by the ability to produce new material through photosynthesis, or (ii) by the ability to utilize it in growth, particularly in the production of new leaf tissue.

Now clearly the biochemical processes involved in photosynthesis and in growth are different, and we should not expect that the ability to commence growth at low temperatures is necessarily associated with the ability to photosynthesize under these conditions. We know very little about what determines the ability to grow at low temperatures, but there is no doubt that differences exist between and within species. Thus, it is common knowledge that species differ widely in the minimum temperature for germination. Similarly, there are wide differences in the time of bud-burst of woody plants, and this again is primarily determined by differences in temperature responses. If we consider herbaceous plants of woodlands, then it is very striking to consider how much earlier the herbaceous plants of the 'prevernal phase', such as celandine (*Ficaria verna*), bluebells (*Endymion non-scripta*), wood anemone (*Oxalis acetosella*), etc., are able to commence growth than are the main woodland tree species.

Although few precise data are available on this matter, there is no doubt that there are wide differences between various native species in ability to grow at low spring temperatures. Natural selection has been operating to produce these differences, and it should therefore be possible to breed crop plants with the same characteristics. Cooper and his associates [9, 16, 25] have obtained some information that differences in temperature responses occur between different geographical races of certain grass species. Thus, Mediterranean races of *Dactylis glomerata*, adapted to relatively mild winter conditions, are able to maintain growth at relatively cool temperatures, whereas Norweign races become dormant in the winter, so that growth ceases, and they require higher temperature conditions for the commencement of leaf growth in the spring than do the Mediterranean races. Similar observations have been made on tall fescue (*Festuca arundinacea*) [30].

What is the basis of these differences in ability to grow at low temperature? Clearly, any growth involves both cell division and cell vacuolation, and species must differ in their ability to maintain metabolic and biochemical activity at low temperatures.

Now, in several of the examples given above of species able to grow at low temperatures, as in the germination of seeds, the growth of tree buds and the growth of spring bulbs, this growth is undoubtedly at the expense of stored food reserves, rather than of current photosynthesis. If we consider annual crop plants, such as cereals, it is clear that once the limited reserves in the seed are exhausted, further growth will depend upon current photosynthesis. What evidence is there for the existence of differences within and between species with respect to their photosynthetic rates at cool temperatures? This is a subject on which there has been remarkably little work in the past, but even so we have sufficient evidence to indicate that there are indeed, marked differences in the responses of photosynthesis to temperature (p. 368).

What determines the shape of the photosynthesis-temperature curves under field conditions, i.e. at a CO_2 concentration of 0.03 per cent and relatively high light-intensities? Under these conditions the overall photosynthetic rate of leaves at the top of the canopy will be limited by the rate of CO_2 fixation, i.e. CO_2 supply is the rate-limiting factor [26]. The rate at which CO_2 can be fixed will in turn depend upon (a) certain *physical* processes, such as the rate of CO_2 diffusion from the boundary layers of the leaf, through the stomata and intercellular spaces to the mesophyll cells and the chloroplasts, and (b) various *biochemical* processes involving the actual fixation of CO_2 in the chloroplasts and its incorporation into sugars and other products. Now, the flat temperature-response curve of photosynthesis in sugar beet over the range $15°-25°C$ [17] and certain other species have been taken to indicate that at high light-intensities and normal atmospheric CO_2 concentrations, photosynthesis is primarily limited by physical diffusion processes, particularly by the 'mesophyll resistance', i.e. the resistance to CO_2 diffusion within the leaf. If this were the case, then if we wish to improve the overall rate of photosynthesis under field conditions, we should concentrate on breeding for reduced 'mesophyll resistance'.

However, recently evidence has been obtained which suggests that the biochemical steps, particularly the carboxylation steps, may also be rate-limiting [37], and if this is so, then we should be breeding for quite different biochemical characters and properties. The work of Treharne and Cooper [35] suggests that there are marked differences in temperature response curves of the enzyme ribulose-1,5, diphosphate (RuDP) carboxylase (which controls the primary CO_2-fixing process), from different temperate grass species. Similar differences have been found between various other crop plants. It is found that in certain species, e.g. oats, turnip, the activity of the enzyme falls off much less rapidly at cool temperatures than in lettuce, tomato and bean [28]. Thus, it is possible that differences in photosynthetic rate at low temperatures may in part depend upon differences in the properties of certain key enzymes, such as RuDP carboxylase. To maintain active photosynthesis and growth at low temperatures, a large number of enzymes will be involved. If only a few of these enzymes are rate-limiting, breeding for increased rates of photosynthesis might not be difficult, but if we had to attempt to breed for changes in the properties of a large number of enzymes, the process of improvement is likely to be very slow. However, the rate of biochemical processes can also be speeded up by increasing the *amount* of the enzymes involved.

Treharne and Eagles [36] have recently published the results of experiments in which races of *Dactylis glomerata* from Norway and Portugal were first grown under different temperature regimes and then the photosynthetic rates and RuDP carboxylase activities were determined for different temperatures of analysis (Figures 26.1, 26.2). It is seen that the temperature at which the plants were previously grown has a marked effect upon the subsequent photosynthetic rates and enzyme activity at different temperatures. In particular, the plants of the Norwegian race grown at 5°C show very much higher photosynthetic rates and enzyme activity per unit of leaf area

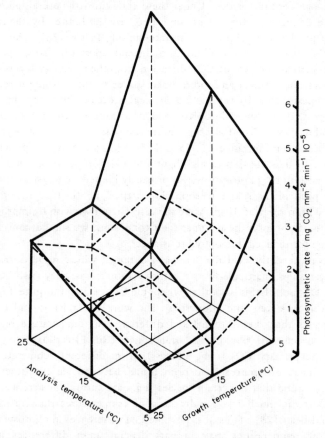

Fig. 26.1   Effect of growth temperature and analysis temperature on the light-saturated photosynthesis of a Norwegian (solid line) and a Portuguese (broken line) population of Dactylis glomerata; from Treharne and Eagles [36].

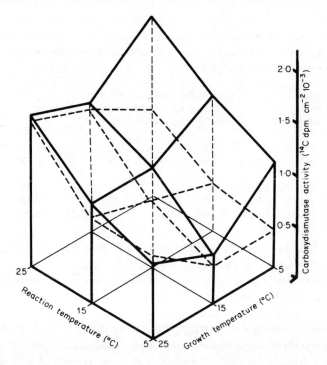

Fig. 26.2   Effect of growth temperature and reaction temperature on the carboxydismutase activity (dpm, where 2200 dpm = 1 nano Curie) of a Norwegian (solid line) and a Portuguese (broken line) population of Dactylis glomerata; from Treharne and Eagles [36].

than plants of the Portuguese race similarly treated. Thus, it would seem that the Norwegian race is capable of adapting itself when grown under cool conditions, so that it is capable of conducting relatively high rates of photosynthesis at 5°C, possibly because there is then more RuDP carboxylase per unit area. However, it has not yet been possible to demonstrate conclusively that there is, in fact, more of the enzyme present in the plants grown at 5°C. It may be significant that the plants grown at 5°C have a markedly higher protein content per unit area of leaf than those grown at 25°C (Table 26.1), although the total protein content per leaf is greater in plants grown at higher temperatures because the leaves are larger, and it would seem likely that protein constitutes a higher proportion of the total dry matter in the plants grown at 5°C. It is possible that the higher protein content indicates a higher overall enzyme content, i.e. that the concentration of all enzymes per unit leaf area is higher in the plants grown at 5°C, due to reduced leaf expansion, which in turn may be controlled by the endogenous hormone levels. Indeed, it would seem simpler to bring about an increase in the amounts of a large number of enzymes by affecting some non-specific

Table 26.1

Effect of temperature on carboxydismutase activity in two populations of Dactylis glomerata, one from Norway (N) and the other from Portugal (P) (From Treharne and Eagles [36]).

Growth temp. (°C)	(mg soluble protein cm^{-1} leaf area)		Carboxydismutase activity (^{14}C dpm mg^{-1} protein x 10^{-4}) Reaction temperature (°C)					
			5°		15°		25°	
	N	P	N	P	N	P	N	P
5	0.253	0.085	4.04	4.72	5.24	5.44	6.96	9.10
15	0.120	0.045	4.00	5.91	8.33	12.60	10.42	18.90
25	0.050	0.043	14.40	16.70	19.80	20.21	28.00	35.73

step in protein synthesis, than for natural selection to bring about increased contents of a number of specific enzymes independently.

This work has been described in some detail, since it appears to indicate that there may be considerable scope for adaptation to growth at cool temperatures in terms of both photosynthesis and leaf expansion. If it should prove possible to breed for early growth in the spring in both grasses and tillage crops, there could be great benefits to British agriculture. Of course, care would have to be taken to ensure that plants capable of early growth were not unduly susceptible to frost damage, since the Mediterranean races of *Dactylis glomerata* and *Festuca arundinacea*, which are capable of growing at low temperatures, are very susceptible to frost damage [31], possibly due to the low sugar content. However, we know very little about the physiological basis of frost resistance and in certain plants, such as rye, growth at low temperatures is associated with high frost resistance.

An alternative strategy would be to breed for the development of storage organs, such as swollen shoot bases, in suitable forage grasses, as suggested by Cooper and Breese [10]. With adequate food reserves, it might be possible to obtain early leaf growth in the spring, at a time when temperature and light conditions may not yet be sufficiently favourable for active photosynthesis. (This, of course, is the biological 'strategy' adopted by many native herbs and woody species). It is possible that in this way, grazing could be started two or three weeks earlier than at present.

Comparative Productivity of Different Crops and Farming Systems

Crop plants clearly differ widely in morphology and physiology – cereal grains, grass, root crops and potatoes, for example – and these differences must markedly affect their performance in the field. Moreover, with some, such as grass, the whole shoot system to the grazed or mown level constitutes the crop, whereas with cereals or potatoes only part of the plant is harvested. Most grasses are perennial plants which remain green throughout the year, whereas tillage crops are typically annual or biennial. Again, the chemical composition of the crop varies widely with respect to the content of carbohydrates, fats and proteins. These considerations render it difficult to make direct comparisons between the productivity of various crops, but due allowance can be made for the various differences in digestibility and the proportion which forms the usable yield.

As Cooper and Breese [10] show very clearly, the annual dry-matter production by a properly managed pasture is very high (up to 20 000 kg ha^{-1} pa^{-1}) and under the best conditions begins to approach the maximum biological potential of a crop canopy. This high productivity can be attributed to two main features of the crop: firstly, it remains green and maintains a high leaf area index throughout the year, so that a relatively high proportion of the incoming radiation is intercepted, compared with many arable crops, which have a low leaf area index in the spring; secondly, a high proportion of the whole shoot system is harvested over the course of the year. One of the main disadvantages of grass as a crop is, of course, that the majority of species do not produce a storage organ in which reserves are accumulated (although some species have swollen stem bases) by contrast with grain, sugar beet and potatoes, so that the grass must be conserved in some way – as hay, silage or by drying equipment – and the attendant losses of dry matter can amount to as much as 40 per cent. Furthermore, only a proportion (70 per cent in young grass) of the dry matter is digestible by ruminants.

By contrast with grass, the productivity of cereals, such as wheat and barley, is relatively low in terms of yield of dry matter of grain, which constitutes only about half of the total dry weight of the shoot system. However, the cereal grain has a high digestibility (over 90 per cent), a low water content and is a 'pre-packaged product', readily amenable to mechanical harvesting and easily transported and stored. The main cause of the relatively low biological productivity of the cereal crop lies in the fact that the material stored in the grain is formed by the photosynthesis occurring only during the six-week period between anthesis (flowering) and ripening. Thus, the cereal crop is relatively inefficient in that only a very small proportion of the total annual period of radiation is utilized. There are good prospects for increasing the yield of cereals by breeding, as seen in the production of high-yielding, short-strawed varieties of wheat, but in this instance the improvement is due to more favourable partition of material between the usable and non-usable part of the plant, rather than to any increase in the total production of dry matter. Other possible ways in which the yield of cereals may be improved are given in the chapter by Bingham [3].

Although the cereal crop is of lower biological efficiency than grass, nevertheless it clearly plays an indispensable role not only for direct human consumption, but also as a complement to grass in supplying animal feed which helps to restore the seasonal imbalance between summer and winter growth of the grass crop, and as feed for non-ruminant animals, for which grass is unsuitable.

Another method of restoring the seasonal imbalance in the grass crop is to use plants which are capable of accumulating considerable amounts of green material in the field, such as kale and root crops, and which can be used as winter feed as required. In terms of production of green fodder, these crops, which are of indeterminate growth habit and can continue photosynthesis well into the autumn when the weather conditions are suitable, are highly efficient producers. Unfortunately, however, these latter crops present other problems, arising from wet conditions in the field for stock, and costly lifting and transport problems.

We now turn to a consideration of the biological efficiency of different farming systems. As we have seen, cereal growing is largely confined to the drier parts of the country, due to the risk of wet harvests and the higher incidence of disease in the wetter regions. However, the wet conditions which render certain areas unsuitable for cereals are a positive advantage, within certain limits, for grass. By contrast, low rainfall in the south-east may seriously limit the growth of grass in some summers [19, 27]. Thus, the predominance of grass in some areas is partly due to their suitability for livestock and grassland farming, and partly to their unsuitability for other forms of agriculture.

However, although high rainfall places constraints upon the cultivation of cereals in the north and west, in terms of biological productivity, this is not an unmitigated disadvantage, in view of the greater yields of dry matter and protein from grass than from cereal crops. Losses of grass in conservation are relatively high, but may be reduced in the future by the use of grass-drying equipment. The digestible matter of young grass, for ruminants, is in the region of 60 to 70 per cent, whereas that of cereal feeds is almost 100 per cent. Nevertheless, as Holmes points out, the overall annual yield of energy and protein from grass, when combined with dairying, or mixed dairying and meat production, far exceeds that from cereals alone [20]. Thus, the climatic disadvantages of the north and west, in terms of radiation and temperature conditions, appears to be offset by the higher efficiency of lowland grass in association with dairy farming. Insofar as cereals are used for winter feed, however, they play a complementary role, and a balance between the two types of crop is clearly needed within the country as a whole. Moreover, there is not a clear-cut demarcation between permanent grass in the north and west, and arable in the south and east, since there is a broad zone of mixed farming in the midlands. Furthermore, there is considerable milk production in the south-east, where proximity to large urban populations is an advantage.

Contrasting with the high productivity of lowland grass-farming, is the poor efficiency of upland grassland and rough grazing, which is largely devoted to sheep farming. The low efficiency of such farming is due both to the poor productivity of the grass itself and to the low efficiency of conversion of energy and protein by sheep under hill conditions [15]. The poor performance of the grass is the result of a series of factors.

    (a) low temperatures (giving a short growing season),
    (b) low solar radiation due to cloud,
    (c) high rainfall, giving a tendency to waterlogged conditions,
    (d) low soil nutrient levels and low soil pH, due both to the nature of the parent rock and to high rates of leaching,
    (e) the low inherent productivity of the indigenous hill grass species.

It has been demonstrated clearly that production can be greatly increased in these areas by adequate use of fertilizers, including lime, and by re-seeding with improved strains of grass, but the areas involved are very large and the return is poor. Alternative ways in which rough grazing areas can be improved are suggested in the chapter by Eadie and Cunningham [15], i.e. seasonal intensification of stocking without re-seeding. However, the question arises as to whether such land is best used for sheep farming or whether it would be biologically more productive under coniferous forest.

Coniferous forest is relatively efficient in dry-matter production, partly because of its evergreen habit and the dense canopy which it presents. There may be other factors tending to high rates of production by conifers. For example, there is evidence that conifers can conduct active photosynthesis at quite low temperatures in the winter and early spring [24] and so build up reserves which can be utilized during subsequent growth. There appears to be a lack of data on the seasonal production of dry matter by conifers and grass under upland conditions in Britain, on which a comparison of the efficiency of the two types of crop could be made. However, decisions as to which type of crop should be used will also be affected by social and economic factors. A detailed economic study of the problem [14] indicated that in some areas the returns from agriculture are greater, and in other areas forestry appears to have the advantage.

By contrast, usually the intensive methods used in horticulture result in yields which are higher than in agriculture and approach more nearly the full biological potential, and as Hudson [21] points out, the trend in horticulture is likely to be towards even more intensive methods.

Future Prospects

Although the yields of agricultural crops have increased steadily over the past two decades, the average yields for most farm crops are still far short of their full potential, so that there is plenty of scope for further improvement. In agriculture, there is little the farmer can do to improve conditions of light and temperature, and at present irrigation is justified only for crops, such as potatoes and other vegetables, giving a high return. Thus, the most immediate prospects for improvement lie in the traditional measures of (a) improving nutrient levels, (b) more effective disease-control, and (c) improvement by breeding.

Yields could be greatly increased by the use of higher levels of fertilizers with tillage crops and especially with grass. However, a greatly increased use of fertilizers on arable land is likely to have undesirable side-effects by increased drainage of nutrients into rivers and lakes, leading to their 'eutrophication'. Another approach is by paying greater attention to the root systems of plants [32], which have been too long neglected, and, if possible, by breeding for root systems which show greater efficiency of uptake of nutrients.

Chemical control of many pests and diseases is effective, but the losses in cereals due to mildew and other fungal diseases are still high [13], and their effective control, possibly by the development of effective systemic fungicides, could lead to greatly increased yields and an extension of the total acreage under cereals.

Breeding still offers great possibilities for many crops, and a more deliberate type of breeding for the physiological and morphological characters determining yield offers great promise in cereals and grasses. In the past, breeding for yield has largely been a 'hit and miss', although very successful, process, but as Watson [38] points out, if continued progress is to be made, it is necessary to identify what are the rate-limiting processes at various stages in the development of the crop. Thus, as we have seen, the major rate-limiting step in the early spring may be leaf growth, whereas at a later stage it may be the photosynthetic rate of the crop; in other words, in some cases the overall growth rate may be limited by the size of the 'sinks' and in other cases by the efficiency of the 'source', and the breeder must plan his programme accordingly.

Several contributors have examined the wheat plant from this standpoint [3, 34, 38], and similar analyses are being made for grasses [10]. Thus, further improvement in grass varieties is likely to result from deliberate breeding for such characters as the ability to start growth and carry on photosynthesis early in the spring, and the more effective use of high light intensities in summer, as well as high digestibility and nutritive value to the animal. In most crops, improved disease resistance offers high returns.

Apart from the further improvement of the traditional crop plants, there is also the possibility of acclimatizing sub-tropical crops, such as maize and soybeans, the existing varieties of which are not suitable for the British climate. A more radical approach would be to attempt the improvement of entirely new crop species, as suggested by Hudson [21]. For example, there is a need for a temperate crop with a high protein yield, and possibly it would be better to attempt the improvement of a native temperate species, rather than to adapt a species, such as soybeans, which originated in warmer climates.

Superimposed upon the long-established methods of improving yields, there are likely to be a number of new technical developments which will have a considerable impact on the pattern and efficiency of agriculture and horticulture, such as the further development of the quick-freezing industry

[7] . A vivid picture of what changes may be expected in horticulture in the next twenty or thirty years has been presented by Hudson [21] .

Some of the most revolutionary changes may include the elimination of the animal in the production of high protein foods, especially meat. The figures given by Holmes (Table 14.4) illustrate strikingly how much more efficient, in terms of protein yield, is the direct human consumption of plant material, compared with the use of animals to process it. The disadvantage of a purely vegetarian diet is, of course, the low protein content of many plant products, in relation to carbohydrate or non-digestible matter; hence the use of the animal to concentrate the protein and yield a palatable product as meat. However, in the case of soybeans, it is feasible to extract the proteins direct and produce a material which is said to have the texture and flavour of meat. It would be a great advantage if a temperate legume with a high yield and high protein content could be developed, and hence the attempts to improve the field bean [3] are of considerable interest. However, Pirie has shown that proteins may be extracted directly from leaves to give a digestible and nutritive product, and if this process could be improved to give more appetising material, we might well see a revolution in our eating habits, and hence in farming. As indicated in the chapter by Pyke [29], the industrial production of microbial protein is also a feasible proposition, especially for the production of animal feedstuffs.

Thus, there is no doubt that more efficient means of producing protein than raising beef-cattle and sheep are available, if we were prepared to accept 'non-natural' foods. It is possible that the world food situation will ultimately require that we accept such foods, whether we like them or not. However, such a development would be in direct conflict with people's present expectations. Firstly, in our predominantly urban and sedentary way of life, there is likely to be an increasing demand for low calorie diets, on health grounds. Secondly, as the general standard of living rises, there is likely to be an increasing demand for high-protein luxury foods. Thus, one might predict that changes in eating habits are likely to lead to increasing demands for high-quality vegetables and fruit, together with high-protein animal products. Whether world economic and political developments will allow us to indulge these tastes remains to be seen, but clearly human eating habits are a most important factor in determining patterns of agriculture.

The use of chemical herbicides is now part of the normal pattern of agriculture in Britain, but we are likely to see the widespread use of chemicals for the regulation of plant growth and development [18]. Synthetic hormones for promoting rooting of cuttings and fruit set, and for delaying fruit fall, have long been used in horticulture, and more recently gibberellins have been used for certain purposes, including the increase of fruit size in seedless grapes. In the past, plant physiologists have been preoccupied with the effects of growth-promoting substances, but it is now realized that growth inhibitors and retardants are at least as important from the practical standpoint as growth promoters. Thus, recently we have seen the introduction of synthetic growth-retardants, such as chlormequat (C.C.C.), which is used for reducing stalk-length in cereals and thereby reduces the risk of lodging. The retardant known as 'dimas' or 'Alar' (B995) leads to increased yields of tubers in potatoes, apparently by reducing shoot growth and thereby leading to a re-distribution of dry matter within the plant [22]. B995 is also being used for several other purposes, including the promotion of flowering in fruit trees [18]. Fatty-acid derivatives can be used to 'stop' chrysanthemums, by killing the terminal growing point and thereby promoting the outgrowth of lateral buds [8]. These compounds have been referred to as 'chemical pruning agents'.

Among the further possible practical applications which could develop from the availability of effective and non-toxic growth-inhibiting substances are the following:

(a) Pre-treatment of crop seed to delay germination in the field, and thereby facilitate the use of pre-emergence herbicides.

(b) Delay of the bud break in fruit trees in the spring, to reduce the risk of frost damage to blossoms.

(c) Prolongation of dormancy of plant materials, such as potatoes, in storage.

(d) Inhibition of growth in hedges and lawns.

(e) Inhibition of flowering, e.g. in grasses.

The gas ethylene, which has long been used to regulate the ripening of fruit, such as bananas, in storage, seems likely to become of increasing importance for several other purposes. The compound known as 'ethrel' decomposes when applied to plant tissues and releases ethylene, and has several possible practical applications [18].

From the foregoing, it is clear that there is considerable interest at present in the potentialities for chemical regulation of growth, and it is likely that further important advances will be made in the foreseeable future.

One of the striking features of present-day crop production is the increasing application of mathematical and computer methods to agricultural problems, as illustrated in several of the earlier chapters [1, 26, 27, 39]. Several authors have developed mathematical 'models' which attempt to express, in equations, complex interactions between various component processes within the plant or within the crop as a whole. At present, the development of such models is in its infancy, and is limited partly by the lack of appropriate observational and experimental information. The ultimate aim is to develop models which will not only describe observed situations, but also make predictions on which agricultural practice can be based. Indeed, it is said that the computer is already being used in the sugar-cane industry to control such field operations as the application of fertilizers and irrigation, and the time of harvesting, based upon information regarding the weather, the sugar content of the cane and so on. Thus, it seems likely that the successful farmer of the future will need to be acquainted with methods of computer programming.

The author is indebted to Dr. J.P. Cooper and Professor W. Ellison for reading the manuscript of this chapter and for their many helpful suggestions.

BIBLIOGRAPHY

1. ACOCK, B., THORNLEY, J.H.M. and WILSON, J. WARREN 'Photosynthesis and energy conversion', Chapter 4, this volume.
2. ALBERDA, Th. 'Potential production of grassland', Chapter 10, this volume.
3. BINGHAM, J. 'Plant breeding – arable crops', Chapter 20, this volume.
4. BROWN, R.M. and BLASER, R.E. 'Leaf area index in pasture growth', *Herbage Abstr.*, 1968, **38**, 1-9.
5. BROUWER, R. 'Distribution of dry matter in the plant', *Inst. Biol. Sch. Ond. van Landbouw. Wag. Med.*, 1962, 203.
6. BULLEN, E.R. 'Farming systems below 25 in. rainfall', Chapter 17, this volume.
7. BUNDY, J.W. 'Environmental limitations in crop production for the quick-freezing industry', Chapter 25, this volume.
8. CATHEY, H.M. and STEFFENS, G.L. 'Relation of the structure of fatty acid derivatives to their action as chemical freezing agents', in *Plant Growth Regulators*, London: Society of Chemical Industry, 1968.
9. COOPER, J.P. 'Climatic variation in forage grasses. I. Leaf development in climatic races of *Lolium* and *Dactylis*', *J. appl. Ecol.*, 1964, **1**, 45-62.
10. COOPER, J.P. and BREESE, E.L. 'Plant breeding – forage crops and legumes', Chapter 21, this volume.
11. COOPER, J.P. and TAINTON, N.M. 'Light and temperature requirements for the growth of tropical and temperate grasses', *Herbage Abstr.*, 1968, **38**, 167-176.
12. COPPOCK, J.T. 'An agricultural atlas of England and Wales', London: Faber and Faber Ltd., 1964.
13. CROWDY, S.H. 'Control of pests and diseases', Chapter 22, this volume.
14. DEPARTMENT OF EDUCATION AND SCIENCE, 'Report of the Land Use Study Group', London: H.M.S.O., 1966.
15. EADIE, J. and CUNNINGHAM, J.M. 'Efficiency of hill sheep production systems', Chapter 16, this volume.
16. EAGLES, C.F. 'Effect of photoperiod on vegetative growth in two natural populations of Cocksfoot, *Dactylis glomerata* L.', *Ann. Bot.*, (in press).
17. GAASTRA, P. 'Photosynthesis of crop plants as influenced by light, carbon dioxide, temperature and stomatal diffusion resistance', *Meded. Landbouwhogeschool (Wageningen)*, 1959, **59**, 1-68.
18. HEYWOOD, B.J. 'Chemical control of plant growth', Chapter 24, this volume.
19. HOGG, W.H. 'Regional and local environments', Chapter 2, this volume.
20. HOLMES, W. 'Efficiency of food production by the animal industries',

Chapter 14, this volume.

21. HUDSON, J.P. 'Horticulture in 2000 A.D.', Chapter 12, this volume.

22. IVINS, J.D. 'The determination of production systems', Chapter 19, this volume.

23. JONES, P.J. 'Farming systems with more than 30 in. rainfall', Chapter 18, this volume.

24. KRAMER, P.J. and KOZLOWSKI, 'Physiology of Trees', New York: McGraw Hill Book Co., 1960.

25. MACCOLL, D. and COOPER, J.P. 'Climatic variation in forage grasses. III. Seasonal changes in growth and assimilation in climatic races of *Lolium, Dactylis* and *Festuca*', *J. appl. Ecol.*, 1967, **4**, 113-127.

26. MONTEITH, J.L. and ELSTON, J.F. 'Microclimatology and crop production', Chapter 3, this volume.

27. PENMAN, H.L. 'Water as a factor in productivity', Chapter 6, this volume.

28. PUGHE, J., TREHARNE, K.J. and WAREING, P.F. (unpublished).

29. PYKE, MAGNUS 'Novel sources of energy and protein', Chapter 13, this volume.

30. ROBSON, M.J. 'A comparison of British and North African varieties of tall fescue, *Festuca arundinacea*. I. Leaf growth during winter and the effect on it of temperature and daylength', *J. app. Ecol.*, 1967, **4**, 475-484.

31. ROBSON, M.J. and JEWISS, O.R. 'A comparison of British and North American varieties of tall fescue, *Festuca arundinacea*. II. Growth during the winter and survival at low temperatures', *J. app. Ecol.*, 1968, **5**, 179-190.

32. RUSSELL, R. SCOTT. 'Root systems and nutrition', Chapter 7, this volume.

33. SIBMA, L. 'Relation between radiation and yield of a number of crops in the Netherlands', *Neth. J. agric. Res.*, (in press)

34. THORNE, G.N. 'Physiological factors limiting the yield of arable crops', Chapter 9, this volume.

35. TREHARNE, K.J. and COOPER, J.P. 'Effect of temperature on the activity of carboxylases in tropical and temperate Gramineae', *J. exp. Bot.*, 1969, **20**, 170-175.

36. TREHARNE, K.J. and EAGLES, C.F. 'Effect of temperature on photosynthetic activity of climatic races of *Dactylis glomerata* L', *Photosynthetica* (in press).

37. WAREING, P.F., KHALIFA, M.M. and TREHARNE, K.J. 'Rate-limiting processes in photosynthesis at saturating light intensities', *Nature,* 1968, **220**, 453-457.

38. WATSON, D.J. 'Size, structure and activity of the productive system of crops', Chapter 5, this volume.

39. WIT, C.T. de, BROUWER, R. and PENNING DE VRIES, F.W.T. 'A dynamic model of plant and crop growth', Chapter 8, this volume.

Author Index

ACOCK, B., 66, 197, 376
ALBERDA, Th., 159, 160, 161, 162, 163, 164, 165, 166, 168, 214, 297, 363
ALGRA, S., 271
ALLISON, J.C.S., 78, 86, 146
ANDERSON, D.B., 27, 31
ANDERSON, M.C., 66
ANON, 203, 323
A.R.C. Report 1967-68, 344, 347
ARCHBOLD, H.K., 30
ARMITAGE, E.R., 298
ASSMANN, E., 178

BAILEY, R.W., 307
BAKER, D., 71
BAPTISTE, E.C.D., 144
BARBER, D.A., 111
BARBER, S.A., 102
BARCLAY, P.C., 308, 313
BARLEY, K.P., 108
BASILEVITCH, N.I., 229
BEAUMONT, A., 18
BEEVERS, H., 132
BEEVERS, L., 31
BEGG, J.E., 44, 60, 63, 66
BELL, G.D.H., 274, 284, 323
BEREZOVA, E.F., 111
BERRY, J., 150
BIDDISCOMBE, E.F., 27
BIDWELL, R.G.S., 152
BINGHAM, J., 149, 151, 274, 275, 276, 277, 371, 374, 375
BINNS, W.O., 183
BIRECKA, H., 84
BISCHOF, W., 25
BJORKMAN, O., 63, 150
BLACK, J.N., 27, 159, 161
BLACK, J.S., 246
BLACKWOOD, G.C., 147, 150
BLASER, R.E., 66, 71, 148, 301, 305, 364
BLAXTER, K.L., 214, 216, 217, 218, 225
BODLAENDER, K.B.A., 271
BOHNING, R.H., 27, 31
BOND, D.A., 290, 291
BOOTH, R.E., 12
BORAH, M.N., 30
BORGGREVE, G.J., 124, 125
BORLAUG, N.E., 277
BORRILL, M., 310, 312, 313
BORUM, D.E., 324
BOUILLENE, R., 81
BOWEN, G.D., 101, 103, 111
BREESE, E.L., 306, 310, 311, 312, 313, 314, 363, 365, 370, 371, 374
BREMNER, P.M., 83, 85, 144, 145, 146
BRITTEN, E.J., 44, 66
BRODY, S., 214
BROOKE, D.W.I., 333
BROUGHAM, R.W., 163, 164, 168, 302

BROUWER, R., 26, 28, 29, 100, 117, 118, 123, 124, 125, 365, 376
BROWN, K.W., 56, 57, 63
BROWN, R., 125
BROWN, R.H., 66, 71, 148, 301, 305, 364
BRUN, W.A., 62, 63, 149
BUDAGOVSKII, A.I., 44
BUDYKO, M.I., 9, 59
BULL, T.A., 27, 36
BUNDY, J.W., 375
BUNTING, A.H., 30
BURT, R.L., 31, 151
BUTLER, G.W., 308

CALDER, D.M., 30
CALDWELL, D.L., 204
CALDWELL, R.M., 278, 287
CAMPBELL, G.K.G., 284
CAMPLING, R.C., 224
CANNON, W.A., 110
CARLE, T.C., 204
CARTER, A.R., 17
CATHEY, H.M., 376
CHADBURN, B.L., 320
CHALUPA, W., 204
CHAPMAN, H.W., 149
CHAPMAN, V., 280
CHARLES, A.H., 306
CHARTIER, P., 44, 55, 56, 58, 59, 61
CLARKSON, D.T., 101, 102, 103
COALES, J.F., 333
COLE, C.S., 288
COOKE, A.R., 349
COOKE, G.W., 100, 103
COOP, I.E., 216, 225, 241
COOPER, J.P., 31, 38, 148, 150, 160, 168, 296, 297, 298, 299, 300, 303, 304, 305, 306, 307, 310, 314, 363, 365, 366, 367, 370, 371, 374
COOPER, R.L., 62, 63, 149
COPPOCK, J.T., 10, 363
CORDES, E.H., 50
CORKE, C., 324
CORKILL, L., 312
COTTON, J., 321
CRANK, J., 102
CROWDY, S.H., 374
CUNNINGHAM, J.M., 372, 373
CURTIS, G.J., 283

DAKK-WLODKOWSKA, L., 84
DAVIDSON, J., 214, 222
DAVIDSON, J.L., 27, 28, 31, 44, 122, 159
DAVIES, ALISON, G., 311
DAVIES, R.O., 240
DAVIES, W.E., 306, 307, 312, 313
DAY, G.J., 8, 15
DAY, P.R., 150
DICKINSON, W., 159

DIJKSHOORN, W., 161
DILLON WESTON, W.A., 12, 111
DOLING, D.A., 320, 321, 322
DOMSCH, K.H., 111
DONALD, C.M., 150, 163, 301, 305, 306
DOODSON, J.K., 320, 322
DOWNES, R.W., 150
DOWNTON, W.J.S., 150, 299
DOVRAT, A., 35
DRAGSTED, J.R., 181, 182
DRAYNER, JEAN M., 278, 289, 291
DRENNAN, D.S.H., 30
DRIESSCHE, R. van den, 183
DUCKHAM, A.N., 214, 225
DUNCAN, W.G., 35, 38, 44, 148, 149, 159
DYSON, P.W., 84
DEPT. EDUCATION AND SCIENCE, 373

EADIE, J., 241, 243, 244, 246, 372, 373
EAGLES, C.F., 31, 38, 149, 300, 303, 304, 366, 368, 369, 370, 374
EAVIS, B.W., 109, 110
ECK, J.C., 205
ECKHART, F.C., 232
EDGINGTON, L.V., 324
EIMERN, J. van, 26, 31, 33
ELLIS, F.B., 105
ELLISON, W., 26
ELSTON, J.F., 364, 365, 367, 376
EL-SAEED, E.A.K., 83
EL-SHARKAWY, M., 48, 60, 61, 62, 63, 66, 150
EVANS, A.F., 85, 151
EVANS, L.T., 34, 134, 138, 149, 151, 152
EVANS, S.A., 347

FARIS, D.G., 149
FARR, E., 102
FARRELL, D.A., 108
FLEMING, G.A., 307
FORD, E.D., 172, 177, 178, 184, 233
FORD, M.A., 30, 31, 87, 146, 148, 151
FORESTRY COMM., 173, 174, 183
FOX, S.W., 211
FRANKEL, O.H., 309
FRANKENBURG, U.C., 111
FRASER, A.I., 172, 177
FREE, J.B., 290
FREELAND, R.C., 184
FRENCH, B.K., 104, 105
FRENCH, S.A.W., 30, 80, 84, 147, 148, 149, 150, 151
FYFE, J.L., 289, 290
FULLER, J.M., 288

GAASTRA, P., 148, 150, 159, 299, 367
GABERT, A.C., 289
GALLIVER, G.B., 210
GARDENER, C.J., 148
GARRETT, S.D., 102, 111
GATES, D.M., 34, 228, 234, 235
GAUDRY, R., 205
GEIGER, D.R., 31
GEIGER, R., 15
GILMOUR, W.D., 332

GIMINGHAM, C.H., 233
GLENDAY, A.C., 308
GLENDINNING, D.R., 287
GLOYNE, R.W., 14, 16, 17
GODDEN, W., 214, 222
GOODE, J.E., 11
GOODMAN, P.J., 83, 85, 145
GORHAM, E., 229, 230
GOSS, M., 109, 110
GREACEN, E.L., 108
GREENWOOD, D.J., 110
GREGORY, F.G., 27, 38
GRENNAN, E., 234
GREYSON, A.J., 183
GRIFFITH, G., 308
GROBBELAAR, W.P., 122, 123, 125

HACKETT, C., 102, 107, 108, 111
HAMILTON, G.J., 178
HAMS, A.F., 321
HANAY, R., 44, 148
HANNA, A.S., 240
HANDLEY, W.R.C., 181
HARADA, K., 211
HARDISON, J.R., 324
HARKINS, J., 248
HAWKINS, R.P., 290
HAYASHI, K., 148
HAYES, J.D., 278, 280
HEATH, O.V.S., 27, 56, 62, 110
HEATHCOTE, G.D., 324
HEITKAMP, D., 231
HESKETH, J.D., 38, 44, 48, 59, 60, 63, 66, 71, 149, 150
HESS, C.E., 107
HETHERINGTON, J.C., 173
HEW, C.S., 152
HEYWOOD, B.J., 375, 376
HILEY, W.E., 175
HILL, J., 311
HILL, R., 55
HIROI, T., 66
HOFSTRA, G., 150
HOGG, W.H., 10, 12, 15, 17, 18, 20, 365, 372
HOLLIDAY, R., 7, 213, 214, 298
HOLLOWAY, A.M., 102, 107, 111
HOLMGREN, P., 48, 63
HOLMES, W., 213, 223, 224, 225, 240, 298, 305, 372
HOSHINO, T., 148
HOUGAS, R.W., 209
HOWARD, H.W., 286, 287, 288
HOWE, E.E., 205
HUBBARD, W.F., 149
HUBER, D.M., 321
HUDSON, J.P., 38, 187, 194, 195, 364, 373, 374, 375
HUGHES, R., 16
HUGHES, R.E., 232
HUGHES, R.G., 348
HULL, R., 284, 324
HUMBERT, R.P., 110
HUMPHREY, A.E., 207
HUMPHRIES, E.C., 29, 85, 122, 151
HUNT, D.R., 333
HUNTER, R.F., 239, 242

HURST, G.W., 11
HUTCHEON, W.L., 105
HUTTON, E.M., 309

IDSO, S.B., 119
INCOLL, L.D., 152
INGRAM, J., 11
I.R.R.I., 146
ITAI, C., 107
ITO, H., 148
IVINS, J.D., 84, 172, 376
IZHAR, S., 149

JAMES, W.C., 321
JAMES, W.O., 134
JARVIS, M.S., 63
JARVIS, P.G., 44, 48, 60, 63, 66
JENNESKENS, P.J., 124, 125
JEWISS, O.R., 38, 303, 370
JOHNSON, R., 280
JOHNSTON, T.J., 148
JONES, D.I.H., 307, 308
JONES, I.T., 278
JONES, J.G.W., 223
JONES, P.J., 363

KASANAGA, H., 159
KASSANIS, B., 286
KEINBERGS, E., 324
KHALIFA, M.M., 150, 152, 367
KING, R.W., 151, 152
KIRA, T., 233, 234
KIRBY, E.J.M., 147
KLEIBER, M., 132, 214, 217
KLEINENDORST, A., 100
KLINCK, H.R., 27
KNOCK, K., 16
KNY, L., 125
KOMBRIS, T., 203
KOPPEN, W., 15
KOZLOWSKI, 373
KRAMER, P.J., 101, 373
KRAUT, H., 208
KRONACKER, P., 81
KROTKOV, G., 152
KRZYSCH, G., 25
KUKKA, M., 323
KUROIWA, S., 244

LAKE, J.V., 48
LANGRIDGE, J., 26
LARGE, E.C., 320
LAW, C.N., 281
LAWES, D.A., 290
LAWRENCE, D.B., 231
LAZENBY, A., 298, 300, 306, 310, 312
LEACH, G.J., 81
LEAFE, E.L., 321
LEAVER, J.D., 224
LEEPER, G.W., 110
LEITCH, I., 214, 222
LEONARD, E.R., 46
LEPLEY, C.F., 139
LEWIS, D., 205
LEWIS, D.G., 103
LEWIS, E.J., 310, 312, 313, 314
LICHENSTEIN, I., 204

LITTLE, R., 278
LLEWELYN, J.C., 270
LLOYD, D.H., 225
LOB, W., 211
LONG, I.F., 104, 105
LONSDALE, C.R., 224
LOOMIS, R.S., 35, 44, 60, 61, 62, 63, 66, 139, 148
LOOMIS, W.E., 149
LOVERN, J.A., 210
LOWE, H.J.B., 285
LUCAS, J.W., 213
LUDWIG, L.J., 134, 138
LUPTON, F.G.H., 149, 151

MACCANCE, R.A., 224, 225
MACCOLL, D., 38, 366
MACCREE, K.J., 131, 132, 133, 134, 165
MACDONALD, M.A., 220
MACGARVIE, Q.D., 32
MACMEEKAN, C.P., 224
MACVEAN, D.N., 233
MACWILLIAM, J.R., 26
MACER, R.C.F., 278
M.A.F.F., 10, 91, 343
MAHLER, H.R., 50
MALCOLM, D.C., 173
MANNERS, J.G., 278, 322
MARVEL, C.S., 205
MARITA, K., 203
MASKELL, E.J., 51, 52, 56
MATHIESON, J., 214, 222
MATSUSHIMA, S., 148
MATTSSON, J.O., 26
MAUDE, R., 324
MAYER, A.M., 14
MAYER, B.S., 27, 31
MAYNARD, J.A., 349
MEIDNER, H., 27, 62, 150
MEIJER, R.J., 337
MIDDLETON, T.H., 214, 225
MILBOURN, G.M., 224
MILES, D.G., 308
MILLAR, H.G., 108, 183
MILLER, G.R., 233, 240
MILLER, S.L., 211
MILNER, C., 232
MILTHORPE, F.L., 23, 27, 28, 30, 31, 38, 122
MILTON, W.E.J., 240
MINDERMAN, G., 230
MITCHELL, K.J., 306
MOLLER, C.M., 181, 182, 233
MONSI, M., 44, 66, 148, 159
MONTEITH, J.L., 6, 7, 25, 30, 35, 44, 55, 58, 59, 63, 152, 159, 232, 364, 365, 367, 376
MORGAN, D.G., 310
MORGAN, K.E., 331, 332, 333, 334, 335, 336
MOSS, D.M., 48, 59, 60, 63, 66
MULLIGAN, T.E., 320, 323
MUNGER, H.M., 149
MUNRO, J.M.M., 16, 59
MUSGRAVE, R.B., 60

NATIONAL INSTITUTE OF AGRIC.
  BOT., 284
NATIONAL RESOURCES TECHNICAL
  COMMUNICATION, 106
NATR, L., 149
NEALES, T.F., 152
NEEDHAM, A.E., 132
NEILSON, K.F., 29
NEILSON, J., 233
NEILSON-JONES, W., 111
NELSON, C.D., 152
NEWBOULD, P., 101, 104, 105, 108
NEWBOULD, P.J., 177, 178, 232
NEWTON, P., 28
NOBLE, M., 321
NOGGLE, J.C., 161
NOSBERGER, J., 151
NUNEZ, A.F., 35
NYE, P.H., 102, 103

O'CALLAGHAN, 332, 333
O'HARE, P.J., 234
O'TOOLE, M.A., 234
ODUM, E.P., 233, 234
OHLORGGE, A.J., 108
OLD, K.M., 321
OLSON, J.S., 232
ORDISH, G., 319
ORMROD, D.P., 149
OVINGTON, J.D., 230, 231, 233

QUIRK, J.P., 103

PAGE, G., 173, 181, 182
PALLAS, J.E., 62
PASSIOURA, J.B., 110
PATIL, B.D., 307, 308
PATON, D., 149
PAYNE, D., 109, 110
PEARCE, R.B., 66, 148
PEARSALL, W.H., 229, 230
PEASLEE, D.E., 63
PELOQUIN, S.J., 289
PENDLETON, J.W., 148
PENMAN, H.L., 9, 23, 25, 89, 92, 93, 95,
  96, 106, 372, 376
PENNING DE VRIES, F.W.T., 117, 376
PHILIP, J.R., 44, 159
PIRIE, N.W., 172
PITT, D., 320
POLJAKOFF-MAYBER, A., 14
POWELSON, R.L., 324
PRICE, C.A., 134
PRICE-JONES, D., 325
PRINZ ZUR LIPPE, A., 134
PROUVIDENTI, R., 279
PUGH, J., 367
PYKE, MAGNUS, 375

RABINOWITCH, E.I., 51, 54
RACKHAM, O., 63
RACZ, G.J., 105
RAE, I.J., 203
RADLEY, R.W., 83, 85
RALSTON, G.W., 174
RANDALL, D.I., 349
RAYMOND, W.F., 306, 307

REESE, A.R., 16
REINBERGS, E., 148
RENNIE, D.A., 105
RICKLESS, P., 125
RILEY, R., 280
RHODES, I., 302, 303, 305
ROBSON, M.J., 38, 303, 366, 370
RODDA, J.C., 9
RODIN, L.E., 229
ROGERS, H.H., 297, 298, 306, 310, 312,
  314
ROO, H.C. de, 105
ROSS, Y.K., 44
ROSSER, W.R., 320
ROUBAIX, J. de, 81
ROVIRA, A.D., 101, 103, 111
ROWELL, J.B., 324
RUSSELL, A.J.F., 243, 244
RUSSELL, G.E., 284, 285
RUSSELL, R. SCOTT, 101, 103, 105,
  110, 374

SAEKI, T., 44, 66, 134, 138, 148
SAKAMOTO, C.M., 71
SAMUEL, C.J.A., 311
SAMTSEVICH, S.A., 111
SANDERSON, G.W., 184
SANDERSON, J., 101, 102, 103
SANGSTER, H.M., 323
SCHARFF, O., 181, 182
SCHMELING, B. von, 323
SCHROEDER, W.T., 229
SCHUPHAN, W., 225
SCOTT, R.K., 83, 144, 145, 272
SEELY, C.I., 324
SHAW, R.H., 71
SHANER, G.E., 324
SHEEHY, J.E., 301
SHIBLES, R.M., 35, 133, 139
SHIDEI, T., 233, 234
SHUL'GIN, A.M., 26
SHURING, C.G., 324
SIBMA, L., 161, 163, 164, 166, 168, 214,
  297, 364
SIDDIQ, M., 194
SIMPSON, G.M., 147
SIMMONDS, N.W., 286, 287
SINCLAIR, J.B., 324
SIVAPALAN, K., 184
SLOPE, B.D., 320, 321
SMITH, D.M., 180
SMITH, G.E., 148
SMITH, K.A., 110
SMITH, L.P., 8, 11, 19
SNOW, L.M., 109
SOUTHNEY, J.F., 320
SPEDDING, C.R.W., 216, 220, 225, 241
STANGEL, H.J., 204
STANHILL, G., 159
STANLEY, R.W., 203
STEFFINS, G.L., 376
STEPPLER, H.A., 27
STEWART, D.M., 204
STEWART, H.E., 108
STILES, W., 94
STOSKOPF, N.C., 27, 148
STOY, V., 149, 151

STRICKLAND, A.M., 320, 321, 323
SUTTON, C.D., 29
SWAN, J.M., 349
SWANSON, C.A., 31
SWEET, G.B., 183
SZEICZ, G., 25

TAHA, M.A., 145, 146
TAINTON, N.M., 299, 300, 303, 365
TAMM, C.O., 234
TAMM, E., 25, 234
TANAKA, T., 148
TANNER, J.W., 148
TAYLER, J.C., 224
TAYLOR, S.M., 8
TEMPLEMAN, W.G., 298
TERRY, N., 27, 28, 31
THORNE, G.N., 30, 31, 80, 84, 85, 87,
    146, 147, 149, 150, 151, 274, 363,
    364, 365, 374
THORNLEY, J.H.M., 66, 376
THRING, M.W., 341
TOMME, M.F., 264
TOOMING, H., 44
TOYNBEE-CLARKE, G., 290
TREGUNNA, E.B., 150, 299
TREHARNE, K.J., 149, 150, 152, 300,
    304, 367, 368, 369, 370, 374
TROUGHTON, A., 107
TROUGHTON, J.H., 131, 132, 165
TROUSE, A.C. Jr., 110
TSUNODA, S., 148, 150
TURNER, W.B., 152

ULRICH, A., 30
U.S. BUREAU OF INTERNAL
    REVENUE, 204
U.S. PATENTS, 205

VAADIA, Y., 107
VAIDYANATHAN, L.V., 102
VERHAGEN, A.M.W., 44, 66
VERHEIJ, E., 199
VIRO, P.J., 183
VOSE, P.B., 306, 308

WAGGONER, P.E., 66
WALLACE, D.H., 149
WALTER, C., 110
WALTERS, R.J.K., 307, 308
WARBURG, O., 52
WARDLAW, I.F., 149, 151, 152
WAREING, P.F., 150, 152, 183, 367
WARNE, L.G.G., 145
WARREN WILSON, J., 27, 28, 60, 66,
    376
WATSON, D.J., 30, 31, 37, 78, 80, 81, 84,
    85, 87, 144, 145, 146, 147, 148, 149,
    150, 151, 183, 235, 363, 364, 365, 374
WATSON, D.M.S., 224
WATSON, M.A., 320, 322, 323
WATSON, R.D., 324
WEAVER, J.E., 102, 105
WEBER, C.R., 35
WELBANK, P.J., 30, 31, 87, 147, 150
WENT, F.W., 30, 122
WESTLAKE, D.F., 229, 297

WHITE, H.C., 205
WHITEHEAD, D.C., 307
WHITEHOUSE, R.N.H., 274
WHITTINGHAM, C.P., 55
WHITTINGTON, W.J., 107
WIDDOWSON, E.H., 224, 225
WIJK, W.R. van, 26
WILFONG, R.T., 71
WILLIAMS, C.N., 27
WILLIAMS, P.M., 209
WILLIAMS, T.E., 94
WILLIAMS, W.A., 35, 44, 60, 61, 62, 63,
    66, 139, 148
WILSON, D., 300
WILSON, J.A., 280
WILSON, J.H., 44, 66, 148
WINTER, S.R., 148
WIT, C.T. de, 44, 117, 118, 119, 120,
    123, 159, 161, 163, 164, 166, 176,
    183, 200, 299, 376
WITTS, K.J., 30, 31, 87, 147, 148
WOLFE, M.S., 278
WOOD, R.K.S., 107

YABUKI, K., 25

ZAHNER, R., 175
ZELITCH, I., 150

Subject Index

Adaptation to
management techniques, 305
Advection, 15
Agricultural developments since 1938, 187
Agricultural labour force, 1, 332
Agricultural output, 1
Agricultural policy, 3
Agricultural research, 1
  aims, 1
  investment in, 1
  mission orientated, 1
Agricultural statistics, 250
  eastern counties of England, 250
Amino acids
  requirements of chicks and pigs, 206
Assimilation
  effect of temperature on, 26, 29
Automatic tractors, 332, 333
Automatic weighing, 335, 336

Barley for beef and milk production, 267
Biological potential
  ryegrass, 297
Biomass, total, 159
Breeding objectives, 299, 300
Breeding techniques, 309

Canopy
photosynthesis, 66
Carbon dioxide exchange rates, 165
Carboxydismutase activity
  effect of temperature, 369, 370
C.C.C., effect on wheat and potatoes, 271, 272
Cereals
  chromosome manipulation, 278
  disease resistance, 278, 279
  exploitation of physiological characters, 274
  frequency in rotation, 268
  hybrid varieties, 279
  shoot production, 275
  winter survival, 275
Cereal production, factors affecting, 252
  diseases, 254
  seed bed, 253
  tilth, 253
  weeds, 254
Chemical composition
  fats, 209
Chemical control
  plant growth, 343
Climatic factors, 363
Combination of characters, 312
  Lolium multiflorum x Festuca arundinacea, 313
  white clover, 312
Comparative costs
  protein from micro-organisms on petrol
    and conventional sources, 208

Comparative productivity, 370
  crops and farming systems, 370
  ecosystems, 228
Consumer expenditure
  food, 352
Conversion efficiency, 213
  factors influencing, 217
  gross energy to animal products, 215, 216, 217
Conversion efficiency (ctd)
  protein, 215, 216, 217
  units of, 213, 214
Crop structure and nutrition interaction, 183
Cutting treatments for maximum production, 168

Diffusion
of CO_2, 45, 46
Digestibility
  of pasture, 243
  seasonal changes, 243
Disease resistance, 278, 279, 284, 287, 291
Distribution
  of assimilates, 303
  grass, 257
Dried distillers solubles, 203
Dry matter
  distribution, 150

Economic yield, 76, 78
Ecosystems
  comparisons, 228
  relevance to agricultural production, 234
Edible yields animals and crops, 224
Efficiency
  effect of animal age, 221
  hill sheep production, 245
  individual animal, 219
  influence of number of lambs, 220
  influence of size of ewe, 220
  of conversion, 219
  photosynthesis, 43
  production systems, 240
  productive systems of crops, 76
  utilization of ingested pasture, 241
  whole farm situations, 221, 222
ELCROS (elementary crop simulator), 117, 118
  programming aspects of, 120, 126
Energy
  novel sources of, 202
Energy conversion, 43, 63, 64, 65
  dependence on light, 70
  dependence on CO_2, 70
Environment
  annual variation, 8
  effects on productive systems, 87

local, 6
major controls of, 6
primary control of, 7
regional, 6
secondary control of, 15
Environmental limitations
for quick freezing industry, 357
Equations of motion, 48
photosynthesis, 58
Even age tree populations, 178
Exploitation of physiological characters, 274

Factors of plant environment, 192
Farming systems, 250, 262, 263, 264, 265
factors affecting, 261
Feed utilization, 217
Field bean, 289
yield of, 291
resistance to pests and diseases, 291
Flowering date
response to selection, 310
Food
conversion efficiency, 217
Food production
by animal industries, 213
Forage grass breeding, 295
Forest crops
growth, 173
potential production, 172, 176, 177
structure, 177
nutrition, 180
Forestry in Holland, 230
Frost
frequency of, 20
Frozen fruit and vegetables
main, 352
sales of, 352, 353
Frozen food industry
development of, 359, 360, 361
Future trends in British agriculture, 1

Genotype environment interactions, 311
Genotypes
response to cutting, 302
Gross energy
conversion to animal products, 215, 216, 217
Growth curves
actual, 166
calculated, 166
Growth
changes with time, 82
chemical control of, 343
leaves, 121, 304
regulators, 343
useful parts, 81

Harvesting equipment, 335
Harvesting problems – row crops, 256
Herbage growth model, 163
Herbage yield and light energy, 163
Hill sheep production, 239
improving efficiency of, 245
Horticulture
basis of productivity, 189
in 2000 A.D., 187

Horticultural industry
developments since 1938, 187
future of, 188, 189
new crops, 188
Human diets
direct utilization of animal feedstuffs, 209
Hybrid varieties
cereals, 279

Incident radiation energy, 193
Industrial by-products, 202
Ingested pasture
efficiency of utilization, 241
Insecticides, 324, 325
Investment in agricultural research, 1
Irrigation
growth under, 91
response to, 91, 97

Land use in Britain, 319
Leaf area index
change with time, 79, 144, 146
optimal, 83, 145
size, 79
profile, 81
Leaf arrangement
effect on photosynthesis, 148
Leaf characteristics, 62
Leaf growth
physiological aspects, 121
Leaf surfaces, 196
Legume breeding, 295
Levels of productivity
wheat, 200
Light
energy, 163
dependence of gross photosynthesis, 43
interception, 301, 303
reflection, 119
transmission, 119
transmission and photosynthesis, 164
Limitations to yield, 269
Liveweight changes in sheep, 243
Losses due to pest and diseases, 320

Major controls of environment, 6
Marketing requirements, quick freezing, 351
Matching crop and site, 191
Measurement of forest crop growth, 173
Mechanization, 331
systems approach, 333
future, 337-341
Metabolizable energy
conversion of, 218
Microclimate responses to
carbon dioxide, 25
radiation, 24
saturation deficit, 25
temperature, 25
wind speed, 25
Micoclimatology, aspects of, 32
Mineral content of grasses and legumes, 308
Model
of plant and crop growth, 35, 117, 163

photosynthesis and respiration, 45, 47, 51, 52, 57, 66
Rabinowitch, 57
Monthly temperatures, 13
Monthly values of solar radiation, 7

Net assimilation rate, 80
changes with time, 80
Net photosynthesis
dependence on CO_2, 53, 61, 62, 68
dependence on light, 53, 61, 62, 68
high light and CO_2, 69
model of, 6
New horticultural crops, 188
Nitrogen fertilizer
effect of high levels, 271
Nitrogen sources
synthetic, 204
Nutrition
forest trees, 182, 183
root systems, 100
Nutritive value, 306

Objectives of agricultural research, 1
Obtainment of vegetables for quick freezing, 355
Organic matter distribution, 181
Output per unit area
animal products, 223
edible yield of animals and crops, 224

Parasites and predators, 325
Pasture
utilization, 244
Patterns of cropping, 261
Peas
harvest changes, 354
Percentage conversion of visible radiation, 152
Perennial ryegrass
biological potential, 297
crop growth rate, 303
energy conversion, 297
leaf area index, 303
seasonal production, 296
variation in light interception, 303
yield of energy and protein, 298
Pests and diseases
control of, 319, 323
losses due to, 320
Petroleum
as a protein source, 206
as a substitute for oil seeds, 208
Photorespiration, 149, 150
Photosynthate
source, 76, 77, 85, 86
sink, 77, 85, 86
Photosynthesis
computation of, 67
dependence on CO_2, 53, 61, 62, 68
dependence on light, 43, 53, 61, 62, 68
effect of crop, 44
effect of environment, 44
effect of leaf arrangement, 148
effect of temperature, 300
efficiency, 43
gross, 164

single leaves, 45, 46, 299
variation within species, 148
Photosynthetic activity
variation in perennial ryegrass, 300
Photosynthetic characteristics
various spp., 63
Photosynthetic rate, 118, 121
Photosynthetic system
size, 79
structure, 81
Physiological characters of sugar beet, 283
Planning according to probable weather, 193
Plant breeding
arable crops, 273
forage grasses and legumes, 295
Plant pathologists
distribution of, 327
Potatoes
acreage treated with herbicides, 347
breeding, 285
disease resistance, 287
effect of temperature, 30
tuber quality, 288
varieties, 282
Potential Production, 159, 362
actual and calculated, 167, 268
definition of, 159
existing varieties of forage grasses and legumes, 295
forest crops, 172, 173, 176
grassland, 159, 160, 161
some conclusions, 362
Primary control of environment, 7
Production
characters of forage plants, 299
definition of, 98
edible protein, 219
estimates, 229
food by animal industries, 213
hill pastures, 240
seasonal herbage, 164
systems, 239, 266
Productive systems of crops
activity, 76
efficiency, 77, 85
limitations and deficits, 82
size, 76
time changes, 78
Productivity
basis of in horticulture, 189
growth in, 3
water as a factor in, 89
Protein
conversion of, 215, 216, 217

Quality
potato tubers, 288
sugar beet, 284
Quick freezing
environmental limitations, 357
crop production for, 351

Reduction of land available for agriculture, 266
Regional environments, 6
Relative growth rate

effect of temperature, 124
Resistance
  to bolting, 283
  to disease, 278, 279, 284, 287, 291
Respiration, 45, 47
  models of, 45, 47, 51, 52
Response
  to irrigation, 91, 97
  to nitrogen by Corsican pine, 182
  to selection for flowering date, 310
Root
  aeration, 110
  depth, 104
  diameter, 103
  environment, 110
  form, 107
  hairs, 103
  length, 103
  structure, 108
Root growth
  critical periods of, 106
  effect of injury, 111
  effect of mechanical impedence, 108, 109, 110
  effect of micro-orgamisms, 111
Root/shoot ratio, 108
Root systems
  efficiency of absorption, 101
  morphology, 101
  nutrition, 101
Row crops, 255
  harvesting, 256
  seed bed, 256

Sales of frozen foods, 352, 353
Saturation deficit, 25
Seasonal herbage production, 164
Secondary control of environment, 15
Selection, 309, 310
Sink, 76, 77, 86
  capacity, 77
  performance, 81
  strength, 77, 85
Soil
  temperature, 14, 32
Space, use of, 198
Specialization v diversification, 270
Solar radiation
  monthly values, 7
Soluble carbohydrate content, 125
  effect of root temperature, 125
Source of photosynthate, 76, 77, 85, 86
Standing crops in British habitats, 230
Stirling engine, 336
Stocking rates
  hill sheep, 239
Structure of photosynthetic system, 81
Sugar beet
  breeding, 281
  disease resistance, 284
  herbicides, 346
  physiological characters, 283
  quality, 284
  resistance to bolting, 283
  varieties, 282
Sunshine, 12
Systemic fungicides, 323

Systems approach to mechanization, 334

Temperature, 25
  effect on assimilation and respiration, 26, 29
  cereals, 30
  grasses, 30
  later growth, 30
  potatoes, 30
  relative growth rate, 27, 29
  root growth, 28
  shoot, 33
  soil, 14, 32
  vegetative growth, 26
Translocation
  calcium, 102
  phosphate, 102
  roots, 102
Topographical modification, 16
Total solar radiation, 9
Tuber quality, 288

Uptake
  calcium, 105
  phosphate, 105
  water, 104
Urea, 204
Useful parts
  changes with time, 82
  growth, 81

Variation
  leaf characteristics, 62
  photosynthetic rate between species, 148
  photosynthetic rate within perennial ryegrass, 300
  productivity of orchard, 190
  root form, 107
Vegetative growth
  effect of temperature, 26

Water requirements, 9, 92
  fruit trees, 11
  grass, 11, 94
  potatoes, 96
Water use
  efficiency of, 90
Wind speed, 25
White clover breeding, 312
World ecosystems, 229

Yields
  animal, 224
  arable crops, 143
  class curves for Sitka spruce, 174
  crops, 224
  digestible energy, 298
  factors limiting, 143, 144, 145, 146
  grain yield characters, 276
  herbage, 163
  hybrid winter beans, 291
  perennial ryegrass, 296, 298
  protein, 298